Arthur George Liddon Rogers, James Edwin Thorold Rogers

The Industrial and Commercial History of England

Arthur George Liddon Rogers, James Edwin Thorold Rogers

The Industrial and Commercial History of England

ISBN/EAN: 9783337338725

Printed in Europe, USA, Canada, Australia, Japan

Cover: Foto ©ninafisch / pixelio.de

More available books at **www.hansebooks.com**

The Industrial and Commercial History of England

(LECTURES DELIVERED TO THE UNIVERSITY OF OXFORD)

BY

THE LATE JAMES E. THOROLD ROGERS

PROFESSOR OF POLITICAL ECONOMY IN THE UNIVERSITY OF OXFORD AND
OF ECONOMIC SCIENCE AND STATISTICS, KING'S COLLEGE, LONDON

EDITED BY HIS SON,
ARTHUR G. L. ROGERS

London
T. FISHER UNWIN
PATERNOSTER SQUARE
MDCCCXCII

PREFACE.

THE discourses in the present volume, which contains almost all the hitherto unpublished comments on the Economic History of England delivered in public by my father, were originally given in the form of lectures in the University of Oxford. They were given in the hall of Worcester College in the autumn of 1888, and the spring of 1889. Although it had been his intention to publish these lectures some day in the form of a book, they were found at his death in the same form as they were composed originally, with the addition of a few pencil notes alone. For, in accordance with a very common practice, he considered it advisable to repeat these two courses before they were finally committed to print. There is always a certain weighty sense of responsibility attached to the work of editing the writings of another. But this feeling is accentuated when the text is not in the condition which the author would have considered final. It would have impaired the value of the book had it been given to the world exactly as it stood, because it was so full of those local and personal allusions, with which my father used to illustrate his arguments, that though the interest might have been increased for a certain class of readers, the point would often have been missed by others. There are passages in the MS. which I am sure my father would not have kept in his proofs. But, on the other hand, it is out of place in an editor to alter the text of his author, if there is any possibility of the reader thereby misinterpreting the meaning, or getting any false impression. And yet I am conscious that there are instances where the progress of economic research, or the march of history, has disproved theories which three years ago were accepted by my father in common with nearly every other man and woman in England. The theory of the causes and methods of the immigration of agricultural labourers to London, as held by everybody in 1889, is recognized now to be incorrect, though so quiet has been the progress of the new theory that few people quite realize how diametrically opposed their ideas on the subject were some years ago to what they are now. I should like to be able to omit the antiquated theory from its place in the chapter on immigration, but it is so woven into the rest of the chapter that it was difficult to pick out one thread without unraveling the whole piece. For the same reason the lectures are printed exactly in the order in which they were delivered, although it is obvious that there is no special connection between some of them, and though from a mere perusal of the titles a different order might appear at first more suitable.

But this, after all, is the less important, as these lectures, like those published under the title of "The Economic Interpretation of History," aimed rather at expounding the methods used by my father in his studies than at announcing new facts, or enunciating new theories. The six volumes on the "History of Prices" contain the extracts from the original authorities he had consulted, and his deductions from them on the economic and social condition of the English people during the greater part of their history. The "Six Centuries of Work and Wages" contain the epitome of his longer work, not only in a more popular form, but also with some direct reference to more political aspect of events. But though I have heard my father say that he believed that by a careful study of the facts published in his "History of Prices," future students would be able to contribute more information to the economic history of the Middle Ages than even he had done, he confined his original research during the last years of his life to the completion of his great work. For I believe he considered it more important to impress his method on students of history and economics than to add more to our fund of information. At the present time by far the greater number of persons interested in economics have no part in either of the two great Universities. Those members of the University who care for the subject have little time to spare from other studies, while little more than an acquaintance with the main theories of the older economists is sufficient for the schools. Let the Professor of Political Economy teach what he will, even the undergraduates who seek honours in the history school, soon drop away. In this way it came about that these lectures were attended by an extremely small audience. Had the Professor of Political Economy given these lectures in some industrial centre, hundreds of workmen would, I believe, have paid to listen to them. But in the home of learning, some dozen men of education attended lectures thrown open, free, to every member of the University.

If any apology were needed for the publication of this book, this alone would suffice. A. G. L. R.

49, BEAUMONT SQUARE, LONDON, E.
November, 1891.

CONTENTS.

I.
THE DEVELOPMENT OF INDUSTRIAL SKILL IN ENGLAND . . . 1

II.
THE CONDITIONS OF ECONOMIC PROGRESS . . . 22

III.
THE PROGRESS OF ENGLISH POPULATION AND THE CAUSES THEREOF 44

IV.
THE DEVELOPMENT OF CREDIT AGENCIES . . 56

V.
THE DEVELOPMENT OF TRANSIT 89

VI.
THE ECONOMIC HISTORY OF CHARTERED TRADE COMPANIES . 113

VII.

THE JOINT-STOCK PRINCIPLE IN CAPITAL . 138

VIII.

THE JOINT-STOCK PRINCIPLE IN LABOUR . 162

SECOND COURSE.

I.

THE ECONOMIC DOCTRINE OF WASTE 184

II.

THE THEORY OF ECONOMIC RENT . . . 205

III.

CONTRACTS FOR THE USE OF LAND . . . 226

IV.

LARGE AND SMALL HOLDINGS . . . 248

V.

MOVEMENTS OF LABOUR.—I. EMIGRATION . 270

VI.

MOVEMENTS OF LABOUR.—II. IMMIGRATION . . . 293

VII.

MOVEMENTS OF CURRENCY.—BIMETALLISM . . 317

VIII.

PEASANT AGRICULTURE AND MANUFACTURE . . . 340

IX.

HOME TRADE AND DOMESTIC COMPETITION . . . 365

X.

HOME TRADE AND INTERNATIONAL COMPETITION . . 390

XI.

ECONOMIC LEGISLATION, 1815–41 . . . 415

XII.

ECONOMIC LEGISLATION SINCE 1841 441

INDUSTRIAL AND COMMERCIAL HISTORY OF ENGLAND.

—◆—

I.

THE DEVELOPMENT OF INDUSTRIAL SKILL IN ENGLAND.

Chauvinism in History—Blunders of economists and amateurs—Backwardness of industry in Mediæval England—Exclusiveness of the English—Foreign influence—Fallacy of the sole market—Arkwright—American and Continental Wars gave increased opportunities to English trade—Effect of Protection abroad on international trade.

It is a common-place with many recent writers to indulge in what I may be allowed to call industrial Chauvinism. The habit, however, of uttering in the treatment of economical questions what is called in the political relations subsisting between different communities, "our country, right or wrong," is not patriotism, except in that sordid aspect of it which Johnson defined, but is constantly a pestilent, economical heresy, in which private advantage is affirmed to be a public benefit. I know no danger which economical progress runs, which is more persistent and more menacing, than the maintenance or even the insinuation of this doctrine is. It is the key to those protectionist fallacies under which the sustentation of particular interests is made a national policy, and the mass of mankind is constrained to suffer in order that a few may be enriched. It is the ground on which the worst vices of our land system are defended, and British agriculture is in ruins. It has not a little to do in this country with the clamour of the unemployed, and the wild schemes which are promulgated about the reconstruction of society. Nor is this vice confined to selfish agitators, like the Fair Trade people, or to interested sycophants, who try to gain popularity by defending abuses, or to the numerous adventurers who seek to get a hearing by flattering social and economical vices. Some of you may remember how vigorously Bentham dealt with the optimism of Blackstone, and his defence of the mass of chicanery to which law pleading had been degraded. In political economy much of this mischievous nonsense was written by MacCulloch, whose general arrogance was in curious and instinctive contrast with his habitual servility towards certain persons and certain interests. But the maintenance of economic truth is a very serious and urgent duty. As time goes on practical politics become increasingly the solution of economic problems, and they who wilfully or ignorantly mislead nations, or pander to the inherent vices of administrations, are among the worst enemies of mankind; just as, on the other hand, the wise economist, who does not allow himself to be swayed by prejudice, or mere partisanship, or authority, is a true benefactor.

Now the present position of Great Britain—I wish I could say the United Kingdom—is set out very clearly in a work which I have more than once commended to you, the second volume of Mr. Giffen's essays. It is true that this very able analyst of economical facts was engaged when he wrote this work in controverting some unfounded and invidious statements, which had been promulgated by ignorance or selfishness. It was not, it appears, his immediate business to point out what are the weak parts of our social or industrial system, but to show that certain allegations were baseless or false. Nor do I intend in the present lecture to deal with that part of this important subject, for I purpose to reserve what has to be said on this topic to my next lecture. It is sufficient on this occasion to say that an analysis of the existing facts, which Mr. Giffen has, in my judgment, successfully carried out, is the best preparation which the student of political economy, in the best sense of the terms, can get for grappling with the solution of those most important problems which Adam Smith happily grouped, under the phrase "The Wealth of Nations." This great writer does not speak of classes, nor of our country. He intends to be comprehensive as regards the whole community, and cosmopolitan as regards other civilized nations, which have entered into the reciprocal relations of trade.

The purpose which is before me in my present lecture is one which is almost entirely historical. I shall try to show you, beginning with the earliest times of which we have industrial evidence, what were the relations in which England, and at a subsequent period Great Britain, stood to other communities. I shall show to the best of my power what were the causes which induced the remarkable backwardness of this country in the industrial arts, and what were the causes which quite recently brought about this extraordinary development in this country, and in Southern Scotland—in which, by the way, the progress was even more recent, but has been proportionately more rapid. In this account of the country, I shall deal with agricultural as well as manufacturing progress, but shall not enter in detail into the development of the carrying trade, since I have reserved this for a special lecture. And perhaps there is hardly any part of political economy which is more indebted to the study of historical and social facts than that which traces the progress of a nation in the arts of life. Much, indeed, which the writers of the principal text-books have said about the production of wealth, with which part of economical analysis you will see that I am at present concerned, is accurate, though even here some of the gravest errors have been committed, partly because the analysis has been incomplete, partly because facts have been disregarded. Thus, for example, the theory of the "distribution of employments"—a phrase very properly substituted by Mr. Gibbon

Wakefield in place of Adam Smith's "division of labour"—has been very fully stated, though even here, nothing is said of the employments in which the distribution is best effected, of those in which it is not effected at all, and, most important of all, the consequences of the process on the respective wages which workmen and employers earn, the latter as superintending the manual dexterity of the former.

Nothing is more marked in the economical history of Western Europe than the mischief which the pirates of Scandinavia did to England, Ireland, and the northern coast of France from the beginning of the ninth to the end of the eleventh centuries. At the conclusion of this period these raids completely cease, and the very district from which these ravages originated becomes shortly afterwards the seat of a powerful commercial association, under the name of the Hanseatic League. It is plain that the impulse which led to this union was one of mutual defence against violence, especially that of sea robbers, and that the trading towns which entered into the alliance collected a common fund for the purpose of securing a common safety. But it is constantly the case, especially during the period in which nearly all our information is derived from monastic chronicles, that no notice is taken of institutions till they are in their full vigour, and then very uncritical accounts are given as to the origin of such established facts. Thus it has been suggested that this famous League was derived from a confederation of the Rhenish towns, against the robber barons, the ruins of whose strongholds top nearly every hill on the banks of the Lower Rhine. But the traffic of the Rhine was eminently of Italian and Eastern produce, while that which the Hanse towns defended was particularly that of the southern and eastern shores of the Baltic, and of Scandinavia, especially its eastern coasts, from which most important produce was derived in mediæval trade. I have little doubt that the league of the Hanse towns had an earlier origin, that its first business was to root out the relics of those habits of piracy, which had been the scourge of Western Europe for nearly three centuries, and that the first notices of the League were made after it had long been active.

Now with the exception of Domesday Book, there is no trustworthy and continuous economical evidence in England till after the middle of the thirteenth century, when this League was certainly in full vigour. After this period, indeed, the evidence is exact and copious, and the student of social life in England has abundant materials for the discovery of what that social life was. Many of you are aware that I have given many years and much labour to the collection of this evidence. I have fondly hoped that the students of these materials would ere this have made some profitable use of them. But just as the righteous souls of Mr. Skeat and Dr. Murray are perpetually vexed by the absurdities of many who attempt philology, so in my poor way I have been astonished and amazed at the ignorance, presumption, and conceit of many, perhaps most, of those who have written on social England, who mistake that to which they refer, and draw grotesque inferences from their inner consciousness. Sometimes they think they have made a discovery, when the find is a common-place to an economic historian, and cackle through a volume or two of print, as a hen does, who, seeming to think that laying an egg is an occurrence of the rarest importance, takes care it should be duly advertised, and carefully reviewed.

The reign of Henry III. is one of great social importance in English life. I will not say that society was organized during the long and, on the whole, peaceful life of this king, for I am persuaded that habits and practices long precede their discovery by constitutional antiquaries. But after the first half of the thirteenth century we get the evidence. I am sure that the discipline of the manor court and the parish meeting long preceded the engrossing of the rolls on which the proceedings of the former assembly are recited. I am confident that formal gatherings, convened by the authority of the crown, which bargained grants for rights, and criticized the administration, are historically older than the records of the Rolls of Parliament, and the notices which antiquaries have collected. But, in the nature of things, conscientious collectors of facts inevitably give a principal value to the date of that which they have discovered. Most properly the editor of the New English Dictionary takes chronological note of the earliest usage of a word. But he would never venture on asserting that the word was not used, was not even familiar before his date, unless he could define the circumstances under which it was borrowed or loaned.

Now let us look at the condition of England just at the time of that famous Parliament which Simon de Montfort collected in this city, 630 years ago, not a hundred yards from the place in which I am speaking. At that time there was only one corporation in Oxford, the University. Not a college was founded, though the University was trustee for some small funds which it distributed among masters, and finally relinquished to University College, a corporation whose real existence is 150 years later than the original gift was. For just as there are people who pretend that their family came over with William the Norman, and just as there are, as there were in the days of St. Paul, lying genealogists who encourage similar delusions, so there have been people who have alleged that the University and a respectable society in High Street were founded by King Alfred. Cambridge, nothing daunted, affirmed that it dated its origin from Edward the Elder.

There were two elementary social units, the parish and the manor. Generally they were conterminous, but it was not infrequently the case that one parish contained two or more manors, with different owners and with separate jurisdictions. The head of the parish was the parson; of the manor, the seneschal or steward. It seems clear that the parish gathering had certain powers of taxation, the two bodies who always existed in the manor, the court baron, which dealt with rights of property, and the court leet which convicted of offences, being the prototypes of the Courts of Common Pleas and the King's Bench. Offenders were presented by one jury and tried by another, just as the grand and petty juries act now.

The principal feature of the parish and manor was their complete isolation. There were hundred courts, probably rape and riding courts, and shire courts. But their action fell early into decay, probably because they had little business to do. Long after they had ceased to be active agents the manor courts survived. But within parish or manor no strangers were permitted to reside. The harbouring them was an offence, and was punished by fine. The people in these primitive and isolated settlements took no thought of what lay beyond their borders. Within the boundary the peace was kept, and this by a very effective police. Outside it, on the no man's law, or in the King's forest, such a phenomenon was by no means universal. Jew, Lombard, foreign merchant, nay, even a travelling abbot, was not at all safe beyond the boundary. There is a curious account in the Rolls of Parliament, and in the petition of Isabel Tresham, widow of the great Speaker of 1450, of the manner in which a gentleman of estate travelled in those days on the king's highway, of the escort which he took, the road he drove, and the perils which he ran. But I am sure that in the troubled times which followed on Tresham's murder, property was not insecure within the boundaries of a parish or manor. It was a large parish which had over fifty inhabitants, a large town which had over 5,000.

Now exactly the same facts which characterized a parish characterized a town. The town, to be sure, generally bought the privilege of electing its own magistrates. It created its own guilds or companies, the charters of these institutions being long subsequent to their foundation. The rule of these corporations was exclusiveness. But I imagine that London was more ready to admit strangers, chiefly through apprenticeship, than the other towns were. Thus the two Chicheles, brothers of the archbishop who founded All Souls, were the sons of a tailor at Higham Ferrers. It is curious that with such an ancestry this college should have a generation ago affected aristocratic exclusiveness. The two Cannyngs, one of them Mayor of London in 1456, the other a rich merchant who built St. Mary, Redcliffe, were Bristol men by birth. But for every reason the cities and towns did not encourage the migration of country folk to within their liberties. And I believe the settlements of strangers in London, as the Italian merchants or money dealers of Lombard Street, and the merchants of the Hanse near the Tower, were there rather by royal grace than by city favour. On the whole, about four-fifths of the English people were country or upland folk, and the residue dwelt for the most part in towns.

There is reason to believe that England exported a considerable quantity of corn, especially from the eastern counties to the Flemish towns, and it is certain that the whole of England largely exported wool. It was perfectly well known, if the manufacture of woollen cloths could only be established in England, that great advantages would follow, and the English kings were eager enough to encourage this development, though with very indifferent success. They strove to get weavers from Flanders, even after they were infected with those heresies, *i.e.*, dissent from established churches, which in some mysterious way always seem to have been rife among a manufacturing population. They exercised a police, immediate or delegated, over such manufactures as existed, and even tried the effects of prohibition, under the only effectual form of those days, a sumptuary law. It was in vain. There was indeed a woollen and linen manufacture in Norfolk, owing, I conclude, to its commercial intercourse with Flanders, though the county has the worst climate in England for woven fabrics, for which a moist atmosphere is all important.

On the south of the German Ocean were the thriving cities of Flanders, any one of which produced more and better cloth than all England did, having indeed the monopoly of these fabrics. Now the estimable people who have studied commercial geography will tell you a great deal about the present condition of great commercial depôts; but they seldom, perhaps never, know why these places have become trading centres, and as rarely why they have, in some cases, ceased to be. And yet, to the historical economist, the circumstances which brought about the rise and fall of Ghent and Bruges are plain and instructive.

The trade in Eastern produce, especially after the caravan routes over Central Asia were blocked by the savages which are still encamped in Asia Minor, Syria, and Northern Greece, centred at Venice and Genoa. The wants of Western Europe were supplied by the carriage of these goods, with the produce of Italy herself, over the passes of the Alps to the upper stream of the Danube and the Rhine. Thence they were conveyed to the Flemish cities, especially to Bruges, and distributed over the west, particularly to France and England. Now trade, just as happened in Holland two or three centuries later, developed manufacturing skill. The cities grew under trade, the population increased, and those who could be spared from trade produced merchandize. The downfall of this trade was due to two causes, almost concurrent. The one was the conquest of Egypt in 1517, and the consequent block of the only remaining overland route from the East; the other was the Spanish Inquisition, begun by Charles V., and carried out by Philip and Alva.

Now it will be plain that this remarkable isolation of English life was a great obstacle to the development of manufacturing enterprise. In early days all the industries were of the villages in the eastern counties. One can see this, at the end of the thirteenth century, in the bailiff's accounts of Bigod's Norfolk estates. The principal seats of the woollen and linen industries were in villages, which grew indeed, but were never gifted with municipal rights, or even with parliamentary representation, and that at times when trumpery hamlets were made freely into boroughs, frequently it appears for political reasons. To be sure, when the greatest manufacture of these boroughs commenced, at or near the middle of the fifteenth century, the eastern counties were firmly attached to the policy of the House of York, and by consequence to its pretensions.

It is highly probable that the remarkable monopoly which England possessed, from the thirteenth century till the sixteenth, may have had a discouraging effect on English manufactures. England, as I have said, was emphatically a rural nation, generally occupied in husbandry. It produced an article of universal demand, and could control its supply. So completely was it the master of this market, that it could, though Parliament imposed a duty of from 100 to 150 per cent. and even more, on wool, without depressing the price at home, or calling another producer into existence. But so great a margin rendered the business of wool producing an exceedingly lucrative one. The landowner or yeoman could win a greater profit from his sheep than from any other agricultural operation. People were quite alive to the fact that a given quantity of wool spun and woven into cloth was worth weight for weight, many times more than the raw material. But you will find that communities which derive great profit from certain callings are slow to enter on new paths, and, if they do enter on them, are slow to improve them. Poverty, not want, as the advocate of this abstraction argues in the Plutus, is the stimulant to the discovery or adaptation of the arts of life, and during the period on which I am dwelling, from 1260 to 1540, poverty was a distant risk in England.

Something, too, must be ascribed to the singular backwardness of the English people, on which, indeed, I have already commented, curiously varied by extraordinary and unexpected outbursts of political anger. Poor as the progress was, which was made in the textile industries of the eastern counties, for the best cloth always came from Flanders, I am persuaded that even this progress would not have been made but for the constant immigration of Flemings into Eastern England. I have frequently seen lists of inhabitants, tenants or owners in villages, which were within the eastern counties, half of whose names were Teutonic. I am sure, had I been at the pains of examining the taxing rolls of the eastern counties, still preserved abundantly in the Record Office, that I should have been able to supply cumulative evidence of the fact to which I call attention. But the organization which in the Flemish towns rendered it possible to produce the most finished fabrics was wanting to England. The guild of the Englishman was narrow, exclusive, local, and was not fitted to bring about results which had become habitual in Flanders. Besides, it is by no means easy to develop a new manufacture, even when the national conditions are present. Of course in those early times, the effectual discouragement of foreign imports was out of the question, and the government wisely imposed only very moderate customs duties.

There are two national products of England the supply of which was inexhaustible as far as the raw material went, the one of which was in the highest degree significant. These are iron and salt. But the domestic produce of iron in England was scanty and of inferior quality, the country depending for what it wanted on Northern Spain and Sweden. The price, too, was prodigiously high. During the fourteenth century iron in mass was worth in money of the time £9 a ton. Now twelve is a very reasonable multiplier on the whole of the fourteenth-century prices. It needs no great acuteness to see what would be the effect on agriculture, and for the matter of that on any industry, if at the present time iron were £108 the ton. So again the national deposits of salt in Worcestershire and Cheshire are enormous. The Romans had certainly made use of the Worcestershire beds. But the art had been lost, and the English were so completely dependent on French supply, that the unrestrained export of salt from France was over and over again stipulated for in diplomatic instruments, and was supposed to be so essential to England, that the restraint of its export was suggested as a military tactic. Its use was essential to the fisheries, and if England could have supplied the Dutch and Flemings with a manufactured product, its monopoly would have been nearly as important as that of wool was. It was not till the end of the seventeenth century that the process of refining rock salt was rediscovered.

Again the art of making brick was lost. There was plenty of Roman brick to be seen in Southern England, and the English did make tiles from an early period ; but they did not make brick till the latter part of the fifteenth century, and then they borrowed the revived art from the Flemings, as usual. A few years ago, in one of the Kensington exhibitions, visitors were shown a mediæval London house. It was built of brick. But I am sure that at the time which that house was supposed to represent brick-making was unknown in England, and no bricks were used for house-building in London. The ordinary English house was a timber frame, on which, within and without, oaken laths were nailed, and covered with a strong plaster of lime, small sifted stones, and hair. After the rediscovery of brick-making, this material was, and for a long time remained, exceedingly dear.

- There is, however, evidence that England possessed early, and long continued to possess, a considerable mercantile marine. The fact is referred to by Frederic Barbarossa in the twelfth, and is allowed by the French herald-at-arms in the fifteenth, century. It appears that it was chiefly employed in the Baltic trade, and with that of Western France and Spain. But it made none of those discoveries which opened up two new worlds at the latter end of the fifteenth century. These were the outcome of Portuguese and Spanish enterprise. Very likely the timid and penurious habits of the first Tudor king may have been a discouragement, but we are expressly told that English ships did not venture into the Mediterranean, when they might easily have chastised the Barbary and Algerine pirates, and have done great service to Christendom. Not indeed that there was lack of enterprise in their own seas. Early in the fifteenth century the Bristol fishermen, by the aid of the mariners' compass, reached the fishing grounds of Iceland, by the Hebrides and the western coast of Scotland.

After the miserable and ruinous reigns of Henry VIII., Edward and Mary Tudor, even the mercantile marine of England shrank into insignificance. An attempt partially successful was made to reach Russia by the north, and Chaloner discovered the White Sea and Archangel, as the port is now called, in the reign of Edward. But for practical purposes the discovery was premature and abortive. There is no period in English history in which the English were poorer and more unenterprising than during the last fifty years of the sixteenth and the first forty of the seventeenth centuries. I am not forgetting the exploits of Drake and Frobisher, Raleigh and Hawkins. But these worthies were no better than pirates, and, a century later, would have been hanged at Execution Dock, as Captain Kidd was most righteously. Of course public approbation went with these old sea dogs, whom Plymouth has recently been eulogizing. It did long afterwards. Blackburn, sometime Archbishop of York (1724–43), is said to have been a buccaneer in his youth, and this long after the days of Kidd. It may not have been true, but it was freely stated during the lifetime of the archbishop, and I have never found out, though I have read a great deal of eighteenth-century literature, that the archbishop resented the charge. It was not, in point of fact, easy in those days, to draw the line between the missionary and the pirate.

The beginnings of English progress were those of the East India trade, on which I hope to comment hereafter. These beginnings were very small and precarious. The Dutch East India Company had eight times the capital of the English. The Dutch were more enterprizing, more intelligent, and being bent, like the English, on securing a sole market, were more successful. There is a famous passage in Clarendon's History, which is highly characteristic of that writer's mendacity. He says, speaking of the dissolution of 1629: "There quickly followed it, so excellent a composure throughout the whole kingdom, that the like peace and plenty and universal tranquillity for ten years were never enjoyed by any nation," and "from the dissolution of the Parliament in the fourth year to the beginning of this Parliament [1640], which was above twelve years, this kingdom and all his Majesty's dominions enjoyed the greatest calm and the fullest measure of felicity, that any people in any age, for so long time together have ever been blessed with, to the wonder and envy of all other parts of Christendom."[1] Now Clarendon may have had in his memory the condition of Germany during the worst period of the Thirty Years' War. I am ready to admit that England was better off than that unhappy country was, of which despotism and bigotry had made havoc. But it has been my business to study the social condition of England during those eleven or twelve years, and I am sure, that with the exception of the long Continental war, at the end of the last and the beginning of the present century, there was no period of recorded history in which the lot of the mass of Englishmen was more degraded, more miserable, and more hopeless. The price of food was generally above the average of the century, and in one year, 1630, was that of an appalling famine. The wages of labour, stinted by the quarter sessions' regulations of the magistrates, were miserably insufficient. The first necessaries of life, food and clothing, were dearer than they now are, and the wages of the labourer were not more than a third of that paid in the poorest agricultural districts. Of course, Clarendon thought that he could utter the false generalities without the risk of detection, and alleges that the despotism which he resisted in his better and earlier days was the golden age of England. You will remember that his famous work was unpublished till the accession of Anne, when it was deemed to have a high political value.

The first movement of English industrial and trade activity was made during the Protectorate of Cromwell. The commercial policy of this remarkable man, undertaken according to the reputed wisdom of the time, was to cripple all possible rivals and to secure a sole market for England, or rather Great Britain. It

[1] Page 122, vol. i. Oxford University Press edition of 1839.

was at this time that the American plantations made great progress, that the East India Company began to obtain enormous dividends, and that generally the mercantile marine of England was revived, strengthened, and extended. "The base mechanic fellow," as the exiled Stuart called him, developed a system, again I say in accordance with the wisdom of the age, which even the restored Stuart could not wholly destroy. From the Protectorate too dates the opulence of London, which even plague and fire could not subvert. The heirs of the Puritans gained that wealth which gave stability to the second Revolution, because it found the new Constitution the necessary supplies.

The most marked features in the industry of the later part of the seventeenth century were the discovery of the processes by which iron, cast and wrought, could be reduced, and the revival of the art by which rock salt could be refined. Iron and glass of the best quality for the time were largely manufactured in Sussex; cast iron, with many of the uses to which this cheap material could be put, became a considerable industry at Dudley. Still wrought iron was more than twice as dear as rolled lead, £36 6s. 8d. a ton; while lead was only £16 7s., and the multiplier at this time being two, in modern money £72 13s. 4d. and £32 14s. It was only when great improvements were made in reducing iron ores, and puddling the best produce, that machinery such as Arkwright, Watt, and Crompton invented would become possible.

Now simultaneously with the improvement in these processes, perhaps in consequence of them, came the new agriculture, and with it a great development of British industry and prosperity, for cheap iron is a prodigious boon to husbandry, and successful agriculture is the healthiest stimulant to manufacturing enterprize. The lamentable condition of British agriculture at the present time has its effects, and those serious enough, on all the other industries of the kingdom, effects so serious that, if private wisdom is not early enough to the rescue, legislation must obviate the efforts of stupid obstinacy. The new agriculture became a universal pursuit, and in some quarters remained a passion till about forty years ago. For nearly a century England was a great corn exporting country. In course of time English agriculture became the object of foreign imitation; for Arthur Young bears witness to the enthusiasm with which he, the student and annalist of the new-system, was welcomed in France and elsewhere. I say English, for no such rapid progress marked the agriculture of the northern part of the island. The fact is, the Scottish lease, which the Duke of Argyll lauds as the quintessence of wisdom and justice, was under its old conditions a very effectual bar to agricultural progress. Greatly as I respect the Duke's abilities, for I value them almost as highly as he does himself, I am constrained to accept the evidence of Sir John Sinclair as to what that most able and useful man saw, in preference to the Duke's ideal. But perhaps you may have read that there were very respectable persons, a couple of generations ago, who thought the unreformed parliament a perfect, almost a heavenly, instrument of government and administration. But one must go out of the world of action if one is to be frightened by paradoxes. There are times in which they sprout as plentifully as weeds do in wet summers, or pictures do for Burlington House, or patents do under the recent law.

I have on a previous occasion set down not a little of the progress made in Great Britain (that of Ireland was rigidly repressed by prohibitive laws) to the peace of Paris in 1763. Nor do I swerve from the position which I laid down, that the effects of that most important political event were a prodigious stimulant to every kind of British enterprize. Chatham had at last succeeded in procuring for Great Britain that which every one taught and believed to be the Eldorado of commerce and manufactures—a sole market. In support of this, Spain and Portugal had alleged that the bulls of Borgia were an integral part of international law. In despite of them, to some extent under their colour, Holland had striven for a sole market, and England had been her rival. Even the Emperor of Germany had imagined that he could, by the Ostend Company, claim, if not the whole, at least a solid share of this great market. But the true rival of England was France. Yet on the conclusion of peace, England rose, according to the theory of the age, the sole winner in the game. France was expelled from India, and practically from North America, while England became, as she has remained, the sole colonizing nation. In these later days, we may know that the sole-market theory, whatever may be said of Greater Britain, is an illusion, that it was rent to pieces within a dozen years after it was affirmed and engrossed, and that the whole of Western Europe, though unable to procure it for themselves, strove successfully against the monopoly which the Seven Years' War aimed at, gained, and seemed to have secured.

There are occasions in the history of nations, especially in their economical history, when delusions are as stimulating as realities. Now here was more than was hoped for. I do not wonder that the English rose to the occasion. The prospect of profit seemed to be instant and prodigious. At the time, however, Great Britain had only one or two successful manufactures. She had at last distanced every rival in the woollen trade, and had held this position for more than half a century; for I have noticed that towards the close of the seventeenth century, the fine cloths of Spain had given place in the market to those of Holland, and at the beginning of the eighteenth the Dutch goods had been superseded by English. North of the Humber and the Mersey, textile manufactures went apace. They had the better part of the New World to supply, and under the colonial system they were alone entitled to supply it. Now no one doubts the benefit of a sole market, if it comes spontaneously, and as a result of the superior excellence of the article manufactured. If we could undersell, or much better, appropriate by the goodness of our products, foreign markets, in a fair and free competition, no rational person would doubt that we had satisfied the highest conditions of production and trade. It was, of course, different when the market was the result of military successes. It was artificial, and therefore precarious.

The pioneers of this new development were our own countrymen. Like the philosophy of Tarsus in the days of Strabo, and the youth of St. Paul, it was entirely of home growth. For the first, or nearly the first, time in our economical history, we were not indebted to foreigners for our improvements, to immigrants from other countries for our new departure. There is an instructive, and I believe accurate, story told about Arkwright. This successful manufacturer was originally a barber and wigmaker at Bolton in Lancashire. Some twenty years ago I came across some of his business cards, printed while he plied this craft, and I gave them to the Bodleian Library, for you know that we ought to carefully preserve all the earliest records we can find of our merchant princes, and while Sir Bernard Banke traces them to Battle Abbey Rolls, we, whose business it is to find how intelligence and industry rise to eminence and opulence, should point our economical moral with the record of this early career. In his later days, Arkwright offered the British Government to incur a large share of the expenses incurred in the Continental War, on condition that his patents were confirmed to him, *i.e.*, his spinning made his own monopoly indefinitely. I do not know why his offer was rejected. Pitt, who committed enormous financial crimes, was at his wit's end for money ; but I presume that the other spinners would not support him any longer if he excluded them from the prospect, just as the landowners refused to condone his foreign policy if he inflicted legacy duties on them. They bore with equanimity the taxes levied on labour and profits, and you may conclude why. But a tax on rents was not to be thought of.

Now my informant was my late friend Sir Thomas Bazley, himself a Bolton cotton spinner. When Arkwright had almost perfected his first power loom, which you probably know meant a process by which the process of the old hand loom could be almost indefinitely multiplied, he found that the yarn as it was delivered through the rollers had an awkward, a fatal trick of curling back. He puzzled over this serious obstacle. At last he took the local blacksmith, who made his early machines, into counsel, and the man, one Strutt, told him that he thought he could cure it. Arkwright asked him his terms. Ten years' partnership and equal profits, was the reply. This was too much for Arkwright, who, like Naaman of old, turned and went away in a rage. But still the yarn curled, and dashed his hopes. At last he reluctantly yielded to the blacksmith. Then occurred another scene. The blacksmith insisted that the deed of partnership should be executed and enrolled. Arkwright stormed, and I regret to say, swore violently. But the local Vulcan was firm. When the deed was signed, the blacksmith went behind the rollers, and apparently rubbed one of them with his hand.

Instantly the yarn was delivered as was wished, and the astonished and enraged Arkwright found that his new partner had only rubbed one of the rollers with a piece of chalk, in other words, proved that one of them should have a different surface from the other. The execrations of the enraged manufacturer were unspeakable. But the compact held, and in the end the blacksmith became Lord Belper.

I tell you this story, in which I trust I have anticipated the excellent Mr. Smiles, in order to illustrate how active the minds of English inventors in the north were during the period which followed on the peace of Paris, when a new world was opened to the energy of the British shopkeeper and merchant. All the invention, to be sure, was centred in the district which lies between the Trent and the Tay, and progressed very unequally in that region; for the hand-loom weavers were by no means friendly to these discoveries, and took energetic means in order to wreck the new system. The manufacturers were even with them, and by help of Parliament hanged the frame-breakers by the score. I regret to say that the progress of British manufacture and trade was as destructive of human life as many battles have been.

Before twelve years had well passed, the doctrine of the sole market received a fatal shock, a *coup de grâce*, in the war of American Independence. Most people dwell on the successful struggle of a principle which that war is said to have represented, that taxation without representation is tyranny. The English Parliament never so understood it, for they taxed abundantly, while they were in no sense representative. To the economist, it is, as it surely was, a struggle against the claim of a sole market, in which not America only, but United Europe, forced the British hand. Of course I am willing to admit that the economical consequences of this war are far less striking than the political. But they are more real and enduring, and in the end, as I shall show you, played the English game. Out of the American struggle came the French Revolution and the Continental war. But out of it also came the total impoverishment of Europe, and the indirect concession of a sole market to Great Britain. Had the United Kingdom kept out of the struggle, the indirect sole market could have come with no 600 millions of debt at the back of it, no beggared and demoralized people among us, and perhaps a few less heroes.

The reverses of the American war were a terrible disappointment. All seemed to be lost. But when great progress has been made in the industrial arts—and unprecedented progress had been made between 1763 and 1775—the occupants of a threatened position do not relinquish their advantages without a struggle. For as soon as great capitals are invested in callings, and the profit of these investments is threatened, the most vigorous efforts are made to avert the disaster. Not to go on, to stand still, is more ruinous than working for a diminished gain, or shrunken profits. The stimulus to invention, that is to economy, grows keener and keener, as the risk of loss is anticipated, and the latter end of the eighteenth century was one of singular activity. Unhappily there was one direction which it took, I mean the enforced labour of the young. Wages were always low in the north, and Arthur Young is an unconscious witness of how inadequate they were in the district from which this new wealth was coming. As years went on, matters became worse; legislation on behalf of children, under the name of Factory Acts, was urgently demanded, and owing to the unfortunate party patronage which it received was as vehemently resisted. Much good came out of the struggle, disfigured as it was by rancour and mendacity. The Factory Acts were passed, and the manufacturers retaliated, by enforcing the repeal of the Corn Laws, and by insisting on the concession of Free Trade. So great good came out of passions which were of ignoble origin.

But before these results were arrived at, British manufacture was established on a firm basis, by the misfortune or folly of the other European States. None of us, in this day, can realize the horror and rage with which the events of 1792 and 1793 were witnessed by the European courts. Philosophers had welcomed the French Revolution, statesmen had applauded it, and it was believed at first that the propaganda of the Rights of Man, would obtain a patient and probably a favourable hearing. But the welcome was speedily followed by execration. Western Europe threw itself in anger on France, and after a short season of doubt, was beaten back, overrun, trampled on. England was the only country which was not invaded, defeated, and held to ransom, and there was a time when it was within this risk. Now war means waste, and when nations have not only to bear their own waste, but to submit to an enemy's waste, and pay ransom in money and men to the conqueror, that community which has only its own waste to pay for is at a prodigious advantage. The Berlin and Milan decrees, prohibiting the importation of British goods into any country under French control, and denouncing the penalties of piracy against shippers who infringed the order, were entirely nugatory. It was proved that, during the time which it might be supposed that they would be effective, Napoleon's soldiers marched to Moscow in clothing purchased from English manufacturers.

The exhaustion of Europe after the peace of 1815, left the British people—I seek to avoid offending Scottish sensitiveness, by using English, and am obliged to use a far absurder ethnic name—as completely the masters of a sole market, as if they had conquered it for themselves. The Continental war had absolutely arrested all continental progress. All the while England was making fresh way in the newer sciences, such as chemistry was, and her rivals were of the future. Of course English trade was crippled by an absurd tariff, and an abominable fiscal system, the first due to the imbecility of such men as Vansittart and Stanhope, the second to the insatiable greed of the landed interest.

The relaxation of the tariff system in England, cautiously undertaken by Huskisson and others, suspended or blundered about by the Whigs and finally effected by Peel, showed what British industry could do when it was freed from these trammels. For instance, very speedily after the abolition of the duty on printed calicos, the price of the finished article fell to less than the duty per yard previously imposed on it. Had not other European nations been more irretrievably depressed by the Continental war, the United Kingdom would have suffered grievously by the foolish pranks of those who handled the finances. I should think that if any single thing would cure the innocent and simple from trusting in administrations, and prove to such persons that they should be severely criticized, the history of the revenue and fiscal expedients during the deplorable epoch from 1790 to 1825 would, if wisely studied, be effectual.

Events which have occurred in the course of the last fifty years in Europe and the United States, during which the former had to some extent recovered from its losses, and the latter had made great progress, but its career was interrupted by the Civil War, made for the British producer. The European wars have been rarely prolonged, but they have been sufficiently destructive, and this country was invited to repair the waste. The development of the United States led to the extensive loan of British capital, and the loans as usual were satisfied by British produce. The enormous waste of the four years' civil war was made up, despite a foolish and mischievous tariff, by British products, for the repair of the losses created so enormous a demand, that the barrier of the tariff, intended to be prohibitive was easily overleaped, and for ten or fifteen years after that war, British manufacture and trade proceeded, as was said at the time, by leaps and bounds.

Even though Europe has profited by peace during two-thirds of a generation, I see no reason to think that British industry and invention are losing their hold on the world's progress, or that, as was the case some centuries ago, our people have to be taught by foreigners. On the contrary, the German has not got beyond the position of an imitator, and not an over honest one either. The United States have made no great discoveries. And so with the rest of the nations. Nor is the cause far to seek. These political communities had deliberately adopted protection. Governments have been too weak or too dishonest to be sensible, and are consequently crippling the intelligence of those whose affairs they administer, by pandering to the foolish, dangerous, and wholly unjust dictum, that private interests are public benefits.

II.

THE CONDITIONS OF ECONOMIC PROGRESS.

Faults of early economists—Importance of study of distribution of wealth —Shortsightedness of some economists as to inventions and value of labour—Division of employments—Skill of agricultural labourers— Agricultural inventions—Babbage on Adam Smith—Effect of division of employments on continuity of labour—Causes of the growth and decay of nations chiefly economic.

I SHALL be engaged this morning in discussing some of the earliest common-places of political economy, positions which though constantly found to be far from exhaustive, are as far as they go accurate. For the conditions of economic progress are very much the same as the analysis of the production of wealth. I have on previous occasions pointed out how grave an error I think it is, to make this part of the analysis precede that of the distribution of wealth, for this latter is the true centre of all economic inquiry. But tradition goes a great distance with most people, and there was an honest reason for this confusion of order. I am not, indeed, quite clear that the excellent people who were responsible for the confusion, as I deem it, either foresaw the consequence, or imagined that the process which they adopted would give force to the very mischief which they strove to expound and condemn. But when people begin to discuss and enlarge upon the processes by which wealth is produced, they are apt to confuse the people who get wealth, a very unimportant, and occasionally a very noxious social element, with those who make wealth, that class on whose exertions not only the progress, but the very existence of society depends. And here, again, I must protest, that the better and more estimable a man is, the more incumbent is it on the honest inquirer to search into and expose such economical errors as he may be led into. You may forgive a man who makes a 'false estimate of another man. But a writer who gives a false view of a social problem must be dealt with on Aristotle's principle—Plato and I, he implies rather than says, are friends, but it is righteous to set truth above Plato and his theories.

Now the authors of the method of political economy, in which the production of wealth is dealt with antecedently to the distribution of products, were the French economists or physiocrats. These excellent men were struck with the stupid hindrances which the French Government put on important industries, and the preposterous favour which it showed to others which were, at least comparatively, trivial. The habits of the time were unfavourable to any criticism as to the way in which France was plundered by a licentious court, and by the vile aristocracy and clergy which were dominant and rapacious. As is the case with many men in many ages, it was necessary to be silent on some scandals, if they were to have any hope of remedying others. In France, as you know, the inevitable temporizing of the economists on the burning question of the distribution of wealth, led to the cataclysm in which the good and the evil were swept into a common destruction. Du Barry with Lavoisier ; the harlots with the philosophers. Let us hope that our history may not be disfigured by any similar catastrophe. We cannot predict, least of all about the English nation, which has not infrequently in its history, exhibited a stubborn ferocity which has startled those complacent people who have been the objects of it.

Nature, says Mr. Mill, gives human beings materials and powers. Both these terms are of enormously wide signification. Of course man cannot make matter. All that he can do is to induce utility in it—utility being employed in the very wide sense of that which is agreeable as well as that which is necessary. But man has first to discover the properties of the different kinds of matter, and next the way in which he can appropriate those properties most rapidly and most efficiently to his service. The properties of matter and the forces, powers, laws of nature, are as nothing till they are distinguished and utilized. There have been ages, it appears, when those qualities of certain kinds of matter which are now familiar to all of us, were utterly unknown. There will be, I do not doubt, discoveries made in the near or remote future, to which our present mastery over nature will seem to be the very infancy of discovery. Now there is nothing on which economists have been so apt to err, as in the limits which they have confidently put on man's powers over nature. Had they known how slowly, even with every apparent stimulus before them, nations which had extraordinary natural advantages, as for example our own people, have utilized them, and had they also known how other nations, with apparently every natural disadvantage to grapple with, have from time to time distanced those who had apparently far greater opportunities; they would, I think, have spoken a little less confidently on the limits of industrial development in mankind. Speculative economists are apt to confound present impossibilities with permanent impossibilities. They who know ever so slightly what has been the course of human invention are aware of how often the impossibility of one age has been the easy process of another. We have no reason to doubt that the same experience will be vouchsafed to future generations. We do not, in short, know all the materials; we are still farther from knowing all the powers. We do know that the materials are utilized, and the powers discovered by labour, and that to such results the idlers contribute nothing. We also know that any given society can maintain only a limited number of idlers, and that these idlers constitute the redundancy of population, the true growth of numbers beyond the means of subsistence—the difficulty of the present, and the danger of the future.

The appropriation, then, of materials, and the discovery and adaptation of powers, natural laws, qualities or properties of matter to human utility is the result of labour. The labour, even when exercised on what seems to be the most ordinary routine, must be intelligent. There is infinitely more distance between a savage and the least skilled labourer—I am using a common-place term—than there is between that least skilled labourer and the most competent and active manager, inventor, and employer. You cannot extemporize labour, that is, you cannot call effective industry into existence by mere demand. It is quite possible to lose what cannot be recalled or recovered, and when people talk glibly of the emigration of the working classes, it is difficult to be patient with them. There are thousands whom we could far better spare than competent agricultural hands and skilful artizans. I do not accept Mr. George's position, that there cannot be a redundancy of genuine workers, but I can so far go with him as to recognize that there may be, and is, a redundancy of people who think themselves very ornamental and very superior.

I defer to a later part of this lecture the exposition of what efficient labour is, and how it can be secured, maintained, and continued. I know no economic problem which is more important than this, none in which more serious practical blunders have been made by shallow metaphysicians. The education of workmen, the instruction of such persons in the conditions of their calling, and in particular in those conditions under which they can get the best possible remuneration for good work, are topics of the highest public interest. I am often amused, till I get irritated, at the self-satisfied way in which certain persons, whose very livelihood, and all that they enjoy, depends on the continuity and efficiency of labour, lecture those whose industry is so all important, threaten them, seek to cajole and frighten them alternately, and imagine that their chatter is not detested and resented. For one cannot get out of this situation, that all wealth is the product of labour, and that the livelihood of all depends on the efficiency of labour. Nay more, the part which capital plays, important as it is in securing the continuity of labour, and comparative uniformity in the value of its products, is small indeed by the service which labour does to mankind. Many of the most familiar functions of capital have been dispensed with in the past history of races, which have made no small figure in the arts of life, and could, perhaps with little inconvenience, be dispensed with again.

One of the earliest phenomena in progress of human societies is that which Adam Smith called the "division of labour." It appears that this great writer was the first person who called attention to the importance of this fact of social life. At least I have not found that the French economists gave prominence to it. But, as Gibbon Wakefield long ago pointed out, the expression is very ambiguous, for the most complete division of labour is exhibited by those persons and classes who least of all come under Smith's principle and his illustrations, and for the sake of clearness, the phrase should be altered into the "division of employments." Nor are the details of Smith's illustrations, and indeed of those who have followed him, exhaustive. Nor has it been pointed out with sufficient clearness how this division of employments has been developed; what are the industries of which it is specially characteristic, and what are the consequences of its development. For in some branches of human industry it is hardly developed at all. In some, at least in Smith's sense, it cannot be. But the analysis of human industry is very imperfect, unless we first discuss the origin and limits of the division of employments.

Even the rudest agriculture produces, as I have more than once stated, more than is sufficient for the wants of the husbandman, unless indeed, as is the case in some parts of Ireland, the narrowness of the holding is the result of certain well-defined causes. Some of you are perhaps aware that these small tenancies were originally manufactured freeholds for life, the motive for which came to an end at the time of Catholic Emancipation, when the Irish freehold franchise was abolished by law, and the life tenancies, having served their purpose, were not renewed. Now unless the landowner contrives to appropriate all but the bare maintenance of the occupier and his family, the excess of produce over necessary wants gives the producer the opportunity of transferring part of the labour which he previously had to give to another who is willing to undertake it, in exchange for a portion of the agricultural produce. In the early days of English agriculture, the husbandman is bidden by those who write about his condition to supply himself as far as possible with the necessary tools and implements of his calling. But very early he must have needed the labour of others in order to carry on his own calling. We may be sure that the smith, the carpenter, and probably the wheelwright had their callings separate from but related to that of the husbandman. It is indeed almost certain that the art of smelting and working metals preceded that of the agriculturist. Now this is the first and the earliest form of the division of employments, and in more recent times it has been quite as phenomenally developed as that which Adam Smith described, and that which he illustrated. There are in our time many occupations, the products of which are in demand, which are in no other sense divided, and in which no progressive partnership, the characteristic of Smith's phenomena, can be developed. This is obviously the case with the higher works of art, in which the conception and execution are entirely the work of one person. But it would be absurd to deny that the prosecution of such callings illustrates the division of employments. There is indeed no surer mark of progressive civilization than the multiplication of such agents. It may indeed be unfortunate that the services of some such persons as obviously come under the definition should be in demand at all; but they exist and do that which they are engaged upon, because the labour of those who procure food can and does maintain them, and persons can be found who will pay them for their services.

It is noteworthy that when these employments were few they were carried to remarkable perfection. Now in England and France the art of architecture was carried to perfection, at a comparatively rude age; in Flanders, architecture and pictorial illumination. We know of English architecture that it was not, except rarely, the work of persons who were specially trained to plan buildings, but of artisans, of masons and carpenters. I know nothing so good as their work in modern times, so faultless in its proportions, so solid, so workmanlike. These workmen are immeasurably superior to modern architects, and the custom went on late. Wadham College was entirely designed by a mason, who had twenty shillings a week for his services, who worked with trowel as well as planned. And so with regard to the miniatures. We have many of these illustrated MSS. Other great libraries have as many or more. But only a fragment of these works has survived to our time. Books of devotion are inevitably worn out as a rule. And it is no use to say that the design and execution of these works were entrusted to men with whom time was no object. One may well doubt the statement. The illuminator was hired to do the work, and no man works longer for his reward than he thinks necessary. Besides, no wealth of time will make up for defects of artistic skill, and it is the artistic skill which characterizes these remarkable products of a bygone time. And one knows how extraordinary was the fertility of some among the earlier artists.

I stated above that the division of employments belongs to only some industries, and to others scarcely at all, except in that broader sense, which belongs to the origines of civilized and settled society. The most marked illustration, to take a common and familiar industry, is that of what is known as a first-class farm hand. Such a person has indeed a distinct occupation, and therefore comes under that elementary division of employments which is characteristic of the earliest social condition, and is increasingly exhibited as human societies become more complex and thereupon more civilized. But his vocation once chosen, or forced upon him, as was the practice when he was made the residuum of all other kinds of labour, his value depends on the number of those operations which he can perform well. Let us consider these functions separately. I will assume that his work is not superseded by machinery, as it cannot be entirely in several important avocations. He must be a good ploughman, *i.e.*, he must not only draw a straight furrow, a work which requires an extraordinary education of the eye, but he must be well acquainted with, and be alive to, the powers of the team which draws his plough. In this latter capacity he is a good deal of a farrier, for however negligent employers may be, careless of the human beings who work for them, it is a plain loss to ill-use or overstrain a horse. He must then know how to drain superfluous moisture off arable land, and give a long ditch that decline which is essential to its efficiency. This has always struck me, who was in my youth familiar with agricultural operations, as a work of no little art. The other preliminary operations of husbandry are less difficult. But in old days, before drilling seed came into fashion, the operation of hand-sowing, with the object it had before it, that of giving exactly the amount of seed which the soil would bear, required a good deal of skill, and in those times was generally carried out by the farmer himself, or by his most trusty hind.

On a well-tilled farm the plough is hardly ever laid aside. It was not six hundred years ago, and it is not now. The earliest writer on English husbandry defines a carucate—and I suppose he knew more about the quantity than the wiseacres do who guess at it periodically in " Notes and Queries "—as the amount of land which a team of horses or oxen with their proper appliances could work on three hundred days in the year. But especially in small farming, say of from fifty to one hundred acres, a distribution of land which has been most unhappily too generally superseded, the good farm hand has to betake himself to other avocations. He will in due course mow, make, carry, and stack hay, and thatch the rick when he has built it. There is some difficulty in building a quadrangular rick, the base of which is less than the superstructure, so that it should be regular in shape, not top-heavy, and so fashioned as to take the minimum amount of thatch consistent with its being water-tight. Similar operations are, or were, carried out in the corn harvest, and in constructing cornricks. One of the operations which he did with great success in which machinery has almost superseded him was that of threshing, so as to get out the whole corn and bruise the straw as little as possible. Then there is no little art in plashing and trimming hedges, so as to make the growth even and to obviate gaps. And though in large farming the tending of sheep was always entrusted to separate hands, you will find that a first-class farm hand can undertake this part of the husbandman's business, if necessary. Of course there is beside the work of the farmyard, the poultry, the piggeries, and some of the rough work of the dairy. These accomplishments the farm hand has to acquire, and to acquire efficiently. You will see, then, that his industry is a marked exception to that division of employments on which Smith insisted as a dominant factor in the progress of human societies. The division belongs, however, to only a limited, and in point of importance, subordinate class of labour. The earliest, most necessary, and most interesting of the industries is little beholden to it.

Now I have pointed out and illustrated this fact at length, partly because it is important to accurately analyse what is said about labour and its incidents, partly because I do not remember to have seen that the particulars on which I have dwelt have been accurately expounded by popular writers, partly, and much more, in order to point out to you how valuable is the industrial element which I have described. I do not here dwell on the political consequences which follow on the forced and ungracious expatriation of those who possess or have inherited this cumulative skill; but it is within my right and my duty to enlarge on the economical consequences of the loss, and the probable substitution for these persons of a less enterprizing or more supple class, who will most inadequately fill their places. The economic progress of society is assuredly not aided by the exit, voluntary or involuntary, of those who are economically the most valuable agents in it. Swift, no doubt, exaggerated when he makes his patriot being of Brobdingnag allege that the person who made two blades of grass grow where one grew before was worth all the politicians in existence. But a little less sweeping assertion is true. And when I say this I am far from endorsing what some economists have alleged about what they are pleased to call certain forms of unproductive consumption. I hold, and I have taught here, that any kind of labour which aids in relieving the strain of life and work is productive, and that that only is unproductive which is selfish and mischievous, and in no sense aids the general energies of society. And here I may add that, in my opinion, it is difficult to account for the rapidity and completeness with which these processes have been learned, except on the principle of hereditary aptitude, an expression which I conceive is more accurate than Galton's hereditary genius, of which, indeed, no evidence has yet been forthcoming.

In manufacture, on the other hand, the principle of the division of employments has been very manifest, and much has been assigned to it by all who have written on it. Here, however, I must make a caution. It is generally imagined that infinitely more progress has been made in manufacturing industry than in agricultural. In some cases this is no doubt the case. But improvements in manufacture are constantly made *per saltum*, and attract attention by their suddenness. Those in agriculture are insensible, partly because the process itself is slow and gradual, partly because it is more gradually adopted. It took a hundred years to naturalize turnip culture in England, nearly as long to diffuse the principle of artificial selection in cattle, sheep, pigs, and poultry. It will, perhaps, take nearly as long to make the practice of ensilage common; but I think I could show you, did occasion permit, abundant illustrations of the manner in which agriculture has progressed.

It has been suggested that there would be an advantage in illustrating the division of employments or labour by speaking of it as co-operation, and Mr. Gibbon Wakefield, an ingenious commentator on the earlier part of Smith's work, has recommended the word co-operation, a term which, in his day, had not been so entirely appropriated as it has in ours. For, says Mr. Gibbon Wakefield, co-operation is of two kinds, simple and compound, both of importance in an economical analysis, the latter sense being that especially which illustrates the division of employments, and he further observes that there is a notable economy in simple co-operation. Two horses, he says in illustration, will draw more than double what one will, as will two sailors working at a windlass, and the like. In compound co-operation each agent is employed on one function only, in the satisfaction of which he acquires extraordinary aptitude and skill.

Now Adam Smith, in discussing his own position, discovers certain advantages in the process. First, "it occasions," he says, "a proportionate increase of the productive powers of labour," or, in other words, "it increases the dexterity of every particular workman;" in the next, "it saves time which is commonly lost in passing from one species of work to another;" and in the third place, it suggests the "invention of labour-saving and labour-easing machines."

Two additions were made to Smith's theory by my late friend Mr. Babbage, and communicated to me a good many years ago. The one is, that in any operation which leads to a manufactured utility there are, however skilful persons may become, different degrees of skill in the operation. Let us take those of the processes of pinmaking in Smith's day. Let one be setting on the head, another grinding the point, a third sorting them into papers or boxes. The first requires more skill than the second, the second much more than the third. But if one person did all three, the commonest labour would be paid at the rate of the most skilful. Now the division of employments renders a graduated scale of pay possible, such a scale being proportioned to the difficulty or easiness of the operation. Now all economies in production are real improvements analogous to labour-saving machines. Mr. Babbage told me that though he had originated as far as he knew this criticism, he subsequently found something very like it in the writings of an Italian economist, who had also examined Smith's theory.

The other addition which my friend claimed to have made to the exposition made by Smith was that the subdivision of employments and the consequent efficiency of labour depended on the width of the market. If, therefore, economists are right in assigning so important a function in manufacture to the division of employments, it is plain that everything which widens the market is an advantage, everything which cripples or curtails it is an evil. Of course the width of the market must be ascertained, and with it the power which the producer has to supply the market. But this knowledge can only be acquired when trade is free, for any attempt to impede the knowledge as to whether a community can compete against any other community precludes the possibility of learning whether we can employ our opportunities to the best advantage. The principle of the division of employments then, taken with the conditions by which it is surrounded, is an unanswerable argument in favour of free trade for ourselves, whatever other nations may do, for in this way we get the best and most solid information as to how we may supply the market, and how we may thereupon make it increasingly wide.

Now what is the effect of the division of employments on the workman, and his power of earning wages? At first sight it would seem that to tie him down to a single operation must be not only to make him ineffective for all other, but to make his calling eminently precarious. Thus we are told that fifty different artisans are engaged in making the different parts of a watch, and all perform operations entirely different from the final act of putting all the parts together. Is not then each of these fifty men rendered useless for any other operation whatever, and is not therefore his special efficiency an injury to him? But in point of fact, his position is not unlike that of the instrument in the production of which he is co-operating with forty-nine others. If watches are to be made, you can no more leave him out of the collective process than you can leave the part which he makes out of the watch. If it be absent the instrument is useless. If he be absent, by parity of reasoning, the whole process is arrested. His apparent weakness is therefore his real strength. To produce, you cannot do without him. It is very probable that in the days of the earlier watchmakers, when the same person finished the watch from wheels and spring to case, the occupation of a skilled workman was more precarious and more capricious than it now is, when he is the master only of the fiftieth part of the collective craft.

I do not doubt, then, that the division of employments has strengthened the position of the workman by making his calling more necessary, and his occupation more steady. Nor are facts wanting to confirm what I have said. There has been in recent years an undoubted depression of manufacturing and agricultural profit. But the loss to the workman has been far greatest in those operations where the division of employments is least dominant, in agricultural as opposed to manufacturing callings. I do not doubt indeed, that the stint of labour in husbandry is a mischief, perhaps a folly. In old days it used to be thought that a farm hand to every twenty acres was good husbandry. If I am rightly informed, the employment is now one in thirty or forty. The Irish are wiser. Irish farmers who cultivate what in that country would be called large farms, *i.e.*, from 200 to 300 acres, have told me, when I have asked them, that they can do nothing on their system except with a man to every ten acres, and this though they are extensive purchasers of modern machinery.

The manufacturer, however, has given far more serious, or at any rate, far more obvious pledges to fortune. Nine cases out of ten it is a less evil to go on than to stop. If he curtails his output he loses on his machinery which lies partly idle, on his plant and buildings. As the husbandman who is slovenly or stingy in cultivating his fields soon finds them become like the garden of the sluggard, though he has the knack of blaming every one but himself for the catastrophe ; so the manufacturer sees that to diminish the effective use of his machinery is to invite something worse than loss of profit. But the workmen in a factory where the division of employments is fully carried out—and where is it not ?—are an organization which cannot be allowed to be idle or to be dispersed any more than the machinery itself can be permitted the suspension of its activity. On the whole, it seems to me, that the division of employments has had a decidedly beneficial effect on the status of the workman.

I have dealt at some length with this elementary part of the production of wealth, and by implication with one of the conditions of economic progress, in order to show to you that in handling these theories we must pursue them, in the light of facts, to their ultimate consequences, as well as see whether the initial analysis is complete.

Nothing is more puzzling to the analyst of economical facts than the question as to how certain sites, famous for progress and opulence, secured this position for themselves. What site, for example, would have seemed more unpromising than that of Venice, built as it is on a heap of barren islets in a lagoon of the Adriatic? But for centuries it was a prosperous city, for a long time it filled a very conspicuous place in the annals of Europe. It is easy to say that it contrived to appropriate all that came from that remarkable movement known as the Crusades, and that till the beginning of the sixteenth century it was the principal *entrepôt* of Eastern commerce. But how was it that other Italian cities, to all appearance equally well situated, failed in the competition? It certainly kept out of the factions which divided Italy, and treated Pope and Emperor with equal indifference. It certainly kept out of European complications, as Genoa did not. The only explanation which I can give here is, that at a very early part of its commercial career, and long before any of its possible rivals did, it developed to a singular extent the machinery of trade. And again, is anything more remarkable in history, than the unrivalled progress of Holland under what seem to have been the greatest disadvantages? Beyond its fisheries, when the War of Independence broke out, it had no manufactures to speak of and little trade. At the end of that war, and at the date of the twelve years' truce in 1609, it was, and remained for near a century and a half, the foremost trading manufacturing and agricultural country in Europe, the teacher of nearly everything to other communities.

Again, it is not easy to assign its place to national character, or the prevalence of courageous opinion. Perhaps after Holland, there is no country which made such rapid progress as those parts of France did where the Calvinists or Huguenots were in the ascendency. These men were the principal cause why, in despite of an execrable government, France became populous and wealthy in the seventeenth century. The men whom Louis XIV. tried to destroy and at last expelled were the true founders of that wealth, and that discipline which gave him so marked an ascendency during the last quarter of that century. But the speculative opinions of the Huguenots did not differ materially from those which were prevalent in the eastern counties of England; and these men certainly, whatever their general merits were, did not produce such an effect on English life and English industry as the French Huguenots did in France. It is very likely that national character depends on circumstances for its development, but it is by no means easy to determine what these circumstances are. The obvious reason in the case of the Dutch is that the very odds against which they struggled, and their almost constant success on sea, as soon as they ventured beyond Europe, gave their daring a promise, and that the position which the Huguenots occupied by the treaty or edict of Nantes made them a garrison within France itself, always circumspect and always enterprising.

No doubt the government of the country, and in particular the relations of that government to economic conditions have to be taken into account in analysing the causes which lead to progress. Governments are almost invariably arbitrary as far as they dare, conceited as to their abilities and their acts, until they are criticized and exposed, and always ready to prolong their existence by base and mischievous alliances. In a well-ordered and progressive community it is wisdom to limit the functions of an administration to the narrowest powers, to be perpetually vigilant over them, and in particular to watch narrowly and critically the conduct of what are called permanent officials, who are apt to do great mischief by mere love of ease and impatience at all intelligent labour. The government or administration of a country is a necessity, for anarchy is nearly as great an evil as a thoroughly bad government, but all authority should be put under the perpetual obligation of proving, as Aristotle said the public speaker should prove, its patriotism, its intelligence, and its devotion to public duty. It is too much to expect these conditions of perfection from any administration, but it is right always to demand them, it is wise to exact as much evidence of them as one can, and it is, or it may be, vital to depose an administration which violates them perpetually and fatally. Let me illustrate what I mean by the history of that ancient civilization which prevailed in Mediterranean Europe from the age of Pericles till the establishment of the Roman Empire, and thenceforward to the fall of the western part of it. The vices which created the empire and destroyed it were all economical. I am not sure that we in modern times can decently charge the Roman people with the lust of conquest, for till a very recent date, most of the European monarchies would be throwing stones from glass houses. But unless the whole of the early history of the Roman Empire is a romance, the warriors of republican Rome were a militia of hardy and frugal husbandmen, whose first energies were turned to the defence of their own holdings. From this the transition to a conquering race, and by a slowly developed wisdom, in which law appears to have been the most powerful factor, an assimilating race, was natural and easy. It is a common-place to say, that the ties which bound them to their subjects must have been strong, even after merciless wars, for Hannibal to have made the very natural mistake, that if they were defeated in the open field, their unwilling subjects would revolt. It is true that they learned the lesson of political assimilation slowly, and after the committal of many errors. But they learnt it.

From the earliest annals or hints of the condition of Rome facts appear, which nothing but the stupid credulity of scepticism could doubt. It may be that there is no solid history of Rome till late in its annals. But no one could have invented the statement, that the peasant farmers bore the brunt of these early wars, and that the aristocracy of Rome appropriated the spoils. For my part I no more doubt the reality of the grievance aimed at by the Licinian rogations, than I do the subsequent efforts of the Gracchi. The aristocracy of Rome, as aristocracies always have done, used their fellow countrymen for battle and divided the spoils among themselves. The ruinous and debasing custom of slavery aided the Roman chivalry in appropriating and securing the plunder, and the constant admission of new men through the channels of office into the existing aristocracy, enabled those who had used the forms of the constitution to appropriate the conquests of the State, to keep a firm grip on what they had seized. For you should remember that the estates of the great nobles of Rome were in theory the property of the State, of which they were in law the precarious tenants, as the early fiefs of Western Europe were. But the people who talk of making the State a universal landlord, have I suspect very little information as to what that means and has been.

Evil however as the age was in which Rome was dispossessing the native Italians, it was as nothing to what happened when the same aristocracy entered upon and administered the prodigious empires of Alexander's generals and successors. Northern Greece, Asia Minor, Syria, Egypt, were crowded with rich and populous cities which, many of them, held the accumulations of ages, the sacred and venerated treasures of uncounted generations. Even those conquests which were made over races with whom Alexander never came in contact, supplied enormous plunder. The gold which Cæsar collected in Gaul is said to have suddenly and permanently doubled prices. Now on this enormous and helpless wealth the Roman aristocracy, once hardy, thrifty, and temperate, was let loose. They became in a generation monsters of licentiousness, extravagance, and greed. The whole machinery of the Roman government played into their hands, and the well-meant restraints on their actions were entirely ineffectual. I can conceive nothing more horrible than the riot and cruelty which prevailed during the last half century of the Republic. The virtuous Brutus, as Adam Smith says, expected Cicero to secure him 48 per cent for his advances to the provincials, and was highly indignant that his friend the great orator should have fixed it at twelve.

Had it not been for the empire, enormous and disastrous evil as a military despotism is, the Roman aristocracy would have made a desert of ancient civilization four centuries before it actually happened. The empire delayed it. It was something that there was only one and not fifty tyrants at work at once. Of course the Roman aristocracy never forgave the empire, and most of the writers of the time, even Tacitus, seem to have had a sentimental feeling that the world was the worse for the change, talked of Brutus and Cassius as the last of the Romans, and dreamed that some pious and liberal emperor would in the end restore the republic. But the ruin though postponed was inevitable. All industry and progress was devoured by the gigantic armies which the empire made a necessity. And the singular fact strikes one that during this long domination, this incessant watchfulness against the savages which were surging on the frontier, Rome made no progress in the art of war. But industry and invention were stifled by slavery. The educated classes were discouraged from labours, which were degraded. Even agriculture, the universal art of the Roman in early times, ceased to be prosecuted by free men, and Virgil's Corycian old man was a pious myth. We do not know very much of the fiscal system of the Roman Empire, but we can learn enough to see that the provinces were slowly drained of all their resources in order that the military system of the empire might be maintained. At last the cataclysm came, and we get the narrative of the barbarism which overspread Western Europe in the earliest chroniclers.

What I have just said, are, I fear you will think, the mere common-places of ancient history. I told the story briefly in order to point out that the primary causes of the catastrophe were economic. Let me take other cases from the history of our own country. I have pointed out how the evil government of our Henry VIII. inflicted injuries on English progress, from which it did not recover for more than a century, and how the brief prosperity of the Commonwealth time was followed by a scandalous and ruinous reaction. Out of that reaction two new forces were developed, the aristocracy and the restored Church. It became an article of religious and political faith to denounce the reign of Cromwell, and the wrangle of the sects; and from the Restoration to the second Revolution, the Dissenters were in evil case. When the Revolution of 1688 arrived, however, these persecuted men were very rich, very strong, and very safe in London, for in old days, English kings who desired to be absolute were very shy of provoking the city. English Nonconformity founded the Bank, lent money to Parliament, and discounted the income from the new taxes. They became indispensable, entirely while the War of the Spanish Succession was being waged, and, as was gradually discovered, while the country was at peace.

The war was no doubt unpopular, the general who gained glory and wealth in it more unpopular, and the administration at home was discredited. At last in 1710 the opportunity came. The reactionary party declared that the Church was in danger, and the people, *i.e.*, the electors believed them. The real motive of St. John, the most restless of the party, was to restore the Stuarts. In this he was aided by Atterbury, probably by Ormonde. There was, I believe, hardly any epoch in English history in which the constitution as settled at the Revolution was in more peril than in the autumn of 1710, when the elections were practically over, and Swift coming to London, on what was an ecclesiastical errand to all appearance, turned over to Harley and St. John—ratted is the later word—and savagely attacked his former friends. Bank stock fell from 130 to 95 in a few weeks, and the stock of the East India Company to nearly the same amount, though the dividend on the former was regularly 7, on the latter 10 per cent. The reason for this panic was, the general belief that the restoration of the Stuarts would be followed by the repudiation of the whole public debt. But the destruction of public credit at this crisis would have been the instant arrest of all manufacture and trade, of the new agriculture which was being commenced, and of that promise from which so much was developed in the eighteenth century. To my mind the history of the price of Bank stock during the three months from October 1, 1710, to January 1, 1711, is more significant than those speculations on the character of public men during the negotiations which led to the Peace of

Utrecht, on which some philosophers of history have been so voluminous.

There are two directions of economic progress, on which much stress has been laid in recent years, and in which much has been done. I allude to the development of sanitary measures, using the expression in the broadest sense, and including in it the restraint of children's labour; the other is the system, slowly and in some directions inadequately carried out, of national, or primary education. The latter of these processes purposes to increase the efficiency of labour, the former to prolong it. By the latter, if the methods are rightly taken, the natural and acquired capacities of the workman are widened and strengthened; by the former, much of the waste of human life, a far more formidable fact than some persons are apt to recognize, is obviated, and what is perhaps in some degree an advantage to the well off, and a motive for action, their risks are also diminished, for no exclusiveness will be an effectual barrier against infection. Dives may neglect Lazarus, but Lazarus has a way of unintentionally avenging himself. Now in both these directions of social reform, my old friend Edwin Chadwick—you can guess how old he must be when I tell you that Cobbett railed at him more than half a century ago—has been energetic and unwearied. I owe him a good deal, for he pointed out to me, many years ago, what was the economic basis of his doctrine.

At the time when Mr. Chadwick commenced his labours some little improvements had been made in London, but hardly anything elsewhere. A few generations before his time a river rushed down the space between Fleet Street and Ludgate Hill, swollen with indescribable abominations. Two similar streams, less in volume, but equally filthy, crossed the Strand. The Thames was nearly as bad as the Fleet Ditch, and remained so till comparatively recent times. The whole of London, especially the City, was polluted by the dead and the living. Small-pox and typhus were perpetual epidemics. The deaths in London were greatly in excess of the births. It took a great deal of trouble to clear away these evils, for it was asserted that some of them were vested interests. Now the only genuine vested interest is that due to a man or class of men who have distinctly done the public a service, under an intelligible contract, the payment for which cannot in justice or equity be decently refused. Compensation for a vested interest is equivalent to the payment of a contract debt, when the creditor's property has been used or consumed by the debtor. A false vested interest is a demand that a nuisance, a social crime, or a wrong, shall not be extinguished without paying the wrong-doer. It is astonishing how confidently nuisance and mischief-makers allege that they have a vested interest.

During the last fifty years London has been turned from one of the unhealthiest to one of the healthiest cities in the world. The progress by which country towns and villages have been purified is more recent, and the machinery by which sanitary reform is enforced is far from satisfactory or complete.

The development of sanitary regulations, though perhaps an invasion of *laissez faire*, has greatly prolonged the efficiency of labour, though much remains to be done, especially in regard to the dwellings of the poor in towns and villages. Now one of the remedies, I strongly believe, is the restriction of the Act of Elizabeth of 1589, under which four acres of land were to be annexed to the cottages of labourers in husbandry, and overcrowding was prohibited under severe penalties.

The education of the children of the poor is insisted on, in order to ensure the greater efficiency of labour. It does not necessarily improve the morals, or increase the prudence of those who receive it. It does not necessarily better their fortunes, for it does not follow that men will earn higher wages because they have gone through the work of a primary school and have passed a particular standard. The knowledge which improves wages is not learned in a school. I doubt whether it will be imparted under any system of technical education which has yet been formulated. It is learned from workmen as it was learned in the best days of the old apprenticeship. No smattering of physics, no study of elementary scientific manuals will give that which, for want of a better word, I call productive knack or handiness. Nor do I believe that effective technical training will be a characteristic of artizans and husbandmen until they themselves insist on acquiring it. I know nothing which should prevent a shrewd, thrifty, and observant mechanic or peasant from being entirely equal, as he was in the Middle Ages, to the abilities of his employer. But he will never achieve the arts of life in a primary school. These he must gather by actual contact with materials. There is reason also to believe that workmen are not particularly ready to embrace the offer of that technical education which is made them. They are, not a few, under the impression that the expedient is intended to secure the employer better work, but with no improvement in the workmen's wages. The struggle between employers and workmen has been so prolonged, and the language which some of the former use about their hands is so bitter and unfair, that there is good cause for distrust on the part of the latter, however unfortunate distrust may be in its consequences.

Now it seems clear to me that a system which constrains a workman to pay for what is not, and is not intended to be, for his personal benefit, is as irrational and unjust as it would be to compel a man at his proper cost to improve another man's property. National education is similar in nature to national defence. Suppose, as is the theory of the law, we were to call on all adult males to undergo military drill, and be enrolled in the militia. With what justice could the State call upon them to do this at their own expense, or rather, not only to find the time for their military instruction, but to pay their drill-sergeants and other officers for teaching them their exercises. To increase the efficiency of the national defences is plainly more in the interests of those who have much property than it is to those who have little, and to a great extent are discouraged from having any. To increase the efficiency of labour is for the benefit of employers, certainly in the first instance, probably in continuity. It surely is the duty of those who own property, and especially capital, to find the means for defraying primary education. And if the efficiency of labour is increased every consumer derives a benefit from the result.

I have only dealt with a few of the conditions of economic progress. But they are by far the most important. They are, in so far as I have discovered them at present, industrial skill or aptitude, in connection with which I have given you a full, and I could fain hope, an exhaustive account of the division of employments, wise and just government, in order to secure which perpetual vigilance and active criticism are necessary, together with those processes which, as I have said, have for their object the prolonged efficiency of labour and its increased efficiency.

III.

THE PROGRESS OF ENGLISH POPULATION AND THE CAUSES THEREOF.

Population of England in the fourteenth, fifteenth, and sixteenth centuries—The coal supply—The poll-tax of 1377—Population of chief towns—Population of Kentish Hundreds—Survey of Gamlingay and Romney—Growth of trade in the seventeenth century—Sole market—Godwin and Malthus—Theories of Malthus and George examined—Redundancy of certain classes of society.

OF recent years, there has been, I must admit, some disposition exhibited on the part of certain writers of what a generous critic calls history, to make some use of facts other than those which are customary or traditional, in what they write and publish, and I presume, sell. In the same way there is some inclination on the part of certain economists to blind evidence with their metaphysics, and to inquire hesitatingly and tentatively with the high priest, Are these things so? I cannot say, however, that as yet the results have been satisfactory. Men are exceedingly unwilling, after they have grown up in an atmosphere of theory, to surrender themselves, their conclusions, their prejudices, their preconceived opinions to the guidance of facts, and patiently submit to the result towards which the facts lead them. Nor is it easy for persons who think that they ought to speak and to write books, to interpret related figures, or even to understand the terms which they use; and thereupon they boldly commit themselves to inferences for which there is no shadow of proof. And in this process they are constantly assisted and encouraged by kindly critics, to the mass of whom, beyond the invaluable assistance accorded by Haydn's "Dictionary of Dates," all facts of more than ten years' old are in the dark ages, and sometimes, I fear, facts of ten days' old. Now in what frame of mind do many such people treat the economical side of history?

They sit down to a writing table with a preconceived notion, to which they cling desperately, as, for example, that the fifteenth century was a period of unparalleled suffering for the mass of the English people. Where they got the notion they cannot tell you, and do not tell you. It may have been gathered in the first place from Mrs. Markham or Mr. Collier, or, as is more probable, it is a bodiless expansion of their own minds. In its inception, there is nothing to support it, nothing even to excuse it. But it is a condition in speculative history, that you must get something which seems like evidence. Sheer dogmatism will not do, except when bimetallism or fair trade are talked about. Authorities must be had, and will be interpreted in a non-natural or transcendental sense. It is sometimes possible to get a seeming proof from an earlier time, and in that self-forgetfulness of those who passionately adhere to a theory, to transfer them to the time of which the author is writing, and the opinion which he wishes to expound. There are some authorities which cannot be so easily got over. There the author misreads, misunderstands, or misquotes. Sometimes he boldly denies their relevance, frequently he ignores them. The writer finds no intention too rash to deter him. I have known such persons quote authorities in what I trust is an unknown tongue to them; the true meaning of whose language is a flat contradiction to the inferences which they draw. So misled are such people by the habit of preconceived opinion, that by some strange fatuity they constantly find proofs where there is nothing but refutation. And it is curious that men, otherwise honourable, diligent, and well-informed, will distort the plainest facts in order to defend their hypothesis. There are writers of history who are like "scientific witnesses," advocates and partizans when they should be searchers after truth.

Now as long as the writer confines his own speculations, and what he calls his proofs, to his own consciousness, and his study table, no person whatever has a right to take offence. If he printed his opinions for private circulation only, as some men do their genealogies, he has not taken the public into his confidence, and cannot be accused of deceiving them by personal fictions. But he ought to pause before he publishes. He could be at once wise and merciful if he committed his MS. to the flames. Better things to be sure have perished in this way, when authors have been rightly fastidious. There is a serious responsibility in the utterance of economic opinion.

Now I am principally led to these observations by what has happened to the subject which I am treating to-day. The wildest guesses have been confidently made about the population of England say in the fourteenth century, about the size of the towns, about the losses from famine, pestilence, and war.

Now my contention is that during the fourteenth, fifteenth, and sixteenth centuries the population of England and Wales was almost stationary, and amounted to between two and a quarter and two and a half millions. I have three grounds for my statement. The first is derived from the average product of agriculture; the second from a return made in 1377, of the number of persons liable to a poll-tax then imposed, a document printed and analysed some century ago in the "Archæologia"; the third from an actual census taken from certain hundreds in Kent in the reign of Henry VIII. I shall be able to add a fourth, from the houses contained in the various surveys taken of the All Souls estate in Warden Hoveden's time, *i.e.*, towards the end of the sixteenth century. Some of you may remember that I showed you a survey made of Gamlingay parish in Cambridgeshire by one Langdon. The same surveyor and another, named Clerke, were employed by All Souls, and both did their work for All Souls, as well as Langdon did for the single Merton estate, which he mapped and planned.

Now I conclude, from most unquestionable data, that five hundred years ago, the average rate of production from seed sown, in wheat, which was then, even more than recently, the staple food of the people, was only four times. I have seen returns of what was actually reaped from a measured quantity of seed sown, in cheap, *i.e.*, abundant, years, and have verified my inference a thousand times. At present the average return from two bushels of seed to the acre, the quantity allowed five centuries ago, is fifteen times. But a greater ratio of seed was consumed then, and it is doubtful whether as much land was under cultivation then as is now. Now a few years since it was reckoned that the present English produce would feed fifteen millions. But five centuries ago, the land under wheat cultivation and bearing a crop, could not have fed more than two and a half millions. From this must be deducted seed, and this may perhaps be compensated by the small admixture of rye or some other grain, which, under the name of maslin or meslyn, was the food of farm servants. I say small, for the breadth of rye sown was very narrow. It must be remembered, too, that in giving a quarter of wheat per head of population, I am very moderate. There were no winter roots, potatoes, turnips, parsnips, carrots, five hundred years ago in England. The monks who dined on parsnips and similar roots, existed in the imagination of figurative historians and novelists only. Historians, you know, will be picturesque. When Macaulay talks of the Irishman of 1692 longing to go back to his potato patch, he speaks of a thing which was not, just as he does when he talks of the oaks of Magdalene, and a host of other details which make up a picture, in which nothing is wanting but facts. Now Macaulay was accurate in a thousand particulars, but this habit of disregarding little facts in detail has made some people doubt his accuracy in greater matters. If I had no other proof than that of the average production of wheat in favourable years, on which I happen to be specially well informed, when I write or speak about the facts of five centuries ago, I should be convinced, that England and Wales did not and could not maintain more than two and a half million souls at that time.

Now in 1377 Parliament gave the old king, Edward III., in the last year of his reign, a poll-tax of fourpence a head, on all lay persons over fourteen years of age, none but known, *i.e.*, registered beggars, being exempted. Beneficed clergymen paid a shilling, all other ecclesiastics, except the mendicant friars, fourpence. Durham and Chester, Wales and Monmouth, not being represented in Parliament, were not taxed by Parliament. The account of the proceeds gives the number of those liable to the tax in forty-two towns. Now if we add a third to the number of those assessed, in order to include the children under fourteen, a very liberal calculation for childhood in the Middle Ages, when the risks of life were far greater, we get 168,720 for the population of the forty-two towns, and 1,207,722 for the other thirty-eight English counties. Durham and Chester may be taken at 51,083, Wales with Monmouth at 131,040. Now add one-third to the country population and you get 1,853,127, or with the town population 2,021,847. There still remain the ecclesiastics and the mendicants. Take them at 162,153, and the population comes out at 2,184,000, or less than two and a quarter millions.

But I cannot yet relieve you of the figures in this instructive return. The largest town of course is London. Perhaps it was healthier than it was in the seventeenth century, when the deaths greatly exceeded the births. With a third added to its taxable population, it had 35,000 inhabitants. The next city is York, with near 11,000. Bristol has about 9,500, Coventry a little above 7,000, Norwich near 6,000, Lincoln about 5,000. No other English town had over 5,000 inhabitants, though thirty-six more are separately assessed, and returned. In Bedford, Surrey, Dorset, Westmoreland, Rutland, Cornwall, Berks, Hunts, Bucks, and Lancashire, no town whatever was thought worthy of a separate return, though they sent many members to the Parliament which granted the tax. England at this time, and for many a year after this date, was essentially rural, and not a little of its economical history is bound up and derived from the country life, which its inhabitants lived for centuries. Besides, though England possessed fortresses and walled towns up to the civil war of the seventeenth century, these were not constructed on scientific lines. There was not an English town which had been protected by such engineering defences as were erected in plenty in Holland, Flanders, and the eastern frontier of France. It would seem from several Acts of Parliament that many towns were falling into decay during the reign of Henry VIII., a fact which has elicited some very grotesque reasoning from Mr. Froude, in his sketch of his patriot king.

Now a good many years ago, I found in the Public Record Office among a mass of miscellaneous papers of Henry VIII.'s reign, an enumeration of the population contained in nine Kentish hundreds, on the eastern side of the county, and an account of the stock of grain possessed by the inhabitants. Kent was, in the first half of the sixteenth century, a decidedly prosperous part of England, and these hundreds are in the most fertile agricultural district of the county. They contained no large town at that time, and contain none now. They are excellent specimens of what was the richest and most settled part of agricultural England at the time. Now the population of the hundreds is 14,813. In 1861 the population was 88,080, or almost exactly six times as much as it was more than three centuries before. Now this proportion almost precisely corresponds with that which I just now stated was derived from the rate of agricultural production and the poll-tax of 1377. I conclude therefore that for upwards of two centuries, just as there had been no improvement in the art of agriculture, so there was no increase in the population.

Now I have long been convinced, for what I may call analytical reasons, that no material increase of the English population took place during the last half of the sixteenth century. I use the expression material increase advisedly. I make no doubt that there was during Elizabeth's reign a considerable immigration of Flemings, chiefly traders, occasionally manufacturers, and that these generally settled in the towns, where alone foreigners could act in concert, perhaps to be safe from hostility and wrong, for the country folk in England had in those days, and to much more recent times, no love for strangers, and they were not even cordially welcomed in the towns. But we know that the woollen manufactures, localized in Norwich and Colchester respectively, that of say and that of baize were brought hither from Flanders. So important was the baize manufacture of Colchester, as a coarse cloth especially fitted for the clothing of working men, that the price of baize is constantly quoted through the early part of the eighteenth century as typical of woollen goods. But I am persuaded that these manufactures of foreign origin did not often spread into the country places.

Recently, however, and from a wholly unexpected source, I have been able to arrive at the same conclusion synthetically, and for reasons very similar to those which enabled me to determine on the population during the first half of the sixteenth century. Some of you may remember that I showed you a survey of the parish of Gamlingay, in Cambridgeshire, chiefly with the object of illustrating the system of cultivation in common fields. This survey was drawn for the purpose of assisting the college in a lawsuit which it had with a family named St. George, between which family and the college, as I know from the Merton archives, there had been litigation for centuries. Now in this survey every house is marked and can be counted, though one has to take care that one does not include outhouses in the number of habitations. At the same time All Souls College entered upon a much more extensive system of surveys. There was a domestic reason for the action. The College, in which one Hoveden, a man of considerable energy and character, was Warden, was very persistently importuned by Elizabeth to grant certain highly beneficial leases to one or more of her courtiers. Elizabeth, like many other excellent and energetic persons, was exceedingly prone to provide if possible for her dependents at other people's expense. She endowed her treasurer Cecil, whom we know as Burleigh, at the cost of the See of Peterborough; her Chancellor, Hatton, at the charge of the Bishop, *i.e.*, the See of Ely; and similarly impoverished the endowments of Exeter and Chichester by the same process and with the same ends. The Colleges at Oxford and Cambridge did not escape, and partly for policy, occasionally on compulsion, granted highly beneficial leases to the Cecils and other people, who no doubt did much public service, but were to a great extent rewarded at the cost of private corporations.

Hoveden appears to have been firm, and to have saved All Souls from temporary, perhaps from permanent, spoliation. In order that the College too might have on record a careful and accurate description of its estates, he employed Langdon and another surveyor named Clerke to map out the College estates to scale, generally sixteen feet to the mile. Now, as before, the houses in the several parishes are marked, and the collection, in five folio volumes, still preserved in the Library, is of great interest and value. Now taking seven of these parishes or properties, and including Gamlingay as an eighth in the list, and assigning four and a half persons to each house—in these days of overcrowding the census gives only five and a half to a house—the population of the eight parishes (all of which were rural twenty-seven years ago, for I still take the census of 1861) there were 280 houses in all, and therefore 1,250 inhabitants. At the census of 1861 there were 8,281 inhabitants, that is more than six and a half times as many people as there were at the close of the sixteenth century, for the survey takes about a dozen years to finish. Now this you will see is a rather less ratio than that of the Kentish hundreds in the reign of Elizabeth's father. One of the surveys, I regret to say, baffled me. It is that of Romney Marsh and its parishes and towns. But the scale was too small. Still, I counted only four houses in Old Romney and thirty-seven in the new town. The population was therefore 186. But in 1861 the population of Old Romney was 151, in place of 18; of New Romney 1,062, in place of 168. Here, then, the increase is over seven times. This kind of evidence, I submit, is overwhelming, and satisfies every condition of proof.

Now it is certain that at the end of the seventeenth century the population is more than double that which I have calculated was in England at the conclusion of the sixteenth. Here, again, we have several proofs. Macaulay has referred to three of them. First, that based on the hearth-tax returns of 1690. The second is an estimate made for William III. of the religious sects in England. The third is a recent estimate by Mr. Finlaison, derived from examining the old registers of baptisms, marriages, and burials. To these then we may add that derived from the produce of grain. In average years, taking into account the enclosures which had been made, I have no doubt that double the amount of corn was reaped that had been a century before, though I am pretty sure that, especially in the north, the people had been forced to subsist on inferior grain. So naturally does this increase of production seem to have been the dominant cause, that at first I concluded that the growth of agriculture was the sole reason why the population increased. But I became convinced as I extended my researches, that though something has to be assigned to this cause, it was far from being the sole origin of the increase. The frequent comments made on the unsatisfactory character of English husbandry are proofs that the growth of agricultural skill had been local and spasmodic.

The most dominant cause, I do not doubt, was the general pacification of the Border and the settlement of the northern counties by weavers. I discovered when I examined the returns of the hearth tax which were given for the several English counties, that, Middlesex and Surrey excepted, the population of the north was as dense as that of the south, and that several of these northern counties had a more numerous population to the square mile than those of the southern counties had. It is true the contribution to taxation which the northern counties made was a good deal less than that exacted from the south. But this inequality was a subject of frequent complaint. And again the charge for maintaining the northern poor was far less to the acreage than that incurred in the south. This was, however, I believe, due to the fact that during the civil war the population pressed into the associated counties. The poor law, too, as we see from the magistrates' assessments, was more severely administered in the north. But, above all, it was during the seventeenth century that weaving, especially woollen weaving, generally migrated to the north, or grew there rapidly. The anonymous author of "The Interest of Scotland," writing in 1732, speaks of the great growth of woollen manufactures in Yorkshire, and of linen and of similar fabrics in Lancashire.

During the eighteenth century population was again nearly doubled. The cause was threefold—the growth of the towns, in many cases owing to the immigration of the banished Huguenots, a body of settlers who were, and continued to be, of the greatest value to the English nation; the extension of the new agriculture, and, I must add, however unjust was the distribution, the numerous enclosures made; and the rapid growth of invention of mechanical skill and of trade. On an earlier occasion I have described to my audience, how this progress was aided by the singular success of British warfare during the Seven Years' War, and the sole market which we obtained as a result of that struggle. It was indeed a brief ascendency, and the sole market was shattered by the War of American Independence. But we got a great start; the attitude taken by France during that war was speedily turned against itself, and the success of British manufacture was, at any rate, if not permanently assured, greatly aided.

At first sight, the acquisition of a sole market seems like that limited protection in young countries which Mill has incautiously, and, as I think, for wholly insufficient reasons, commended. But the difference between the two is fundamental. The acquisition of a sole market gives the possessor of it the opportunity, with entire competition among his fellows, and therefore with every stimulant to invention and thereby labour-saving and profit-making expedients, to hinder foreign rivals from entering on the market which has been won for the trader. The adoption of protection does not, and by the very terms of its existence cannot, aid in procuring a foreign market, but, on the contrary, excludes the protected industry from that foreign market, unless the protected manufacturer sells at a loss on production, that is, at the expense of the consumers in his own protected market. It is possible that American calicoes and German iron occasionally compete against our products in neutral markets. But I am certain that, in the very nature of things, the trade could not be carried on, unless the American and German consumer paid the expenses of the trial. It is also clear that the power of competition by dealers who work under protection is very narrow; for if the trade grew to any dimensions, the burden on the domestic market would be at once intolerable, and traced to its true causes.

Of course, I hold that the sole market was a blunder, and that Chatham in seeking to obtain it was chasing an *ignis fatuus*. But like many unwise economical acts, it had a defence and a plausible one. English statesmen saw that Spain had clung passionately to the monopolies which the Bull of Borgia, pontiff and profligate, had conferred on her, and had done all in her power to exclude the British trader from the New World. They had seen that the Dutch, the teachers of Europe in maritime enterprise and successful trade, had with De Witt believed that the "true interest of Holland was to maintain her trade monopolies." Now statesmen are rarely wiser than the times in which they live. They are apt to say that what they do not foresee and are not ready for does not come within the range of practical politics. I do not find fault with them for their hesitation. They have to consider what they can do, and they know that what they can do will be certainly criticized adversely, even by those who if they were in office would imitate them exactly, and claim originality for the imitation. And then the market was won. It seemed the height of Quixotry to vindicate the freedom of the seas and the freedom of the market for those who had taken no part in the struggle. And then sliding inevitably into the pernicious doctrine that private advantage is a public benefit, they complacently put the cost of acquisition on one set of shoulders, extracting the charge from other people's pockets, and coolly, and almost with conscious virtue, shovelled the gains of the acquisition into their own.

As population grew towards the close of the eighteenth century so it sank deeper and deeper into misery. In Gregory King's time the workmen who, even in these remote times, were seen to be in some shadowy way the sole creators of wealth, were, notwithstanding, declared by that acute reasoner to be a burden on the wealth of the country, because without assistance from the poor rate, the wages paid them were insufficient for their support. Their lot was lightened greatly during the first sixty or seventy years of the eighteenth century, for the new agriculture procured abundance, and, as is always the case, wages rose during those cheap times. But at the end of the century their misery was as marked as their earlier and temporary affluence. It became necessary, so insufficient was the pittance which was paid them, to quarter them permanently on the rates under the allowance system. But no one seems to have dreamed of the machinery which had beggared them. Sir Frederic Eden, with the most appalling facts before him, wrote the history of the poor, collected the justices' assessments as far as he could, and calmly surveyed the surface, not giving the slightest heed to the manifest causes of the situation.

I have done my best to make people better informed. The misery of the poor was the deliberate act of the legislature, of the justices' assessments, of the enclosures, the appropriation of commons, and the determination, as Mr. Mill has said, on the part of the landowners to appropriate everything, even the air we breathe, if it could only be brought about. Nor is it wonderful that population increased under this misery. Misery is a far more powerful incentive to population than a check to it, as Adam Smith saw, and Malthus did not. In the interest, as they fondly believed, of rent, the English legislature, composed of landowners, by statute, had utterly impoverished and pauperized the British labourer. Now, the eighteenth century was an eminently sceptical age, and had become entirely unheroic. It was, among other things, blindly and blunderingly, I must admit, with the great exception of Adam Smith, groping after economical verities, and men often mistook their own just indignation for the discovery of remedial measures. Of this school was Godwin, and an illustration of it is his "Political Justice."

Godwin, like many other persons of his age, was struck by the miserable condition to which labour was reduced, and the undeserved hardships which it underwent. He had witnessed with keen interest, as nearly every honest man had, notably Arthur Young, the uprising of the workers against the shameful oppression of the old French *régime*. Great things were hoped from the events of 1789, and there was but little sympathy with the old noblesse when in the autumn of that year, the uprising of the peasants took place. The well-wishers to human progress were terribly disappointed, when the September massacres came, the Directory and the Terror. But the brutalities of the French Revolution were the outcome, the inevitable outcome of long centuries of evil doing. They were exasperated by the consciousness that the rest of Europe was either conspiring against France, or being leagued for the purpose of armed intervention. Recent discoveries among French archives have proved that Pitt, while he still professed amity to France, was secretly supplying her domestic enemies with funds. Perhaps we shall at some future time learn how it was that the splendid services of Burke were rewarded, and how it was that that eminent personage suddenly became a considerable landowner, for the history of Burke's fortunes is one of the mysteries of that epoch.

Now Godwin erred in treating the subject which he undertook in the way in which all persons at that time erred. He discussed the situation on the lines of abstract principles, on lines which the House of Commons calls academical, and I have been accustomed to describe as metaphysical. This method of handling social questions is, I venture on asserting, always nugatory. I will not say that nothing besides talk came out of the reasonings of Rousseau, for I am pretty clear that a great deal of mischievous and in the end disastrous action came from it. And the reason is plain. Such a line of argument as Rousseau brought into fashion, and Paine with Godwin introduced to Englishmen, has no result but one, against which every habit and every interest is always, and I believe rightly, arrayed. It aims at nothing short of the reconstruction of society, of an entire social revolution. Unless all history is studied in vain, attempts after this ideal involve discomfiture and discredit, or ruin. The worst enemy of human progress, often I allow the unconscious enemy, is the man who works for a social revolution, to be accomplished by violent or even Parliamentary means. But you cannot, to use the schoolmen's phrase, discover a *materia prima* in social life. You cannot arrest its action, while you submit to a remodling. The only thing which wise men will attempt to do is to remove manifest and provable wrongs, which under the guise of law have crept into the social state, and have distorted it. Had Godwin betaken himself to a discovery of the causes which had brought about the deplorable condition of the English workman, at the time in which he and Eden were simultaneously writing, he would have given a very different complexion to the controversy between him and Malthus. As it was, he saved Malthus the trouble of inquiring into the sufficiency of the causes, and gave him the opportunity of bringing forward a theory which was utterly irrelevant to the subject, but was, for sufficient reasons, entirely acceptable to those who wished to find a satisfactory solution of the situation. Now the explanation which Malthus gave was highly satisfactory. It has been accepted by most economists with some slight modifications. It is the backbone of the political economy of Ricardo, of the elder and of the younger Mill. It has seemed to prove that the misery of the poor is inevitable, not to say providential, and has blinded people to the true laws of population, and the occasional or permanent phenomena of its redundancy. I cannot say that on the present occasion I can give an exhaustive examination of the principles which Malthus enunciated, and economists have generally accepted, any more than I can give within the limits imposed on me, a similar examination of Mr. George's counter-hypothesis; but I trust that I shall be able to make a few general principles clear to you. Ricardo and Mill or Malthus are the parents of German socialism, in the pages of Marx and Lassalle.

Malthus was an estimable and excellent man. He was really struck as profoundly as Godwin and others were with the deplorable spectacle of many people starving and all workmen miserable, in a population of less than ten million persons, for so the unions revealed the facts in 1801. But he did not grapple with the social causes of the phenomena. He tried to find their origin in certain natural laws. So much exception must be taken to his theory that a careful analysis shows it to be well-nigh worthless, so numerous are the objections even from his own point of view which might be taken to his theory. I may add that Malthus was professor of Political Economy at Haileybury, and apart from controversy, there was some reason in his attempt to grapple with a question which is always of interest in Hindostan, even at the time when he wrote, when the population was hardly a third of what it now is.

Malthus began by assuming from the analogy of other forms of animal, and he might have added of vegetable, life, that there is a struggle for existence, and thus he was the indirect author of the familiar doctrine known to economists as the margin of cultivation theory. Up to this line of the means of existence population always tends to press, increasing till it becomes perilously near it. He did not say the means of comfortable existence, and perhaps the state of things which he lived in, and witnessed, would scarcely have suggested the gloss. The boundary would be inevitably and incessantly overpassed were it not for those correctives which he called vice, misery, and voluntary restraint, the last factor being subsequently altered into moral restraint, perhaps out of deference to his professional position, for Malthus was a clergyman.

Now here appeared to be an explanation sufficient, perhaps exhaustive, of the situation. It was inexpressibly soothing to those who had brought about the situation, for it seemed to show that nature not man was the cause of it, that it was the result of an inexorable natural law, and in no sense the result of positive and partial legislation. It gave, I grant, great annoyance to some ardent philanthropists, who coupled the name of Malthus with those of some other unpleasant entities. But none of the good man's critics took the pains to study the statute book, and discuss the origin of what have been called rights, and I am constrained to describe as wrongs. The doctrine that in countries which are fully settled, a phrase which by the way has no meaning, population is always pressing on the means of subsistence, was accepted as indisputable, and that consequently the misery of labour is of its own creation. So satisfied was Malthus of his teaching, and so satisfied were his disciples, I am bound to say, with it, that the economist went so far as to recommend, in order to assist his positive checks, as he called the first two, distinguishing them from the preventive check as he called the last, that all legal relief to destitution should be at once and peremptorily put an end to. I do not think that he came to the conclusion that the processes which he described resulted in the survival of the fittest. That would have been too ironical. He only took into account simple numbers, and a hypothetical limit to the means of existence.

Now it must I think be admitted that there are such marked differences between the human race and the inferior animals as we call them, that it is unphilosophical and unnatural to consider them parallel or even analogous, when we consider social facts. In the first place, the nonage of the human offspring is remarkably extended. Other animals equal in bulk to him come to maturity and independence at an early age. Man often needs a period of from fifteen to twenty times as long. The increase cannot then be as rapid, is foreseen and felt. Whether it precedes or follows on the increased means of subsistence, is a matter we shall see further on. Again the very nature of his life and its conditions enforces a prescience of the circumstances which surround it. Such a forethought is manifest in the customs of the lowest savages. It is greatly intensified among races, for we can only speak generally, in which the standard of subsistence is a high one. So far is it from being the case, as Malthus thought, entirely on abstract grounds, that misery checks population, that it is perhaps the most powerful stimulant to it, quite apart from the provision on which Malthus laid so much stress, the legal relief from destitution. The fact is abundantly illustrated by the social history of Ireland. Up to 1845–6 Ireland had no poor law. But the misery of Ireland was excessive, and is witnessed to by writers like Swift and Arthur Young. At the outbreak of the potato disease in the autumn of 1845 the population of the island was over eight millions, most of them dependent on a single means of subsistence, and that the cheapest, lowest, and most perishable. Now though nothing so terrible as the famine of 1845 had ever occurred in Irish social history, famine was endemic in Ireland. The people were miserably oppressed and therefore reckless. It is very difficult to get at any information about fertile and infertile families. We know something about noble families, and how they die out in the male line. We know a little about the singular fecundity of the criminal classes, for inquirers have been startled at the numerous descendants of thieves. We know, too, that hardly any persons of great literary acquirements, especially those who have been distinguished for imaginative gifts, have left descendants in the fourth generation. Perhaps in time to come, a law will be discovered on this phenomenon, and the fact that a poet has left a long line of descendants will be more fatal to his reputation than any assaults of any number of critics.

Now let us turn to the facts of English social history. From the earliest times the staple food of the English people has been wheaten bread. Wheat is the costliest, and on the whole the most precarious of our corn crops. Now I consider a famine to be a scarcity in which the price of wheat rises to more than twice its average price, a dearth when the additional price is from one half the ordinary price to double. I should add to this that the contingency is increased when the law tampers with wages, as it did successfully in 1563 and onwards. Now I have in my possession a record of every harvest in England since 1259, *i.e.*, for 628 years. The resultant inferences are, to be sure, affected by the free-trade measure of 1846, though it took a much longer time than people foresaw, or even now understand, to create a corn trade. Now in the last forty-two years of the thirteenth century there was no famine. There was in the fourteenth, in 1315, 1316, 1321, and 1369, for in these years wheat was more than double the average price, and once was five times above it. Then people as we are expressly told perished from hunger. In the fifteenth century there was only one year of famine, 1438, and only one year of dearth, 1482. In the sixteenth there was a year of famine in 1527, and after Henry had committed the enormous crime of issuing base money, famine was endemic. But the most dismal record is that of the seventeenth century, when severe dearths, consequent on deficient harvests were endured by the English, Hartlib, an excellent observer, saying that people in numbers died of starvation. Among these evil years, too numerous to burden you with, the worst was 1661. I don't know whether in those days, the newspapers, such as they were, had adopted the phrase of the king's weather, though there is plenty of adulation in them. For the first sixty or seventy years of the eighteenth century, there were on the whole abundant crops, a result greatly to be attributed to the new agriculture. But the famine of 1709 in France—we suffered seriously in England—did more to break down the French arms than the victories of Marlborough did, and you may perhaps remember that the last of his great fights, Malplaquet, was not much of a victory, and this occurred in that disastrous year 1709, after the hope of the harvest was well-nigh destroyed in Western Europe. People who write about history and dilate on the philosophy of prominent characters, are exceedingly apt to neglect that which is, after all, true history, the indisputable facts of social life. I am willing to admit the judgment of the first Napoleon, that Marlborough was about the greatest military genius which the world has produced, the more willingly because I do not pretend to be a judge. His greatness has cost us dear. But I always feel myself on safer ground, when I find that opinion is fortified by facts, and philosophy gives a place to intelligible statistics. Of course people may handle statistics foolishly. But you will find as you live that many persons arrive at conclusions and judgments for which they would be incompetent to discover premises. The habit however gives a kind of variety to human life.

The most disastrous period however through which population

passed was that which intervened between the close of the eighteenth century and the first twenty years of the nineteenth. Then, as Malthus was writing, famine raged. But it was artificial. The harvests were bad, but the laws forbad the importation of food. It seems to me, that almost the only human trait in Pitt's career, the heaven-born minister you will remember with his admirers, was his forcing, by rather questionable means in 1800, grain ships which might be driven into English harbours, to discharge their cargoes there. In those days we exercised the right of search, and we did it with a witness. But, unluckily, expedients of this kind are temporary, and the experience of them acts as a deterrent.

Vice and misery, then, the preventive checks of the theory which Malthus announced, are not found to be preventive of all. Thieves are inconveniently prolific; so are the miserable. Nor is it likely that moral restraint is likely to operate on such people. The former class entirely repudiate it by the very circumstances of their calling. The latter do not entertain it, for despair knows no control. And the curious thing about the whole business was this, that while Malthus with the best intentions was consoling the oppressors of the poor, with the assertion that the poor, though the sole workers of wealth, were the sole cause also of their own calamities, he did not take the smallest pains to investigate economical causes. But the fact is, that Malthus was a metaphysical economist, and the only prediction which you can make about the conclusions of a metaphysical economist, is that he is almost certain to be in the wrong.

Mr. George in his attack on Malthus, and by implication on Mr. Mill's endorsement of this famous theory, points to the fact that densely-peopled countries are always, absolutely and relatively, the most opulent. And he further points to the fact that in early and scantily settled countries, such as some among the Western States of the Union, while all can secure abundance, there are few that can live at leisure. And he adds, truly enough, that this result is not due to the mere accumulation of wealth, understanding by this those forms of it which assist in the continuity of present labour, for that these are very destructible, and have on the whole a very brief existence. And he concludes rather incautiously that mere numbers make wealth, without examining sufficiently what are the conditions on which numbers make wealth.

The result depends on the efficiency of labour, the astonishing growth of skill in manipulating materials which progressive societies exhibit. One form of this is no doubt the division of employments to which I have already adverted in an earlier lecture. But the dexterity which makes wealth rapidly is exhibited in all labour, in that which does not admit of division as well as that which does. But it is exceedingly difficult to estimate industry and its efficiency at different epochs of economical history. Closely as I have followed and studied it, I got a very scanty conception of it, and need in order to get any conception of it at all, to constantly refer myself to related prices. Now in modern estimates over a necessarily narrow range, the results of researches such as those of Dawson, Newmarch, and Jevons, very capable persons indeed, are by no means satisfactory, after they have been at great pains to develop and accentuate what they call index numbers, that is, money values of the principal necessaries and conveniences of life. I am perpetually asked to interpret for inquirers what is the value of money five, four, three, two, one centuries ago, and after I have been at great pains to explain the facts, I have generally found that I had sown my seed on the highway.

Two conditions, the efficiency of labour being postulated, make the risks of general over-population among the industrial classes remote. The one is the establishment of a high standard of living, the other is perfect freedom on the part of the workmen to interpret the terms under which they will accept employment. There is no risk that they will destroy the contingencies of their industry. No combination of English working men has ever attempted to improve the capitalist employer out of existence, and I see no likelihood that they will ever fall under so gross and suicidal a delusion. Of course they have never attained to the conditions which I have referred to. There are still laws in existence which permit certain persons to take excessive toll on industry, even to imperil its efficiency, and these are frequently called rights. The combination or association of workmen is still partial and imperfect, and when the union men meet they are apt, like all the rest of us, to run after the red herrings of logomachy. I wish that people would not, following an evil example, talk so much about the rights of men. They would find ample room for their energies, if they grappled with the wrongs. Law, I repeat, can do little positive good. Its highest and best efforts are those in which it puts a stop to evil.

I cannot agree, then, with the reasoning by which Mr. George attacks the Malthusian theory. He alleges that it contravenes the facts, but he does not analyze the facts, any more than Malthus does, when he commented upon what people sometimes call good old England. That it was old I have no inclination to deny. But to call it good is an abuse of language. It is surprising, however, to note how soon practices, exceedingly bad and injurious, become poetical, and the property of the romancer. The epoch of Malthus's theory is the very worst, the most cruel, heartless, and discreditable in the annals of England. It is wonderful enough that the British race ever recovered from it. But every day which makes us more remote in spirit and character from it, and much remains to be done, removes further back the risks of over-population.

But though I do not think that we need be much alarmed at Mr. Malthus and his theory, yet it must be conceded that partial or local or special over-population is a recurrent risk, and sometimes a very serious one. Human societies cannot without danger maintain more than a certain quantity of idlers, or in the language of economists, unproductive consumers. Nor should it, I think, allow these people to consider and vaunt themselves, to use Mr. Disraeli's phrase, as superior persons. They always will if they can, for this is the best defence which they can allege for their existence. I seem to remember having read that the Jewish rabbis invariably insisted that every member of the race, from prince to peasant, should have a calling, and that to leave a man without a calling is to make him a thief, that is to incur the risk of his becoming a Bedaween or a brigand. I have heard the same thing said of the Turks. I may be wrong, but it appears that the wholesome rule has become obsolete, regrettably so.

The redundant population of the fifteenth century, otherwise so prosperous, was that of the younger sons. They joined the forces in that horrible vendetta which raged from the year 1455 to 1485, and as they extinguished themselves for a time, they extinguished or suspended with their own existence, no loss, all but the forms of the English constitution. The place-hunters of the Restoration and the second Revolution were exceedingly redundant. For there is no service which should be rewarded except that which deserves to be rewarded, just as there is no true vested interest but that the public benefit and profit of which can be conclusively demonstrated.

The people who prey on society are always redundant. Most people admit this of the criminal classes. They who, by misfortune and incapacity, are a burden on the public charity, are redundant, superfluous, but should be gently and kindly dealt with. I wish I could find out about the unemployed. I have never arrived at more than the fringe of information, and that had been in unexpected quarters. It is a little suspicious that the phenomenon reappears very speedily after the sporting season is over. It would be, I am sure, well if inquiries were made about the status and origin of these unfortunates. They seem to present the phenomena of over-population, and if I can believe Mr. Peek, who has had exceptional opportunities for learning the facts, "the workless, the thriftless, and the worthless," are a sorry lot, for whom there is little hope, a mere army of utterly unproductive consumers.

I cannot, indeed, pretend to particularize classes here. I can only refer to them historically, as Juvenal advises, those who are buried by the Latin and Flaminian Ways. But so far I agree with Mr. George. I could witness, I will say no more, with extreme complacency, the emigration of many superior persons. For the risk of over-population does not reside in skill and industry, but in the proportion which those bear to skill and industry who do nothing. They have been described with appalling frankness, as they who toil not, neither do they spin. In the abstract I suppose one may class these as redundant. But I am fortunately exempt in this place, from designating them in the concrete. I do not pretend to indicate where we should search for the residuum, but I am sure that we are none the stronger for keeping that, and losing the most useful of our people.

IV.

THE DEVELOPMENT OF CREDIT AGENCIES.

Antiquity of Credit Agencies and Commercial Law—Effect of credit on wealth and prices—The career of the South Sea Scheme—The South American craze of 1825—The railway mania of 1847—The rise in agricultural rents, 1860-70—Causes and duration of inflations and panics.

WHEN I addressed an audience last year in this hall, I dealt among other subjects with paper currencies, and I strove to give a general and exact account of the process by which banking was carried on in remote and in recent times. Now a banker is a credit agent, the most important and significant of agents in transactions involving credit. His calling requires him to exhibit two qualities, caution and integrity. The development of the former is a very long and arduous business, though time and attention have enabled the banker to guide his method by a few principles. They were stated, I believe, for the first time, with frank, and almost amusing simplicity, by the late Mr. Gilbert. Bankers are exceedingly tolerant of theory. Some of them have been conspicuous and influential theorists, and the disputes among them about the principles of their craft have been prolonged, acute, and highly controversial. The school of Lord Overstone, Mr. Norman, and Col. Torrens is entirely opposed to that of Mr. Tooke and

Mr. Newmarch. The reasonings of the former satisfied Sir Robert Peel, and were accepted in the Act of 1844. But there are economists, and I enrol myself in the number, who accept, like Cato, the opinions of the vanquished party. I know nothing in the whole range of monetary science so acute and so conclusive as the arguments of Mr. Tooke are, none which were more speedily confirmed by facts. But Mr. Tooke was a careful student of evidence, and though a study of evidence will not always keep a man right, if he happens to be a dolt, it is a miracle if the shrewdest man, who has no evidence, does not go wrong.

But the theories which the banker listens to patiently never come within the range of his practice. The most voluminous and the most confident writer will not make him turn aside from his traditions. I remember hearing the late Lord Overstone say, that genius was a dangerous gift to a banker. He ought, the noble lord continued, to be emphatically common-place, to be wedded to a beaten track. There were, he continued, occasional anxieties in a banker's career, when he must needs—the metaphor was his—oil the machine. But ordinarily it should be automatic. But it would be an error to conceive that pains and care, even a foresight akin to genius, were not needed in order to perfect the machine. If the Bank of England of to-day were to do what the Bank did in 1697, in 1710, and in 1720, not to trouble you at present with more instances, it would rapidly lose the confidence which it so justly possesses. The mechanism which the directors preside over in Threadneedle Street is the perfection of trained and traditional skill, and the managers are almost as automatic an engine as the Mint is, or as some tell us the pork factories of Chicago are, where a live pig enters at one door, and emerges through various machines from another as pickled and packed pork. So I heard at Chicago, though I had not the curiosity to inspect the process.

Credit agencies existed in countries, all the annals of which have been lost, even in countries which did not possess a coinage. The succession of Babylonian monarchs is at best a list of obscure and disputable names, but antiquaries have discovered the strong rooms of bankers whose business was probably arrested in that capture of the city which Herodotus describes with such vigour, and I must add, imagination. There must have been credit agencies between countries, all of whose memorials have perished. It is certain that such agencies existed between Tyre, Carthage, and Cadiz. Polybius has preserved in one of his ancient treaties between early Rome, royal or republican is not clear, not only the evidence of credit agencies, but a provision for enforcing contracts. So entirely were these agencies familiar to the Greek mind, that Aristotle employs the name of the instrument to signify a moral process. In that strange country, where it seems every Teutonic or Aryan settlement (I do not quite know what word is in fashion now) was early hardened into an autonomous and pugnacious municipality, which could hardly conceive, and very rarely develope a collective sentiment, trade, and with it credit, which always comes with trade, were exceedingly active. To exclude a neighbour from trade in any market was an act of war resented as an international offence. But though we know that it must have existed, we know but little of Greek mercantile law. I have designed indeed to make it, if I can collect materials enough, the subject of a special lecture hereafter. I do not doubt, to quote a similar instance, that many wise Greeks deplored the disunion of Hellas, and foresaw that in time some monarchy would consume it in detail. But I never read but one practical suggestion in favour of a common Greek purpose, and that, oddly enough, is in the Lysistrate of Aristophanes. When the Romans gave them freedom it was too late, for the freedom of Greece was really intended to be an act of literary gratitude, and the failure was expressed, in one case at least, by a proverb too coarse for translation.

All-important as it is, to civilization and international comity, credit is a matter of slow growth, and needs for its development the powerful protection of municipal law. I am not an adept or, in the least degree a judge, of the sufficiency which is said to reside in Mr. Darwin's speculations or proofs as to the origin of species. I can only admire the patience and integrity—a matter needed to men of science—with which he worked out his theories. But there is yet a field open for investigation in analyzing the origin of what I may perhaps call social morality. For many wrong things may be done by the *jus Quiritium*, which cannot be permitted by the *jus gentium*. The autocrat, whose power seems boundless, is a stranger out of his own country. He is like his own money, which is mere bullion when it leaves his borders. There is no sovereign who seems to be more absolute than the Tzar of Russia. But in matters of international business he has to conform as absolutely to the rules and regulations, to the caprices and suspicions of the Stock Exchange, as the pettiest state has. I do not pretend to have a great admiration for Stock Exchange people, but their action, and the rules by which they bind themselves and others, are the best illustrations which I know of international morality.

The machinery by which contracts are enforced, and credit is sustained, is exhibited in the old law of debt. In any country, it has been exceedingly, and, I presume, necessarily severe during the earlier days of credit. Lawgivers, like Draco and the Decemvirs, the authorities of the Pandects, and our Edward I. and Henry VIII., were, I am sure, convinced that the strict maintenance of commercial contracts was a condition precedent to all trade. The ancient Roman was probably, when he dared, a stubborn cheat. I have little doubt that there were many Athenian gentlemen, like Strepsiades in the "Clouds," who had an invincible repugnance to refunding what they had borrowed. The vigorous law of statute merchant and statute staple was Edward's remedy against commercial fraud. The legislation of Henry VIII., under which entails were forfeited for bankruptcy, was no doubt deemed necessary. Compare our own old law on contract debts with the far milder process under which distraint was the very precarious and only remedy for default in paying the landlord's rent, and one will see how differently the two were viewed. There is a striking passage in Fitzherbert, where he compares the remedies against breach of contract with failure to meet the landlord's dues. In course of time these severe laws have been mitigated, only, I conclude, because in the general growth of commercial morality they had become superfluous. Their modern analogue is a bankruptcy law, and curiously enough, the least protected creditor of ancient times, the landlord, is the most protected now.

Commercial law, that is, the law which protects, and intends to preserve credit if possible, is of most ancient origin. It was coexistent with the municipal or local law of Rome and Greece. As you are probably aware, the civil law had an historical beginning, was gradually consolidated, and at last codified under the authority of Justinian. Our own common law, though its origines are lost in barbarism, was, by the peculiarities of its details, the simple work of a half-savage race. These early codes were collected by Balue and the Grimms, and are a rugged but interesting study. But commercial law transcends them all in antiquity. Its beginnings are lost in the unrecorded past. But it has had an unbroken continuity, for it could not be dispensed with. The intercourse of civilized man, even of imperfectly civilized man, has been continuous, and the obligatory usages of such an intercourse are necessarily continuous too. The code of Carthage and Rhodes has been transferred from the civil law into our common law.

I have promised myself, at some future time, to read you a lecture on the Italian trading towns of the early Middle Ages. No country has ever been so overrun by savages as Italy has. No country has ever so humanized its victors. Goth and Lombard, Saracen, German, Frenchman, Spaniard, have occupied and ravaged it. But the invaders have never destroyed its municipalities. Some, like Venice, maintained themselves against all comers. And the annals of Genoa, Pisa, and Florence, are nearly as distinct and brilliant. At last Italy became divided as Greece was, and remained till recently, as Napoleon called it, a geographical expression.

I know no writer who is more laborious and more copious than Muratori. He puts to shame our puny collections. He is even more industrious than our Prynne was. His materials for Italian history can never be exhausted. Their amount is appalling. I am mainly concerned for the present with one, his " Antiquitates Medii Oevi." I owe a good many facts to it in connection with my researches into ancient currencies, and the relative value of the two precious metals. But to those who read it carefully, there comes out the commercial life and the commercial law, *i.e.*, the protection of credit in those dark times, and from these volumes I have gathered my proof as to the continuity of commercial law.

I learned from Muratori what I concluded must be the meaning of the commercial treaty between Rome and Carthage, which is preserved by Polybius. The great work of this writer contains many thousands of treaties, conceding, defining, and guaranteeing the rights of merchants as creditors between the numerous trading cities of Italy. For as soon as ever trade ceases to be mere barter, the function of credit commences, the employment of money as a means of exchange, when the money is not intended to take the place of mere merchandise or bullion, a limited and elementary form of credit arises, for the money currency of a foreign state may be accepted in exchange on the faith that the issuing country will duly honour that which it has put into circulation. The fact that in the modern bullion trade, the currency of a country when it leaves the country of its origin, becomes bullion, may obscure certain primitive understandings as to the pledge implied in a currency.

Now credit is the power which a person, or a state, has of attracting to him or itself wealth, either in the passive or active form from other persons or other communities, under the condition that the loan or advance will be liquidated by the virtual borrower. In fact, the loans or credits obtained by mercantile persons precede historically those procured by non-traders, and both kinds of advances precede the credits obtained by nations or governments. Let us take as an instance of the first class commercial bills, of the second bank-notes, of the third government loans. The origin of commercial bills is lost in the darkness of antiquity. The beginnings of bank-notes, either in the form with which we are familiar, commences with the origin of the Bank of Genoa, or of England; or in the form of warrants pledging the recipient or his assignee to the restoration of the actual moneys deposited, with the foundation of the Banks at Venice, Amsterdam, and Hamburgh. But the development of national or government credit is of far more recent growth, and is hardly two centuries old. That governments issued and discounted their own acceptances and acknowledgments of indebtedness, and so anticipated their own resources or revenues, from very early times, is true enough. Philip of Spain did so with Genoa. Earlier still our third Edward did so with the Florentine bankers, the guardians of Edward VI. with the Antwerp bankers, and most of the sovereigns made default. As late as the War of the Spanish Succession, as we learn from Peterborough's despatches, English government bills were negotiated at Genoa for the Spanish campaigns ; and the commercial notes of newspapers and other similar publications, quote notes of exchange between Great Britian and divers foreign countries. Then, again, credit is internal as well as external, is inevitably developed between the members of a community as well as between members of different communities from very early times. In our own experience, the liquidation of what are called ready-money transactions is constantly based on credit. If we buy goods and pay for them over the counter with notes, the trader accepts the exchange, because he is confident of the solvency of the issuing banker ; if we pay for them by our cheques, the transaction is theoretically completed, because he can rely on the solvency of the drawer, though, of course, it is not practically completed as far as purchasers are concerned till the cheque is honoured. Even then, nine cases out of ten, or ninety-nine out of a hundred, the recipient of the cheque makes it the means of developing another form of credit, in the form of a balance at his own bankers.

As human societies have been educated in functions of credit, and see daily how all-pervading and significant they are, it has been natural to assign to credit qualities and powers which it is far from universally possessing, to say nothing of others which it does not possess at all. It is really part of the mechanism by which wealth is mobilized, even in its most stationary forms. Take, for example, the old forms of obligation conveyed under a statute merchant or a statute staple, and the recognition of such pledges as exceptional, by the law of Edward I. A landowner sought to procure funds for the prosecution of a commercial venture. The law allowed him for this end to pledge his land and his personal liberty, before the chief officer of a trading or a staple town. He raised a loan on this security and traded. It is plain that he was transmuting during the period of the loan, the passive wealth which he possessed in his estate into the active wealth of another person. He was creating no new wealth, though the fact that he was about to do so lies at the bottom of his transaction.

He was simply displacing it, mobilizing it, giving it a new efficiency. He might, indeed, have lost by the transaction, and forfeited his estate. The security which he offered is *ex hypothesi*, unimpaired, but the wealth which he secured by the pledge is lost.

Some people allege that credit creates new wealth. It does so no more than bank-notes make more money. What it does is to utilize, to mobilize wealth, and make it more efficient. I remember to have heard that, when an enthusiastic advocate of the functions of credit was dwelling on its creative powers in the House of Commons, the late Sir Robert Peel congratulated him on his eloquence and his mastery over one theory of the currency, but added, not perhaps without some tinge of personal sarcasm, that he would sooner have the orator's money than his credit. And Peel had done the country an infinite service by insisting on the restoration of genuine credit, on the resumption of cash payments, in opposition to those who wish to develope the currency. When by proper exercise and diet, to use an illustration, you bring human strength to its fullest efficiency in an individual body, you do not make two bodies. And so, when by judicious substitutes, in the form of commercial obligations, the fullest efficiency is given to the monetary resources of a country, you do not make another mass of money. If you did, the more instruments of credit you made, the more you pile up indebtedness, the more property do you create. You might as well allege, as a very active and enthusiastic, not to say positive, writer appears to assert, that if you had a thousand pounds, and owed a thousand pounds, you were worth two thousand pounds. To my mind you are worth just nothing under such circumstances.

There is an obvious question which it is not easy or accurate to answer with a yes or no, which is, does credit affect prices? Now no doubt price is due to demand. Articles rise in price, because the demand appears to fall short of the supply, and fall in price, because the supply seems immediately or prospectively to exceed the demand. How the possession of credit may enable one person who determines on producing an article an opportunity of competing against another, who will go without it if the other gets it. But here the credit does not raise the price which the purchaser gives, it simply, and for the time, enables the purchaser to satisfy his demand. Sooner or later, generally very soon, it will be found that the purchaser has used his credit temporarily, and that he must give value for his acquisition. He has merely anticipated for a brief space what the article was worth.

Take, again, a commercial speculation. Persons will strain their powers and their credit among their powers, in purchasing a commodity, cotton, copper, tin, the supply of which they think that they can estimate, the demand for which they assume that they can interpret. They are simply engaged, if their calculations are sound, in anticipating that which is sure to arise, and in appropriating that exaltation of price which others have not been acute enough to foresee. In such a case, credit is not raising prices, it is merely enabling an individual to take early advantage of an inevitable rise. Hence, speculations of this kind are looked on with much leniency. They are supposed, and with much show of reason, to stimulate supply. It is also alleged that if they are mistaken they bring their Nemesis with them, and that no trader, or combination of traders, is strong enough to exercise more than a very temporary control over the market. Whether, indeed, the law or the custom of mercantile transactions is not over lenient to speculative failures, is a question of considerable gravity. Whether it is possible for combination to produce a monopoly, for a monopoly to defy competition, and for monopoly to exact an over-heavy charge, not for intelligent apprehension, but by the sheer force of what may be called a commercial conspiracy, is a question which is by no means easily answered. The law does contemplate such possibilities, as, for example, in the costs of railway transit, and take precautions against them, in the just interests of consumers. It has done so in the case of certain labourers, whose demands, with the alternative of the cessation of work, might paralyze society at a crisis, and therefore insists on the continuity of contracts made by such persons. It seems easy to conclude that such action is just. Under a voluntary system of enlistment, men may refuse or accept the pay and prospects of the public service. But for an army to strike for higher pay, at the commencement of a campaign or an engagement, would be fatal, and could not be entertained. But the sudden abandonment of a calling where continuity was essential to the well-being of society, as, for example, some years since of the gas stokers in London, was treated as an offence.

Of course if a government deliberately permits or creates a monopoly in any necessary article, it enables—nay stimulates—the producer to create an artificial price. Such is the case with the English land system, which, in towns at least, affords an artificial price to the owner of extensive areas, by creating what is virtually, to use commercial slang, a land ring. I do not affirm that the particulars of our land system which produce this result were designed to bring it about. It is sufficient that they do, and that they are directly responsible for some of the worst conditions, at any rate in past time, which have affected the housing of the poor in large towns. Nor is it just that unoccupied houses and areas should be exempt from local charges. The State is under no obligation to assist such owners in finding tenants at artificial rents, as it virtually does by excusing them from their liabilities during the period of non-user.

Protection to producers, always to certain producers, for if it were extended all round it would assuredly defeat itself, is again one of the means by which prices are artificially heightened. No one should be forced to sell at the optional price of a purchaser, for it is clear that such a rule would be spoliation, and a fatal discouragement to industry. But by parity of reason, nobody should be forced to buy at the optional price of the vendor, for such a practice is just as much spoliation, nay, impudent plunder, and that of the most feeble and helpless. And so it has come to pass, and that quite naturally, that in the United States, where protection is maintained by terrorism where possible, and by the most barefaced falsehoods where it is not, the protected capitalist detects in all combinations of workmen in all discontent at wages, a danger to his monopoly, which he must remorselessly persecute. I know few things in the modern history of labour and capital more startling than the machinery employed to terrorize workmen among the ironmasters of Pennsylvania, and recorded in the published documents of that state.

But scarcity interpreted by dealers or speculators, advantages permitted by governments, and protective laws forced on communities by selfish and powerful interests, are the principal causes, if not the only causes of exalted prices. Of course I am leaving out of consideration the permanent cause of high and low prices, the cheapness or dearness of the metal which forms the standard of economy. But in these three causes credit is concerned with the first only as an independent factor, and that only partially or temporarily. To deny that credit has any effect whatever on prices is to contradict experience. But it is very easy and very obvious to exaggerate the effect. And if it be employed to stave off a serious fall it is simply undertaking the common functions of capital with this difference, that the capitalist has only his own counsel to take, while the man who sustains his operations by credit has to take, as he sometimes finds to his cost and disappointment, counsel with others.

There are occasions under which very extensive credit operations may be entered on, in which, however, no effect whatever is traceable on real prices, that is, the price of the necessaries of life. I will illustrate this by a brief history of the great South Sea Bubble of 1720, an economical phenomenon which is not entirely without parallel in the history of other countries, and indeed of our own. But it has never been exhibited in such proportion since. I have some special opportunities for commenting on it, for I have recently gleaned from the copious collection of newspapers during that period, which is contained in the Bodleian Library, a daily register of the price of stock in the South Sea Fund from the beginning of the process, during the time of its inflation, and at the crisis of its rapid and complete collapse. Most historians who have commented on it have very imperfectly understood the facts. The nearest analogues to it are the speculations entered into at the rise of the Republics in Central and Southern America in 1825 and the railway mania in 1847.

Now in the early years of George I. the public debt, contracted during the wars of the English and Spanish successions, was held in a very different way from that in which it now is. This debt, of course, represented the credit of the nation in Parliament. Much of it constituted the stock of the Bank of England, the East India Company, and, above all, the South Sea Company, which, after 1713, had secured as part of their bargain the trade in negro slaves with the Spanish Plantations, under what is known in history as the Assiento treaty. Not a little of the debt was in annuities granted for life or terms of years. Some was a floating debt renewed in the form of Exchequer bills, and generally put into circulation through the Bank. Now in itself the system was cumbrous and wasteful. Wealth had been rapidly growing through the trade of London, and no doubt while Walpole was still in the Ministry he had ventilated those projects of his for consolidating the public debt which he was in after years to mature. But Walpole had been ejected from office in 1717, and was succeeded by Stanhope, who gave way to Sunderland, under whom were Aislabie, Chancellor of the Exchequer, and Craggs, Secretary of State.

Now in order to effect this change, it seemed obvious that one or the other of the great chartered companies, the Bank of England or the South Sea Company, should undertake the commission. The East India Company was out of the question. Now the Bank regularly paid its shareholders 8 per cent., the South Sea 6, and the ordinary price of the two stocks was 140 to 150 for the Bank, 105 to 110 for the South Sea. The two companies bid for the bargain, and the South Sea offered to transact the affair for less than the Bank thought prudent. It is doubtful whether it was wise to allow a trading or banking company to ingraft so enormous a stock on its capital as more than thirty millions additional, and imperfect as the knowledge of finance was at the time, I think it very doubtful whether, had Walpole been in office, he would have lent himself to the negotiation. For the business was exceedingly complicated by the vast quantity of debt which was secured to annuitants, and it would certainly be unsuccessful unless the annuitants were persuaded to accept the value of their interest in some stock or the other, or cash could be found to pay them off at a fair valuation.

Now how was the South Sea Company to effect this result. They had a trade, it is true, which the Spanish Government strove to curtail within the narrowest limits, the South Sea Company to expand. One would have thought, after the experience of the Mississippi scheme in France the year before, that the prospects of the American trade would have been seriously discounted.

But the collapse in France was set down to Louis' bank, not to the trading scheme, the shares of which, as I see from the papers of the time, still bore a respectable price. It was then upon pledges as to the enormously profitable character of this speculation and really meagre trade, that the promoters and directors of the scheme proposed to build up success. The stock rose during the negotiations and advanced rapidly when they were completed. Nor were the English capitalists and speculators alone tempted. The stock was purchased largely in Holland.

The Government promised the company 5 per cent. for a time, to be reduced after the lapse of a few years to 4 per cent., no particularly tempting offer at a time when the ordinary rate was from 5 to 6. The Directorate, to be sure, contained many considerable names in the mercantile world of London, and four members of Parliament. The King was the governor. The papers discussed, or at least expounded the scheme, which promised enormous dividends, and a considerable number of annuitants were induced to take stock in the company in exchange for their bargains. As far as the Government went, the transfer of its liabilities was on paper only, but some annuitants, and these represented a considerable sum, elected to be paid off. How was the money to be raised in order to sustain the credit of the company, for you see that the operation was entirely one of credit, or of confidence in the management of those who undertook the operation? It is true that some of the papers, rarely at that time supplying their readers with anything but mere news, doubted the success of the scheme, and warned the public. But as is clear from the fluctuations of the stock, many persons realized their gains, and it soon became known that this and that man had achieved a fortune by his speculations. It was when the stock had risen from $123\frac{1}{2}$, its price on December 3, 1719, to 310 on April 1st, the highest of the day, that the directors took the step of endorsing by their own action the public craze.

On April 14th they offered new stock to subscribers at 300, the amount being $2\frac{1}{4}$ millions nominal, and the payment being spread over a considerable time. Next, on April 21st, they announced a dividend of 10 per cent. for the half-year, to be paid in stock at par, this being, you will see, at the rate of 60 per cent. per annum on the original stock. On April 29th they issued a fresh million of stock at 400, the payments being distributed over a longer period than the first issue was. But it was three weeks—I am writing with the daily register of prices before me—before the public rose to this price, though on June 1st the highest price was 755. On June 16th the directors issued new stock for the third time, and in the same manner. This time the amount was five millions, and the price was £1,000 for every 100 subscribed. On June 25th the highest price was reached, 1,060. In order to assist subscribers, the directors offered to lend ten millions of their own capital on the security of their own stock, and, I presume, at the prices which they had themselves fixed. That price, as was stated subsequently, was calculated to exceed the whole selling value of all the land in the kingdom.

Now most of the history books which you read will tell you that the great Bubble collapsed immediately after the company, on August 16th, began to prosecute the unlicensed projectors who were trying, and, it is said, with much success, to attract some of the gains of those fortunate gamblers who had cleared out of the project when prices were at the highest. But the register of prices contradicts this. The stock continued high all through August, in which month the whole of the first new issue was paid up. It was not, to be sure, at the height at which it stood on June 25th, but the highest price on the last of August was 810. In September the fall began, the fluctuations being exceedingly violent. Thus on September 30th prices ranged from 190 to 320. On the 8th of September the directors issued a notice that they would pledge themselves to pay a dividend of 30 per cent. for the year 1720, and 50 per cent. for the next twelve years, and this in money. I presume that some stockholders trusted to this promise, for the stock does not fall below 500 till September 17th.

From this time the collapse was rapid and complete. The directors had some hopes that the Bank would come to the rescue, and the Bank showed some inclination to do so. But apparently, in order to back up the pledge of September 8th, the directors stood out for assistance on far too favourable terms, with the result that no assistance of an effectual kind could be rendered them. The South Sea Company had a security, a good security, one that remained good for more than a century after this famous year, but it was not worth anything like that value which the directors gave it. Parliament was obliged to intervene. Walpole, the only person able, as it seemed, to grapple with the situation, was recalled to office. The fraudulent Chancellor of the Exchequer, Aislabie, who survived the catastrophe, for Secretary Craggs was expelled the House, the last member of a Cabinet who has been expelled—I cannot say the last who deserved to be—and a Bill was brought in and carried, which to some extent compensated the dupes of the Bubble out of the private fortunes and illgotten gains of the projectors. The process which Walpole adopted (he had greatly increased his own fortune by buying and selling judiciously) is part of general English history, and except in one particular I need not comment on it. There is, I believe, no other instance in our history in which a fraud has been punished by an *ex post facto* law, for the attempt to punish Duncombe in 1698 for forging Exchequer Bills was defeated by a single vote in the Lords, and the Lords have been very properly commended for their action, for it needs a very strong case indeed to justify an *ex post facto* law, and there is no justification for an *ex post facto* administration of law.

Gibbon, the historian, was the grandson of a man who had been a Commissioner of Customs, and a director of the South Sea Company during its inflation. He was one of the victims of the Parliament. He had acquired a fortune of £60,000, and he was stripped of it, a single thousand being left him, says his biographer, though Parliament assigned him £10,000. His son, the father of the historian, who sat in Parliament, was, as we may well anticipate, a bitter enemy of Walpole, and the grandson has commented with great severity, and with the great resources of language at his command, on the measures which Parliament took. The ordinary comment on the transaction which you will see in the common histories is the tradition of Gibbon's discontent. We need not be surprised at the anger of a man whose family was reduced from affluence to comparatively narrow means by such a process as Walpole took, but he is hardly a disinterested commentator. If Parliament acted with severity, it discriminated between the offenders.

I cannot but think that the doctrine which was laid down by Macaulay that no *ex post facto* legislation is permissible, with all deference to so great, wise, and just a man, savours of paradox. I cannot think that a stupendous, impudent, and distinctive fraud should go unpunished, because the legislature has not yet anticipated the possibility of the offence. Nor do I think the doctrine to be constitutional. We have provided in our history, and have used against offenders whom no existing penalties would have reached, the mechanism of impeachment. The mechanism is, I allow, clumsy, absurd, and, in these days, impracticable, for who would dream of summoning a jury of 500 persons or more, few of them having had even the training of a juryman, to decide on the guilt of a great criminal. It is one thing to say that impeachment has become practically obsolete. It is another thing to say that what it implies should be abandoned without an attempt to refer it to a court which, being properly constituted, should command public respect. But in the absence of such a court, great offences would either pass unpunished or must be met by Acts of Pains and Penalties. In 1720 Walpole resorted to Parliament in order to punish the South Sea directors. In 1721 he employed the same enginery against Atterbury, whose published correspondence shows that he, sworn as Lord of Parliament and bishop to the existing government, was plotting against the institutions to which he had pledged his allegiance and owed his rank and place. And if it be alleged that a wicked minister or administration has violated the constitution and committed crimes against public liberty, it is, I think, dangerous to that constitution and its liberties if he is to go unpunished because the quibbles of law decline to bring him within the reach of a punishable offence, and that he is sufficiently chastised if he be excluded from office. It is not by a doctrine like this that the liberties of this country have been won ; and if such a doctrine is to be accepted as final, there is danger that those liberties, common to all, may not be maintained.

Now during the whole period of inflation, though credit, baseless I admit, had been apparently increased ten times at least, prices (the record lies before me) were entirely unchanged. The purchasing power of the country, according to the theory of some economists had been increased tenfold, and according to all analogy, prices should have been powerfully affected. But, in fact, the wealth of the country remained as it was. Property changed hands. Many were ruined, many were enriched, but the aggregate of riches, some waste considered and accounted for, remained unaltered. No doubt the distress was very general. It always is when credit is inflated by folly and temporarily destroyed by inevitable panic. People often wonder at the rapid recovery from monetary disasters. The true explanation is that what is lost is impersonal; individual, not collective. There may be a serious strain, there is for a time a formidable collapse. But what is substantial is not gone, and will soon recover its efficiency.

You will then agree with me, that the proper interpretation of credit is derived, as is common with economical phenomena, from negative inductions. But to frame negative inductions you require facts, as much as you do in affirmative inductions. Men learn what they can do, by discovering, occasionally after a painful and dangerous experience, what they cannot do. The lesson people have to learn extends through all human action, from the highest efforts of political and social agencies to the ordinary business of every-day life. But I am sure that this cannot ever be learned in an arm-chair, at a study table, and with nothing but metaphysics to guide one.

The British nation is the only civilized community, and the criticism does not of course extend to uncivilized communities, which has kept unbroken, undeviating faith with its public and private creditors. There have been, it is true, temptations and tempters, both plausible enough, but they have not been listened to with effect. There have been occasions on which, relying on this honest sensitiveness, rogues have attempted and with success to palm indefensible claims on the British public, under the guise of vested interests. I told you on a previous occasion what is the only vested interest which an economist can allow. But I suppose that it is better in the long run, to be stupid and honest, than to run the risk of being called clever and unscrupulous. But if one is honest, one need not be stupid, and one may discover that one is encouraging knaves, if one listens with over-much compliance to their claims. There is and there cannot be any other definition of

7

a vested interest than honest compensation for an unquestionable public service, when that service has been done, with a full understanding between the doer of the service and the public that compensation may be due.

The best illustration which can be given from English commercial life of a just appreciation of the functions of credit, and a wise regulation of its concession, is the conduct of the Bank of England, an institution now near two centuries old. I do not say that this institution, alone among similar establishments for unblemished good faith, has never committed errors. It has committed grave errors, as its best advocates would admit. But its errors are those of good faith, and therefore have never been fatal. And now its manipulation of commercial credit is almost as automatic as its issues are under the Act of 1844. Its action has been criticized, as the action of all great social instruments is. But experience has proved that it is wiser than its critics. To my mind its relations to the finance of government are infinitely more valuable and more honest than that of any department of state. It has enjoyed no considerable pecuniary reward. To a great extent it protects against risk those who have been its rivals, and divides profits which do not equal the half of those corporations which would look to it for succour, if their own indiscretion led them into a trap. For it cannot be disputed that the Bank is the centre and pivot of British credit.

One cannot look with similar confidence on some of these institutions of credit. The evil may be of difficult cure, for Lord Thring, the draftsman for many years of Government Bills, and in particular of the Limited Liability Acts, assured me the other day, that he knew of no process which could secure a *bona-fide* audit of accounts. And of course it is obvious, that no accountant could vouch for the goodness of all the commercial Bills, *i.e.*, instruments of credit, which being discounted by a bank, are held in its portfolio. The danger, I imagine, to these institutions of credit lies in the inclination to suppress or qualify a loss, but the indiscreet exposure of it would have an injurious effect on deposits. But, on the other hand, commercial espionage has become almost a fine art. For a guinea a year, you can learn at discretion and in confidence, everything about the commercial character of your neighbours.

THE DEVELOPMENT OF CREDIT AGENCIES. 83

The second great commercial craze, over a hundred years after the great battle, was the epoch of loans in 1825, particularly to the Spanish republics of the New World. The occasion of Canning's celebrated platitude, a far more serious piece of rhodomontade than the friend of humanity's address to the needy knife-grinder. The English capitalists, and their number is legion, their wisdom being occasionally not higher than the swine into which the legion entered, lent to these emancipated peoples, and the emancipated peoples took their money with genuine Spanish dignity. The fact is, they did not know how to use it. Their old masters had carefully excluded them from every function of government, and they had to learn the very rudiments of a civil polity, and among other things the philosophy of credit. So the English capitalist lost the money, and the Spanish republican lost not credit, which he never had, but the contingency of credit. It is not a little instructive that the same region gave occasion to the Bubble of 1720, and that of 1825.

The railway mania of 1847 was the most anxious, and at the same time the most pardonable, of these crazes. Almost suddenly a means of land transit was perfected, which gave indefinite, because unknown, opportunities of hope. There was no mistake about the fact, the error lay in ignorance as to the conditions under which the fact could become a practical reality. I cannot discover trustworthy evidence for the amount which individuals had subscribed for, or for the amount of their losses, but the effects were nearly as disastrous as those which we can read of as to the collapse of the South Sea Scheme in 1720.

Of course the greater part of commercial business carried on, even in these periods of inflation, is prudent and honest. With the mass of people engaged in trade there is no abuse of credit, for otherwise general business would become impossible. But there is always a risk with individuals. Men, says Adam Smith, habitually overrate their own good fortune and intelligence. If they did not, bookmakers at races, and speculating jobbers on Stock Exchanges could not make fortunes by their craft. If they can succeed in impressing the notion that they are farseeing and fortunate on the holders of loanable capital, that is, extend their credit, they may overshoot the mark. Somebody must have trusted men who become bankrupt, and have trusted them unwisely. Occasionally people have acquired a character for honest dealing and solvency which is wholly undeserved. Many years ago, I suffered a severe prospective loss by the failure of Paul's Bank. Sir John Paul had been insolvent all his life, but by an ostentation of profound religious conviction, he continued to hoodwink a number of people, and to persistently rob them. In our own time similar tactics were adopted by the Greenways, with the same success and the same results.

Occasionally, the phenomena of a serious collapse of credit, which, did it occur in ordinary business, would create a panic, arises from an improvident extension of credit to a particular class of traders. From the end of the Crimean War, to the final adjustment of Europe after the Franco-German War, the rent of English land was greatly exalted. I have referred to it before. It is derivable of course, from the income-tax returns of farmers' rents. It amounted to $26\frac{1}{2}$ per cent. in twenty years, and I have quoted these figures in order to substantiate other inferences. Now during this period of inflation, banks in agricultural districts made very free advances to farmers. It seemed obvious that men who could compete for occupancy so freely and so boldly, must have a wide margin to meet liabilities. At last, as we all know, the crisis came, and rents began to fall and farmers to be bankrupts. In two years, 10 per cent. of the British farmers, taking the Bankruptcy returns and the census together, were swept away by failure. Now at this time I was going to town with a well-known London banker, and in conversation I suggested that the country bankers had made great losses by farming failures. "On the contrary," said he, "they have been the principal agents in the collapse of the farming interest and the depression of rents. They had, as you seem to see, made very large advances to the farming class. But they began to be alarmed for their security. The landlord, they knew, was protected, come what might, by the law of distraint. But the banker had only a second or deferred security. So they began to call in their advances, and precipitated the ruin which was perhaps impending." Now, bankers' advances are obviously a form of credit. But it is quite certain that the staunchest advocate of our land system, and the most energetic defender of the landowner's rights, would not allow these sentiments and sympathies to warp his judgment, when he got into his bank, turned over his ledger, and noted the ominous growth of his farming customers' liabilities.

There are occasions when the acuteness of a trader or a class of traders in the same commodity leads them to anticipate a scarcity, and that rise in prices which follows on a scarcity. Such persons strain their credit to get a command of the market, and sometimes succeed. But they more frequently fail, and for the reason which I have quoted from Adam Smith. But their failure may involve great losses to those who have unwisely assisted them. Such was the case with the great leather failures some twenty years ago. It is the fashion—I believe the use of the word is transatlantic—to call these transactions rings or corners. Sometimes, again, persons have divided great gain from the operation of an economical law, which I believe that I was the first person to announce a quarter of a century ago. I noticed in collecting prices that when there was a scarcity in an article of prime necessity, the rise in price is always greatest in the commoner or cheaper kinds of the article. The cause is plain enough. The stint in the article causes a greater demand for inferior kinds. Now I have known persons who have greatly prospered by dealing on such occasions in what had previously been cheap goods. I do not think that they formulated the law, but they got hold of the fact.

More fortunate still is the person who by divination or private information gets information that a change is meditated in the customs. Some time ago the Government reduced the tea duties by 6d. in the pound. The intended change came to the knowledge of a dealer in Mincing Lane. How the knowledge was obtained was never, I believe, publicly divulged. Suspicion, however, fell on a prominent official, who suddenly and completely escaped from known embarrassments. The innocent or guilty recipient of the intelligence at once strained his capital (a large one) and his credit, which naturally stood high, in the purchase of tea. He knew that the lessening of the duty would be followed by a rise in price. Suppose that 2d. in the sixpence went to the dealer, and the public saved the 4d. It would not be difficult for a large and powerful operator to make £100,000 by this safe operation, and, I must add, it might be expedient to pay handsomely for the sole information. The result of this reputed transaction with the official, and real speculation of the tea dealer, was to introduce a custom into administrations, under which the particulars of the Budget are made known to the Cabinet only the night before the Budget is introduced into the House of Commons. The story which I have told you was given to me as an explanation of this singular, and sometimes inconvenient, practice—inconvenient because our coldness and over-timidity in finance are found embarrassing to parties. But nothing under ordinary circumstances can exceed the anxieties with which traders seek to anticipate the financial measures of the Government.

Sometimes, indeed, a general collapse of ordinary credit ensues, and this almost unexpectedly. This state of things has been called a panic or a crisis, and is rarely or never foreseen. Now, I have already referred to two of these by name only, *i.e.*, the panics of 1825 and 1847. In both cases the catastrophe was due to a sudden distrust of commercial credit, particularly of the country banks ; for on both occasions, when credit was almost universally shaken, the reputation of the Bank remained intact. But the acutest men of business were very much divided in opinion as to the causes which had really brought about the calamity, and still more divided as to the cause of its cessation. A panic rarely lasts long. In 1825, according to Mr. Tooke, an eye-witness of the circumstances, its endurance was three weeks only. In 1847 the same acute observer declares that there were two panics, one in April, the other in October, and each of somewhat longer duration.

The true cause, I conclude, of a credit panic is the close interlacing of monetary interests. If Ucalegon's house catches fire, his neighbours are in extreme risk of the conflagration extending. The incaution of one banking house has led to its failure, and similar incaution is ascribed to other houses which have been cautious. But, as it is the essence of banking that it puts its credit into circulation, distrust induced on that credit leads to a demand for that which it represents, and in the crisis of 1825 it is admitted that the form which the demand took was gold for internal use. Fortunately the public was entirely convinced of the soundness of the Bank of England, and was ready not only to take its notes, but to exchange the gold which it had drawn out, through the bankers in which it had distrusted, for the notes of the Bank. Thus, when a London bank failed on December 8th, there at once arose a run on the other London banks on the two following days. But these banks were prepared, and the alarm subsided. On the 12th, however, another London bank failed, and the run re-commenced. On this occasion the Bank of England began a practice which before it had steadily refused to adopt—that of lending money on its own or on Government stocks. But during the intensity of the crisis, the Bank made free loans of its own notes, and humoured the panic so effectually that it reduced its own stock of coin and bullion to little over a million, to as low an amount as the cover stood in the memorable 1797. But the Bank knew that the gold coin was in the country, and that, the trouble over, it would rapidly return. For, though credit was suspended, and it was impossible without serious loss to turn securities into cash, the property and the securities were there, and the Bank was able to fortify the credit of others by an enormous advance of its own notes on security. It is noteworthy that during this period the Bank raised its rate of interest only once from 4 to 5 per cent., and, indeed, for the first century and a quarter of its career its rate of discount was generally invariable.

Three years before the trouble of 1847, Sir Robert Peel, then at the height of his reputation—well-deserved, indeed—and leading a large and united party, passed the Act under which the Bank of England is still regulated. I cannot enter here on the criticism of that Act. It is perhaps the strongest meat in all economics, and requires the most energetic digestion. I do not as yet venture on discussing the provisions of a statute on which more has been written adversely and eulogistically than on any other Act of legislation. It is sufficient to say that while its advocates declare it to be the quintessence of monetary wisdom, the most acute and dispassionate of its critics says that it is the " most wanton, ill-advised, pedantic, and rash piece of legislation which ever came within his observation." The Act has been frequently suspended, and under circumstances where it was meant to be operative, and it has been imitated by no other civilized community.

The Bank is constrained to curtail its issues, and thus to contract it accommodation, its own reputation remaining intact, at the very time when its assistance is most wanted. Hence, when the stringency has been at its height, the law has been suspended, and the Bank empowered to make an excess of issue. The Bank, of course, cannot, and should not, support those who are provably insolvent, as it never has knowingly done through its long history. Its function is to help at a period of unreasoning and unreasonable distrust those who are solvent. And the proof that the suspension of the Act is imperative, as well as discreet, is in the fact, invariably recurrent, that the panic ceases as soon as the Bank is allowed a discretionary issue. In the interval, much undeserved hardship has occurred, not in the cost of accommodation, for this is comparatively trivial and temporary, but in the stint of accommodation when this has been urgently needed.

A good deal of metaphysics has been written about credit. I have only glanced at this method of treating the subject in the present lecture. The true theory of the subject has not only been obscured by them, but by the wrongheadedness of many, some great names, who would not admit that their inductions were erroneous and one-sided, and by misconception as to what credit will do. You will be safe, in my opinion, if you recognize it as the mobilization of capital with a view to increasing its efficiency, and that it tends to make that fluid and elastic which is naturally rigid and unyielding.

V.

THE DEVELOPMENT OF TRANSIT.

Development of marine transit in ancient and mediæval ages—The discovery of America and the Cape Passage—Rise of Dutch trade—Rivalry of the English—Hindrance to the development of English shipping—Progress under free trade—Mill's pessimism refuted by experience—Modern economies in the cost of transit.

THE annals of no country illustrate more conclusively what trade will do for a community than those of Holland. It was not till it began to assert its independence, or, at least, to affirm that it had chartered liberties, which it was not competent for its Count to revoke at his pleasure, though this Count happened to be King of Spain and Portugal and lord of the East and the West, that it possessed either trade or manufactures to any notable extent. These were centred in the great cities of Flanders—Bruges, Ghent, Antwerp, and a hundred more. It was in those towns that the clothing of the west of Europe was manufactured, at least, all but home-spun, and it was from Bruges that the spices of the East were distributed over the same region. Antwerp, of course, by the relative pre-eminence of its trade, was also the city where the commercial bills of the same district were negotiated and discounted, for in the fifteenth and the first half of the sixteenth centuries Antwerp, always considerable for its connection with the

Hanseatic League and the Baltic trade, was appropriating much of the commerce which Venice and Genoa had formerly enjoyed. The Eastern commerce of Bruges was seriously crippled by the conquest of Egypt in the first quarter of the sixteenth century, and the consequent block of the Alexandrian trade, and Flanders was, as you all know, ruined by Alva, the Spanish Inquisition, and the wars of religion. But the ruin of Flanders was the making of Holland. It would not even under the circumstances have been made had it not been for the character of its people. But in estimating the progress of nations you must always take circumstances into consideration. Men are not, as fools and poltroons say, the creatures of circumstances, but it sometimes happens that very obscure or unrecorded causes have had much to do with personal, local, and even national ·prosperity. I do not think that Holland would have been so great if Flanders, after it had lost its ancient spirit, had not ceased to be the commercial rival of its would-be liberator. But I shall have occasion to refer to the place which Holland took in the history of trade transit as I deal with my present subject.

The trade of ancient civilization was, with one exception—that of Carthage—bounded by the shores of the Mediterranean, and we infer that the Phœnicians passed through the pillars of Hercules into the Atlantic, rather than possess proof of it. But the trade, and by implication the transit of goods from city to city, was bounded within narrow limits. Athens was the most enterprizing of the Greek cities in the East, and there is not much evidence that Athenian vessels went beyond Byzantium in ordinary trade. In the Western Mediterranean Marsilia was the principal centre of trade, but there is reason to believe that its principal business was done with the Gallic tribes of the interior, and that through this port the Phœnicians derived their tin by an overland passage through Gaul and the short sea route of the English Channel. In the absence of evidence one cannot affirm or deny that they passed up by the coast of Spain, ventured on the Bay of Biscay, and thence kept along the coast of Gaul to Western Britain. The Cornishmen believe that they did, and I was told that there still remain evidences of Phœnician moorings in the numerous creeks of Falmouth Harbour. There are some people to whom the evidence of Cade's follower, that the bricks are alive to this day to show it, is conclusive. That tin was procured is certain, that it came from Western Britain is nearly certain, though tin is found in the Iberian peninsula, but history is silent as to the route by which it came.

The English race, particularly in the south, early developed a marine. But there are charges, not perhaps entirely unfounded, that these sailors were more given to freebooting than to trade. Quite apart from any differences between the two countries, which were indeed from after the middle of the eleventh up to near the middle of the fifteenth, with no doubt a considerable interruption in the thirteenth, under one sovereign, the mariners of Northern France and those of Southern England carried on incessant warfare with each other. Now piracy to be successful requires that some attention should be given to the arts of shipbuilding and navigation, for it is of importance to the pirate that he should escape with his booty. There is some evidence in the stories of sea fights, as that of Eustace the monk, with the Cinque Ports in 1217, and that of the fleet which our Edward III. collected, principally from the southern ports, in order to the battle of Sluys, that the English in these early days handled their barks shrewdly. But the English hardly ventured out of their own channel, except on the eastern side of the island, where they went in quest of fish, all along the Scottish coast, and probably as far as Iceland.

Towards the middle of the fifteenth century the Bristol fish curers determined to attempt the western route to the Iceland cod fisheries. The author of the "Libel of English Policy," who, as I have been told by the present librarian of the British Museum, was almost certainly Adam du Molyns, Bishop of Chichester, murdered or lynched, for he seems to have had a kind of rough trial at Portsmouth, early in 1450, says that in his day this expedition was first attempted by the use of the mariners' compass. I have little doubt that this successful venture was the principal stimulus to Bristol enterprise, and I doubt not that it was out of the riches gained in this and similar voyages that Cannyng made the wealth, the dedication of a portion of which remains visible to this day in the beautiful church of St. Mary, Redcliffe. To my mind it would be well if the students of commercial geography, instead of merely announcing the present conditions and statistics of commercial centres, were to search a little into the causes which led to certain localities becoming commercial centres.

Certain evidence, however, survives that in early times attempts were made to explore that mysterious ocean which lay outside the Mediterranean. Herodotus tells us of a Persian who was forced in expiation of an offence to explore, and makes a statement as to what the traveller saw, which is at least a proof that some mariner must have crossed the equator and sailed into the southern hemisphere. There is the voyage of Hanno the Carthaginian, and Scylax, and there is still preserved to us the narrative of the expedition which Nearchus made down the Indus and into the Arabian Sea. But the geography of antiquity is very vague, and like its navigation gets very little beyond the basin of the Mediterranean. Strabo, the most voluminous writer on ancient geography, and if you can read Greek, a most agreeable author, for he fills his descriptions with the most curious facts and statements, takes Homer as his principal authority. But one of the most remarkable facts in ancient civilization is its rapid and amazing development in art, and its early ascent in everything else. Of course the Greeks filled this unknown region of ocean with mysterious continents and islands, some submerged, others far and happily removed from the incessant aggressions and turmoils of ancient life.

These ancient stories and legends no doubt led to the enterprize of Henry, Prince of Portugal, the grandson of our John of Gaunt, who, in the middle of the fifteenth century, ventured on the unknown sea, and explored the coast of Northern Africa. Thenceforward maritime enterprize became a tradition at the Portuguese court, which fortified itself by a bull of Roderic Borgia, also Alexander VI., in which the full sovereignty of all possessions discovered in the eastern side of the great ocean was conferred on Portugal. The example was contagious, and Isabella of Castile supplied the ships and funds for the voyage of Columbus. The doubling of the Cape and the discovery of Hispaniola were effected almost at the same time. Our Henry VII. stood aloof from the enterprize. But the Bristol merchants discovered Newfoundland, the nearest part of America to Europe.

The Cape passage and the sea route to India were not discovered a day too soon. In 1515, the Turkish scourge fell on Egypt, nearly destroyed it, and blocked the only remaining land route to the East. I know no historical event which has brought about more signal and more enduring changes than the conquest of Egypt by Selim I. But nothing has been more entirely ignored by our paste and scissors historians than this event and its consequences. I have dwelt on them before; I have pointed out that they are the key to many a European problem in the first quarter of the sixteenth century. I need not dwell on them here, and only refer to them in order to show how powerful a stimulus necessity was to the development of the sea route to India and the improvement of the transit trade.

Now at the time when Borgia issued his Bulls Western Europe still believed in the Pope, though his doings and those of his family were inconsistent, to say the least, with his function and profession. I believe that an attempt has been made to whitewash his daughter Lucretia. I am not sure whether something of the same kind has not been done for his son Cæsar, and even for the Pope himself. But these are the customary pranks of the philosophy of history. After possession had followed on the Bulls, the occupants were, or seemed, too strong for dispossession, and, to say the truth, the Spanish soldier of the sixteenth century was a very formidable person when he was properly led and paid with fair regularity. It was a long time before any of the European nations ventured to dispute the ownership of the New and the Old World as enjoyed by Spain and Portugal respectively.

Now this bears upon my subject, the development of the art of transit. Provided a vessel was seaworthy, speed was no object to these monopolists. They had virtually, at least as far as Portugal went, the sole market of the Eastern world and its most desirable products. Their vessels were huge unwieldy structures; but apart from their knowledge of gunpowder and its uses, which was formidable as a terror, if for little else, their visits were to peoples which were not seafaring, or, at most, familiar with nothing better than a canoe. So the Portuguese fairly established themselves in the Spice Islands, and had factories on the western coast of India. When it was too late, the Turks tried in their clumsy and barbarous fashion to restore the trade which they had ruined. But the land route to Aleppo had no chance against the long sea voyage, slow and capricious as it was.

The English were still a seafaring people. They seemed to have frequented the Baltic. But during the reign of Henry VIII. they did not go further south than Seville. Their first distant venture—I omit that of the voyage to Newfoundland—was an attempt made under Sir Hugh Willoughby in the reign of Edward VI. to discover a north-east passage along the Arctic Sea and the coast. Sir H. Willoughby with two of his crews was caught and perished in the Arctic winter, the third reached what we now know as Archangel, and established our first commercial relations with Russia. They did not attempt to navigate the Mediterranean till towards the end of the sixteenth century, and then they had but little success in that region, for the Levant Company which Elizabeth chartered was a failure to the adventurers, and a loss to the Crown.

Now to carry on distant navigation with safety it is necessary to know several things. The Portuguese had learned something about the trade winds, the peculiarities of the Southern and Indian Oceans, and had surveyed, and in a rude way constructed charts of these seas. These were, however, State secrets, like an Emperor's diary. It was in the last degree important to get at them, to copy them, and to put copies of them into safe hands in Europe. Now there was war between Spain and Holland, of which I shall say a little hereafter, but till Philip II. succeeded to the Portuguese throne, peace between Holland and Portugal. If Philip had not succeeded to this new kingdom and its vast possessions it is difficult to understand how Holland could have got a foothold on the Spice Islands. The necessary information was procured for them by one Linschoten, a Dutchman.

I know nothing in the romance of history more curious than this man's career. I never read but of one other Dutchman whose fortunes were so romantic. I refer to that of Ripperda in the eighteenth century. But that person was not so respectable, and he ended in failure. Linschoten had taken up his residence in Portugal. He got into the service of the Archbishop of Goa, and accompanied him to the Portuguese settlement in the western coast of Hindostan. Here he began to collect all the important evidence which he could put together, the mystery of the trade winds, the geography of the Eastern Archipelago, where the most important of the Portuguese factories were, the botany of the district, the navigation of the channels, and the character of the natives. Finally, he got hold of the maps which the Portuguese had drawn, copied which could be procured, and carefully secreted them. During the long period of his eastern residence, Portugal, with its dependencies passed into the hands of the King of Spain, and Linschoten, though he had to work with still more secrecy and care, had the satisfaction of knowing that he was not only engaged in instructing his countrymen, provided he could get back with his treasures, in the way to enrich themselves, but was countermining against the national enemy. He must have had rare gifts of dissimulation. At last he completed his research, contrived to quit his patron's service without suspicion, and returned to Holland. Here he speedily published his "New Map of the Indies," to which our own Shakespeare makes reference, and instructed his countrymen in the new field of adventure which he had informed them of. He must have let them know how readily their quicker and more easily managed craft could grapple with the great clumsy galleons in which Spain carried on its trade.

But before Linschoten's maps were published Dutchmen and Englishmen had successfully achieved the circumnavigation of the world, and so solved a problem which was insoluble to the earlier geographers. The English expedition was effected by Drake. This resolute and able navigator was by no means indifferent to accidental opportunities. Whatever Philip's secret intentions were, however well they were divined by Walsingham and disclosed to Elizabeth, there is no reason to believe that the Plymouth sailor was made acquainted with them. Drake, however, takes matters into his own hands. He had personal reasons for dislike to Spain and its government; but, I imagine, that if no such reasons had existed, he would have harried Spanish commerce. In plain English, Drake had all the instincts of a pirate, the best opportunities, and the fullest inclination to avail himself of them. One cannot defend his action, but it was eminently useful. Out of his great voyage he learnt how to attack the Spanish fleet in Cadiz, and to deal with the Armada. For in those days, and after so long a decline in the naval enterprize of England, after the disgust which had come over everything, owing to the action of Henry, his son's guardians, and his elder daughter, it was necessary that the seaman should be schooled into confidence. The story about Drake and the game of bowls at the Hoo may be a fiction, but it must have been a verisimilitude.

Now, you will see that, in order to effect the settlement of their factories in the East, and to overawe such potentates as might be disposed to resist them, and to conquer the native races of America, it was sufficient that the two powers of Spain and Portugal should have seaworthy vessels, and should make some study of navigation. The races with whom they came in contact were not seafaring, except to a trivial extent, and were wholly unacquainted with the means of modern warfare. Nor was time a matter of serious consideration to these earlier traders; they obtained a monopoly of the articles in which they designed to traffic, for any other route was cut off when they began their career; and when the Turks tried, as I have told you they did, to revive the overland traffic, they found, as other people besides Turks have found, that it is much easier to destroy than to revive. The produce of the East when it reached Europe was sold at ten times the price which it cost in the country of its origin, and, even then, was cheaper and better than the produce which was carried by land. Besides, in aid of this monopoly, long after certain European races had ceased to respect the Pope and his Bulls, the power of Spain was very formidable in the eyes of Western Europe. There was a real and a rational dread of Philip II. a century later, and there was the same dread of Louis XIV. A century further on and the career of French conquest began, and Europe, with no little reason, was greatly afraid of Napoleon. Experience in all these cases dispelled the alarm. The Dutch, after a severe struggle, disposed of Philip II. The English and Dutch a century later disposed of Louis XIV. The career of Napoleon was first arrested by Russia, then by uprisen

Germany, and finally this country took a conspicuous and resolute attitude with that remarkable individual, whom our fathers and grandfathers were fond of calling the Corsican tyrant. Now I mention these obvious and trite particulars, the common-places of history manuals, because we should remember, that international scares, though frequently discreditable to poltroonery, are real states of mind with some people, and have to be taken account of, in the economic interpretation of history. It needs no little courage to confront a general scare, and the nation or state which does it, when the scare is at its height, exhibits a courage which may be called almost desperate.

Now this was what the Dutch did. Aided by Linschoten's information, and made confident by their success at sea, for the battle of Dutch independence was mainly fought at sea, the Hollanders determined to essay the Indian Seas and the Indian Archipelago. But to do this they needed: (1) the requisite knowledge of navigation; (2) greater skill in ship-building, especially in view of the fact that a trading vessel was originally also a vessel of war; and (3) confidence. The Dutch were a very curious people in their wars. They fought the King of Spain to the death, and they traded with him and his subjects all the time. Trade, free trade with the whole world was essential to their very existence. In the seventeenth and the first two years of the eighteenth century they hated and dreaded Louis XIV. a great deal more than they had Philip II. in the sixteenth, but they could not understand why the English should insist during the War of the Spanish Succession on a cessation of all trade with France. They yielded to English demands in 1703, but with a very ill grace, and I suspect that their deference was mainly outward show. I am sure it was in England. French brandy and French silks, although prohibited, were plentifully purchased. The London traders, though heartily attached to the Revolution and the Protestant succession, were great dealers in smuggled French goods, and all the effect of the policy which our people thought wise in those days was, that the goods came in and the government did not get the customs on them. It is exceedingly difficult to baffle the smuggler when the sympathies of the public are with his calling, and I am old enough to remember when those sympathies were active and friendly.

Now the Dutch entirely contrived to satisfy those conditions of which I have spoken. They routed, captured, sunk Spanish war vessels which were three times their tonnage, and carried three times their weight of guns. And the peculiarity of this warfare was that they inflicted these losses without incurring any notable injury themselves. The details of Dutch history are full of these extraordinary exploits. The Dutch became as formidable on sea as the Northmen and the Danes, and the Hanseatic League curbed the Northmen and Danes much more effectually, I suspect, than their conversion to Christianity tamed them. The profession of Christianity, I fear, has not deterred nations from piracy and buccaneering and privateering, and aggressive, unjust wars.

That the Dutch built the best ships of the age, knew the art of navigation better than any one else did, and improved that art by the most careful and elaborate processes, is proved by the fact that within fifty years after their independence was acknowledged they became the carriers of the civilized world. Dutch vessels, manned by Dutchmen, were in every port of Europe. Now the art of navigation has been built up more slowly than any of the economic arts. It has laid all kinds of human knowledge under contribution. Its first requisites are a knowledge, as far as the sea is concerned, of physical geography. For centuries it has been compiling observations, in the days of sailing vessels more important than now, of ocean winds and ocean currents. Then it enlisted the services of the mechanician, the astronomer, the chemist, for the art of preserving ships from decay and the attacks of numerous sea enemies, has been a vast stimulus to the discovery of practical results. Galileo, using his new telescope, discovered the satellites of Jupiter, and forthwith laid the foundation of an entirely new art of navigation. But it was in Holland that this art took its first new steps, and the mariners of England went to Amsterdam to get the new devices for swift and safe navigation.

Like any other European state, the Dutch aimed at securing a sole market. We were no wiser than they. To make Great Britain and Ireland and the British Colonies free ports for the world was a theory which only a few wise, and therefore discredited, people elaborated. I only remember one statesman who held this opinion in the eighteenth century, and that was Henry Fox. Now Henry Fox was a man whom everybody disliked. He was believed to be the most corrupt and greedy man conceivable in a very corrupt and greedy age, and I don't think that this character, a pretty just estimate, assisted the force of his opinions. And you must not imagine that this foolish delusion—a sole market—is defunct. The French, though they have not succeeded very well in their efforts, are under this illusion. So are their rivals and enemies, the Germans. It appears, however, that their project of establishing African factories is not particularly promising. In old days, our own Chatham was fully pursuaded of the prudence of this kind of policy, and certainly seemed to have secured its accomplishment by the Seven Years' War. I have my suspicion that his strange conduct towards its conclusion was due to his being at his wits' end to see how the interest on the loans contracted during that war could be provided for. His successors certainly did not, and made matters worse. But I do not intend to investigate Chatham's motives and manners. They are part of the philosophy of history, a branch of human speculation to which I never took kindly.

A sole market, as you will easily anticipate, is a form of protection, and it has the inherent vice which characterizes all forms of protection, that it makes the object of it slow and stupid. To give a man a secure market is to shorten his faculties and weaken his powers. I do not doubt that if the Dutch had secured, as they seemed likely to secure, a sole market in the Eastern seas, they would never had been, despite their free-trade theories in Holland, the carriers of the world. We have got an old proverb, certainly as old as the Greek world, for the extension of it in detail is the substance of a good part of the Plutus of Aristophanes, "that necessity is the mother of invention." Take away the necessity and the invention goes with it, is the argument of the Greek poet, and it is true from that time to this.

Now the necessity came from English rivalry. However much they might have desired it themselves, and they fought long and desperately for it, they had no mind to see another nation affirm and secure it. The Dutch were for two centuries the

English allies, and very useful allies the English found them. But it was another thing to give way to their pretensions and abandon one's own. So the English became the ill friends of Holland in the Eastern Archipelago, and there were awkward doings there—doings long remembered and made the politic plea for hard bargaining. But this rivalry put the Dutch on their mettle. They fought against their competitors in the approved mode, but they fought against them by invention and sharpened wits. You will remember that when Peter the Great determined on giving his people practical instruction in the arts of life he undertook to learn them himself, and go through the only practical course which there is of technical learning. So he went as a ship's carpenter to Amsterdam, and worked in the yards with his own hands. He came, it is true, to England, and inhabited Evelyn's house, much to that excellent man's subsequent disgust; for Muscovite habits, even in the highest ranks, were decidedly and permanently repulsive; but he learnt his craft in Holland.

I shall deal with the two East India Companies in a later lecture, merely stating here that the Dutch Association was conceived and carried out on a far greater scale than that of England, and that the Dutch were traders as well as conquerors, while our people, if we can take the first chairman of the East India Company as a specimen, I mean Clifford Lord Sunderland, were scarcely conquerors and decidedly buccaneers. But the process of rivalry, peaceful or piratical as the case may be, was too slow for the passions of the British merchants, and Cromwell indulged them with the Navigation Act, another form of protection, under which trade to England or its dependencies was limited to English-built ships, manned by a large majority of English sailors. They did not absolutely exclude all foreign sailors; that would have been suicidal, as they still had a good deal to learn from them. The Navigation Act was the most foolish piece of Cromwell's whole legislation, and was therefore, very naturally, the only part which was re-enacted after the Restoration. There is a characteristic flavour of baseness in the re-enactment, for it was aimed at the Dutch, who had befriended, sheltered, and assisted Charles during his exile. Charles must have relished it.

The Navigation Act, like every other form of protection, injured the Dutch, but did not benefit England. It diminished, as far as this country was concerned, the carrying trade of the Dutch, but it is an exaggeration to say that it ruined it. It merely made it more effective in other quarters. The ultimate decline of the Dutch carrying trade was due to totally different causes. The States permitted themselves to be involved in European wars in which they had absolutely no concern, notably that of the Austrian succession, mainly that they might secure their sole market by getting rid of the Ostend Company, and by incurring, for the same visionary end, enormous and ruinous charges in the Eastern Archipelago. And as for us, under the Navigation Act and the merry monarch, merry as Nero was, the Dutch burnt the fleet in the Medway and insulted London. After Charles, with the perfidy of his race, garnished by levity of his own, declared unprovoked and sudden war on Holland in 1672. Human beings have reverenced strange rulers, but the endurance of Charles II. is a puzzle to me. And yet the newspapers kept up the farce of applauding him till the beginning of Hanoverian epoch, when some of them, to the disgust of the Highflyers and Perkinites, as they called the adherents of the exiled dynasty, began to draw conclusions. At the present time, I should think that even his descendants would hardly respect his memory.

As I have mentioned to my hearers more than once before, the two great efforts of persons engaged in commercial intercourse between nations are to lessen the cost of production, and to lessen the cost of transit. Of course, if one were to succeed in getting a sole market from which all rivalry is shut out, these impulses are greatly attenuated. Trade regulations of a protective character, like a conventional currency, instantly cease over the boundaries of local or municipal law. You may injure your neighbours by such expedients in the home market, but you are powerless in neutral markets. Here competition has its own way, and the protected producer has to hold his own if he can, and this is rarely his fortune against the genuine free trader. But there is only one way in which the protected producer can, and then only to a limited extent, undersell his free-trade rival. This is to put the charge of his experiment on the wretched people who are constrained to deal with him, either by charging higher prices on genuine articles, or equal prices on fraudulent and inferior articles. For what is the need of protection if in international and competitive commerce you can sell your own products as cheaply, the quality being equal, as your rivals can? But the experiment can only be on a limited scale. If it were on a large scale, the domestic burden would become intolerable, attract notice, and except under an autocratic government, or among an entirely deluded and besotted people, would be removed.

Even during the period in which the craze of the sole market was crippling invention, and generally checking the development of the industrial arts, the British Government was alive to the necessity of improving the art of navigation. It offered substantial rewards for the discovery of the longitude, and for the improvement of marine timepieces or chronometers. But the British Parliament, absurdly jealous as it was of a standing army, never manifested any jealousy of the navy. The navy was not, indeed, in a very satisfactory condition, if the description which Smollett gives of the king's ships in "Roderick Random" is in any sense a correct portrait. But crimped or pressed as the sailors were, brutally ill-used as they were by the despots who ruled them, they would fight. Even the captains were very rarely guilty of cowardice. I can only recall the case of Benbow's captains to memory, as manifestly guilty of poltroonery; and it is not quite clear that in 1702, some of these captains had not taken bribes from Louis XIV., for that most Christian monarch was perfectly ready to corrupt any one with his money. Now in order to maintain the naval supremacy of England, it was necessary that her navy should be furnished with every appliance which could assist rapid navigation, quick evolution, and safety. Read the account of any of the great naval battles of England, from that of Cape Passaro onwards, and you will find that success was expected from the adoption at sea of the one great rule of land warfare—that of breaking the enemy's line, and destroying him in detail.

There does not, however, seem to have been much improvement in the navigation of the mercantile marine, except the adoption for reasons of economy and safety, of those expedients which the Admiralty had secured for the armed marine. Hence, when war broke out, the danger which merchant vessels ran from privateers was very great. The exploits of these rovers who, during the war of American Independence materially assisted the issue, are still remembered. To build quick sailing ships, manned with a resolute crew, and provided with a few well-managed guns, was forced upon the colonists, and was soon a marked success. I imagine that the superior skill of the Americans in building racing yachts is in succession from those privateering times.

But, in fact, the art of navigation in England was blighted by its surroundings, the sole-market theory, the differential system, the monopoly of the great chartered companies, of which I hope to speak hereafter, and the Navigation Act. Under the two forms of the first of these we obtained war materials at a higher cost, on the plea that in this manner we fostered the colonial lumber trade. Under the second British trade among the general body of English shipowners was excluded from that part of the world which had been assigned to the chartered companies, one of which, the East India, had continued to get the China tea trade into its hands to the great injury of the English consumer, and for the matter of that to the customs revenue. By the third the material for shipbuilding, as then practised, was rendered artificially dear. I can well remember what an impulse the tea trade took when the virtual monopoly of the old company was put an end to, and how the price rapidly fell.

It is only when you take cases and follow them out that you can detect the disaster which a protective policy induces on industry. It excludes its objects from light and knowledge. The progress of English agriculture was rapid while the corn laws were, owing to good crops and abundant supplies, inoperative. In the woollen, the cotton, the iron trade, the impetus given by the possibility of foreign competition has removed the actuality of that competition. I cannot, of course, allege that domestic competition has not cut down profits, as is the case in the salt and soda ash trade. I have heard that a similar competition has reduced the profits of colliery owners, though here the situation is by no means so simple as they who say they smart under it contend. Similar allegations are made about the iron trade, and it is gravely suggested that the whole supply of these articles, perhaps only among others, shall be regulated and the price fixed by a syndicate, association, or gigantic company, which shall reproduce some of the phenomena of what the Americans call a ring or corner.

But the power of regulating prices possessed by producers is very narrow. It is always open to competition on the part of those who have not taken part in the association, who would assuredly, if the prospect were open to them, make a rush for the extra profits which such an association is intended to guarantee. And if this takes place, and a fresh supply is added to that which the promoters of the scheme allege is already excessive, the expedient becomes nugatory, and the latter end is worse than the beginning. I have never yet heard, in modern times at least, of one man or any association of men, being able to dictate the terms under which a free industry shall be carried on, and a price secured to the regulated produce. Of course, if the State confers a monopoly by patent, the price can be secured to the patentee, being that at which he is able to undersell successfully all produces under a common and old process. But the monopoly granted by protection does not affect an exalted profit. As long as the Government does not go to the length of protecting individual producers, and allows the area which it fences for the industry to be open to all, the inevitable tendency of profits to an equality will do its work. I very much doubt whether the profits obtained by the New England cotton spinners and woollen weavers, and the reputed gains of the Pennsylvanian iron masters are due to the aid which the Government gives them by a protective tariff. The population of the United States increases at an enormous rate, mainly by immigration. There is consequently an ever-increasing body of local consumers, whom the cost of freight and the habit of the market, bind to the domestic producer. And if there be any truth in the complaints made about the cotton and woollen trades, domestic competition has reduced profits in New England as fully as in the old country; and as for the pauper labour of Europe, in contrast with the high wages of the States, an examination of the statistics laboriously and most conscientiously compiled and printed by the States and the Federal Government, as to the wages of labour and even the numbers of the unemployed, the description of the tenement houses, and the narrative of the terrorism exercised by the Pennsylvanian iron masters over their hands under the black-list system, prove that the United States are not the paradise of labour which interested knaves allege that they are, and that not a little of the confidence expressed by the advocates of the present system in its efficacy and usefulness is, when it comes to be examined, no better than bounce.

When this country boldly and definitely adopted free-trade principles the doctrine of the chartered monopoly had become obsolete, or nearly so. But there still remained the differential duty on colonial products and the Navigation Act. We were told, of course, when we urged that sugar or timber, whatever their origin was, should be put on the same level of duty payment or freedom, that we were about to sacrifice our colonies their allegiance, and whatever there was that could be called Imperial in their relations to us. But the shrewd men of the day were not frightened. Some of them remembered the fact that when the American plantations obtained their independence they were better customers by far of English manufactures than they had been when they were in the bonds of a colonial system. But, in fact, the interests which were saved by the differential duties on sugar were not the free labourers of the sugar colonies, but the planters. Half and more than half the present trouble in Jamaica is due to the fact that, certainly up to three or four years ago, when I verified the fact for use in debate, the planters were levying export duties on sugar and import duties on food, and resolutely refusing, as is their wont, to pay anything towards the expenses of government by a direct land tax on their property. The lumber trade of Canada was similarly in the hands of certain squatters, who got, or thought they got, an advantage out of the differential duties. The interests of labour are never advantaged by protection, and, from the nature of things, those of capital only slightly and temporarily. Those of land are only benefited in so far as the produce is a necessary of life, and high prices induce fools to think that they can pay high rents accordingly.

But when we proceeded to assail the Navigation Act there was indeed a hubbub. We were charged with betraying the national defences by destroying the calling of seafaring men. We were bidden to hesitate before we attacked that system to which England and Great Britain owed its greatness, which had been believed to be the safeguard of the nation from the days of Cromwell to the days of Canning, and had been eulogized by every statesman of patriotism and sense. But some of us even in that day had read a little of history and knew that the Navigation Act, for everything but spiteful and malicious ends, was an illusion. We had heard of the Dutch fleet in the Medway, and of its exploits despite the Navigation Act, and we knew enough political economy at the time to allege with abundant evidence our argument that protected interests never thrive, and that they cannot thrive. So the Navigation Act went the way of the other forms of protection, and one thing at least is certain that the mercantile marine of this country is by no means ruined. What the condition of the armed marine is I cannot guess. The admirals tell us, despite the enormous expenditure on it, that it is inadequate, unseaworthy, and incapable of the national defence. If this were an accurate account of the situation, and I, for my part, have long given up any belief in the assertions of experts, an inquiry into the system ought to be conducted under the forms and with the objects of a criminal investigation.

We have thrown open the ports of all our possessions over which we retain the power of control to the mercantile marine of every nation which possesses a ship. They are liable to just the same charges as, and no more than, British vessels are. The market is free and the carrier is free. With but little time and expense, as I have been told by great shipowners, the mercantile marine could be very effectively armour clad. For we do under this carrying trade, and on a free system, two-thirds of the freight of the world. British yards (for governments, whatever they may do with private interests by protective laws and regulations, will never allow themselves to spend more for what they want than they can help) are supplying the armour clads of foreign powers. A generation or two ago the exportation of a machine, and of the materials which might be used for warfare, and even the emigration of an artisan to a foreign and possibly hostile country, was a grave offence and severely punishable.

Nearly all the other foreign nations and the United States have clung to navigation laws. They adhere to that which we have deliberately abandoned, the evidence of what has followed from our abandonment being manifest. At one time the United States promised to be our rivals in ocean-carrying vessels. Seduced by the persuasions, or frightened by the threats of Mr. Morrill and his followers, they have enacted Navigation laws, and their mercantile marine is a thing of the past. What a satire on "trimuphant democracy" it is when the things which the American people were assured were for their health have been to them an occasion of falling, when an industry which was to be fostered into greatness by a well-defined process is extirpated by it!

Protection, as I have told you, is of no avail when it comes into collision with foreign competition. The subtlest arts of your Bismarcks and your Blaines, and the other economic quacks who have pretended to regulate production and trade on behalf of municipal or local interests are, outside the limits of the country whose affairs, to the misfortune of their patients, they are allowed to administer, of no significance. And I shall be exceedingly surprised if the profits of Tonquin trade and Madagascar trade on the one hand, of New Guinea and Zanzibar on the other, are 1 per cent. of the cost to which France and Germany will be put to acquire them.

There are, however, one or two facts connected with the development of freight which I must dwell on for a few minutes. I think it will be clear to you without further detail that we owe the remarkable pre-eminence of our mercantile marine to the fact that the process of producing and using it has been entirely unshackled, and that we have utterly repudiated those illusions to which other nations cling. I do not deny that the operation of these illusions is injurious to us, as well as mischievous to the victims of them. Hindrances to trade add to the cost of freight, and whatever adds to the cost of freight induces an artificial sterility on the trade of those articles which are produced and shipped under the greatest disadvantage. And though in what I have said I have dwelt mainly on the mercantile marine, the same facts hold good in railway transit. The development of the British railway system, in many directions exceedingly premature and foolish, was the immediate outcome of Sir R. Peel's free-trade policy. And here I may observe that the principal inventions which have lowered the cost of railway freight are of British origin. How great and how beneficial those inventions are I shall be able to point out. For it is free trade which gives invention full play, protection deadens and stupefies it.

Of course shippers may over-estimate the profits of the carrying trade at any particular time. All production, every kind of industry is undertaken in the hope of a market, and the hope may be disappointed. What the general said, that he is the most accomplished commander who makes the gravest mistakes, is true of every enterprise. Some callings, for reasons which I need not expound to you, appears to be permanently overstocked. This is said, for example, to be the case with the calling of a barrister. But I take it that all industries which form part of the necessary and invariable business of a civilized community are only temporarily overstocked. I am not, I believe, over-sanguine as to the future of industrial society, but I cannot share the gloomy anticipations of our earlier economists. Three or four years ago we were told that British shipping was a good deal ahead of the demand for freight, and that the whole interest was in imminent peril of congestion. We were not indeed advised to revive in any shape our old Navigation laws, but it was commonly said that we ought to exercise a vigorous police over unseaworthy foreign vessels who competed against our shippers, who are under Board of Trade rules, in entire freedom from any restriction whatever. But a glance at the tonnage of the British mercantile marine, developed and growing under the police of the Board of Trade, would show, and did show, that this was a grumble with very little reason in it.

Some forty years ago when my late friend, Mr. Mill, first published his "Political Economy," a work which he subjected to very little revision during his life, he was filled with alarm at the contingency that the mechanism of freight would be insufficient for the supply of a growing nation like our own. At the present time its development is the principal cause of alarm to home producers of food, and is the perpetual topic of fair-trade predictions. And this freight, be it observed, is rendered as far as the sea passage, and to some extent the land transit as well, is made more costly by protective regulations. It is plain if the British shipper could earn a profit on the out-voyage as well as the home, he could do either at less cost. It is also plain that if, owing to restrictive regulations, the transit profits of a railway are decided only from freight outwards, that the single loaded journey must in the end bear the cost of the returned empty waggons. I have little doubt that the exceeding cheapness of Indian wheat is not a little due to the double freights which shippers earn to and from that country.

Even under these circumstances the alarmist and sinister predictions of Mr. Mill have been signally refuted by the facts of experience. There is perhaps no branch of human industry in which the economy of cost has been so obviously exhibited as in the supply of transit. The vessel, we will say, is made of iron. It costs about a third what it used to cost to make any kind of iron-work. The voyage across the Atlantic is completed in less than half the time it took when Mr. Mill wrote his work, a great saving in motive power and labour. The same is true—I am not thinking of the Suez Canal—of voyages to and from India, China, and other distant places. The process of loading and unloading ships does not take a third of the time, a third of the labour, and a third of the cost which it did a few years ago. Now it is as foolish to predict future possibilities as it is to negative them from present possibilities, but the prophet of the future has a good many facts to go on, enough at least to prevent him from prophesying stagnation, as our older writers did.

The improvements in what is called the permanent way are as marked. A quarter of a century ago the rails were of wrought iron, which wore out rapidly, especially at stations and sidings, the weight of the carriages peeling off strips from the rails. The life of those old rails was very brief. Mr. Bessemer not only discovers the process by which to make impure and unmanageable iron ore purify itself, but turn itself into steel. I do not say that the modern steel rail is immortal, but its life is very enduring, and you do not see where such rails are employed the strips peeling off as used to be. The permanent way, again, is more solid and steady. Now everything which induces oscillation on a carriage is an element of wear and disintegration. I do not remember ever to have consulted a railway engineer as to the saving which has been induced by these new appliances, nor do I feel it particularly necessary that I should, for all that I need to insist on is that the cost of freight is gradually, and yet greatly, diminishing, and with it the extension of freight is effected. Of course nations may be premature. We were in 1847. Unless they are misrepresented, some of our colonies have been too much in a hurry, and have constructed railways over ground from which there is no produce to carry.

There is another direction in which human ingenuity has recently been exceedingly successful. This is the carriage of fresh meat in refrigerated chambers from distant regions. The chemist has discovered that no change can go on in animal structures if the product is kept at a temperature below a certain point. The shipper has taken advantage of this information, and though the trade in fresh meat is as yet only of moderate proportions, it certainly has a considerable future before it. In point of fact, the diminished cost of freight is bringing about, not indeed an equality of prices, for the cost is, and will remain, considerable, but an approximation to quality. The results of this process are very far reaching. If they do not affect certain interests permanently, it is because such interests have not prepared themselves for the new departure which is inevitable. The cost of production and the cost of freight being diminished, a fall in prices is sure to follow. And it should be noted that trade speculations find little or no place in the processes of production which are continuous. The speculator may be under the impression that some scarcity is at hand, and he takes his measures accordingly. But the period during which his judgment is to be verified or falsified is very brief. A few months will bring him profit or loss. With the producer the case is entirely different. He too anticipates the future, but his hopes are prolonged. A set of speculators in copper may cause a vast temporary elevation in price. The continuous elevation of it is subject to the permanent demand for it, and that is a matter of rough calculation.

In conclusion I must repeat in brief what I said last year in detail. It may be new to some of you, and it is most important, for there is no subject on which, consciously or unconsciously, more fallacies are uttered than on that which I am referring to. When a community like our own is exceedingly successful in the carrying trade, so successful that it entirely distances its rivals, its success induces some very striking and, to ill-informed people, very alarming phenomena in the balance of exports and imports. Now people have taken advantage of these facts, and predict calamitous consequences from what is, when properly interpreted, the evidence of prosperous trade.

In the trade of every country with the rest of the world, if the community is doing well, the imports are always in excess of the exports, when interpreted in money values or prices. If they were not—I assume that the prices are correct—the trader would be making no profit. In all trade, in order to make a profit, you must sell for more than you gave for the goods. And this, which will be obvious to you in the course of ordinary trade, where say a grocer buys £1,000 worth of goods and sells them for £1,100, is equally true if the goods are bought with goods instead of money, the money value being stated. There are people who buy what they cannot pay for, and there are nations which do so. In this case the individual runs into debt if he can get any one to trust him. But we do not give trust to nations, we demand securities, and in the case which I have given securities come back in place of goods, only they are not put in the public or Board of Trade accounts. There are plenty of sharp people, however, who know when they are coming.

But a man does not carry goods except with an expectation, and in the end with the certainty, of profits. If the British shipper, as is proved by his tonnage, carries two-thirds of the goods which are conveyed from country to country, and certainly not of the least value, he gets paid for it. But in the exports the cost of carriage does not appear in the price, for the exports and imports are all valued, say in London, and when the price is declared the service is not yet performed, and therefore cannot be charged for. But on the imports the service has been performed, and therefore the cost of carriage appears in the price. A vessel takes out say 1,000 tons of machinery, which is valued at £20,000 in London. This has to pay the cost of freight, and the merchant's profit, and neither of these appears in the value given.

He brings back £20,000 worth, say of sugar, so declared when it leaves the place of origin; but when it is landed in the London docks the cost of freight and certain initial profits are added to the money value. The difference remains with the shipper and the merchant. But unless the facts are analyzed and explained, they are puzzling and sometimes startling. Now this is what Mr. Giffen, with much felicity of expression, calls the invisible export and import. It is much less now than it was once, when freight was slow and costly. But it is, and always will be, an element of cost.

VI.

THE ECONOMIC HISTORY OF CHARTERED TRADE COMPANIES.

Antiquity of maritime laws—Regulated and joint-stock companies—Their origin and excuse—The East India Company—The Bank of England—The South Sea Company—The variations in the price of Stock—Collapse of the South Sea Company—The suppression of the East India Company—The Bank Act of 1844.

THERE is no trace, as far as I know, and I have read with much interest that vast repository of facts, the geography of Strabo, of joint-stock enterprise in antiquity, still less of the policy by which government attempts to develop trade by conferring a monopoly upon a body of projectors or adventurers. The utmost which we may be said to know was that the Island of Rhodes was the first to codify international maritime law, and that from the precedents collected and reduced to system by this enterprizing and prosperous seat of commerce, the commercial part of the civil code was ultimately compiled, and, much more important, that of the principles of international maritime law. But there is no hint that the societas, or collegium mercatorum, went beyond the limits of a guild. I shall have, indeed, in dealing with trade companies, to examine one of the forms of these trade guilds.

Now I do not think it difficult to discover the reason why the trade company remained undeveloped in antiquity. The area of mercantile business was narrow. That the Carthaginians went beyond the Pillars of Hercules or the Straits of Gibraltar is indisputable, for they founded factories, or colonies, in Andalusia. But it is far from proved to my satisfaction that they reached the British islands by sea, though they certainly from early times trafficked in its produce. But, on the whole, antiquity made no considerable, or at least no permanent, geographical discoveries. The trade of the age was not sufficient to maintain the ancient canal from the Mediterranean to the Red Sea, a waterway which was, it seems, created by the Pharaohs, but suffered to fall into decay after the conquest of Egypt by Persia.

As I have mentioned to you before, it was near a century before the English mariners took advantage of the discoveries which had been made by the Spaniards and the Portuguese. The empire of Charles V., the vast dominions of Philip II., were a terror till the resistance of the Dutch proved how entirely hollow was the power of Spain. The English did reach the northern port of Russia, and much was hoped from this new market. But the project came to nothing after the death of Ivan the Terrible. It does not appear that English vessels ventured into the Mediterranean till quite the conclusion of the sixteenth century. There was considerable peril in the attempt, for the Southern Mediterranean swarmed with corsairs from Morocco to Tunis. Even after the trade began the peril was very serious. In the first quarter of the seventeenth century, Lord Craven devised certain estates to trustees. Half the income was to go for the redemption of English captives from the Algerine pirates, the other moiety was to be divided between the two Universities to found scholarships in them. It was only after Lord Exmouth destroyed the Algerine pirates in 1816, that the first moiety found no objects, and the whole income of the estate was devoted to the second purpose. When Noy invented or rediscovered the liability which we know in history as Ship Money, the plea, during the time which Clarendon says was one of unexampled prosperity, was the mischief inflicted on British shipping in the English Channel by the Barbary pirates. Now though Charles I. was not a very truthful person, he would hardly have justified an illegal, or at best an irregular impost, on a plea which, if wholly false, would have easily been met by a flat denial. I have no doubt that during the paradisiacal epoch of Clarendon, these rovers did venture even into the English Channel. You may remember, too, that the Sallee rover is a figure in the earlier pages of "Robinson Crusoe," and Defoe always wrote verisimilitudes; indeed the greater part of his art consisted in publishing fictions which seemed like personal experiences.

In Adam Smith's time there were two forms of chartered companies—those which were called regulated, and those which went by the name of joint stock. Of these the former were the earliest. The regulated company is a system obviously derived from the trading guild. In it, the trader paid a fixed fee for the license of carrying on, at his personal risk, the business in his district, and for the special trade, which the company undertook to protect and to promote. Such were the Levant, Turkey, and, later on, the Russian companies. Of these the first was an experiment made by Elizabeth, towards the conclusion of her reign. The great Queen strove in its grievous decadence or decay to revive the mercantile marine of England, once so strong and famous. Hence she conferred considerable immunities on the companies which traded to the Mediterranean, remitting, in exchange for a trifling annual payment, the customs on goods imported by these projectors. In her lifetime the company was unprosperous, and she lost the annuity as well as the customs. But the company did better in the reign of James, and the imports which it made were the objects of Cecil's Book of Rates, that first attempt at discretionary taxation, which ended so disastrously in the next reign. I presume that the fund paid for the licenses was laid out in protection accorded to the traders, or if insufficient for this, at least for the payment of consuls at foreign ports. Some of these regulated companies still existed in Adam Smith's time, who enumerates five of them. You will find his criticism on this practice and policy in the first chapter of his fifth book. From the first these companies did not maintain forts or garrisons. They did support an ambassador in Turkey to some extent, and, as I have said, a few consuls. But when the new African company was established on this principle in 1750, the associated merchants were constrained, by Act of Parliament, to maintain the forts and garrisons on the western coast. All these companies are, however, obsolete now. In the first place, the duty of maintaining officials, and of building and garrisoning forts, was transferred to the Exchequer; and in the next, the privilege which the companies possessed of granting licenses of trade was done away with, and as far as the area of their operations and monopolies extended, was thrown open to all British traders.

While I think it quite true that at the time in which Smith wrote, the system of regulated companies was indefensible, and that this great man's criticism was justified, I am still of opinion that the system was inevitable at its inception. At the time when these companies were founded, when it was conceived expedient to extend, if possible, British commerce, the country was practically destitute of a naval force. The ships which did battle with the Spanish Armada were, in the main, vessels owned by private persons, hastily armed with such artillery as could be supplied. The Crown had a scanty and an inelastic revenue. Even in the munitions of war, it had to rely on private subscriptions. I have collected and printed from private accounts which I have read, at the date of the Armada, what were the subscriptions and purchases of certain private persons and corporations, how one person bought powder, and another laid in a stock of arms. It was therefore premature to argue that the State should defend commerce, when the State was almost too poor to defend the island itself from attack. Long after the age of the Armada, the marine force of England was small and of little importance, as is shown by the fact referred to above, the appearance of Barbary rovers in the Channel. The real founder of the modern British navy was Cromwell. Had his life been prolonged—he was only fifty-eight years old when he died—I do not doubt that the exploits of a generation or more later, would have characterized his administration. The restored king, to be sure, did his best to ruin the restored navy, as he did everything which he could stint in order to obtain the means for his orgies. It is the one respectable trait in the character of his brother, that he did his best to save the relics of the navy.

I cannot see, then, how the defence of commerce could have been at all effected, even in scanty measure, except under the machinery of these regulated companies. The merchants of the time were not wealthy enough for joint-stock enterprise, and even had they been wealthy enough, I do not see how they could have developed sufficient confidence in each other, for the successful vindication of the joint-stock principle. I can well believe, as Adam Smith alleges, that the directors or managers of these regulated companies put a heavy charge for admission on those who wished to obtain the commercial advantages which they had, or professed to have, and squandered the receipts to their own advantage and enjoyment. Such a result is, I suppose, inevitable in a guild, at least it was characteristic enough of the City Companies up to recent experience, when they have in many cases offered ransom from the accumulations. And I cannot but conclude that when Parliament fixed the fines by which admission to the company was secured, it was simply carrying out its old policy, and merely preventing an extravagant or abusive manipulation of the privileges. For it was not till the latter end of the seventeenth century that England really had a navy, and there are grievous complaints in the next century as to how the captains of the king's ships abused the privilege of impressment, and were a terror rather than a protection to the mercantile marine. Besides, as I have often mentioned to you, it was not easy in the seventeenth century to distinguish a respectable trader from a buccaneer. The regulated company was, therefore, I conclude, an original necessity, and had grown obsolete and mischievous in the time when Smith wrote. But we may dismiss this form of chartered trade companies. I only conclude that as an existing force or process must have an origin, so it must have a motive, and although to later criticism the force is misdirected and the process erroneous, or mischievous, it probably, nay, almost certainly, had the justification of necessity at its earlier development. And this, I am confident, is a rule of interpretation in dealing with bygone conditions which we cannot safely neglect. It is very likely that the origin of a custom, a rule, a law, is obscured in its later manifestations by self-interest or malpractice; it is even probable that it may have been bad and dishonest from the beginning, but we must, if we would interpret economical action, take into account the circumstances, as well as disregard that ancient maxim first formulated as is certain by a knave who feared detection, that one should not impute motives. But the imputation of motives is the analysis of action.

The joint-stock company created by charter, and therefore having to all appearance an administrative sanction, latterly subjected to Parliament, and having, therefore, the legislative reputation of a vested interest, is an affair of far greater significance, and in the economical history of English, and, indeed, of European life, of profound and far-reaching consequence. It has done temporary good, and has inflicted enormous evil. Parliament, in its early forms, looked on it with grave suspicion, for it expected and sometimes discovered and resented, the evils of monopoly in it. You will remember, no doubt, how Elizabeth strove to supplement the poverty of her exchequer, by the grant of monopolies. She encountered the respectful but energetic opposition of her faithful Commons, men to whom, even in these days, we owe much in the way of precedents, and she yielded with grace. Her foolish and unclean successor was more obstinate, and had to yield with a bad grace. For it is perfectly clear that, when Elizabeth gave a monopoly to Raleigh, and James gave another to Mompesson, these men were only the figure-heads to a ring, just as some directors of joint-stock companies are in our days. There is nothing modern in dishonesty except its forms.

The first of the joint-stock companies was that created in 1600, by charter from Elizabeth, for trade to the East Indies. The chairman of it was Clifford, Earl of Cumberland, an ancient buccaneer, whose portrait, hairy and hatted, is still in the Bodleian gallery. It was a small affair. The country was very poor, and the capital of the company was very slender. But it contained the germ of the greatest and the most lasting conquest which has ever been made on sea-board, that of the acquisition of Hindostan, which has been, not without misgivings, translated in our own time, into the Indian Empire. Never has so gigantic a result been achieved from such small, such insignificant, such inadequate beginnings. The first capital of the East India Company, as developed in 1600, was £72,000, and its first voyage was in 1601.

The ships did not return till after the great Queen's death. Shortly after this the Dutch established an East India Company, with a capital of £600,000, with a far higher reputation, and with far better appliances.

Everything which could be said of the regulated company in defence of its origin, could be said with far greater force of the joint-stock company. From the beginning, in this kind of mercantile association, the adventurer could not reclaim his capital from the direction, he could only dispose of it to any one who was willing to buy it. His liability, it is true, was limited to the amount of his subscription, but ill success might extinguish all that. But the collective wealth of mercantile England at the close of the sixteenth century was not equal, estimated by the subscription, to the mercantile wealth of Scotland, less than a hundred years after, to judge from the subscriptions to the Darien scheme. The desire to obtain the gains of commercial enterprise was keen enough, for they were large, well known, and easily appraised. It was the capital which was lacking, not the will.

Notwithstanding its small beginnings, the East India Company grew rich rapidly. The margin of profit which it was able to exact from those who purchased the goods imported in the Company's ships was very wide, and the resultant gains were enormous. Ten years after its foundation, James gave it a second charter, which, as far as words went, was perpetual. The proceedings are described, though not in detail, by Mun and others, who wrote in order to plead for a remission of the rate against the export of specie in the case of the East India trade, urging, and with reason, that unless permission were given to export silver, commerce with India was impossible, and that the sale of imports would secure the country a far greater balance of the precious metals than the exported silver amounted to. The early trade then of the Company was the first breach in that balance-of-bargain theory, which Adam Smith calls the mercantile system, a system which prevailed long after the days in which Mun, Child, and Roger North advocated a more rational theory of trade than had hitherto prevailed.

Of course the Company took sharp measures with traders outside their own organization, or interlopers as they called them.

They argued, and the reasoning was very plausible: "Quite independently of our chartered rights, secured to us by the grants of successive monarchs, whose right to confer monopolies of trade, with countries outside their own authority, has never been disputed, whatever may be said about monopolies of domestic trade; we have, at our own expense, built forts and factories, entered into diplomatic relations with native sovereigns, and laid out much of our capital, and not a little of our legitimate gains, in founding the trade which we enjoy. There may be reason in controlling the regulated companies, which have not incurred such outlay, and therefore have nothing to show for the fines which they levy on those whom they admit to their partnership. But the case is quite different with the East India Company. We are engaged, no doubt on business principles, in securing for the English people a part of that trade which has been successively the monopoly of the Portuguese, the Spaniards, and the Dutch. No doubt the produce which we bring is dear. But we have reduced the price. Had it not been for our efforts, Englishmen would have had to pay whatever price the Dutchmen might choose to exact. The expansion of our trade is, moreover, the expansion of English enterprise. We train seamen by hundreds, we have, it being necessary for our trade, an armed marine which is part of the national forces, as it assuredly would be used, did need arise, for the national defence. But it is impossible for us to continue this system, from which we contend great public advantage ensues, if any person at his pleasure can enter on the fruit of our labour and expense, without contributing anything whatever to either." Such was the reasoning employed. But, on the other hand, the factories of the old company were few and scattered. There were many parts of the Indian peninsula and the islands which they had not pretended to occupy, and even do business with, and it seemed to be a matter of very doubtful right that they should not only exclude independent traders from visiting their factories, but from any commercial intercourse whatever with places and peoples where the company had no business relations of any kind. And when they proceeded further to fine, imprison, and even put to death persons whom they caught in what they were pleased to call their monopoly, the defence of their action and monopoly were alike untenable. They were, in short, doing what no civilized community ever dreams of permitting, establishing a paper blockade, which they could not, or would not, make effectual.

It was for reasons like this that Cromwell, who was in many particulars of his administration greatly in advance of his age, annulled the charter of the Company in 1654, and made the trade to the Indies free. Of course this action of his did not confiscate their factories, or give any Englishman, and, for the matter of that, Scot or Irishman, the right to use the Company's property. You will remember that Cromwell bestowed all the advantages of English trade on the Scotch and Irish, a privilege which did not last longer than his life; but was very fully remembered when the Scottish Union was negotiated. The short interval, however, during which the Eastern trade was thrown open, gave occasion to that remarkable constitutional struggle between the two Houses, which is known in constitutional history as Skinner's case. Skinner had taken advantage of the new situation, had traded to India, had purchased, as he said, an island from a native prince, and had set up trade on his own account. The Company, during the period in which their charter was suspended, had despoiled and imprisoned him. Skinner, as you probably know, appealed to the Lords, who at that time claimed original as well as appellate jurisdiction, and a very pretty quarrel ensued between the two Houses. The problem was an insoluble one. Skinner was unquestionably wronged, but the Lords did not possess the function of righting him. On the other hand, the Commons were wrong in disputing his claim to compensation, and in the right in affirming that he had applied to the wrong tribunal.

Charles, however, had recognized and restored the Company's charter, no doubt holding that Cromwell's action was a usurpation. He did more; he gave them that part of the dowry of Catherine of Braganza which consisted of Goa, and what afterwards became Bombay. Her other possession, Tangier, he held till he was tired of it. In consideration of these white elephants, the Parliament gave her a very handsome annuity, which she lived long to enjoy. But the settlement on the western coast of India was of considerable advantage to the Company, and during the reign of Charles the profits of the shareholders were very great, Child being virtually the autocrat of the directors. As the Company had been depressed by the Puritans and reinstated by the Cavaliers, the bias of the directorate was towards the Court party, which afterwards developed into the Tory party, and Child entered deeply into the corruption which began with the Pensionary Parliament, and gathered strength after the Revolution of 1688. The directors flew at high game, and were found out. They bribed Trevor the Speaker, Seymour the leader of the Tory party, and the Duke of Leeds, who had reached to fortune and rank by a few good acts and much flagitious conduct. Trevor was expelled from the House, Seymour and Leeds were discredited. They suffered the penalty of being found out, and I am convinced considered themselves ill used. But the disclosure of their practices led to very serious consequences to the Company, and to the affirmation of a parliamentary rule of high constitutional significance. I shall revert to it in a short time, for before it was affirmed another and a far more distinguished joint-stock company was formed.

Long before the Revolution, the example of the Bank of Amsterdam—its astonishing success, and the powerful influence which it wielded—had suggested to English merchants the policy of founding a public bank. Two projects of this kind had been discussed and commended during the Protectorate, the leading idea in both being that the management of the bank should be entrusted to the Corporation of London, as that of Holland was to the Corporation of Amsterdam. But the two municipalities were very different bodies. The Corporation of London was not then corrupt, I believe. But it could not resist the depravity of the Restoration, and some of the most impudent and scandalous jobs ever perpetrated by that institution—and they have been numerous—were brought to light after the Revolution, as the leases of the Conduit Meads, the maladministration of the orphans' fund, and the embezzlement of the collections made in aid of the Huguenot clergy. I allow that there were men of great worth in the Corporation, and that for a long time the City retained some flavour of that spirit which made them so energetic in defence of the Long Parliament and its policy. Had they possessed their ancient character, neither Charles nor his tool

Jeffries could have extorted their charter from them in 1683. They were utterly unfit to manage an institution of credit.

On the other hand, the burghers of Amsterdam, even when the power of the princes of Orange was at its highest, were a haughty, self-contained republic, who looked upon the stadtholder merely as a magistrate, retaining his power at their pleasure and during good behaviour. The constitution of Holland had many faults, not the least being the disintegration involved in the union of a number of small republics, which were exceedingly apt to quarrel when a common danger was abated. It was not without reason, then, that people commonly said that a bank, that is, an establishment of credit, and monarchy, *i.e.*, the restored Stuart line, were incompatible. If one wished to confirm the generality by a prerogative instance, the theft of the Goldsmiths' money by Charles in 1672 was overwhelming proof, and yet Charles was popular, and the Stuarts had a party. Surely loyalty to them was the most incomprehensible and irrational of passions.

The Bank of England owed its origin and its charter in 1694 to the exigencies of the Government and to a loan. The expediency of a joint-stock bank, governed by a body of elected directors, each with a considerable qualification, was urged by Paterson, a Scotchman, and Michael Godfrey, an Englishman, and brother of that Edmund Bury Godfrey, whose mysterious death gave occasion to the fictions of Oates, Dangerfield, and others. The occasion was Montague's necessities. The loan was £1,200,000 at 8 per cent., and it is highly probable that Francis, the gossiping chronicler of the Bank, is accurate when he says that for a long time the dividends of the Bank came from the interest paid by Government, the profits of the banking business being absorbed in the management. This is also my impression gathered from the prices of its stock, which I am registering for a long period. But I trust that on some future occasion I shall find it possible to enter in minuter detail into the fortunes of this remarkable institution than I can at present. I only say now, that the price of Bank stock is to a greater extent the history of England in the eighteenth century than any other record, as I could show you from many crucial instances. The Bank Act of 1694 was amended in 1696-7, and remained in general its constitution till 1844, when Peel entirely reconstructed it.

Now the Acts of Parliament under which these and other joint-stock companies, now entirely forgotten, were created, suggested to Montague the affirmation of that principle, which had so great an influence on the fortunes of joint-stock enterprise in Great Britain. It was that Parliament alone could grant joint-stock companies a monopoly of trade. This resolution, which William was by no means disposed to resist, cut the ground from under the feet of the old company. It took nothing away from them which they actually possessed—their fleet, their forts, their factories, their business. But it stripped them of their right of excluding every one from the sole market which they had hitherto treated as theirs, and gave any association which obtained the requisite sanction as much right to traffic in Hindostan and the Spice Islands as the original company possessed, provided the new association did not intrude on absolutely occupied ground. Now I have no early and authentic account of the price of India Stock during its palmy days. It is doubtful whether any record subsists earlier than 1692, though the archives of the Company, no doubt, if they still exist, contains a register of its dividends. Now, on March 30, 1692, which is my first entry, the price of East India Stock was 158. On January 1, 1699, when Montague had launched his parliamentary company, under the name of the New or English East India Company, the price was $41\frac{1}{4}$; and six months before this, when the scheme of the new company was being matured, it had sunk as low as $33\frac{1}{4}$; now we read that in its palmy days the stock was up to 300 or 400.

But the old company did not despair, and despite the rivalry of its more prosperous and younger sister, it recovered a considerable position in two or three years. Of course amalgamation under the Parliamentary title was sooner or later inevitable, and it came in 1708. Under the new system the greater part of the Company's capital, as was wholly the case with the Bank of England, was a debt due from Government, on which interest was paid, at first high, but greatly reduced during the long and commercially prosperous administration of Walpole. But the privilege in each institution was bought dearly. The Bank and the East India Company wanted a trading, not a dead capital. Besides which the expectation of business profit is on an average pretty permanent, for I imagine that though generally from 10 to 15 per cent. was all that was expected in the beginning of the eighteenth century, as it is at the end of the nineteenth, the rate of interest on loan capital has been steadily falling since that earlier time. In Montague's days the Government had to give 8 per cent. for advances; in Walpole's, forty years later, it could get it in plenty at 4 per cent. Hence, on every occasion on which the Bank negotiated a fresh loan to the public, in return for the extension of its parliamentary privileges, it had to submit to worse terms. Not only on its new advances, but on the old ones as well. I have no doubt that not a little of the trouble into which the East India Company fell at or about the time of the Seven Years' War, was due to the enormous amount of its capital, which was represented by advances to the Government. So after the South Sea Bubble, when the Bank dividend fell from 8 per cent. to 6 per cent., and the East India Company dividend from 10 per cent. to 8 per cent. I should not assign this falling-off to the shock which had been given to credit, but to the decreasing rate of interest which these companies were forced to receive for their advances to Government.

The third of the great joint-stock companies, destined speedily to have a very infamous reputation and memory, was the South Sea Company, founded by Harley, Lord Oxford, in 1711. Harley, it seems, was desirous of emulating the reputation of Montague, by founding a gigantic trading company, and making the principal part of its stock to consist of public debt. The new company were to hold near nine and a half millions of the public debt, and to receive 6 per cent. and £8,000 a year for charges of management. They were to have a sole market on the east side of all South America, and on the west of the whole continent. The scheme, which Oxford's friends called his masterpiece, was borrowed from the Bank and English East India Company projects of Montague.

There was in reality no new capital, no new subscription in the scheme. What was really done was the consolidation of the floating debt into a permanent stock, called South Sea Stock, the management of which was undertaken by an association, the funds being provided by the State. To be sure, a small amount of new debt, £500,000, was created; but this was a trifling matter, and was soon represented by bonds of the new company. But I do not believe that the Tory administration, which came into office after the election of 1710, and remained, though in a great state of dissension, till near upon Anne's death in 1714, could have negotiated a general loan. In all the annals of the Bank of England since 1697, I have never noticed such a panic as prevailed at and after the election of the Tory Parliament in 1710. In November, 1710, when the elections were over, and the character of the new House of Commons could be estimated, and it was known that the Lords would be swamped by the wholesale creation of peerages, Bank stock, which had stood at $127\frac{3}{4}$ in March fell to 97. Even when in 1711 the company was created, and visions of indefinite trade were dangled before the holders of the new company, the price of the South Sea stock, bearing 6 per cent. interest, was only $77\frac{1}{4}$. The third number of *The Spectator*, containing the vision of the Bank of England, the appearance of the Pretender, and the instant collapse of credit, is dated March 3, 1711, and accurately represents, as I do not doubt, the prevalent anxiety and alarm, being the only paper in that week which has a strong political meaning. Early in that month Bank stock was under 104, and everybody must have seen and sympathized with what Addison meant when he prefigured the danger which public credit was running. I am persuaded that much of the indecision and procrastination which his contemporaries, and especially his associates, noted and resented in Harley's character, was due to the distrust which the joint-stock companies felt towards him and his party. The clergy could keep shouting that the Church was in danger; the country squires could get fuddled by drinking confusion to the Whigs in bumpers of October and bowls of punch; and mobs could easily be instigated to wreck dissenting chapels, while they hiccoughed out blessings on the Church, the Queen, and Dr. Sacheverel, whom his own friends held to be a vain and empty coxcomb; but there was the counterpart to these triumphs, viz., the decline in the value of public securities to an alarming extent. So Harley remained timid and irresolute to the end of his career, fortunately for him, cut short by the fiery Bolingbroke, though in the lampoons of the time, the Ox and the

Bull, with the other Perkinites, as the advocates of the exile were called, were warned that the other party was on the alert, and would frustrate them. The stocks never entirely recovered till the death of Anne, when they suddenly rose 10 per cent.

Facts and figures like these appear to me to throw more light on the acts of public men, and the motives which impelled and controlled them, than the speculative estimates which the philosophy of history formulates, to be torn to pieces in another estimate by some other historical philosopher, and so on through the ages. And it is because I see this perpetual shifting of the characters, I have, I must confess, very little interest in these ingenious, but entirely psychological, speculations. After all, we shall never be able to collect all the facts which make up an epoch. But it is infinitely better to collect what facts we can than to be constantly ventilating airy hypotheses. To me the fall of near 30 per cent. in 1710, consequent on the election of the Tory Parliament, and the establishment of a Tory Government—these are, of course, the historic Tories, and have no modern counterparts—is worth a thousand guesses at the motives of Swift and Atterbury, Harley and St. John, Harcourt and Masham, and the whole procession of dim shadows which pass over the stage of history at this age. And similarly I am more instructed by the rise of 10 per cent. at the death of Anne, than I am at the picture of the Whig peers pressing into the council chamber as Anne was in her last lethargy, and forcing from her almost unconscious hand the nomination of Shrewsbury to the office of Treasurer, and the repudiation of the Pretender and his hopes. It is more to the purpose than the maledictions of Atterbury, when the disappointed intriguer exclaimed, not without some unclerical ejaculations, "There goes the best of causes for want of a little courage."

Had the Tory party wished to carry on the War of the Spanish Succession, peace was a necessity for them, for my studies of finance at the time prove to me that they could hardly have raised a loan. So the Treaty of Utrecht was speedily brought about, in which England did not gain, beyond Gibraltar and Minorca, scarcely one advantage. I must not indeed forget one, on which so much turned subsequently.

When the Treaty of Utrecht was passed, a supplementary treaty was entered into between Philip of Spain and the English sovereign under the name of the Assiento Treaty, by which Anne and her successors were empowered to assign to such persons as they might designate the right of importing in a ship annually despatched four hundred negro slaves into the Spanish colonies of the New World. The Spanish settlers had nearly destroyed the native population by forcing them to labour in the mines, and the benevolent bishop, Las Casas, in order to save some relics of the native population, had advocated the importation of negroes from the African coast. The process seemed humane to the good bishop, and was plainly lucrative to the planters, and the alliance of benevolence and self-interest was speedily carried into execution. But the Spanish mercantile marine was decayed, and indeed every impulse to enterprise, as Alberoni soon discovered when he tried to resuscitate Spain; while that of England was abundant, enterprising, perhaps redundant. So Anne negotiated the treaty, handed over her interest to the South Sea Company, began the slave trade for the English people, encouraged it in our own plantations, gave in the centuries afterwards occasion to the most sanguinary civil war which was ever waged, and immediately promoted the instincts which led to the South Sea Bubble. The South Sea Company gladly received the boon, for they had visions before them of forcing and appropriating the South Sea trade, not with the single ship of the Assiento Treaty, but with a fleet which should range from the Oronoco to Terra del Fuego, and thence to the Aleutian Archipelago through the Pacific. Why not discover another Peru and another Mexico, and rival the exploits of Cortes and Pizarro?

The Whigs returned to office after the death of Anne, and were the masters of the English constitution up to the accession of George III., when Jacobitism, the spectre of the early eighteenth century, had become a sentiment, and Hanoverian Toryism, in George III.'s case without Hanover, took its place. The Hanoverian sovereigns, indeed, like men who have long been in possession, began to show good feeling towards the refugees, or victims of the earlier days of the dynasty, to reverse attainders, and restore titles and estates, especially when the estates, to the habits of the time, before deer forests, hotels, and sentiment, were not worth much. If I am not in error George IV. masqueraded in a kilt, a habit which his great-grandfather had proscribed as a heathenish costume, savouring of rebellion, and the Lowland Scots, with much reason, detested as the regular garb of a thief. But the Tories during the last years of Anne's reign, had left the finances in confusion. I may mention here that the rising of 1715 has scarce left a trace on the price of stocks. It was to induce order on the finances, and to consolidate the debt, that Stanhope, a weak, well-meaning man, with some sharpers who were his companions in office, notably Aislabie and Craggs, entered into negotiations with the Bank of England and the South Sea Company with a view to engrafting the public debt on their stock. The Bank of England negotiated, hesitated, made some timid offers, and then wisely left the field to the younger company. Fortunately for his reputation, or unfortunately for the country, Walpole was out of office.

In my lecture on the development of credit I stated all that was needed about the career of the South Sea Company and the marvellous year 1720. But the collapse brought about a singular result, or at least was followed by it, a general lowering of the rate of interest. The long-continued peace, the growth of wealth, the great prosperity of the agriculturists, and the paucity of public stocks for investment, were probably the causes of this singular development. The Bank dividend became habitually 6 instead of 8, East India Company 8 instead of 10, and South Sea stock 5 instead of 6. The general price of Bank stock was 127, of East India Company 147, of South Sea 100, and in June, 1727, the interest on every kind of Government stock was to be reduced by 1 per cent.

The South Sea Company still undertook trade, and had a fleet, but it appears that the expenses were so great that little or no margin of profit was left, and ultimately this company, from which so much had been expected, sank into a mere department of the National Debt Office. The East India Company did carry on a trade, and carried it on to a profit, for they dealt in articles of familiar use to the world, and on their own terms. About the beginning of the eighteenth century tea drinking began to be common in England, at first, of course, among the richer classes in London. It appears to have been supplied by the Company. Now there is no reason to believe that the price of tea in China was higher in the reign of Anne than it was in the reign of Victoria. But the cost of freight and the profits were enormous. Bohea—I have made my notes from the accounts of rich Londoners and a few country gentlemen—was at first 42s. a pound, green tea 20s. It was generally the practice of purchasers to buy a China teapot when they bought tea, and give a shilling for it, and I do not doubt that the very numerous old melon-shaped China teapots which are in existence are the relics of this custom. In ten years, however, the price fell to 16s. or 14s., and 10s. The earlier price may have been due to the uncertainty of the market. But as long as the tea trade was included in the Company's monopoly tea remained dear, and when the trade was thrown open about fifty years ago the price began to fall. Nothing, in short, illustrates the effect of trade monopolies such as those conferred by the charters granted to trade companies, than the history of tea prices. It is noteworthy that in the last quarter of the century tea-drinking became common among the working classes, greatly to the disgust of Arthur Young, who comments in his tomes on the practice with alarm and contempt.

The creation of a gigantic empire, which early became the position of the Company, and was inevitable from the time when Clive began his victories to the time when Wellesley, afterwards the Duke of Wellington, broke the last serious opposition to British arms in India, was incompatible with the trade transactions, on behalf of which the Company was first chartered, transactions continued long after they had ceased to be profitable to the shareholders, and were highly injurious to British consumers. The difficulties of Indian finance, consequent on the seven years' war which Great Britain waged chiefly in Hindostan and North America, led to the expedients of Granville and North for taxing the American plantations, and coercing the colonists when they refused to pay the Stamp Act, and declined to purchase the Company's tea. The inevitable control of a company by Parliament, as soon as that company was forced to rely on Parliament for assistance in its difficulties, led to Fox's India Bill, the defeat of the Bill, not on its merits, by the passionate intrigues of George III., who wished, as long as he was sane, to substitute personal government for that parliamentary system by which his family had been raised from an obscure German principality to the foremost throne in Europe, and to the substitution of the younger Pitt for Fox, and with this the abandonment of the principles for which Chatham, Pitt's father, had contended. Then came Pitt's India Bill, which differed so little from that of Fox that the intrigue to which I have referred is manifest from this alone, if there were not other and conclusive evidence on the subject. It is said that monarchy aids in the maintenance of national unity. If so the reign of George III. was an amazing failure in this direction, for his obstinacy led to the successful revolt of the American plantations and to a new colonial policy. In our days an attempt is being made to bring about a closer union between Great Britain and her colonies, and the symbol of it is the Imperial Institute. No one can wish more heartily than I do for the success of the movement, and few, I fear, are more despondent about it ; for the social system, the fiscal system, and every particular of life in the colonies, is in violent contrast with what prevails in the United Kingdom, and I cannot see how one can expect unity from inharmonious elements.

The Indian Mutiny led to the suppression of the East India Company as an independent and imperial corporation. The Company had achieved a great empire, I do not doubt of necessity, for victory begets conquest. Its career was without a parallel in the world's history, and though the last scenes of its existence tarnished the greatness of its reputation, it is still the fact that its heir entered on an inheritance which the Company had won anew and reconstructed. I do not suppose that any person sincerely regretted the extinction of its trade monopoly ; but there are, and have been, many persons who have doubted the justice and expediency of extinguishing an institution which had played so conspicuous a part in the history of our race ; and though I cannot in this place deal with the political exigencies which were supposed to have compelled its extinction, it may well be doubted whether the India Office, and the languid debate on the Indian Budget, for which it is exceedingly difficult to get a House together, are the best equivalents conceivable for that Directorate which exercised the most diligent and unremitting scrutiny into the affairs which it had to administer. In all that I have ever heard and learned the Indian Council is a farce, and the administration is a despotism shared between the Indian Secretary and the permanent officials. I may add that the only parallel to an empire being founded by a trading company even on a small scale was the Bank of St. George in Genoa, which sold Corsica to France.

Only one of these great chartered companies survives. This is the Bank of England. The credit of the Bank grew during the eighteenth century, and this mainly by two circumstances—one the foundation of the Rest at the end of the first quarter of that century, the other the abandonment of note issues by the London bankers at varying duties after the middle of the same century. The happy thought that it was expedient in order to give stability to the Bank's credit to create a fund out of surplus profits, which should gradually accumulate till it became a substantial sum, was evidently suggested by the collapse of 1720. It was for some years, however, before the directors could begin the process, and more years before it assumed anything like its present proportions. The country owes about fifteen millions to the Bank, and this institution has saved out of its earnings, and set aside, under the name of the Rest, a sum equal to more than one-fifth of its capital. Of course this is profit, the property of the existing owners of Bank stock, which they might, if they pleased, divide among themselves. It amounts to about two and a half years ordinary dividend at the present time. But the Rest is as fundamental a part of the Bank system as the law is under which it lives, and the traditions under which it is managed. It is known that the Bank has accumulated profits to the amount which I have stated, and these accumulated profits are seen to be a further element of security in the statement of its assets and liabilities. It seems to me plain that the existence of the Rest is the reason why, in these historic occasions, when mercantile credit has been put to the severest strains, as, for instance, in 1825, the solvency and power of the Bank was never doubted, and it was able to help solvent persons, whose credit was shaken in the general crisis, without being itself affected by the general distrust. They who have made a study of monetary science, in its most concrete form, have always attached the highest interest to the Rest, or accumulated and undivided profits, of the Bank.

The abandonment of their issue of notes by the London bankers, led to the note issue of the metropolis being concentrated at the Bank. The notes of the Bank were not of low amount, for it was late in the century that they issued them for £5, while the £1 note, necessitated by the circumstances of the time, did not appear till the suspension of cash payments after 1797. But the fact that the Bank became the sole source of paper money in the metropolis, enabled them to enlarge their issues, and thereon to increase their profits. These notes were of course only issued against value, as for example trade bills and securities. But they circulated as money, and for many reasons were more safe and convenient than metallic money is. They operated also in international trade as short dated bills of exchange, and of course during their existence they were a profit-bearing issue to the Bank. The average existence indeed of a note of large amount is very brief, almost momentary, for the Bank invariably cancels every note which is returned to it. Nor is that of the smallest note, which it now puts into circulation, as prolonged as we should think when we look at the date of notes which are circulated in the country. But it is a sensible and significant time, and during that period the Bank is making profit on its issue, as it does not give them, except in exchange for deposits and securities.

For exactly a century and a half, the Bank possessed the power of discretionary issue, that is, the circulation of notes to those who wished for them, of course in exchange for negotiable securities, to any amount. It is not, of course, to be believed that it did not put a practical check on its issues whenever such a course was deemed expedient. But it had the power, when the occasion arose, to help straitened credit, when the person straitened had adequate security to offer, and it did so, at most important and dangerous crises. It was at a crisis, not commercial, but political, that the first breach was made in its reputation. I am referring to the suspension of cash payments.

Pitt revived the policy, which had been adopted in the War of the Austrian Succession, and of the Seven Years' War, of subsidizing the German emperor and knights. The practice indeed may be said to have been begun earlier, for William III. is constantly complaining of the rapacity of these personages during his own war, Peterborough dwelling on the same topic during the Spanish campaign, and Marlborough during his experiences, though to be sure the great captain was not above imitating them. But value was received for what he got, little or no value from what was got by the Serene Highnesses. In Pitt's day the subsidies were greater, and the results most disappointing. Now, in order to pay these people, cash was wanted. Pitt could and did impose what taxes he pleased through a sham Parliament, but he wanted ready money. So the heaven-born minister drew on the Bank till he had nearly drained it of its treasure, and the Bank began to be alarmed; I presume at the likelihood of its being repaid its advances, for it had made its loans, not upon securities of unquestionable value and accuracy, but upon the proceeds of future and experimental taxation. He determined, therefore, to direct the Bank not to honour its notes, and obtained from Parliament an indemnity for their action, which was intrinsically one of bankruptcy, just as he could have procured from that assembly the suspension of the ten commandments had he so minded.

So high, however, was the credit of the Bank, that in a very short time it had collected money enough to have enabled it to resume its liabilities and cash its notes. But the Government had found out how useful its metallic reserves might be in the war which it was carrying on, and refused to allow it to recover its reputation. Still, for a long time, either because its reputation still stood high, or because it limited its issues to the ascertained wants of the public, the note remained at par, the indication of the fact being supplied principally by the foreign exchanges. In course of time, however, as the war assumed greater and greater proportions, as the waste of wealth went on, and the sufferings of everybody, except those of state jobbers and financiers, increased, the Bank was tempted by the prospect of trade profit to issue its notes in excess of public requirements. They did not return on the Bank, for the issue was forced and inconvertible. Then came the inevitable. The note was depreciated, that is, fell below the gold standard, though it had to be taken at its nominal value. The opinion, and a very natural opinion it was, got abroad that the Bank was deluging the country with its paper in order to get a profit on the excess of issue. It was predicted that the Bank would never resume cash payments, and Cobbett, who saw pretty clearly what the situation was, after circulating certain letters to the public in which he denounced the Bank and the Government, published a periodical called the *Gridiron*, in which he asserted his willingness to be roasted on that implement if the Bank ever honoured its liabilities. And when the time came it required all the address and courage of Peel, who then did a notable service to his country in saving it from following the advice of men who, having been unconscious fools a few years before, were now unconscious knaves.

The memory of those twenty-two dismal years clung to the great Corporation, for it was supposed to have fallen in with the project under which it made its gain out of the public loss and misery of the great war, the main gains of which to the British nation was an enormous debt, a few costly acquisitions, and a State prisoner at St. Helena. But during the period which intervened between the recoinage and the resumption of cash payments in 1818, and the Bank Act of 1844, the Corporation more than once did great services to public and private credit. It had become the centre of the world's finance. In an eloquent passage, my late friend, Mr. Cobden, describes the intense eagerness with which the announcement of the Bank's rate of discount was watched for in the commercial centres of the further East. It was supposed to possess in its hands the gains or losses of trade, and that on the decisions which its directors came to in their parlour—the language of the earliest days of the Bank are still traditional with it—depended the success or failure of commerce.

Peel totally changed its constitution by the Act of 1844. The alteration was a subject of much controversy at the time, and even now that the warfare of words has somewhat abated, and the nation is ready to accept the new condition of things, the last word has not been said upon the subject. But the question of the currency is the strong meat of economics, and it is perhaps dangerous to offer it to beginners in the science, seeing how it has tried the digestive powers of many who would fain be considered authorities. Be that as it may, it was a measure which, of its kind, was as great a departure from tradition as any of the Acts framed by that great statesman, and marks a new era in politics.

The days indeed of chartered joint-stock enterprise have long passed away. The South Sea Company, as a trading association, had a brief and shameful career. That of the East India Company was long, splendid, and unique. Both, I believe, if trade was to be carried on, were necessary in their day. I do not think it would have been possible in the seventeenth century to have achieved trade with the East by private enterprise. Skinner may have been an ill-used man, but he intended really to trade under the ægis of the Company, whose monopoly for a time superseded, he ventured to intrude on. Jenkins of the Ear would not, I apprehend, have suffered in the service of the South Sea Company. He was no doubt trading on his own account, and when he had to endure, as he said, the mutilation he had certainly undergone, he did not seek succour from the South Sea Company, but, as he alleged, from God and his country. Of course, as people at that time knew, there were divers processes under which ears were lost, and the unabashed Defoe, novelist and pamphleteer, was not the only earless person to be seen. But the trading of these companies soon became a public scandal and a public loss. Long before its dissolution, Parliament had to distinguish between the East India Company as an empire and as a trading concern. The monopoly of the latter became intolerable.

The Bank of England, with the exception of that episode in its history, on which I have commented, when it should have had the firmness to resist temptation, and to have insisted on its own account, that it should give proof of its solvency, has been continuously useful and honourable. Its political services, on which of course I do not comment, have been as significant, as profound, and as important as its economical career has been. It has endured for nearly two hundred years, and it is infinitely stronger than when it began its career of usefulness. It has been criticized, but always with respect and confidence. To my mind, the English constitution has been as much guarded and developed in Grocers' Hall and Threadneedle Street as in the palace of Westminster.

VII.

THE JOINT-STOCK PRINCIPLE IN CAPITAL.

Origin of the guilds of the Middle Ages—The regulated companies of the seventeenth and eighteenth centuries—Limited liability companies of this century—Dialogue for and against the principle of limited liability—Industrial partnerships in Cornwall—Bankruptcy and co-operation regarded in their relation to the joint-stock principle in capital.

THERE has been a time in the economic history of England when a peculiar form of what may be called joint-stock enterprise in capital prevailed universally. I am referring to the trade guilds of the Middle Ages. How universal was the spirit of association can be gathered from the names of the various London Companies, once combined for purposes of mutual defence and assistance, and constantly recognized by Parliaments and Governments, both for the purpose of exercising a police over the craft which they represented, or for serving the State in reference to certain duties or functions. It is not very clear when these Companies, of which only the London guilds survive, began to dissociate themselves from the craft with which they were originally identified, and to admit members who had no relation to what was called their mystery, beyond association with it. But up to the Corporation Reform Act, it was a rule of prescription, if not of law, that no person could carry on trade in a corporate town unless he were a freeman of the borough, or in London, unless he belonged to one of the City Companies. Even now these freemen have a parliamentary franchise, which is not conditioned by residence or property. Certainly by the time of the Revolution of 1688, the City Companies possessed a number of members who were in no way connected with the trade which they represented.

I have found no evidence that at any time of their career these corporations carried on manufacture and trade with a common stock, at least as regards the London Companies; but there were associations, such as the Merchant Adventurers of Bristol, which seem to have done so at an early age; however, the Companies became possessed of considerable wealth. In the last volume of my "History of Prices," I printed from the Rawlinson Papers a fragment of the Common Council Book of London, in which the loans made by the Companies to James and Charles are described, security being given in land for the debt. In this way, I make no doubt, the Companies obtained their Irish estates, not, I conceive, by a round sum paid down, but by advances from time to time, made to the Crown. James, though pacific, was exceedingly extravagant, and Charles was constantly in debt and difficulty, a fact which explains though it may not excuse much of his action.

I do not, however, intend in this lecture to dwell on these associations. I have done so already on an earlier occasion. It is sufficient to say that these guilds, companies, or associations, may be traced back to the *collegia* or *sodalitia* of the Roman Republic and Empire. The aristocratic party in the State looked suspiciously on these companies, and constantly extinguished all but those which, being of venerable antiquity, were ascribed to the policy of Numa. The plea generally was that associations of traders and artificers were collections of artisans and workmen whose very existence was a degradation to the majesty of Rome. Cicero in his "Offices" is very sharp upon them, alleging that the retail trader, for example, can get no profit except by falsehood. But there are grounds for believing that a political reason was the main cause of this hostility, and that when Clodius favoured and organized them, he intended to make them the instrument of what he called democracy. The principal interest to me, however, in these ancient *collegia*, is that they formed a characteristic part of the later Roman *municipium*, and that from these *municipia*, with their existing institutions, were derived the chartered towns of France and England. I am only concerned at present with those voluntary associations in England, known as partnership and joint-stock enterprise, the latter having been recently developed by very modern Acts, and constituting a most important aspect of modern production and trade, the principles and practice of it being sometimes very adversely criticized, and quite as frequently eulogized.

Partnership, and the regulation of partnership by law, must have been as early as trade and mercantile law. In English law, from early to recent times, the liability of the partners, whether they entered into a private arrangement, or adopted as far as possible a joint-stock principle, was unlimited, each partner or shareholder being responsible for all the defalcations or debts of the firm or association. Now it was early seen that certain forms of trade or production could not be carried on, or even exist, on this principle. The stock of the Bank of England carried no liability to its partners beyond the amount of each person's subscription or holding, and this, I conclude, was the reason why the greater part, if not the whole of the capital, beyond the freehold premises of the Bank, was invested in Government securities. When, in 1816, the Rest of the Bank of England amounted to near nine millions, (you will remember that the Rest is the difference between the assets and liabilities of the Bank), that accumulated profit was undoubtedly invested in securities; and when in that year the directors, with the sanction of the proprietors, added 25 per cent. to the capital stock of the proprietors as a bonus, the form which the new stock took was a security. Similarly, when the South Sea Company was formed in 1711, and expanded in 1719, the whole of the stock was in public securities, and so far was a guarantee to the subscribers, whose liability was limited to the amount of their subscription or holding.

It would have been plainly impossible for the great works which have been carried out by private or joint-stock enterprise in England, to have been even contemplated, if the old law of partnership liability had prevailed in them. Undertakings like the London Water Companies, and the railroads, would have been impracticable, if every shareholder was liable for the whole costs of failure, while his gains were limited of course to his share in the undertaking. The process adopted in these and analogous cases was to define the undertaking and the responsibilities of the promoters and subscribers by private Acts of Parliament, and in consequence great industrial undertakings in the United Kingdom, have been saddled with enormous initial costs, and under certain rules of procedure with outrageous subsequent costs. Compensation was awarded to landowners, when private property was dealt with, on a prodigious scale, and some of the great railways have never recovered from the pillage. When, however, as in the case of some among the London Water Companies, the source of supply was public property—in this case the Thames—the charges put upon the projectors was trivial. In the case of the railways, the result has been that the cost of carriage of passengers and goods has been necessarily increased by this factitious capital, and the concentration of all public business in the Westminster Parliament has led to great and unnecessary outlay. In the case of Ireland, matters were far worse. In that, an agricultural country, the railways were constructed on a broad-gauge system, in perfect ignorance, it would seem, of what the natural conditions of the country were. And then, the committees gave these trading companies a grotesque maximum of profit, which the proprietors have of course interpreted as a guaranteed dividend, and actually claim compensation for, as a vested interest of the highest class.

These numerous partnerships with limited liability necessarily went to Parliament. The English law, as law books are fond of telling us, does not vest the *absolutum* or *directum dominium* of land in any subject whatever, and perhaps it is as well that it does not. But it does vest the perpetual usufruct, which differs only metaphysically from the lordship which the law denies. This usufruct, when honestly acquired, the law rightly confirms to the owner, and as rightly insists that either Parliament itself or some authority, the powers of which are delegated by Parliament, and can be revoked by the authority which gave them, should possess, under a just compensation, the privilege of invading such rights of usufruct, and transferring them to others. This delegation is not unknown. Urban authorities have been empowered to take houses and land for street improvements, or for sanitary reasons. In country towns this power is given, *ab initio*, to the civic authorities. In the metropolis, and under the now defunct Board of Works, Parliament wisely reserved to itself the power of reviewing, while accepting or rejecting the schemes which the London Board prescribed. It was not always easy to keep these schemes free from jobbery even in Parliament, but I do not remember any case in which the House of Commons was tainted with suspicion. But neither House is able to repress the enormous expense which attends private bill legislation, and is virtually a denial of equity to new undertakings, by the initial and unremunerative charges with which it loads them.

I have referred to these facts, because I wish to point out to you that the principle of limited liability is by no means the novelty which some persons affect to consider it, and in itself by no means deserve the injurious and invidious criticism with which it has been assailed. It is old, and it has been advantageous. Of course no human undertaking is exempt from the risks of failure, and it is a common-place in political economy to say that there is no escape from risk, except by insurance, *i.e.*, by distributing the liability. People constantly tell you that you can, in these modern times, insure anything. But it may be doubted whether you could insure against the risks of commercial business, or to be more accurate, define the conditions under which the risks can be insured. For insurance is always based on averages, and I do not think that any one has yet, and I do not think that any one could, calculate the risks of success or failure. Nothing at one time seemed more stable than canals and turnpike trusts. But except in rare cases, the former have been either failures, or nearly failures, and I know no case of the latter in which there has not been a failure. And I do not think that even in their best days, any one could have guaranteed a permanent and invariable income from either.

There was in comparatively early times a good deal of joint-stock enterprise. The earliest lists of Stock Exchange values enumerate a large mass of securities, once thought solid, but long since ruined and forgotten. For example, there was a lutestring company, established in England soon after the Revolution, the object of which was to utilize the skill of the refugee French artisans, in the manufacture of silk goods. It was thought to be exceedingly promising, but within twenty years it spent all its capital, abandoned its business, and has long since disappeared into oblivion. Again, there was a sword-blade company, which was destined to a longer, but, in the end, to a not more prosperous existence. A century and more ago, a sword was considered part of the civil dress of a gentleman, and perhaps was drawn a little too freely. The sword-blade company, after a time, disappeared. In Scotland, some patriotic individuals attempted to improve the Scottish linen trade, and established the British Linen Company. But in a very short time, national shrewdness, which is certainly as strong a Scottish characteristic as patriotism—I do not say this in reproach, for I own to some Scottish blood—induced these manufacturers to lay aside their design, and to turn their looms and factories into a bank. But the institution still bears its original name, and as a bank has had a long, honourable, and useful career; for it has performed a notable part in that ingenious and useful mechanism of credit, which is known as the Scotch banking system, a system to which much of Scottish progress in the last and the present century is admittedly due. It may be briefly described as a practice which has indued the cumulative responsibility of endorsed bills of exchange on the balances and credits of its customers.

The whole law of partnership with its unlimited liability, however numerous were the partners or shareholders, unless the liability was restrained by a special Act of the legislature was no doubt incorporated into the practice of the English law from the civil code. The principles and practice of the Roman law will be found in the Digest, Book xvii. Tit. II. I dare say that those who are engaged in the University study of law make themselves familiar with the long and subtle practice by which the rules of partnership were defended. I refer to them here, in order to point out how great the difficulty naturally was, in reversing a branch of law which had so respectable an antiquity, and had been so thoroughly engrafted on that English custom which is called common law. Even now, the question as to whether the legislature has been wise in permitting the creation of joint-stock companies with limited liability is disputed. Of course the question is entirely an economical one. If the law is too lax, so lax that it permits fraud to go unpunished—a very general complaint—the objection, if it can be substantiated, seems to point rather against certain details in the two principal acts, rather than against their principle. But before one enters upon the general merits of the system, it may be well to say a little of its modern origin, as regards general trade. Our law of limited liability was borrowed originally from a particular phase of French practice, and was commended to the legislature long before it was accepted as an integral part of commercial law. The hesitation was natural, for I can well remember that when the legislation was initiated there were many misgivings as to the consequences.

The French have a very severe bankruptcy law. It is almost pedantic in its rigidity, and contains a characteristic of French sentiment, which I do not reprobate, under which a descendant may rehabilitate the commercial character of a deceased progenitor. Such a process would of course be entirely alien to our system of family settlements, under which the liabilities of a debtor do not survive beyond his life, and that part of his personal estate which may be attached by his creditors, nor do I think that until a total change takes place in the devolution of English property, would such a strain of integrity be welcomed in England. The French law visits with serious penalties, such as *travaux forcès*, acts on the part of bankrupts which are treated with extraordinary leniency by the English courts. It is held, I believe, that in a manufacturing and commercial country like the United Kingdom, it is better to run the risk of occasional excessive speculation, than to check enterprise by severity on failure. I am convinced that we carry this theory too far, and that gambling in goods ought to be much more severely handled than it is. If such practices are to be too readily condoned, the speculator has the advantage of winning a heavy stake from the public as a consequence of success, and of making the public pay for his failure.

The French law of limited liability is of two kinds. One is when the directors and certain partners in an association for trade purposes, are still liable on failure to the extent of their means, while the ordinary shareholder who takes no part in the management is responsible to the extent of his venture only ; the other in which the whole of the subscribers are responsible to the extent of their shares only. In the United Kingdom we have adopted the latter system, though in practice, the extreme vigour of the courts of law upon the conduct of directors, both in the initial stage of the partnership, and in its subsequent management, gives the existing law not a little of the characteristics of the first system. Of course this only takes place when the partnership gets into court, and if all one hears is accurate, fraudulent projectors of companies, and directors, too, calculate on the unlikelihood of prosecution, for the suffering shareholders are naturally unwilling, even when they know what has happened, to follow up the business in a law court, and, in their own language, throw good money after bad. I may add that all the company law, as at present existing, was drafted by Lord Thring, who was for many years Parliamentary draftsman of Government Bills, and is an exceedingly acute and able person. In his opinion, as I have heard him say, the blemish in company law lies far more in the administration of the courts, than in the principles and details of the law itself. That the English judges mean well I do not doubt. That they are entirely uncorrupt, and defer entirely to rules of professional honour, I am ready to allow. But it does not follow that they are entirely wise in the administration of the law which they expound.

Now in connection with this new system of joint-stock enterprise with limited liability, the objectors argued : " The law is responsible for inevitable slovenliness in the conduct of business, exaggerated and unwise competition, and many of the evils of depreciation. In an undertaking where the shareholder merely stands upon a fixed stake, the responsibility of his subscription only, not a little of the gambling spirit is aroused. But it is a very serious thing for people to undertake business when they stake everything which they possess, and this alone is a guarantee that the undertaking will be conducted cautiously. Such a fact is illustrated by the far higher reputation of a company in which there is a large unpaid capital, than that of one in which the future responsibility of the shareholders is exhausted. Undertakings which under unlimited liability have, and should have, no chance of success, are constantly floated, to the injury of trade, to the loss of creditors, and, a smaller matter, to the loss of those who assisted in floating them, under this new system. The concession of limited liability is the harvest of adventurers, who would have, and ought to have, no place in honest and legitimate business. In the same way, after the dupes, who have been invited to speculate, are cleared out of what they have subscribed, advantage is taken of some difficulty, perhaps temporary, perhaps inherent, to wind up the concern by unscrupulous attorneys and equally unscrupulous liquidators. There are legal firms in London which have a scandalous notoriety for this practice. They are known by a rigorous metaphor as wreckers. Besides, it constantly happens that owing to a failure in such undertakings, quantities of property are thrown on the market, disposed of by forced sales, at an entirely inadequate price, and in this way depress the value of stocks and property possessed by old-fashioned and legitimate traders. You cannot deny that the tendency of profits is to an equality. But it follows from this rule that if property purchased at an inadequate price, falls into new hands, it tends to diminish the profits of those who gauge their business and their profits, by the only legitimate canon which trade affords, the cost of production under the most favourable conditions and the most intelligent supervision.

"Nor is this all. As profits tend to an equality, so does the interest of capital. In those undertakings with limited liability, the subscriber has no reason to expect, and as a rule, cannot get for his shares more than the average rate of interest plus a further amount to represent his risk, in so far as it can be calculated. It is notorious that in investments such as railways, the average rate of dividend, calculated in the price of the companies' stocks, and spread in the shape of admitted earnings over the whole of these undertakings is not more than the interest on Government securities. It is less notorious, but equally true, that the same result would be found to ensue if a capitalist invested largely on the faith of circulars in joint-stock companies. The occasional large profit, always heralded and constantly exaggerated, may fall into the hands of a successful gambler, but depend on it, it is fully counterbalanced by unacknowledged or concealed losses. In brief, the system of joint-stock enterprise, with limited liability, does not differ materially from those State lotteries, which every respectable Government, struck with the mischief which they caused, has put down."—"I remember," said one of the critics of these acts to me, himself a director of the Bank of England, "that when I wanted a secretary an applicant called on me. I asked him for his qualification, and he told me, mentioning the name of a person who was notorious, I might almost say infamous, for his association with these new undertakings; that he had been for years engaged in collecting out of the books of the Bank of England, the great railway companies, and similar undertakings, the list of whose shareholders is accessible to all comers, the names of all clergymen, retired military and naval officers, barristers, and lawyers, who had £200 and upwards in the undertakings." Such persons were plied with circulars, because it was known that if they could be induced to take stock in proportion to their holding they would be good for the calls. My friend did not engage that clerk.—"Besides, does not the importunity with which these circulars are pressed on you suggest suspicion that the announcements of the future are over-florid, even if one had not the evidence of failure to confirm the suspicion?

"It is perfectly true that certain great undertakings would have been impossible but for the principle of limited liability. But it is not difficult to define those branches of business in which the permission should be given without making that permission universal. In undertakings which no individual and no partnership could contract for and complete, but one of supreme public utility, the rule may be allowed. Here, too, you have something enduring to show for your money. Grant that the railway companies have received too little profit for their outlay, the London Water Companies too much, they have at least made and worked a permanent way, and created the supply. It is quite a different thing to allow the principle to be adopted and carried out in buying and selling, in which a turn of the market may induce a total loss, and a total loss considerable injury to creditors and legitimate traders. The old law may have been severe, but it contained wholesome checks. The new law is exceedingly lax, and has practically no checks at all."

I have heard persons argue against joint-stock enterprise, with limited liability on the above grounds. Of course there is a rejoinder to them. "You run the risk," people answer, " of suffering from the failures and blemishes of a system, inseparable from all human undertakings, to the whole class of similar undertakings. Before you can come to so sweeping a conclusion you should have, what the logicians call, a prerogative instance, and show that what you can allege in some cases only, inevitably runs through all examples of the same species. But this cannot be asserted, either from the facts of the case, or from anticipations as to the future. There is a great deal of business carried on under the Companies' Acts. Most of it is carried on satisfactorily, smoothly, discreetly. We may be sure that if failure was abnormally conspicuous in such undertakings, they would receive nearly as sharp a check as prohibition or a reversion to the old system would be. Let us admit that some projectors are rogues, and some shareholders are dupes. Let us grant that unscrupulous people get up these undertakings and unscrupulous sharks wreck them. It does not seem to us that this is a valid reason for prohibiting them, but does seem a good ground for amending the law and stopping the game, the gains, and the frauds of these people. It might be a little expensive to undertake the State prosecution of a few among these adventurers; but the money in the end would be cheaply laid out, for it would deter people from these practices. It is, we believe, the duty of the legislature, when it provides that certain powers should be given, to see that these powers are not abused, and made the mechanism by which dishonest persons may prey on society.

"It is not clear that the old mechanism provided against the evils which you dread. A person under unlimited liability may be more reckless than one who has his risks defined. He knows that everything will be gone if he fails, fortune, reputation, credit, and he strains every chance, nay, simulates every gesture of solvency, when he is fairly conscious that any reasonable chance is gone, and that he is hopelessly insolvent. Under the law of unlimited liability you cannot demand that he shall submit the state of his affairs, not only to all interested in his doings and his solvency, but to all comers. But you do this, as far as human power can publish the result of an independent audit, under limited liability. We are aware that balance sheets may be fraudulent, and that an independent audit is in most cases a condition which cannot be absolutely satisfied. Indeed some of the most scandalous frauds which have been perpetrated in times recent and in times comparatively remote, are imitations of genuine solvency, perpetrated by traders under unlimited liability. Sir John Dean Paul, the head of a banking firm whose failure caused great loss and dismay about thirty years ago, swore that his father's personal estate was worth, if I remember rightly, £150,000, by his father's dying advice, when it was not worth sixpence, but a good deal less than sixpence. The Greenways, of Leamington, when they became bankrupt, confessed that they began business about the time of Paul's failure, with a capital of £600, and on the faith of their previous reputation, kept up a local note circulation of £30,000 on it. Now it does not seem easy to see how they could have done this under the limited liability Acts. Nor indeed is joint-stock enterprise, conducted under unlimited liability, free from the risks of a disastrous crash. The Glasgow Bank was directed by men of effusive, perhaps ostentatious, piety, and of reputed wealth. Its collapse brought ruin to a thousand homes, a ruin more disastrous than a bombardment. Instances of the same kind could be multiplied. Now before you infer generally to the peculiar risks which ensue from the doctrine of limited liability, you must show that the older system is free from these risks. But it is clear that you cannot let us confine ourselves to banking houses. They went down by dozens, by hundreds at the close of the eighteenth century. The great panic of 1825 was principally caused by the failure of banks. The disaster which came on after the Overend and Gurney business, shook the financial world of London to its centre. Now in all these cases the principle of unlimited liability was dominant, and the creditors of the unfortunate undertakings got very little consolation from the unlimited liability of their debtors when they found out that their resources were virtually exhausted before the crash came.

" It is perfectly true that an undertaking in which a large amount of capital is uncalled, even when the liability is limited, is in a better position, as far as credit is concerned, than another is in which there is none left to call. But the affairs of every trading company are liable to temporary strains. Uncalled capital is not the best security to offer for advances, but it is a security which no bank which does regular business with the company would, up to a certain point, hesitate to accept. But a private undertaking, with unlimited liability, and with no complete evidence as to the solidity of its assets, has not this to offer. Now the proof that the facts are as is stated is seen in those joint-stock banks, which, in addition to their six-monthly balance sheets, have a large amount of uncalled capital, when they all, or nearly all, a year or so ago registered themselves anew under limited liability. Their deposits have not fallen off, their business has not declined, though they have certainly diminished the security which they offered to their creditors. This uncalled share capital too is as nothing to the liabilities which they have incurred, and have, I do not doubt, amply covered. It does not seem, therefore, that in this, the most critical instance of joint-stock enterprise, considering the enormous interests which are involved in success and failure, that the customers of these banks felt any alarm at the limitation of the shareholders' risks.

"There is one part of your case against the new law, which is we may admit, at least apparently made out. It would appear that joint-stock enterprise in trade and production does tend to assimilate the rate of profit to the rate of interest, and that the cost of direction being satisfied, and the charges of hired management being paid, with perhaps a little margin for risk, shareholders are satisfied with less dividends than a trader expects in his business. It may be admitted too that the second or third purchaser of an uncompleted undertaking, which has gone through the hands of one or two liquidators, may make a good, and if a good, a rare bargain; for if such failures characterized joint-stock enterprise, a very effectual and rapid check would be put on it. I am disposed to think that the best and most frequent purchases of this kind have been made by railways of branch lines, which have certainly been bought for next to nothing, and have been turned into paying sections when they are manipulated by the trunk lines in the general interest.

" But there is an answer to even this part of the objection. In the first place, the supervision of a board and hired servants is never so effective as the master's eye. I have heard traders over and over again assert that they have nothing to fear from co-operative stores, and I suspect that the principal outcry against them is from those London traders, whose connection suggests to them, or constrains them to, the expediency of giving credit. The more courageous traders allege that the store cannot buy so well as they do, sell so well as they do, and effect economies as well as they do. They might cite instances. Some years ago a co-operative store was started under the name of the Universities Co-operative Association. It had large premises in a convenient, and it may be supposed not over-expensive, part of London, and it received large support, in capital and custom, from the clients which it expected to attract. It very rapidly collapsed in complete ruin, for the management from the beginning was as bad as it could be. And it does not by any means follow that if a man opens a shop he has good grounds for expecting an assured custom. It is quite possible to overstock a district with retail traders. It is highly probable that among people of that class the phenomena of over-population are more frequently manifested than in any other class of industrial agents, with perhaps the exception of barristers. Besides, it is quite clear that traders in a good way of business are seldom content with one shop. Many of them have a dozen, sometimes in half a dozen towns. Now it is impossible, except they are like Sir Boyle Roche's famous bird, that they can be in two places at once, and *a fortiori* in a dozen. It is plain, then, that in these subordinate places of retail selling—the modern, and I suppose polite, fashion is to drop the word shop and call them establishments, even nonconformist tradesmen using the objectionable word—the owner must delegate his functions and incur the very risk which, as he alleges, has such a compensative power in that joint-stock shop.

" It would appear, then, from these considerations, that the principle of limited liability does not deserve the sweeping criticism which is constantly uttered about it. It would seem that it is really less likely to be reckless than that person, or set of persons, who carry on business with unlimited liability, and that the law has put hindrances to this danger. It is probable, too, that bankruptcy has a larger effect in the lowering of prices than joint-stock trading has, for individuals who are in fear for the future will buy desperately, and sell desperately, and if they have sufficient shrewdness will escape the snare of the bankruptcy law. And in this reply nothing has been done but to meet objections. The benefits of the new law have to be shown."

I have given you this sketch of the situation, and of the attack and defence on the joint-stock principle in capital at some length, the defence naturally at greater length, since the defence is in the nature of things more elaborate than the attack, because it seems to me that nothing is more useful to the student of social problems than to exhibit the case in what I may call a debate. Nor do I think I need make an apology for adopting what you may perhaps consider a parliamentary manner, in putting the case before you, and in arguing for and against a principle or practice. For though much time is wasted in the House of Commons in discussions on foregone conclusions, there are subjects on which parties are indifferent, to use an excellent word in its earliest and best sense, and really do discuss a question from both sides. And you will find it excellent practice in economic and social questions to consider both sides of the case, and to see what can be said from either aspect. You will find it more profitable to deal with the facts of actual life, than like the Roman youth to handle the philosophy of history, and like Juvenal, in his undergraduate days, "give counsel to Sulla, as to his retirement into private life, in search of sound sleep."

I do not think it can be doubted that the recent Joint-stock Companies Act has had a great effect on industrial activity in England. It is true that many of those who have entered upon this system of manufacture and business, have been restive, impatient, and in these latter days, minatory about royalties. Now of course you know that land and its incidents have always been considered the undoubted and peculiar field for the economist. The lawyer is merely an agent in dealing with it. The statesman, when he ceases to be a partisan, arbitrates on it; but the economist considers that he is justified in analyzing the origin of its ownership, the causes and effects of its rent, and all the accidents of its owner's tenure. Now when the Royal Commission on the Depression of Trade was sitting, witness after witness, and among them some of the most extensive joint-stock miners and smelters, gave evidence as to the depressing effect of royalties, alleged to be excessive in this country upon mining operations. They treated the phenomena as natural and inevitable, but as a serious hindrance to the industry which they represented, even under the modern conditions of limited liability. And I see now that many persons are alleging that, as in France, Belgium, and Spain, all minerals are the property of the State, so they should be declared in the United Kingdom. I have constantly pointed out to you that rights abused are sure to suggest communism and violent reconstruction.

I have recently been studying the mining district in Cornwall, and particularly that narrow district in which the copper and tin deposits are found and raised. Here mining is carried on, under the unlimited liability system, and with very singular results. The products sought for are copper and tin, the former generally lying near the surface, the latter in the deeper veins, though habits of observation, no doubt hereditary, guide the adventurer in mining to anticipations which are generally realized, though the realization often leads to formidable losses in quantity. The metal, I mean, may be there, but in insufficient amount. But mining for these metals is plainly a local passion. The lucky man may make a great fortune, though I suspect if all were put together, and an average drawn, it would be found that losses overrun profits, especially under the system. And not only is the distribution of these minerals exceedingly capricious, but the market price is liable to great fluctuations. A few years ago, copper was, as the phrase goes, a drug. Within the last year its price is trebled. Tin again was not much more than £60 a ton, a year ago, and now it is £135, or was when I was there a month since (1889). These fluctuations greatly stimulate the spirit of enterprise, or as people are apt to say, gambling with the future. And it is curious to notice how naturally these people witness the decay or destruction of fortune in the case of those who are persistent, and persistently unlucky. There was a gentleman there, who had lost, I was told, £80,000 by these ventures, and his neighbours evinced no surprise. He was buoyant, jubilant and now thought he had at last come to his luck.

Cornwall is a county in which the rights or claims of the landowners are carried to an extent which I have never found paralleled elsewhere, though I have seen some curious instances of them in Ireland. Not only is every inch of common land appropriated, but the streams, and in many cases the harbours, have been usurped into private property. It is impossible, so I was told, to purchase a freehold, and the only occupancy is an exceedingly severe one. Landowners will not grant a lease for years for house building, but concede only a building lease on lives, by which their prospects of appropriating the occupier's outlay are greatly accelerated. I have had instances quoted to me, in which a building has fallen back, through the ill-luck of the lessee, and the unexpected falling of the lives, into the hands of the landowner at the end of twelve years. Now many of these miners emigrate for a time to Colorado, or the Transvaal, or Australia, get heavy wages, save, and by that indestructible instinct, which seems to be inveterate in the Celtic race— Irish, Gaelic, Welsh, Breton, Cornish—return to the place, as Shakespeare says, where they were kindled. They are the apt victims of the landlords, and after they have built their houses on these conditions, they venture the residue on a mining lease, generally in joint-stock, and all but invariably on unlimited liability. The spectacle of all but universal ill-success makes them reckless, perhaps patient.

The mining leases are generally for short terms, say twenty years or less. The adventurer has to pay a rent, and a royalty, varying from one-tenth to a twenty-fifth of the produce, not the profits, and beyond sinking a shaft, has to set up adequate machinery for pumping and ventilating the mine. Of course he is responsible for the term, and his plant follows the judge-made rule, *cujus est solum, ejus est usque ad cœlum*, and for the percentage of the produce, at whatever cost it is acquired. If, as sometimes happens, his venture is successful, he may make a good thing of it during his lease. The landowner is, as you will see, entirely protected, for in addition to his term, he has the hold of unlimited liability, and he can hardly ever be persuaded to accept the more modern arrangement. If the venture succeeds, he can raise his fine, his rent, his proportion of the produce, so as to squeeze as much as possible out of the occupier. When the lease is drawing to a close, the negotiations are long and anxious. The occupying tenant has only one resource. He can spoil the mine, by obliterating the signs of the deposits, and by flooding it. Cornwall is full of springs, and the latter process is secured by neglect. I can conceive no system which is more mischievous, more rapacious, and more certain to stimulate to the highest extent, the gambling spirit in industry. Mining is more speculative than any other industry, and does not need incentives.

The calling of the miner is dangerous. Though the risks of the collier are absent from his labour, unless the air is constantly renewed, it gets foul, the workman digs and blasts in the wet, and in deep mines works in a suffocating heat. Many men are maimed and especially blinded by the explosions. A miner attired for his underground journey—I saw them by hundreds—is a strange, hardly a human object, if he were not so lively and cheerful. His wages are no great temptation, rarely exceeding 18s. a week. Now notice how complete an answer it is to those people who go about telling these workmen that if prices rise wages rise. Within twelve months the price of tin has risen about 120 per cent., and wages have not risen a penny. The fact is, the miners are not yet enrolled in trade unions. And yet, strange enough, so general is the dislike to the ground landlords, that the employers, unlike their practice in other places, are particularly anxious that the men should enter into their labour partnerships, because they conclude that in this way only they shall be able to modify the extortionate terms, as they allege, under which they take their leases, and renew them.

The concession of the Acts permitting limited liability has been followed by a great extension of the system, both in manufacture and trading. No doubt advantage has been taken of the law to put out artful and florid prospects of the benefit which those will obtain who trust their money to the venture. But though it comes in a different form, it may be doubted whether there is as much deception practised in joint-stock enterprise as there is in private trading. The loss, to be sure, is limited, but the loss is total. I never heard of any assets being recovered from a liquidator. But unless we are greatly misinformed, the assets of a bankrupt are never entirely recovered by his creditors, and if so, such a person is virtually trading under limited liability, for all the technicalities which law may allege. And in proof of this I may cite the extraordinary success which has attended one of these companies, the Assets Realization Company, the principle of which is to offer the creditors a percentage in the pound on their debts, and to undertake the realization of the estate by the company. Besides, the severity of the law against a defaulting debtor is as nothing to the severity of the law, as the courts expound it, with a negligent director, even though he may be proved to have derived no advantage from his superintendence, and even to have incurred considerable loss by his negligence. Lord Thring, when the subject was discussed with considerable fulness at the London Political Economy Club, the members of which are not *prima facie*, presumably interested in the success of the new system, dwelt with great severity on the harshness with which law treats unintentional breaches of company law, as compared with its attitude towards bankrupts. For, in fact, company law is one of the most difficult branches of commercial law, as I am informed by those who are more or less familiar with it, and is full of contradictions, traps, and pitfalls.

But to pass from this subject. The most interesting, significant, and important departure in the new system is the development of co-operative trade, and subsequently co-operative production among the artisan classes and factory hands. The narrative of this movement has been told in a simple, and yet exhaustive, manner by Mr. Holyoake. Its beginnings in Rochdale were watched with great interest by my distinguished friends Mr. Cobden and Mr. Bright, who augured great moral good from the experiment. Its progress has been noted and commended by such excellent persons as Mr. Thomas Hughes, Mr. Vansittart Neale, and others. But it may be doubted whether the acutest persons, who witnessed the beginning of the movement, could have foreseen the social and economical effects of the extension of co-operation, *i.e.*, virtually a working-men's partnership under limited liability, on those who undertook the function. It began in an attempt to achieve two things—a ready-money business among factory hands, these being a class naturally prone to run into debt in small shops; and to secure genuine articles of consumption, for it is not surprising that the small shops are not over-scrupulous in the quality of the articles which they sell, as poverty enforces cheapness. The movement, the history of which I do not pretend to narrate, adopted a singular rule at its commencement, which I believe it has generally continued. It did not undersell the ordinary trader, but fixed its prices at ordinary rates. Probably it did not wish to provoke enmity. Certainly, working men are not enamoured of competition. But I conceive that the ruling motive in the practice which was adopted was to assist the factory hands in the habit of saving, by an almost unconscious process, for the managers divided the profits of the business among its customers, in proportion to the amount of purchases made at the common shop. It was in this way that the capital was increased, for the societies were always ready to receive these savings and to reinvest them.

The step from shopkeeping to production or manufacture was taken, though cautiously and slowly. It was especially adopted at Oldham in the cotton manufacture, and at Leicester in the stocking trade. I have not followed the numerical increase of these undertakings, though I know that it has been large. Now it is said, and that by persons strongly disposed to criticize these ventures, that in the competition of business the co-operative factory, after getting rid of some initial errors, natural enough, has been able to hold its own against the private manufacturing firms. The principal initial errors were in discovering that in a factory order and obedience were absolutely necessary, that though the workman was a proprietor, sometimes for his class a considerable proprietor of stock, he must not bring the impulses of an owner into his work, but must behave just as though he were as he was originally, and still is, as far as the manufacture is concerned, entirely a factory hand. The other difficulty or error was, that after recognizing the necessity of a manager or superintendent, and of obedience to his directions, to see that one must pay for skill. It was hard to induce the shareholders to believe that management, as long as it is necessary, must be paid for, and, to be efficient, must be paid for well. Of course, as soon as ever the associated workmen are one and all competent to undertake the work of management, the rarity of managerial ability has ceased, and with it the necessity of hiring and paying for it. This has not, it seems, come yet, though it will come in the future. Those whom I have consulted on co-operative manufacture assure me that the principal cause of their success is the rigid prosecution of small economies in management, and the careful elimination of waste. The danger, I have also been told, which they run, is in the magnitude of the capital forced, so to speak, on them, in accordance with their rule, always to accept and utilize workmen's savings.

These, however, though interesting incidents in the calling of co-operative production, are by no means the most important or suggestive to the economist. The least agreeable fact which one sees in the modern history of labour, a result distinctly traceable to past wrongs, deliberately inflicted and continued upon workmen, is the tendency which such persons have to live from hand to mouth, and even to decline work, when a limited number of days in the week secures to the workman his maintenance and small enjoyments, though a more prolonged industry would, in prudent hands, have a margin over. Now, as a spontaneous and organized effort, the movement for an eight-hours day has my entire sympathy. I am persuaded that employers of labour would get, on the hypothesis that the labourer really exercised his skill and energy on an eight-hours day, more out of such a limitation than they do for longer labour. I utterly discredit and disbelieve the shallow and interested utterances of some people that English labour runs serious risk of rivalry by the long hours of the French and German artisan. Given equal conditions, I would defy any person to substantiate by facts what has become an exceedingly common, and to use the mildest language, an exceedingly reckless averment. But I entirely disbelieve in the notion, too commonly entertained by the indolent and impatient, that the common boon should be achieved by the action of the legislature. I have constantly stated that attempts on the part of the law to do positive good generally result in the incidence of more positive evil. The artisans of the Middle Ages got an eight-hours day by their own combinations, and maintained it till a series of great crimes committed against labour and the public good by kings and parliaments, left the workmen helpless, because disunited.

Co-operative production is a powerful educating force in what working men need to be taught most thoroughly, community of purpose. Getting, as they must get under the system of the division of employments, a familiar insight into the harmony of interests in the business of their life, they learn that they are strong when united, weak when divided. I have been told that in co-operative production, the disputes which arise between capital and labour are all but unknown, and that the union of the two functions in the same person gives a rapid and successful lesson in the true relations of the parties. Now, when the hostility to capital ceases, it is very difficult for persons to accept crude notions about the duty or necessity of nationalizing capital. But everything which instructs people in the fact that all legitimate interests are at harmony is a lesson of no little value. There is, and there will be, till the causes are removed, no little discontent at existing practices and privileges which appear to give unreasonable and unwarrantable advantages to certain interests.

I have already commented on the fact that Mr. George, while his enmity to rent is thorough, his anticipations as to its extinction are sanguine, and his predictions as to the boon which his process will confer on labour are, to say the least, confident, has no antipathy to capital. He has witnessed, as he believes, with indignation, the rapid growth of wealth among those who have got hold of the land, but he does not detect a similarly spontaneous development of wealth in those who are technically said to possess capital. But I have been told that there are persons in the United States who look on the manner in which the wealth of the Vanderbilts has grown, to take the most obvious instance, with the liveliest alarm and with but a little indignation. Some part of the process, if I may infer from a narrative of the family, recently published, and on the side of admiration, would, I think, in the United Kingdom, have been met with very effectual checks. But, except in so far as it comes from the possession of land, I do not remember that Mr. George denounces the gains of these millionaires. Here, at least, you have a type of socialism which is not led into the theory of nationalizing capital and establishing employment for all by the agency of a government office.

I take it that the demand for the reconstruction of society, by a violent modification of its present conditions, has few attractions to those who labour on the co-operative principle. These people, in so far as they demand reforms, generally go in the direction of giving more ease to the materials and forces which human industry utilizes and clothes with utility. They may, for example, conclude that much that characterizes our land system is wrong, and allege that it handicaps industry in the effort to confer exceptional advantages on individuals. They do not think that you will mobilize capital by frightening it, or that the accumulation of wealth is assisted by insecurity. But they see also that capital and labour may be starved by injudicious and unfair restraints on the universal instrument or material of all capital and labour—land.

One of the most pleasing features in the history of co-operative production is that the competition of working-men producers has not, after perhaps a brief interval, provoked the jealousy of capitalist producers. Some years ago I happened to be residing at Leicester for a few hours in the house of a local manufacturer. Now I knew that in this town co-operative production had completely established itself, and I inquired cautiously of my host in what position those workers stood. To my surprise I found him extremely friendly to the movement, for he had come to the conclusion that the success of these undertakings was sure to bring about harmony between employers and workmen, since even those who had not taken part in the undertaking saw what were the conditions under which successful industry could, and indeed must, be carried on. And he went on to say that an association of co-operative stocking weavers, knowing that he was friendly to their system, called upon him with a request that he would assist their comparative inexperience by an inspection of their books and their works, for that they were sure that they had missed one or more of the conditions of successful business. He complied and advised them, in what direction I do not exactly remember, but he asserted, with complete success. Now, such confidence on the part of the workmen, and alacrity on the part of the capitalist, strike me as particularly commendable and hopeful.

I know no phenomenon of industry which is a more characteristic fact to modern experience than the recent development of the joint-stock principle in capital. I could give you numerous instances of social benefits and social economies which could never have come into existence but for this modern force. I am quite convinced that in extensive districts in Great Britain it has been of great advantage to workmen and industry. It is true that it has not yet got much beyond manufacture. But there is reason to believe that it will in time be introduced into agriculture, and in this way solve many difficult and serious social problems.

VIII.

THE JOINT-STOCK PRINCIPLE IN LABOUR.

Trade unions—The regulated company as a trade union—Must the law always be obeyed?—An appeal to history—Jusification of trade unions—History of English trade unions to 1563—Unions compared with syndicates—Effect of increased wages on prices in the coal and match trades.

You will probably anticipate that, by this heading to my lecture of to-day, I intend to refer to those organizations by which men, working through or under the direction of a capitalist employer, by their own action seek to better their position, both by increasing their wages and by rendering as far as possible that increase stable, if not permanent. The title which working men give these organizations, at least in modern times, is that of trade unions, a term which is, I believe, quite late, though in the language of their several crafts the word trade is assumed in a technical sense, as denoting any kind of skilled labour, the plying of which has generally been preceded by an apprenticeship, at least till recent times. This usage of the word trade is, I do not doubt, ancient, and that the more recent sense which is given to it is long subsequent to that which prevailed in earlier times. I understand by this organization also one which seeks to achieve its ends by peaceful means, which collects its members by voluntary action, which does not attempt to use violence towards those who decline association with the purposes of the combination, however keenly the members may feel that the outsiders are getting an advantage from the sacrifices and energy of those who enter the association, and does not attempt any other process but persuasion with those who may be, consciously or unconsciously, baffling the objects which the association has before it. The only remedies which the organization has at its disposal are a refusal to work on the terms offered, and, if they are strong enough to do so, a refusal to work with those who do not enter into the association and compete with them simultaneously for employment. But, of course, the occasions of discontent may be numerous, and a recent publication of the labour bureau in the state of New York gives very many details as to the motives which have led to strikes in that state. Among others, one of the most frequent is the impression that employers and managers have dealt unfairly with individual workmen, the discipline of the association demanding that the combination may be wronged by the ill usage of a member. Practically, indeed, the combination of workmen has only one remedy, known familiarly as a strike.

The action of workmen in these combinations is economically identical with those mercantile associations which, under the name of regulated companies, were at one time no small favourites with the legislature, though Parliament was constantly on the watch to prevent their being turned into oppressive monopolies. They also closely resemble those trading companies which still survive, though under very altered conditions, in the city of London. In both these associations there was a common fund collected from the subscriptions of those who entered on the union and shared its privileges. But the object of this fund was to defend the privileges of the company against interlopers. Neither the regulated company nor the City company had a joint-stock capital for trading, but simply a common fund for defence. In just the same way one of the most ancient payments made by the members of the university of all degrees was collected for the purpose of defending the privileges of the university when they might happen to be attacked. It was a capitation tax, in short. When the first commission sat on the

Universities, now about forty years ago, this word greatly exercised the members of the commission. Till they published their report I did not know what was their difficulty, though had I learned of it I could have explained it to them. In brief, the University of Oxford was a trade union which constrained all those who claimed admission to its privileges to subscribe for the defence of those privileges. So, again, the City companies claimed to impose fines on those of their members who did what in their judgment was unneighbourly or unfair to other members. I have quoted a case which I was able to extract from the archives of the Grocers' Company, in which a very substantial fine was imposed on two of the fraternity for what would, I suppose, be called in Ireland shop grabbing, in this case offering a higher rent for a tenement than the occupier was paying.

English law or custom has sanctioned penalties inflicted by corporations or quasi-corporations on persons who are guilty of unprofessional conduct. The benchers of an inn may disbar a counsel for misbehaviour. The medical council can take away his status from a practitioner, and recently has done so in the case of a person who published an obnoxious book. The archbishop of a province can deprive a bishop under his jurisdiction for an ecclesiastical offence. The precedents are not numerous, but they are decisive. Pecok, Bishop of Chichester, was thus deprived by Bourchier in 1457. Watson, Bishop of St. Davids, was suspended in 1694 by Tillotson, and deprived in 1699 by Tenison; and in the present century an Irish bishop was similarly deprived by the Primate of All Ireland. It is by no means an uncommon practice with professional men and traders to decline intercourse with such members of the several callings, as decline to be bound by an etiquette or rule. We have no doubt got a new word in "boycott," but the word covers a very ancient, time-honoured, and recognized practice. Perhaps in the course of the investigation with which I am concerned to-day, we may be able to discover why a practice which has been deemed necessary and therefore harmless in certain directions, has excited so much horror and indignation in others.

Of all the questions which puzzle practical men, politicians, and even economists, none is greater than that of the extent to which an existing law is to be obeyed. The moralist, and the man in possession, to whom the existing law is a private, perhaps an unfair advantage, answer that the obedience should be accorded, the former with some hesitation, the latter, as might be expected, with no hesitation whatever. It is alleged that obedience to the law is of more importance to civil society, than the wrongs are which exist in the law, and are resisted in it. There are some occasions in which good persons, in these days, affirm that resistance is always indefensible. Such, for example, was the defiance of the persecuting statutes in the days of Henry VIII. and Mary Tudor. We have put up monuments to those who broke these laws. I do not think that many persons in our time would seriously condemn those Irish Catholics who evaded the consequences of Chancellor Brodrick's penal code. For law is not only liable to be mistaken, but is exceedingly apt to be designedly unfair. If it escapes from these pitfalls, it runs a further risk in a judge's interpretation, which may be pedantic and wrong-headed. I could enumerate many deep-seated social evils, which have been entirely originated by judicial dicta, such as, *cujus est solum, ejus est usque ad cœlum*, the foundation of the system under which the ground landlord has been able to plunder the occupier. We have been lately reading of a suburban householder, who has stood a siege, and apparently gained a victory, because the tithe-owner of the parish demanded payment from him of the whole tithe which issued from the land, of which he merely occupied a small portion. Depend on it, he relied on some absurd construction put on the law of tithes in Westminster Hall. But the householder who withstood the tithe-owner had the sympathy of those who heard of his plan of campaign, and the congratulations of those who, knowing him personally, saw that in the end the siege was raised. Of course there are stronger cases. If oaths and declarations of law meant anything, no monarch's position seemed more secure than that of James II. His exclamation on receiving the bishops' memorable petition appears to me, on looking at what Parliament and the Church had inculcated, natural, and even necessary. It was he alleged a standard of rebellion. Within six months he was deserted and repudiated by nearly all his subjects. It seems to me that they broke the law, but I cannot assert that they went wrong in doing so. On the contrary, I am constrained to conclude that they would have done more wrong in obeying it. And you will remember that during the reign of James, the judges were on his side, with scarcely an exception, and with hardly any misgivings. Perhaps they thought that the fate of Tresilian was an obsolete risk.

The case is rendered still more difficult when you deal with criminal law, in which the judge must await and abide by the decision of a jury. In early times, the jury were the witnesses to the facts, and declared evidence on oath. If they gave under these circumstances a false verdict, they were obviously guilty of perjury, and justly suffered the penalties of an attaint, as the process for chastising a dishonest and perjured jury of the old time was called. In course of time, how is by no means clear, the jury became judges of evidence which was laid before them, and ceased to tender it themselves. The authorities strove to render them liable to the old law, as during Mary Tudor's time, in the Throgmorton case. The last attempt to make a jury liable for a verdict, was in Penn the Quaker's case, in Charles II.'s time, when the jury virtually acquitted Penn in the teeth of the evidence. On that occasion Chief Justice Vaughan as we all know, affirmed the immunity of juries, and now all that a dissatisfied judge can do is to rate the twelve gentlemen soundly for going against his ruling. In this, I venture on thinking that he oversteps his province. Even in laying down the law, he is an adviser and not an authority, though he is exceedingly apt to put on the airs of authority.

After the Revolution of 1688, the law became atrociously severe. No doubt as wealth increased, people in high places became convinced that it must be secured by penalties from depredators. There was every motive for this conclusion, except the evidence of experience, and that other evidence which is still more important, the analysis of the causes which make crimes frequent. I really believe from reading the papers of the early Georgian epoch, that more people in England perished on the gallows than were killed in Marlborough's campaigns. Monday was the principal day in London, and gangs of wretches were carted to Tyburn, amidst I fear the sympathies of the spectators. There arose among certain men of fashion, a horrible appetite for these spectacles. George Selwyn the wit never missed an execution. But the number which was condemned and executed was only a portion of those offenders against whom the law denounced capital punishment. If one examines the calendars of provincial crime in towns like Reading and Oxford—and these calendars are frequently printed in the papers—neither of which towns had more than five thousand inhabitants in the days of the first two Georges, he would be amazed at the numbers which were raked together for the assizes. But the juries were more merciful than the law. They refused to find more than a low value on goods stolen, when the law inflicted the penalty of death on stealing over thirteen-pence halfpenny—the price of a box of pills—from a dwelling-house. In consequence, the administration of the criminal law became exceedingly uncertain, and crime was stimulated rather than checked by severity on paper. But it took a long time for Parliament to see that its ferocious penalties defeated their own ends, and it required all the energy of Romilly and Mackintosh to get the necessary alteration in our criminal law. It is very hard to induce a British Parliament to see that remedies are more deterrent than penalties.

The forgery of Bank notes and Exchequer Bills was made a capital felony. In other offences of the same kind, *e.g.*, wills and deeds, the offender was left to the statute of Elizabeth which prescribed the pillory, mutilation, and branding, penalties which I have seen were inflicted as late as 1731. In course of time, juries again refused to convict, though the clearest evidence was brought before them, and at last, the bankers who had procured the capital sentence in the first case, petitioned Parliament for a modification of the penalties, on the plea that the practice of juries was giving an immunity to crime. Now looking at the result which ensued from this refusal of juries to convict, viz., the amendment of the criminal law, at once in the direction of humanity, and the diminution of crime, it is not, you will see, quite easy to allege that unconditional obedience to municipal law is an imperative duty. I am ready enough to admit that the alternative is very serious, and to some high-handed resolute persons is exceedingly irritating, but one must be blind to some of the best-known facts in the social history of our country, perhaps in its political history, if one fails to discern that there have been occasions in which resistance to authority has had more beneficial effects than obedience to it. And moreover it may be fairly alleged, that the blame rests more with those who have indirectly compelled the violation, than it does with those who have vindicated an irregular but necessary justice against an unwise, oppressive, and it may be even a dishonest law.

I am conscious that this is a very long preface to a lecture on the joint-stock principle in labour, *i.e.*, a dissertation on the history of trade unions or labour partnerships and their economical defence. But I have no doubt that in what I have to say, you will see that the sketch which I have given you is relevant to the development of a system, whose future bids fair to assume far greater proportions than it hitherto has, whose influence in the distribution of wealth will probably be exceedingly effective. It is prudent to see what these labour associations can do, should do, cannot do, and should not do, when we are taking account of a social force which has long been suppressed, long distrusted, but is slowly, as I believe, surely being educated into a just interpretation of what, to use a phrase of the workmen, are the rights of labour. Let us first look at the history of these associations, and then give an economic analysis of them. It is not a little remarkable that they are generally ignored by writers on economic subjects or of economic systems, though I cannot but think that this practice, though authors may have the abundant defence of ignorance, is very unwise and very irritating.

The distinction made between the work of an artisan and of a farm hand is, in my judgment, as unphilosophical and as misleading as the contrast which some people heedlessly make between the agricultural, the manufacturing, and trading interests. Not only is it true that all legitimate interests are in harmony, and are reciprocally beneficial, but it should never be forgotten, that the wanton injury of our industrial interest—and by wanton I mean a removable injury induced by custom or law—is an injury by implication to all other interests. If the husbandman suffers by rapacity and ignorance, the home manufacture suffers. He finds a poor instead of a prosperous customer, and the cost of filling up the void of agricultural produce, requires more energy and more sacrifice. If the trader, and I am assuming that his presence is natural, and not artificial, and is therefore necessary, is crippled and tampered in the work of distributing goods, if his calling is made precarious by exactions, by unfair taxation or unjust assessments, or by unnatural charges for freight, I am convinced that the agriculturist and the manufacturer get a worse market for their produce. Of course the trader may, nay, frequently does, overstock his own market, and several men are trying to share work which would be better, more cheaply, and more profitably done by fewer hands. For there is a form of overcrowding in employments which nothing can obviate, unless we ruled, which would be a reactionary, unwise, and unsatisfactory step, that the number of persons engaged in a calling should be limited to the wants of the market. In past times, and indeed in recent times, attempts have been made to effect these results, but with consequences which do not suggest or encourage imitation. All legitimate interests, then, are at harmony, and, as the French economists said with perfect truth, it can never be to the interest of one class or calling to oppress any other class or calling. By this of course they meant, men who are of use. Idlers, profligates, criminals are, by the very terms of their being, noxious, intrusive, and should be checked, suppressed, or if you like oppressed.

Now a workman has something to sell. This is his labour. Society cannot exist without him, for the prolonged cessation of his industry would be ruinous to all. His labour, too, is of necessity intelligent, *i.e.*, capable of effecting that to the supply of which he has been trained, a notable outlay being made in order to secure this training. It should be always remembered too that, especially in modern times, when population is dense, and employments are greatly divided, the workman who proffers his labour has rarely any other means than the sale of that which he offers. He cannot, if he fails of employment, betake himself to other avocations, a fact too frequently lost sight of when people are discussing labour and its claims. In some cases, when this absence of any alternative is put before him, he is not to blame for the result, but the wrongheadedness, the perversity, the malignity of those who have been able to materially modify his lot. He has also the most perishable of all articles which can be offered for sale. A day lost, when he wishes for work, and is willing to undertake it, is lost irrecoverably. A trader who has goods in his shop may decline to sell, and may be wise, for he may be able to secure his price by waiting. In the practice of law, the sale of goods by a shopkeeper at less than they cost him is a suspicious, a punishable offence. The workman is, therefore, when he offers his labour, under a peculiar urgency. Of all people living he is most of all constrained to sell. For not only is it a permanent loss if he does not sell, but his article, unlike any other article offered, must be kept out of the market at a double cost, the cost of wasted time and, more serious still, maintenance, as long as the sale is uncompleted. There is no industrial agency to which a bye or second opportunity is more needed than it is to the workman, none whose situation has been more aggravated, in comparatively modern times, by his being cut off from that second calling. His power of holding out till he gets better terms is seriously curtailed at the present time, if it be compared with the situation in earlier ages.

I have stated that in those earlier times agriculture was the alternative which most artisans had, and I mean by this agriculture on the workman's own holding. In my researches into the history of English labour I have constantly noted that artisans, employed say in building a college or a church, were also owners in husbandry. When the Fellows of Merton were building the tower of the church, in the fifteenth century, they bought hay and straw from the foreman of their works. So did Dorothy Wadham in the seventeenth century. In Lord Lovell's account of his farming operations, early in the eighteenth century, he deals largely with his own workmen. The records, of course, of peasant and artisan husbandry have perished, and they only, who have read extensively in other accounts, and have a keen eye for social facts and phenomena, will detect these relations. And these facts explain why an artisan's wages are always so much higher in London than elsewhere. Here, to be sure, he was more certain of employment. But here he was also debarred from bye industries. And here, too, one may notice that the day wages of the workmen in harvest time are generally quite up to those of artisans, for artisans were constantly engaged in harvest work, nay by divers statutes, were compellable to serve in the harvest field. But they would have resented this obligation if their ordinary wages had been lessened, and they inevitably dragged up the wages of the ordinary labourers in husbandry during this important season.

I have often commented on the extreme harshness with which the magistrates in quarter sessions interpreted the Labourers' Act of 1563. The law, to be sure, gave them an opportunity of wrongdoing, and put no check on their action, and if the law enables people to do injustice, law and right may become very wide apart. But, in commenting on the history of labour, and particularly on the oppression to which it was subjected, I have never forgotten, or omitted to state, that he had many indirect advantages, which were as yet his legal rights. He could turn his cow, or few sheep, and, at least, his geese, into the common pasture, which generally belonged to him as surely, though, as events proved, not as securely as it did to the lord. The payment for the pannage of pigs in the lord's wood, which was nearly if not quite as much his right as the use of the common, was small and customary. But, besides, he had the right of snaring wild animals on the common pasture or waste. I have collected overwhelming evidence of the fact from the purchases of game in the sixteenth and seventeenth centuries by Lords Spencer, Pembroke, and others, and by corporations such as Winchester and Eton Colleges. If the animals, including all game but deer and hare, had been captured on their own land, the landlords need not have paid for them, if on the land of others, their purchase encouraged trespass. They must have, therefore, been procured from regions over which the peasantry had as much right as the lord. When Markham published his treatise, "Hunger's Prevention, or the whole art of Fowling," he gives no hint that game was reserved for the richer classes. When a statute prohibiting the practice was passed in the reign of James I., the right of the peasant is not disputed, but the reputed effect on his diligence and usefulness is recited. Now what the peasant sold, he might better his own provisions with. In our day, no doubt, a poacher is not only a very offensive phenomenon to the game preserver, but a disreputable and evil personage. But, for all that, he represents the free exercise of an ancient right, which the law has never ventured to entirely repudiate, and cannot as long as it does not recognize that property in wild animals which it does in their domestic varieties.

But, besides, the peasant generally possessed, though probably in later times only on a precarious tenancy, a small plot of land, which he cultivated with his own hands, as a bye industry. The Allotments Act of 1589 was, I am certain, an attempt to check the restraint of labourers in husbandry to a cottage and wages, as well as a well-meaning attempt to check pauperism and over-crowding. It endured till 1773, when it was repealed on the plea that it checked enclosures. Now the benefit of such tenures, as a bye industry, as supplementary to wages, and as a check to agricultural pauperism is, in my experience, very great. In my native place, where it prevailed in a shrunken form, it almost extinguished destitution. Its advantage is that the peasant can subsist to a great extent on the produce of his small holding. When Mr. Clare Read, according to Dr. Jessopp, said that no labourer in Norfolk would take five acres of land on the ordinary tenure of a farmer, he was, of course, thinking of the farmer as a salesman. But the farmer, as a consumer of his own produce, is a very different person from a trader in produce. But the whole question of peasant farming deserves separate treatment.

In Ulster the process, as I found when I carefully examined its agriculture a year ago, was reversed. There the bye industry was domestic spinning and weaving. A generation ago, as I was told by those who had been brought up under the system, every little farmhouse had its spinning-wheel and hand-loom. The peasant farmers grew the flax, and carried it through all the processes into strong coarse home-spun, generally producing two pieces a year. Now, as long as the sale of such a domestic produce paid the rent, they were indifferent as to whether the rent was high or low. Even now, I was told, the industry was by no means extinct, though it was far from general. As a consequence, the rents which could be easily paid under the old system became impossible under the new. And yet, so negligent are those who undertake the administration of affairs in getting necessary information, that I have never heard that this most important fact has ever been taken into account in the interpretation of the Irish land question. My late valued friend, Mr. Fawcett, was not a profound nor a learned economist. But he was an exceedingly acute, sympathetic, and observant person, and I well remember his insisting with great emphasis to me on the superficial way in which economists dwelt on industrial changes. He asserted, and with great truth, that one of the most powerful causes of poverty was the fact that traditional avocations constantly become obsolete, and that the change presses invariably, and with great severity, on those who have been practically ousted from their old calling.

It is important, in order to really understand the position of labour, to note the progressive disadvantages to which it has been subjected. But there are, we must not forget, countervailing advantages, especially in new callings, and in those in which the division of employments has made the greatest way. As time has progressed, the organization of the workmen under the circumstances referred to, has become indispensable to the capitalist. The machine of human industry has become as complicated as the mechanism which the workman superintends and guides. The gradation of labour has been effected, but with the result that all the factors are collectively and individually essential to the due and easy working of the organization. Workmen have, I suspect, seen this more clearly than employers have, but none too clearly. The apparent weakness of the workers' position has been discovered to be one of great, but hidden strength. I conclude that much of the continuity of occupation in times when business profits are reduced is due to the fact that it would be a greater loss to stop than to continue, and I imagine that the consciousness of this inherent and increasing weakness in modern industries, which are carried on in a vast scale, has had a powerful effect in bringing about a better understanding as to the relations of workmen and their employers. In older and less complicated times the employment of labour in such callings as were carried on, so to speak, under the principle of the division of employment, was far more optional than it now is. I cannot say that the discoveries of mechanical and engineering science have enslaved capital to labour, but I am pretty certain that they have made the harmony of the two factors more necessary, more obvious, and more inevitable, and more speedy.

But I must proceed to the historical facts with which, as usual, I design to illustrate my treatment of the subject. Nothing threw so novel a light to me, at least, as the social condition of England in the Middle Ages, if modern pedantry will permit me to use this convenient phrase, as the universality of labour combinations. They came, I do not doubt, in the first instance, from the interlaced interests of all who resided in the same social microcosm, the parish and manor, and from the early practice of creating benefit societies out of the surplus of the charges made for religious offices. The main of these permanent donations probably went to the monasteries. But the secular clergy, who had no great love for the monks, competed for the employment which these endowments gave, and even, when the function was not permanent, but temporary, there is evidence, which I have discovered, of a competition for the office. The surplus, if any, and it is pretty certain that there nearly always was a surplus, went to the guild or association of workmen, which, in country places, would have chiefly consisted of labourers in husbandry. In the course of centuries especially in a time when purchases of small parcels of land were common, and custom supplied cheap evidence of ownership, these accumulations became considerable, and beyond question, were the fund from which destitution was relieved. And although the life of the individual was ordinarily bounded by the parish or manor in which he resided, there were occasions on which the peasant was introduced to a wider world. We know that there was a gradation of courts from that of the parish to that of the county, and that there were opportunities afforded for concerted action, and we need not be surprised that the preamble of the statute, in which the franchise was limited or restrained in 1432, complains of the excessive and outrageous number of persons who congregated to, and took part in, the election of knights of the shire. Thus the gatherings at fairs were an exceedingly important agency for the development of common purposes. Walter de Henley, writing in the middle of the thirteenth century, assigns a good many days a year to these gatherings, which were indeed the principal markets of the time. In Oxford I have traced the usage of the Wednesday and Saturday market days almost to the time in which Walter de Henley was writing, and I know from the bailiff rolls that the farmers frequented these markets for the purpose of buying and selling. In fact, I am disposed to believe that there was more intercourse between the peasantry of different parishes six hundred years ago than there now is, and therefore more opportunities for concerted action.

But, besides, the people were brought greatly into contact with the migratory clergy. It was a tenet with these people that the priest who was bound to an order was a more efficacious intercessor than one who had been merely associated with parochial duties, and was therefore called a secular clerk, with some little contempt. Gascoigne, in the fifteenth century, complains greatly of the effects induced by this tenet. Now for some time, perhaps not more than a century and a half, this opinion gained credence, especially in relation to the two orders of mendicant friars, the Dominicans and Franciscans. It is true that later on Wiklif and the Lollards denounced them. But their migratory practices continued till the Reformation, when, especially in the "Supplication of the Beggars," a calculation is made as to the sums of money which the friars annually collected from the people. In other words, the occasional appearance of those personages in villages must have been familiar, and it would seem that public opinion was not unfavourable to their migrations. I cannot indeed say that they constituted a channel of communication between the workmen in different districts. The institution of Wiklif's poor priests seems to suggest that in this bold reformer's eyes a new agency was necessary. This he supplied, and armed with the far-reaching tenet, that dominion is founded on grace, which, interpreted by himself in his lately recovered treatise, means that deference to authority is based on the worthiness of him who exercises the authority. Now this is a gloss which subjects all institutions to searching, perhaps to destructive, criticism.

Social institutions, like constitutional precedents, generally become known to us by some strain which brings the fact into prominence, the practice, though no record be taken of it, long preceding the record of its activity. The first intimation which I have found of labour combinations is in Kingston, and this in connection with the events of 1350 and of 1381. But I am convinced that it would be an error to conclude that these associations had no earlier existence. In London they were probably as old at least as the time of Longbeard, in the days of Richard I. It is certain that the City guilds were in existence as more or less irregular associations long before the earliest charters which they possess. But prominence is given them in the earliest struggles between employers and workmen. A grotesque antiquity is given to that modern association, which under the name of freemasonry is, I believe, justly associated with nothing but high feeding and benevolence. The student of social forces discovers its origin in those congregations, chapels, and conventions of free masons, against which the Lancastrian kings denounced the penalties of felony. The form of the institution, as far as an outsider can judge, has greatly changed. No doubt the modern craft is as unlike the proscribed association of the Middle Ages as a City company in its modern shape is to the artisans and shopkeepers who founded the worshipful guilds of mercers and goldsmiths, tailors and grocers, fishmongers and haberdashers, and I know not what.

The industrial life of England down to the Reformation, especially that carried out by Somerset, was one especially of trade combinations. The system was so powerful and so universal that the legislature was wholly unable to grapple with it. It broke down under a set of circumstances which I have often described, and was rapidly extirpated, under these new conditions, by the law of 1563. From that date to 1825 the trades union was effectually proscribed, and I am persuaded that the memory of the ancient system, once so universal and so vigorous, had entirely passed away, till at last an antiquarian economist, as I suppose I may call myself, rediscovered it, and traced it back to its early activity and efficiency. I will not say that what I found out entirely changed my views as to those relations of labour and capital which I have found in the earlier economists, but I gained an insight into bygone conditions, in which a substantial deference to the claims of labour was, as I found, not incompatible with general and even national prosperity. The conclusions at which I arrived were by no means weakened, as I followed up the consequences of the Act of 1563, and traced the growing misery of the workman from the middle of the sixteenth century down to almost recent experience, long after the repeal of the old labour statutes, when the workman was left to the tender mercies of the judge-made law of conspiracy.

A trade union is really an industrial partnership, or if you will, the adaptation of the joint-stock principle to labour. In ordinary joint-stock action as recognized, protected, and adjudicated on by law, the owner of property pledges his means in part or in whole to the undertaking which attracts him. To external appearance the member of a trade union, which is only recognized by law, and rather grudgingly recognized, does not in the same way pledge property or capital. Yet he does not possess that in any notable degree, which the shareholder in a joint-stock enterprise, by the very terms of his engagement, does pledge. But he enters into similar, perhaps more onerous obligations, because more searching and unquestioned liabilities with the only thing which he has to sell or dispose of, his labour. Unlike the holder of joint stock, the law does not bind him to his obligations, and he can withdraw from the association at his pleasure. His combination or partnership more nearly resembles the old regulated company than it does anything else, with this difference, that the workman's association is, while not banned by the law, unable to invoke the law in order to give effect to its purposes.

The object of a trade union is to steady and if possible to increase the share in the price of the produce which the workman receives. I have frequently stated that the true, and in reality the most beneficial, function of capital is that of securing the continuity of industry, and as far as possible an anticipated level of price. The first of these functions is the permanent service which capital does to society; the second is a necessary condition in the long run to the industrial prosperity of the individual. It is not infrequently the case that by general misconception the capitalist may pursue a calling with little profit. This has been, I believe, the fact to a great extent with the lessees of collieries up to very recent times, and I believe that I have on other occasions pointed out the historical origin of this unprofitable competition. I cannot see in what particular the function and the action of those who engage in these labour associations differ from the policy of the capitalist employer. He knows that to sell his produce below its cost is to invite ruin, and he is justly charged with rashness if he enters on an undertaking without foreseeing or at least guarding against the risk. The workman is as laudably anxious not to sell the only thing which he has to sell at a less price than that at which he can reasonably afford to offer it, and this by every economical analysis should contain a notable margin over his maintenance. The capitalist employer is blamed if he sells at a price which does not give him back his outlay and a profit. The workman, on the other hand, was once coerced, then severely chidden, and even now meets with very sinister criticism, if he attempts to do that which it is proper wisdom and forethought in his employer to achieve. And if an exalted price is the consequence, it is not honest and it is not just, for reasons which I shall state further on, to put all this on the workman. For I shall be able to give you evidence from what is, I believe, a competent and really disinterested source about the analysis of exalted prices, and show you (1) that the enhanced price precedes the increase of wages, and that (2) the increase is but a moderate fraction of the enhanced price.

There must be some reason why a process which is, as I contend, identical in the case of employer and workman, is looked on with approval in the case of the former, with disfavour in the case of the latter. Part of this feeling, I do not doubt, is the tradition of the old times, in which the law denied the workman anything but a bare maintenance. Nor do I doubt that the language of economists of the middle school, by which I wish to distinguish Adam Smith from his successors, and the latter from what I would fain hope are fuller and truer exponents of social forces, has had not a little to do with the sentiment. Mr. Mill no doubt developed the wage fund as part of the argument by which he sought to prove that unproductive consumption or waste was in no sense a benefit to society. But there are parts of his great work in which he betrays a faint bias towards what once was current opinion, as when, for example, he lays it down, that an improvement in the wages of workmen can only be attained at the expense of profits. Of course this statement is incorrect. It may be, and perhaps sometimes is, obtained at the expense of the consumer, though generally as a consequent of the consumer's expense being enhanced before the workman's wages are. It may be met, as it commonly is, by a diminished cost of production, by labour-saving appliances, and similar economies. For I conclude, and I believe with perfect correctness, that the loss of profits is much more due to the competition of capitalists than it ever has been or ever will be by the demands of workmen! Even now, however, the salt syndicate of Cheshire is looked on with far greater favour than a trade union of miners or engineers. And yet, unless I am greatly mistaken, very large fortunes have been made by men who have been engaged in these salt works under the old *régime* of sharp competition, though the beginnings of such successful people have been very humble.

The feeling, instinct, alarm, aversion, or whatever else we may call the sentiment which is unfriendly to trade combinations, from which the most dispassionate persons are not free, which it requires much robust and exhaustive knowledge of the facts to rid oneself, is, I believe, due to the consciousness, that the progress of society depends a good deal more on the continuity of labour than it does on the continuity of capital. In human societies the means of life is annual produce. On the perpetual supply of this depends the existence of every one, of the workman, I grant, himself among others. It seems as though this Samson, however blind he may be to his true powers, however bound he may be in the prison-house of poverty, can pull down, if he exerted himself, the temple of Dagon on himself indeed, but on the lords of Philistia also. And in a way Mr. George has, I think, seen how much society depends on labour, perhaps how much society loses by the expatriation of labour, and how strong society is, when labour is orderly and contented. We see the fact in minor matters. Some years ago, a strike of the cabdrivers paralyzed that part of the business men of London, to whom rapid locomotion was a matter of money, besides inflicting much inconvenience on travellers and railways. On another occasion a strike of stokers in the London gasworks seemed likely to hand over the metropolis an easy prey to the predatory classes. Only the other day, when there was threatened an extensive strike of the colliers, the papers were full of sinister predictions as to the paralysis of British industry which would follow on the action of the workmen, and with some adroitness the workmen were bidden to reflect on the distress which they would assuredly bring on those of their fellow-labourers, millions in number, to whom an adequate supply of coal was a prime necessity. You will remember that the rise in price, some two or three shillings a ton preceded the action of the workmen. That rise was witnessed with complacency, perhaps with congratulation. But the attitude of the colliers gave occasion to general and undisguised alarm. Fortunately, and at least to a great extent, the alarm was brief, for the workmen secured their advance.

Now I thought it very much to the purpose to write to my friend Mr. Burt, who has been for many years in the House of Commons as Member for Morpeth, who is intimately acquainted with all colliery topics, and whose moderation and judgment has won him the esteem of all persons from all parties; and to ask him the plain question, what increment does the 10 per cent. added to the workmen's wages induce on the price of coal? His letter is before me, and entirely carries out my anticipations. I will read you that part of it which bears on my question. "The prices for coal-getting vary very much in every district, and almost in every mine. It is therefore difficult to say how much 10 per cent. advance in the wages of the miners will put on the price of a ton of coal. I see that Mr. Pickard stated it at twopence a ton. The employers, on the other hand, contend that this would only apply to the actual coal-getters, and that when other classes of labour are included the amount will be nearer fourpence a ton. I have just been talking to a large Derbyshire coal-owner, who sets the amount at fourpence a ton. My opinion is that threepence per ton will cover the extra cost. It is important to bear in mind (*a*) that the advance, so far, has only been in a portion of the mining districts, including less than half of the persons employed; and (*b*) that the demand for increase of pay followed, and did not precede, the increase in the price of coal." If these statements are accurate, and they bear, in my opinion, all the conditions of accuracy about them, I think that you will agree in my conclusion that an increase of 10 per cent. in the colliers' wages, an increase which may probably be well met, and more than met, by economies in production, is not a very serious burden on the consumer, to be in need of the article for domestic use, or for the generation of force. And if it be said that the dealer must compensate himself for the enhanced price, the answer is obvious. I buy coal from the London exchange, and pay ready money to a middleman, who gives a three or six months' bill to the producer. In just the same way a bookseller thinks he makes you a grand offer in taking off threepence in the shilling on books, when he gets fourpence allowed, and while you pay him over the counter, he claims six months' credit from the publisher. The middleman in England is very rapacious, very plausible, and generally very ignorant. I confess I never saw much merit in the process by which some eminent people have got rich, *i.e.*, by buying at eightpence and selling at a shilling.

A good deal of attention has been directed of late to the processes adopted by what are called sweaters, *i.e.*, middlemen who prey on the ignorance and misery of poor workmen. Now recently the case of the match girls, earning from seven to eight shillings a week, has been handled. Near twenty years ago Mr. Lowe, then Chancellor of the Exchequer, proposed to tax matches; I fancy sometimes because he wanted to puzzle people with the motto of his projected stamp, *ex luce lucellum*. On that occasion Messrs. Bryant and May marshalled their workwomen, got them to go in procession to Westminster Hall, and extinguished the project by a judicious mixture of pathos and ridicule. But this estimable firm got all the profit of the demonstration. A few months ago Mrs. Besant called attention to the wretched earnings of these people, and an attempt at making their condition better known was made by some of our University people at Toynbee Hall. The London Trades Council also lent their authority to arbitration. After a good deal of fencing the firm yielded, and I am glad to hear that now the wages of the match girls are more than doubled, and that they are able to lead respectable lives. But I don't think that matches are dearer and profits are less. The new departure only required a little management and tact. Some people, however, seem to have a peculiar pleasure in making their workmen beggarly and keeping them so.

I do not indeed assert that all the improvement in the condition of workmen has come from the establishment of labour partnerships, but I do not know any other cause for a phenomenon, in which, imperfect as it yet is, I feel a strong satisfaction. The Amalgamated Society of Engineers is an association which fought with determination for its ends, enrolled nearly all the artisans which come under the definition of engineers, and, after a prolonged struggle, succeeded in all they claimed. For as time goes on the strike, which is the last expedient in this social warfare, becomes rarer. They are far commoner in the United States than with us, and far bitterer, as the Government returns show. For the possibility of such an expedient becomes ultimately as great a deterrent to unfair advantage as the reality of it, and arbitration is seen to be a far more rational expedient than a quarrel. In many cases already a sliding scale, based on the two elements of cost and price, is adopted. Of course the cost is that which is general in the calling. No one can by any action intercept the reduction of cost which comes from the improvement in a process as long as the producer is guaranteed by a patent. For, as I have stated to you before, the benefit of improvement to the workman and the consumer comes slowly, to the rent receiver last of all, and only when the new process is diffused. When that happens he gets his turn, and, as some people think, gets far more than he deserves.

I have already stated in another lecture, and must here restate, for economical facts are manysided, and therefore illustrate various economical principles, that I never saw a district in which the absence of all labour partnerships have so markedly an injurious effect on the wages of labour as in the Cornish mining district. The wages of workmen in this district are, I believe, taking the calling and all its dangers into account, lower than in any other English industry. Trade unions are entirely unknown, and the workmen, though massed together, are oppressed in detail. The industry they represent is one of singular significance, for the economical importance of the metal which they chiefly produce, tin, is great and permanent. It is at any rate clear that organization among the workmen would secure far better terms to them than they now get, and probably would lead to economies in the separation and reduction of the metal, the process now being excessively rude and wasteful, and the industry being carried on under conditions so noxious that nothing but the oppression of the miners could render them possible and continuous.

There is no fear that working men will abuse the strength which they obtain by their labour partnerships by the adoption of the joint-stock principle to their own industry. They are always doing battle at a great disadvantage, for their powers of waiting are, by the circumstances of the case, necessarily limited. Besides they understand, I am convinced, what are the true functions of capital far better than that economist who constantly dogmatizes on it without the possession of the facts ; or even than the employer, whose natural impulse is to magnify his own importance ; or than the public, which is constantly twisted by shallow newspaper sophistries, the constant outcome of arrogance, conceit, and sycophancy. I confess that I am struck, and constantly have been, at the patience with which, to all appearance, working men hear or read the calumnies which are uttered about them, and the sinister predictions with which their efforts to better themselves and their fellows are met.

The trade union is a peculiar product of English social life. It can be traced back to the dawn of economic history in this country. It was proscribed for nearly five centuries, at first ineffectually, at last with complete success. But the memory of the association never quite died out. At last the old laws were considered obsolete, as at least to be quite superfluous in the light of the judge-made law of conspiracy. When they were permitted as far as the law allowed, it must be conceded that the revival was attended by not a few scandals, as, for example, those revealed at Sheffield. I set these down partly to the passionate manner in which they had been proscribed, partly to the conspiracy laws, partly to the national ignorance and impatience of those who had won a boon, and did not know how to use it. At last the legislature became wise, and undeterred by the revelations made by Broadhead and his associates, gave these partnerships a most generous recognition, though even now it is half-hearted.

SECOND COURSE.

I.

THE ECONOMIC DOCTRINE OF WASTE.

Popularity of wasteful persons explained—Policy of Colbert—Theories of the Physiocrats; their effect on the French Revolution—Turgot and Adam Smith—" Unproductive labour"—Quesnai—Mill—Waste of labour, of health, of machinery, in agriculture—Scientific waste—Political waste—Gastronomic waste.

EVERY one admits that waste is an economic evil, and, in certain well-understood cases, a moral offence, though not always a punishable one, for the theory of law in our days is that a mischief done by one man must be provably injurious to some other particular person before it can conveniently be brought within the restraint of law. An individual may ruin his health, waste his resources, disable himself from earning his own livelihood, and thus plant himself on the public charity of the Poor Laws, without, in the process, bringing himself within the reach of any civil penalty. He may, even indirectly, induce the greatest wrongs on the innocent and helpless members of his own household without running the risk of punishment. He may go a great way in putting direct wrongs on them, and those of a serious kind, with but little peril. The motive for this leniency, I suppose, is the disinclination which people feel towards enlarging the operations of positive law, because they have too good reason to distrust its administration, and an unwillingness to restrain individual liberty, when the offences of the individual affect himself and his own family only. Besides, it may be hoped that self-restraint and shame will be correctives in the individual's own case, natural affection and duty for the relations in which he stands to his own family.

Perhaps, again, the State hesitates on punishing or checking economic waste, because administrations are and have been themselves the greatest offenders in this direction. Adam Smith had good reason in contrasting the impertinence of sumptuary laws with the wanton and lavish expenditure of those who enacted such regulations. Nations, he alleged, are never ruined by their own expenditure, their peril comes from the governments which undertake their affairs, and manage them wastefully or ruinously. The great economist might have appealed to overwhelming evidence in support of this contention. Mighty empires, possessed of no little art and much civilization, have passed away into nothingness because the government of the country was evil. That culture with which all university students are supposed to be more or less familiar became a wreck, entirely owing to the vices of its government, though the ruin of the Roman Empire was not so complete as that of the races which inhabited Central and Western Asia.

Wasteful people are, however, generally popular. The most selfish enjoyments are seldom entirely personal. A spendthrift can rarely so arrange matters as that no other person can make gain of his extravagance. It is true that society at large does not profit by him so much as it does from the action of his thrifty neighbour. But in the spendthrift's case the advantage which the few gain is sensible, in that of the man who saves from superfluities the benefit is larger, but hidden. Henry VII. was the most covetous and thrifty of the English kings. His son was the most exacting and the most extravagant. The English people were singularly prosperous during the reign of the father. They were impoverished, whole classes of them beggared, by the action of the son. But I have no doubt that in their several times the parsimony of the father was unpopular, the prodigality of the son was acceptable. The waste of Henry was the means by which a new nobility was created, and the king found favour in the eyes of those to whom he cast contemptuously some of his spoils. Charles II. was probably the most flagitious person who ever ruled in England. But he was certainly popular. His brother James, whose life was far more decorous, appears to have been always disliked. And what applies to kings applies to private men. There are incessant apologies made for the reckless and unthrifty, even when their practices have been selfish and vicious. In my youth the biographies and exploits of these wastrels were popular books. I do not know whether the taste survives, though the success of a recent publication seems to imply that it does. It would be quite in human nature if it did. But setting aside these sympathies, if we share them, it will, I hope, be possible to discover in what economic waste or unproductive consumption consists. The expression, in the latter form, has an historic origin, and not a little of the difficulty which has been traditional in the interpretation of it, is due to the arbitrary sense, as I think, in which it was first employed and subsequently justified, a sense which, as it seems to me, is misleading, both in Adam Smith and in Mill.

The policy of Colbert, under which subventions or bounties were given to articles in which Frenchmen have shown conspicuous taste and elegant fancy, was not only supposed to have made France, and especially Paris, the centre of the world of fashion, but to have created such a taste for French goods as secured them a ready market wherever any tendency to refinement prevailed. It cannot, I think, be doubted that the very effective patronage of the fine arts, which the policy of Colbert bestowed on them, conferred no little advantage on the court of Louis XIV., and indirectly aided in no slight degree that predominating influence which the French acquired at the close of the seventeenth century. Of course the circumstances were exceedingly favourable. France was nearly the only European or continental state which emerged from the terrible Thirty Years' War with no loss, and with considerable gain, not only in its internal resources, but by the extension of its frontier. England was for a short time under the military rule of a successful adventurer, whom Mazarin assiduously courted and conciliated. But after his death, on his 59th birthday, the government was for near a quarter of a century in the hands of a cynical voluptuary, and in the scandalous and corrupt camarilla which he gathered about him. You may learn what Paris was to the rest of the world in the numerous memoirs of the time, and a reflection of some of its worst features in England, in the literature of our own country, for instance, in the memoirs of Grammont. The policy of Colbert was so identified with the age of Louis XIV., that even when it had ceased to fulfil the purposes of its projectors it remained an ideal from which France was loath to part. It is not a little remarkable that the principal agents in this new industrial departure were the Huguenots, whom in his later years the French king banished.

Now about the middle of the eighteenth century, when everything in France was sacrificed to those State-supported industries, a class of writers arose who were really, though with many errors, the founders of the modern science or philosophy of political economy, and supplied Adam Smith, during his residence in France, with not a few of the principles which are found in his capital work, "The Wealth of Nations." The fiscal system of France was the most vicious conceivable. The taxes were in the last degree oppressive, and the mode of collecting them increased the oppression. There was not even trade between the old Parliament provinces of France, and the people in one district might be starving while those in another might be impoverished, in consequence of a ruinous, because artificially unsaleable, plenty. In particular, the estates of the nobles and the Church were exempt from taxation, while the tenure of the peasant was made liable to arbitrary inaction, to say nothing of the feudal dues which were squeezed from his poverty under the old *régime*. Unhappily the economists, as the new sect of philosophers was called, preached in the desert, and the wrongs of the French peasants were terribly avenged by the Revolution and the Terror. Arthur Young describes the early days of the Great Change, not without a secret sympathy with those who retaliated in the latter end of 1789, on the nobility which had so long oppressed them. I know no one who has stated the situation more exactly, and predicted its outcome more accurately than Smollett did in his letter of March 23, 1765, and the thirty-sixth in the collection. But Smollett was one of the keenest observers in the eighteenth century. I cannot recommend his history or his poetry, but his novels are excellent pictures of eighteenth-century life, and his letters are full of information.

Now the economists discovered and announced one economical truth of the greatest importance. It is that the existence of every class of persons, artisans, in the ordinary sense of the word, men of leisure, men of science, men of religion, men engaged in warfare and in the arts, and the dependents and domestics of these people, depended on the extent to which the products of agriculture were in excess of what was needed for the maintenance of the agriculturist, and for the continuity of his calling. On this foundation, as they saw clearly, rested the whole of the social structure. If it failed, the whole which was above it vanished into nothingness. It was plain, then, that what impoverished the peasant threatened mischief to the nation, and I need not say that in the existing state of trade and transport, almost the sole reliance for everything beyond the maintenance of the peasant lay in the efficiency of the peasant's labour and the abundance of his crops. To these men, therefore, agriculture was as sacred as it was to Cato and to Cicero. Perhaps the views which they entertained were as cordially acknowledged by the public men at the time, who had as abstract a respect for agriculture as Cicero had, and as practical a dislike to any change which could alone make agriculture effective. Unfortunately, too, the Economists of the eighteenth century, after grasping this and a few co-ordinate economical truths, wandered off, as economists have always been apt to do, into metaphysics.

The agricultural system of the French Economists is expounded and criticized by Adam Smith in the ninth chapter of his fourth book. I do not know whether, in this age of experimental study, you are advised to read Adam Smith, or are counselled to master authors who know but little of the errors committed in past times, and have but little insight into the errors of the time or the country in which they live. But I can assure you that in my opinion, whatever that may be worth, Adam Smith is much more frequently in the right than his commentators and critics are, and that, in particular, he had the advantage of a just and unprejudiced judgment, to say nothing of an entirely fearless candour, at a time when it was difficult to form a sound opinion and dangerous to utter it. The true economist, until Utopia is reached and settled is, I fear, always destined to the duty of aggression. We have made great progress in this country, but we are far from having realized all the causes which induce the wealth of nations, not to say that to which we belong. At one time it is necessary to do battle with a mischievous privilege, which is sheltered by tradition and self-interest, at another to combat an anarchical theory, which under the pretence, perhaps with the intention, of righting social wrongs, would effectually, if it were adopted, reach society itself.

Now the Economists recognized that the agriculturists needed two kinds of forms of capital, which they called original (*primitive*) and annual (*annuelle*), these terms corresponding to what are familiar to you as the fixed and circulating forms of capital, but would be better divided, or at least be more suggestive, if they were called permanent and recurrent. They also saw, that occasionally the proprietor, when the occupier was a tenant on a rent, expended capital on permanent improvements, essential or contributory to agricultural success. They insisted that these two kinds of agricultural capital must be kept sacred from all exactions, and that only when they were thus secured, would it be possible, without future and serious loss, to pay rent, taxes, or dues. All this is perfectly true, as true in this year as it was more than four generations ago, when these French Economists were writing; and you may depend on it, the violation, even though it may be unconscious, of these conditions of successful agriculture, is as disastrous now as it was then.

These agriculturists thus secured in the continuity of their industry, Turgot, the most systematic writer of the school, called productive, and every one else, without exception, from the highest to the lowest, from the king on his throne to the lackey, whom you know no doubt from your knowledge of the French plays of the time, existed, like the slaves of the Roman comedy, only to be caned, kicked, and pommelled, he declared to be sterile. Into this vast and all-absorbing economic limbo every one went, the churchman, the lawyer, the doctor, the courtier, the landowner (except in so far as he made agricultural improvements only), the merchant, the trader, the artisan, the darlings of Colbert, and the darlings of Louis Dieudonné, even the philosophers, and among them even Turgot and his allies in the economic analysis, the statesman, the professors at the Sorbonne, and the Encyclopædists, their rivals, Voltaire, Rousseau, *et id genus omne*. No one escaped. They were all, with the exception of the roturiers, and the improving landowners, swept into the barathrum of the sterile, into the gloomy and discredited army of unproductive consumers. Consumers they certainly were, for did they not exist, some of them only too well?

Smith did not fail to attack these unpalatable metaphysics. It was a startling utterance, when all the people who considered themselves the best of Frenchmen, and thereupon the best people in the world, were branded with economical sterility. It was turning the tables with a witness. Now, beyond doubt, the reasoning, such as it was, had a lasting effect, for part of it was exceedingly true, and the class, which had hitherto been considered the natural victims of society, was now shown to be, on the contrary, the saviours of society. I have no doubt that the reasonings of the Economists had more influence in that movement of 1789, than all the wit of Voltaire, all the political philosophy of Rousseau, and all the scepticism of Diderot and the Encyclopædists. It should be observed, too, that the Economists rightly divined that the evidence of a progressive agriculture, progressive because protected from rapine, was to be detected in the national development of rent. An improving and a considerate landowner had his reward. He was to be honoured as one of the productive classes, and he was on the road to a justly improving rent.

Adam Smith states, with commendable gravity, the residue of Turgot's theory. Artificers and manufacturers, the especial objects of Colbert's case, were in Turgot's eyes wholly barren and unproductive. Their labour merely produces that which they have consumed in their calling and in their maintenance. They add nothing to the sum of annual wealth, for even the profit which they and their employers divide is simply extracted through the demands of another sterile person, of that which might be employed for a further productive end. The cultivator of the soil cannot but feel as he consumes the produce of his labour, that he is increasing the national resources, and therefore the wealth, of his country. The merchant and artificer can only effect this desirable end by parsimony and privation, and even then they are only securing, in the distribution of those products, in the production of which the agriculturist is the only beneficent agent, a certain share to themselves. "They are employed and maintained altogether at the expense of the proprietors and the cultivators, who pay their wages and provide their profits." The outside that can be alleged on their behalf is, that by their industry and dexterity, they do that neatly and quickly which those productive agents, if left to themselves, would do clumsily and slowly. Hence the two parties have reciprocal interests. Let the cultivator leave the artisan and his employer alone, and he will get whatever he wants more cheaply. Let the unproductive class leave the productive alone, for the more prosperous and energetic his labour is, the more margin is there in his hands with which to employ artisan, manufacturer, and merchant. It follows then, the Economists concluded, that the only adjustment of all interests, both between the members of any one community and between all communities, will be found in perfect freedom of trade, domestic and foreign. Quesnai, one of Turgot's associates in this new social philosophy, was a physician, and illustrated his theory of the social state by ingenious parallels drawn from the orderly regimen, which keeps the physical organization of men in a healthy condition.

Of course the work of the artisan, the manufacturer, and the merchant contributes in no slight degree to the efficiency of the husbandman's industry. The progress which agriculture has made from the earliest record of its energies, by which it produces three times its old acreage at one-fourth the relative cost, and over three times a wider area, is due to the fact that the instruments furnished by the artisan have increased the efficiency of the agriculturist thirty or forty-fold. There has been an unseen, but a virtual partnership between the two classes, a reciprocity of services, none the less real because it has not been formulated. It is true that at the time when the Economists wrote, the economics of invention were in their infancy. But they were already visible, not perhaps as much in France as in England, for, as I have said, the principal stimulants of Colbert were applied not to the industrial arts of life, but to those which ministered to mere luxury, or fashion in fobs and wigs, china and tapestry. But in the nature of things, even when wealth is largely accumulated, the number of artisans and manufacturers who minister merely to the enjoyments of the richer spending classes, at home and abroad, is small. We shall see presently what this expenditure means.

In dealing with the sweeping conclusion to which the Economists came, as to the unproductive character of the labour exercised by artisans, manufacturers, and merchants, Smith does not attempt to analyse the relation in which by far the largest number of the functionaries stand to the community in general, to its essential resources, and to the agriculturist in particular. He recognizes the superior productiveness of the agricultural class, though he claims for the others that they do produce, that they replace at least that which they consume, and *pro tanto* therefore are no loss to society, as domestic servants are, and that as far as the increase of national wealth goes, this altogether depends on parsimony, an economic virtue from which hardly any individual, whatever be his place in the distribution of wealth, should be exempt. And it is singular that in the analysis of those factors which produce national wealth, he does not go more fully into the case which was constantly before his experience, and constantly appealed to by him, as the means for illustrating his conclusions. This was Holland.

It was a common-place with those who studied social questions nearly a century before the time of Adam Smith, to refer to the Dutch Republic and its economical history, as the best illustration conceivable of the benefits which successful trade confers on a community. Holland was intrinsically a poor country. It was stated, frequently and familiarly, that the grain produce of Holland would not keep all its inhabitants for a single month out of the whole twelve. It had no timber, no stone for its public and private buildings. And yet there was no country in which grain was more abundant than it was in Holland, and more at a uniform price. The wharves of Holland were crowded with a produce which was not of Dutch origin. The dockyards of England and France purchased their timber at Amsterdam, as is proved by the correspondence of Pepys with Houblon, now preserved in the Bodleian library. From the same place came the most valuable kinds of marble. In nearly all commodities Holland gave the price, and it did so because its towns had a free market, to which all the world resorted, for such a condition of things only can make the regular quotation of trade prices permanently useful to dealers. The Dutch, I admit, were manufacturers, in some articles the successful manufacturing rivals of England; but their principal source of wealth, of that wealth, abundance of good products, on which alone the capacity for any other industry can be based, was to be traced to trade, and the policy of free trade. They got their live stock from the Danish peninsula, says Smith, and "their corn from almost all the different countries of Europe." Now it is a sheer paradox to say that those callings, which secured plenty to the Dutch consumer, and an ever-increasing wealth to the Dutch burghers, could be exhibitions of unproductive consumption. To make such an assertion is to indulge in the most barren form of metaphysics, to dispute or disdain the evidence of facts, because they do not square with an hypothesis.

As has often occurred in the history of economic science, the extravagant conclusions at which the Economists arrived were in great part due to the mischievous practices which they combated. In just the same way, the excessive harshness of the doctrine of *laissez faire* was a reaction against the incessant and vexatious meddlesomeness of governments. It is very often thought to be necessary, or at least expedient, to prove men and their practices to be much more in the wrong than they really are, in order to provoke that criticism which corrects the mischief which they actually do. The Economists found the agriculturist degraded and harassed. So they did not so much exaggerate his social value, as they unduly depreciated the social value of every one else, in order that they might get him some little consideration, and ensure him some justice. By adroitly showing that it was the interest of the rent receiver to take some thought of the person who earned rent, a hint which from time to time landowners have been slow to take, they got a few of his most notorious and indefensible grievances redressed. They got the term extended during which the grant of a lease would be valid against a future proprietor, by descent or purchase. They procured that the restraint of traffic in agricultural produce between province and province should be abrogated, and that freedom of export should be granted. Naturally they overrated the value of their own labours, the thoroughness of their own reforms. The elder Mirabeau, dwelling on the services of M. Quesnai, contrasts to its advantage the Economical Talk, as the conclusions of the Economists were called, with the capital discoveries of writing and the use of money. A few years later, however, and nearly every one was agreed that these reforms were insufficient; and in the autumn of 1789 the *Tiers Etat*, by a stroke of the pen, destroyed the whole system on which the cultivator stood to the rent receiver. The best account of this situation, after the French feudal dues were extinguished, is to be found in Arthur Young's French tour, for he witnessed the violence of the reaction.

Mr. Mill, in the third chapter of his first book, appears to conclude that the expression "unproductive labour" is so common as to have become classical, or in other words, to have taken so solid a hold on the minds of those who study economical topics, that it cannot, even at the risk of offence, be dispensed with. The most obvious restriction of the word "productive" is to those who are agents in producing material wealth, by which is, I suppose, meant, such tangible and visible products as satisfy some intelligible, even if it be an unintelligent demand, and are therefore, however unwisely, perhaps mischievously, possessed of merchantable value, and therefore classed as utilities. It would be easy to discover examples, among unquestionable utilities, from the merchantable point of view, which a brief inquiry would declare mischievous, or odious, and even criminal, and though I am far from saying that the economist should be guided by moral or political considerations in either his formulas or in his inferences, I am nevertheless entirely sure that his inquiries cover the same ground which is occupied by the moralist and the statesman. To carry on his investigations from his own point of view is doubtlessly essential to the completeness of his theory, but what he calls wasteful is in the end what the student of ethics calls immoral, and what the politician, who is worthy of the name, desires to check by such expedients as his experience of men, of administration, and of legislation, instructs him in, or suggests to him.

After having said that by productive labour must be meant "those kinds of enertia which produce utilities embodied in material objects," Mr. Mill is not, I think, consistent with his own definition. He instantly says that he "shall avail himself to the full extent of the restricted application, and shall not refuse the appellation 'productive' to labour which yields no material product as its direct result, provided that an increase of material products is its ultimate consequence." He gives as illustrations, the acquisition of manufacturing skill—I presume as much in the teacher as in the agent—and the officers of government, "because without them material wealth, in anything like its present abundance, could not exist." He says that these are "indirectly or mediately productive, and his test of such agents is that they leave the community richer in material products than they found it, that they increase, or tend to increase, material wealth." He then proceeds to illustrate his theory, by saying that the labour of saving a man's life is not productive, unless the man saved produces more than he consumes; that the work of the missionary is not productive, though he credits such persons with the best intentions; that the more "a nation expends in keeping agriculturists and manufacturers at work, the more it will have for every other purpose, and the more clergymen, &c., it keeps, the less it will have." He admits that unproductive labour may be as useful as productive, it may be more useful, even in point of permanent advantage, or again it may be absolute waste; and he concludes "that the services of the labourers," such as he enumerates, "if useful, were obtained at a sacrifice to the world of a portion of material wealth; if useless, all that these labourers consumed was waste."

The door which Mr. Mill opens, when he concedes that labour may be called productive when "an increase of material products is its ultimate consequence," is exceedingly wide. It is difficult to see what, under certain circumstances, can be excluded from this class of operations. We may assume that the ideal state of the specially productive labourer, be he labourer with skilled hands, or employer with skilled head, is one in which every muscular and every nervous energy is kept in the most efficient and vigorous condition. If that agriculturist, as Swift said, with excusable exaggeration, is worth more than all the statesmen in existence, who makes two blades of grass grow where one grew before, surely a man or an agency which makes the workman able to do in an hour what might have taken him two, without this assistance, is as productive a person as the typical agriculturist of Swift's patriotic and gigantic king. But what, and how many, are the agents which effect this result? The teacher of method to childhood and youth do so; the person who inculcates good manners, orderliness, and obedience, do so; and here is room for the clergyman and missionary, whatever phrase he gives to his work; the physician who saves strength and health does so. The science which shortens processes, and the economist who teaches the true relation of capital and labour do so. But this is by no means all. Breaks in the continuity of labour are necessary, innocent recreation is necessary, adequate exercise is necessary, even a periodical cessation of all labour is necessary, in order that labour shall be as efficient as possible. The most hopeful student in the Universities is not the youth who mopes, and is, I believe, described here and elsewhere by suggestive names, but the young man who is active and athletic, who judiciously divides his time between recreation and study. But what is true of intellectual labour is true of physical labour, if indeed you can, except in thought, separate the act of mind from any productive or efficient labour whatever. Take away rest, recreation, innocent pleasure, and you will assuredly sacrifice efficiency. Of course all these relaxations may become pursuits. If they are pursued for their own sake only, they may be nearly as harmful to the efficiency as their total absence is. Or they may be pursued professionally, for judicious recreation must be taught, just as taste must be educated. I cannot deny to the musician, to the artist, to the actor, and even to the singer, his place in Mr. Mill's definition, if the consequence of such agencies is to make the producer of material wealth more efficient. I am disposed to admit that the skill of the cricketer, the football player, the oarsman, may bestow as substantial a contribution even to merely mechanical processes, in their degree and manner, as those other educational and preservative agencies do. For the efficiency and the due continuity of industrial energies is, and always has been, a very complicated business, to the completion of which, relative as that completion still is, many agencies have contributed, towards which many new agencies have to be found out, and frequently are found out by people who are merely drawing inferences from observation. The restraint of children's labour, the introduction of the half-time system, the discovery of the fact that short hours of work are constantly cheaper in the end than long hours, may be, and as I think, have been, as economically useful as the inventions of steam power and spinning machinery. What we are in search of, indeed, is not unproductive consumption, which is, I hope I have made clear, a mere metaphysical phrase, but waste, which is the great economical evil, which the economist detects, if he has the skill to do so, and criticizes, if he has the adequate courage for his utterances. This waste arises from many causes, some inevitable, some excusable, some corrigible, some entirely and wholly indefensible, some justly punishable by the action of government. Let us look at a few of these separately.

There is a kind of waste which belongs in some form or another to all organic energy, and to every substitute for organic energy. This, in the latter, is friction; in the former, the gradual weakening of vital powers; and, I should add, the variable period of nonage, which precedes the fullest manifestation of vital power. In every human being, in every animal which has been pressed into the service of man, a certain time must elapse before the agent can be useful. Human skill has been engaged in shortening this time, and great progress has been made in selecting and maturing animals which serve for human food, and in selecting and strengthening those who are employed in substitution for human labour. But in human labour, where the development of mental is more important than that of mere physical strength, though the latter cannot be lost sight of, the process of securing the maximum of utility, is found on economical grounds to be bettered by retarding rather than hastening it. Two or three generations ago, human beings were put to work in extreme youth, to the manifest injury of economical utility; what seemed to be industrial activity was found to be economical waste, and better counsels prevail in our time. So again sanitary science has greatly contributed to economy in human energy. We cannot escape the cost of nonage, we cannot obviate the certainty of ultimate decay; but we may greatly prolong the period of full activity, and by implication of economical utility. Two centuries ago the deaths in London, chiefly by infectious diseases, were greatly in excess of the births, sometimes, during periods of special unhealthiness, were double the number. At present the average death-rate by the thousand is not half what it was at the time of the second Revolution. During this time the waste was chiefly of child life, where the loss is total. But it was very considerable in adult life, where it is real but partial. Even at the present time the skill of man is unable to obviate the whole of this waste. But it has been reduced within more manageable limits. There is a waste of this kind on which I must comment. It is the maintenance of those who cannot possibly become industrial agents at all, or cannot recover the industrial capacity which they have lost. Such are congenital idiots, incurable lunatics, and the entirely disabled destitute. But here, when the economist shows that their existence is sheer waste, the moralist and the statesman rightly assert that they shall be, and ought to be, a charge on society, because humanity is better than economy, and public or private charity should not be entirely sacrificed to public or private thrift.

In those mechanical appliances which are substitutes for human labour, friction is waste. Now the victory of mechanical science over friction cannot by the nature of things ever be complete. The most carefully adjusted, and the most cautiously protected machinery will wear, though the wear may be so infinitesimal that the efficiency of the mechanism may be very prolonged. Certain buildings, especially those which are buried in the earth, are very enduring. The Roman forum, and the low-lying ground, known still as the Velabrum of Rome, are still drained by the cloaca, which was constructed in prehistoric times, and probably will be drained by the same agency in the most distant future. But other works of human skill have a far briefer industrial existence. Machinery wears out by natural causes. It is superseded by improvements, and the wear as well as the supervision are economical waste. Perhaps the fact that the duration of the best among these substitutes has but a limited existence is a powerful stimulant to invention and improvement. The value of machinery, buildings, &c., in the assets of a trader or manufacturer, is, or should always be, annually lessened by a sinking fund, and the life of the instrument should be recognized to be brief. There is inevitable waste in a metallic currency. At times, as in 1562 and 1698, this waste has brought about a financial crisis. Now it is the business of the private producer, and the business of an intelligent government, to anticipate and interpret as far as possible inevitable waste, and as far as each can, to reduce or narrow the amount. Invention and improvement have done this to a remarkable degree in private enterprise. I am afraid that I cannot bestow the same commendation on all the acts of any administration, whatever its complexion has been.

There is another direction in which physical, and especially chemical, research has obviated waste. You have, no doubt, often heard of these processes, of how the cost of materials in familiar use has been amazingly reduced, of how bye-products in particular industries, as, for example, in the manufacture of coal gas, and in the purification of rock salt, have been turned from being mere waste into valuable economical products. Similar inventions have attended the art of agriculture, the art of navigation, and a thousand other sciences. As I told you at the beginning of these lectures, we know that there is a limit beyond which human invention and adaptation cannot go; but there is no knowledge of what that limit is, and what are the victories still reserved for scientific research.

Is the rent of land, that is, toll taken for the user of the soil, and the license charge for exercising agricultural skill, apart from the outlay of the owner, waste? My hypothesis, you will see, assumes that the legal owner contributes nothing to the mechanism of industry, that he simply extracts from the demand of the occupier as much of increased value from outlay, as is in excess of replaced capital, personal maintenance, and reasonable profits. The problem must be faced, for it is of no avail to meet sceptics by simply asserting the right of property in a natural but limited agent or instrument. Now I think the economist must admit that rent, as I have described it, is waste. But it is a factor to which, given perfect freedom of supply, and just rights to the occupier, no person can have any higher title than the legal owner. He has bought it, and has a natural claim to whatever innocent use he can make of his property. The cultivator has no right to it. The State has no right to it, whatever it may have had in time past, for if one begins to challenge the justice of past engagements knowingly entered into and sanctioned, all society would be in confusion, credit would fail, property would be soon made insecure, and every motive to labour, and to save, beyond the vague, and, I am sure, weak stimulus of social duty, would be extinguished. I may entertain a very sincere respect for the intentions of those who wish to employ the force of government in order to entirely reconstruct society, and to annul all the motives which, at any rate, have hitherto made notable progress, in bettering the general condition of social man. But I may be pardoned for resisting, to the best of my judgment, a practical trial of so astounding an experiment. Respect for a speculative theory is very different from respect for a practical proposition. I am so ignorant of physics, that I hear with equanimity the news that you and I are descended from a brainless and long-tailed aquatic animal. But I have no inclination to plunge into the mid depths of ocean, in the search after my long-lost kinsfolk. The pedigree may be ancient. It is not flattering; though what is this to truth, especially to physical truth, which is to be our future guide, in opinion; never, I sincerely hope, in practice.

Some waste is excusable. Of this kind, the waste of experiment is most excusable, the most beneficent, the most instructive. There is no department of human knowledge in which it does not occur. There is no department of human action in which it is not inevitable. You must risk waste, in order to secure anything; from Christianity down to joint-stock enterprise and limited liability. Your chance is very wide, from crucifixion, through plank beds, down to a composition with creditors, to say nothing of despairing and therefore merciful creditors. *Humanum est errare*, and all our race, except women, who never err, are merciful to the erroneous. All progress is due to experiment, and will be. The waste, the unproductive consumption, is a blunder to the metaphysician, is a hope to the economist. Let us never despise experiment. It may answer, if we deal with ants and bees, and the origins of the human race. It is dangerous, if you challenge vested interests. But youth, and especially Oxford youth, is very considerate of those interests. It has a proper respect for age, even for disreputable age. It is impossible for me not to appreciate the sympathy of what, I trust, is reputable in any case. I do not, however, see why we should be considerate of institutions. In my mind, it is the best education to criticize them.

There is, however, one kind of waste, generally conceived to be excusable, but of which the recent history is most inexcusable, and the most dishonest. I am referring to the premature development of industrial undertakings. In the United Kingdom such things have happened, but we can bear them. In our colonies they bid fair to ruin the fairest hopes. I think that I can easily illustrate what I mean.

Let us conceive a German Jew (I have no objection to origin or race, and think that what is objectionable in either, if it exists, is kept alive by an intolerance), who, having kept a grogshop at Ballarat in the gold-digging times, and having dealt profitably with the miners, and deleteriously with their health, transfers his gains to a neighbouring colony. He is the smartest of the smart, and makes it his business to ingratiate himself with the people, few and busy, who are seeking to acquire a rapid fortune in their new home. Now there is one direction in which such people can be readily influenced. This is to dwell with emphasis and enthusiasm on the illimitable but undeveloped resources of the new country, and to suggest the immediate and extensive development of new harbours, docks, and railroads, the capital being borrowed in the United Kingdom, and the income assured from the earnings of these public works, and further covered by protective customs duties. The colonists are invited to discount their future expectations, and to load themselves with debt, while the country of their origin is met, after advancing the loan, with the grateful tribute of a hostile tariff. As a reward for his services in making the colony stagger under a debt, which might have been incurred fifty years hence with advantage, but under present circumstances will cripple the country for more than fifty years to come, and for having carried as its inevitable consequence a Protective tariff injurious to colonial progress and unfriendly to the country which has guaranteed, often at great expense, the infancy of the colony, this worthless and ignorant adventurer is rewarded with the dignity of a knighthood in the Order of St. Michael and St. George. I know no greater evil that has befallen the British colonies than the habit they have of listening to those who dwell on the boundless and undeveloped resources of the colony. Undeveloped resources are not resources at all. They are like the strength or the intellect of a child, and to anticipate them, by treating them as actual when they are only hypothetically potential, is as profound an act of folly, as it is for a private individual to launch into limitless expenditure in the hope that at some future time he may come into a fortune. Most of our colonies have succumbed to these temptations, and some of them are already half ruined. *Pessimum genus inimicorum laudentes*, says Tacitus. Mr. Mill has touched on this form of waste.

Rest and recreation are not waste. Neither is the moderate indulgence in refined pleasures. We cannot always trace the extent to which industrial energies are invigorated by these relaxations, but we may generally conclude that as long as they are invigorated, the expenditure is economically defensible. On the other hand, indulgences which do not and cannot have this effect are waste. So is also the employment of unnecessary intermediaries. In the early days of economic science, when *laissez faire* was so supreme, that it had almost adopted the maxim that whatever is is best, the defence of these multiplied intermediaries who get but do not make wealth, was taken for granted. In the latter days of unchecked competition, which you will remember always goes on between nations, however much it may be denounced in the domestic life of a people, the usefulness of these people is increasingly challenged. It is being seen that many of them are mere waste, and we are told on many sides that the true producer and his ultimate customer are seriously mulcted by the number of hands, each claiming a commission though which the produce passes before it reaches its destination.

Attempts are being made, with what success I do not yet know, to bring producer and consumer into more immediate relations, and thereupon to eliminate the middle man ; and we are assured that the recovery of manufacturing and even of agricultural profits, would be possible if the machinery of production and consumption were simplified. In the meantime, all needless intermediaries are waste. All processes which are foisted on business relations, such as complicated documents on the transfer of property, are waste. Every device which in the course of international competition straitens national energies is waste. Now such waste is corrigible, and while it is the interest of private persons to get rid of superfluous intermediaries, it is the duty of government to remove needless burdens from the processes of business. I need not detain you with punishable waste. It will be perfectly obvious. Crime and vice are in the highest degree waste. Some of these mischiefs are to be checked by the severity of law. Some are best coerced by the exercise of local authority. Some may perhaps be discouraged by public sentiment, and an improved social tone.

Only one other topic remains which I may briefly refer to. To what extent is the expenditure of the rich the employment of the poor? The banquets of the Mansion House and the Halls of the Companies have repeatedly been defended on the plea that these dinners give employment. Of course they do. But to whom? Measured by price, it takes as much labour to grow a hothouse pine as it does to produce two quarters of wheat, a sheep and a half, or some equally large products of what is confessedly useful. Now the maintenance of those who provide luxuries must be obtained from that source of occupation which economists call the common fund of industrial capital. The more there are of such producers and consumers as purvey for these City banquets the less there will be for others who are engaged in the homelier but more important avocations. Now I do not doubt that in the analysis of industry you have already discovered that voluntary consumption is a powerful stimulus to invention and improvement, and that extreme simplicity of life to a somewhat unprogressive condition of things. Even religious orders, bound by vows of poverty, have devoted themselves to the manufacture of costly and excellent liqueurs, and the monks of La Trappe, the Chartreuse, and the Benedictines have allowed themselves to be in touch with the City gourmand. But the expenditure of the rich is not in itself the employment of the poor. It is the stint of their employment. It will be plain that if the capital which is devoted to the supply of luxuries were diverted into the employment of those who supply necessaries and common comforts, that the demand for labour would increase and the wages of labour would be enhanced. But the luxury of the rich may be perhaps defended without being excused or economically justified. It is the outcome in the main of industrial efficiency. When the efficiency of labour is low, there is little opportunity for such expenditure as I have referred to, because there is but little margin for the production of anything beyond necessary use. The possibility of that luxury is due to the fact that economical waste has been greatly obviated in other directions, and Mr. Mill is in the right when he says that the existence of such expenditure is a proof that the community has much to spare from its necessities, while he regrets that the surplus is distributed with "prodigious inequality," that "the objects to which great part of it is devoted are of little worth, and that the large share of it falls to the lot of persons who render no equivalent service in return." This is rather adverse criticism on those who bid us recognize the intrinsic benevolence of their expenditure, and I am afraid that the criticism cannot be conveniently rebutted.

II.

THE THEORY OF ECONOMIC RENT.

Extreme opinions on the question of rent—Limited ownership of the soil in England—History of the rise of rent in arable and pasture lands, and in building sites—The Ricardian doctrine of rent—Mill and the unearned increment—Henry George's "Progress and Poverty"—A defence of rent.

You are no doubt aware that in recent years the right of private ownership in land has been very vigorously, and very generally, attacked, sometimes with every consideration for existing interests, though under the apologetic plea that it would do more harm to society to disregard those interests than it would be advantageous to extinguish them, on the ground that they were in their beginnings mere usurpations. In the case of an able and very sympathetic writer, whose treatment of the subject has, I suspect, won him more followers, or admirers, than the solidity of his reasoning justifies, the immediate and total confiscation of all rent is asserted to be not only just, but necessary, in all the interests of society. Now in treating this topic I avoid a cognate, but different subject, the regulation of rent, and the other question, the distribution of land—a topic which opens up a large number of interesting relations. In brief, I purpose to deal with land in its varied aspects, and with the theory of vested interests. You will anticipate that these several subjects are very closely related, though it is necessary, for reasons of time, to handle them separately.

Not only have the right of ownership in land, and the reputed interests which are connected with it, been energetically assailed by Mr. Mill and by Mr. George, but there are very active associations which, covertly as I think, aim at least at a part of the object which Mr. George has advocated with so much warmth. I have found advocates of the last writer's theories in very unexpected places. Very respectable politicians are insisting on the exceptional taxation of ground rents, and on the compulsory enfranchisement of leaseholds. Now to exceptionally tax one kind of property on the plea, correct or incorrect, that it is the creation of other agencies than those which are exhibited by the person who obtains the advantage, does not differ, except in degree, from the total and sweeping confiscation of Mr. George. The milder proposal of enfranchising leaseholds is not indeed so sweeping, and, as I think, not so disputable in principle, but it is intended to extinguish those advantages which the lessor is supposed to be likely to acquire at the extinction of the lease, and to secure to the lessee or the occupier, as the case may be, the improvements which he has himself effected. In brief, there is a very widespread conviction that the position of the landowner in the United Kingdom is a violation of natural justice, and this quite apart from the consideration of real or reputed wrongdoing on the part of this class in certain districts of the United Kingdom. The right of ownership in land is, in the minds of many, perhaps by an increasing number, by no means so sacred and indisputable as it was conceived to be thirty or forty years ago. I shall try to point out in the course of this lecture what have been the grounds on which these opinions have been developed; what is the economical authority for the theory from which they have been unquestionably derived; what is the economical value of that theory, and how far, in case it can be shown to be untenable, is the attack on the ownership of private property in land possessed of, or destitute of, any economical force.

Now it cannot be doubted, if the language of those who wrote in early ages on the common law of England has any force whatever, that in theory the largest rights of the private owner of land were very limited and qualified. The doctrine that no subject has the "absolutum et directum dominium" of land, that the Crown was the paramount owner, with the consequences of escheat and forfeiture, positions affirmed when the power of alienation was scanty and indirect, are not the mere verbiage of lawyers, borrowed from the formularies of mediæval logic. Nor are they principles intended to serve the police of government, by being a deterrent to offenders against the King's peace and dignity. They must, I think, be taken to mean that when the principles of the common law were affirmed, the ownership of land was qualified and limited, that the King's Council, and later on the King's Parliament, could alter and perhaps extinguish it, and that however unpopular and dangerous it might be to strain the rights of the Crown in Council or in Parliament, the existence of those rights could not be gainsaid. Perhaps one of the most striking illustrations of acts of Parliament enshrining this principle is to be seen in the dissolution of the monasteries, where the rights of founders to the reversion of their grants, implied, if not expressed, in the charters of foundation, and held to be real less than a century before, were entirely ignored in the concession to Henry VIII.

I have in an earlier lecture pointed out how entirely dissatisfied the public was when the official estate of the Crown was diminished by large or unwise alienations, and how important a part was played in the politics of countries by the doctrine of resumptions, even up to the middle of the eighteenth century, and the passage of the Nullum Tempus Act in 1768. But the doctrine that private ownership could, and should, be superseded, with or without compensation in real or reputed public interests, could be illustrated by a thousand examples in our social history. The largest instance in comparatively modern times of such parliamentary action is that contained in the first clause of the Statute of Frauds, under which occupiers who had no documentary evidence on which to support their interests, even though those interests were freehold, were declared to be tenants at will. I know that my position has been disputed by men who will look at the seventeenth century and its action with the eyes of the nineteenth, but I have discovered abundant proof in the rentals of colleges that my interpretation of this famous act is correct.

The doctrine that the ownership of the land is limited, and that by the common law, at least, a man may not in the case of land, as the Duke of Newcastle thought, "do what he wills with his own," is no mere antiquarian utterance. It has been appealed to by those who have attacked the ownership of land, as it is commonly understood, not indeed as a principal, but as a powerful subsidiary argument. What that principal argument is I proceed to state.

The owner of land has not only, it has been imagined, exacted in the first place a price for occupancy, under the name of rent, but has made the claim without according any consideration to the tenant. From this point of view Adam Smith believed that rent was originally a tax, imposed by the stronger on the weaker. Now it is certain that even the rudest agriculture produces more than is necessary for the occupier's subsistence, the replacement of his outlay, and even provision against risk, and that therefore this surplus can be exacted by the over-lord. Nor is it quite correct to say that the payment was made without any equivalent. The history of English agriculture refutes such an inference, and it is with English agriculture, and its economic situation, that I am concerned. The English landowner of the thirteenth and fourteenth centuries did two things for the savage tenant. He guaranteed the King's peace, that is the continuity of the farmer's industry free from the risks of brigandage, and he taught him by his own example and practice the best system of agriculture which the age could develop. In the age when rent seems most like a tax, because it was to all intents a fixed and maximum charge, *i.e.*, from the middle of the thirteenth to the middle of the sixteenth century, the English landowner, whatever his faults, was concerned in keeping the peace, and securing the farmer in the continuity of his calling. From the middle of the sixteenth till the middle of the seventeenth rackrenting of a very harsh kind occurred, and with very disastrous effects. Another system prevailed during the greater part of the eighteenth century. At the end of it the rackrenting was revived, and occasionally with great severity, till the close of the Continental War. For a time the farmer had little to complain of, except well-meant but blundering efforts to secure him in his new position till after the repeal of the Corn Laws. Then the rackrenting recommenced, and continued till more than ten years ago ; then the whole system collapsed in a common ruin, and to the amazement of those who had been ignorantly concerned in it.

Now the history of rent is not a little striking. Good arable land was let in the fourteenth century at 6d. an acre. I have never found a higher price. In the seventeenth it rose generally to 4s. 6d. an acre, not without grievous complaint. During the eighteenth it rose to 7s. in the first quarter, to 10s. in the last. In the nineteenth, up to the middle of the century, it rose to about 35s., and during the twenty years, 1853–1872, on an average $26\frac{1}{4}$ per cent. more. Since 1879 the reaction has been rapid, and I think that I can point out its cause. My authority, for the last time, is Mr. James Howard, of Bedford, who has made the land question in Great Britain his peculiar study, and can be entirely relied on. The rise in the rent of pasture land is far less considerable. The low-lying meadows on the Cherwell, partly enclosed in the Parks, partly continued as you go down the principal stream of the Cherwell on the right, let in 1309 at 9s. 6d. an acre. I doubt whether they fetched more than £4 to £4 10s. when the University bought the land. The rent of arable land, therefore, till the time of the present troubles, rose eighty-eight times, that of pasture nine times. I must ask you to attend to these figures, for much depends on them.

But the rise in the rent of arable land is as nothing to the rise in the rent of building land, and building sites in growing and thriving towns. In the early period to which I have referred, such land was worth little more than arable. London was by far the most densely peopled and busy place in the kingdom, but it was full of gardens and waste places. But unless I were to put before you numerous instances, you could not realize the growth of the rents derived from town sites. Some few years ago I was informed by a zealous inquirer into departmental abuses, that a site had been let in Cockspur Street by the Woods and Forests, *i.e.*, Crown land, by private arrangement. My informant scented a job, and wanted me to ask a question. But prudent men do not ask a question if they can get at the facts. So I went to the Woods and Forests office in Whitehall and inquired. I found that a forty years' lease at £40 a year had just expired, one granted say in 1845, and that the land was now re-let at £800 a year ground rent. I did not ask the question, for whatever else the Commissioners had done, they had certainly not neglected the interests of the office. But the rise of twenty times in forty years is as nothing to the rise from the time when Cockspur Street was a field with cow-sheds on it, and fine ladies went into the Mall and drank curds and whey. In the seventeenth century the site was probably worth about two-thirds of a farthing, or the 1·1440th of a pound sterling. You may make your calculation as to its growth in value since.

Now I daresay that no one who has undertaken to criticize adversely modern rents, has provided himself with such facts as I have given. Arable land has risen in rent eighty-eight times, pasture nine, and building sites incalculably, for I think it probable that the Cockspur Street site is not more than a tenth the ground rent of a similar site near the Royal Exchange. A good many years ago, I have been told, a working goldsmith, whose home was not the pleasantest, left the freehold site of his shop in Lombard Street to the Goldsmiths Company, in memory of the cheerful evenings which he spent at the livery, and with the intention of bettering their potations. The modern rent—Glyn's Bank occupies the site—would give, I was told, all the worshipful people among the goldsmiths a bath of Tokay. In a vague way these things are known. My informant was a very considerable economist, a bank manager, and a goldsmith. Of course he thought it a creditable bequest, and an exceedingly natural result. He was, I think I shall show, right in the latter inference.

But how does all this show to the general public? I will try to state the case as it appears to them, and the inferences that they naturally draw from the facts. And I venture on anticipating that no case could be quoted which more thoroughly illustrates what I have always striven to put before you, the wisdom of completely examining all the bearings of an economical theory, than this rent question does. For to anticipate what I shall hope to prove presently, the most dangerous, the most mischievous theories of social reconstruction have been based on the misconception of rent, and to these theories the most honoured teachers of political economy have rashly, and I believe unconsciously, lent themselves. But political economy is the last science in which you can allow dogmatism or authority, and I may add metaphysics, or sentiment.

Now to a large, and, I believe, an increasing number of persons the recipient of rent appears as a person whose income is increasing spontaneously, without labour or merits of his own. "He toils not," in the words of an eminent statesmen, "neither does he spin." The labours of others are engaged in continually pouring wealth into his pockets. Unfortunately for his reputation, he is continually engaged in shirking his obvious duties, putting on others, by his influence in the legislature, the cost and the business of improving his estate, and of making, perforce, every occupier an altruist, as the modern plilosophers say. "Here is a natural estate," such people allege, "which neither God nor nature nor man can have seriously intended to give over to these people. In the whole range of economic facts and principles, the fundamental condition of which is labour of head or educated hand, this fortunate person attains an ever-increasing share without outlay on his own part. He is the sole inheritor of other men's toils. To him they pay tribute; to him they are enslaved; by his permission they exercise the industries under which they live and he thrives. His share in the distribution of wealth is not only inordinate, but it is indispensable. We will not inquire too curiously or too insidiously into the question of how his ancestors obtained it. But we have a right to criticize the process by which its occupant has grown to such gigantic dimensions. We are justified in emancipating ourselves from the onerous conditions of occupancy, of resuming what a past generation never intended to give, and had no right to give even if they had intended it."

"Let us consider," they go on to say, "to what this strained and unnatural assertion of ownership of land is tending. If it is to be unchecked, allowed, conceded, the whole of society will rapidly become tenant at will to a few persons, who will exercise their usurpation remorselessly. We are in the condition, rapidly becoming worse, of a city in an eternal state of siege, in which the struggle for the means of existence is yearly becoming sharper, the competition more fierce, in which we allow the unfittest, the do-nothings, to survive at the expense of those who are engaged in the great work of national defence. These people have got hold of a necessary of life, the land, as Bishop Hatto, in the German story, got hold of the granaries. These people exact a famine price for their usurped possessions, and by the operation of well-known economical laws, exact the severest terms from the poor, from those who are least able to withstand them. In vain does a statesman attempt fiscal reforms. The benefit is intercepted and goes into the coffers of all-devouring rent. A tax is remitted; but the landlord claps it on the rent before the relief is sensible. His power of exaction is unlimited. Now it is clear that in a besieged town no person would concede that the owners of the necessaries of life should be allowed to extort anything from the necessities of a straitened population, least of all the non-combatants or non-workers from the workers or combatants, for the very existence of society being in danger, the rights of private property are at least to be suspended by those upon whose good-will and forbearance alone private property only has relied. Besides, do not all economists, wise and unwise, hard and considerate, agree that the laws regulating the distribution of wealth are of human institution only, created by society, maintained by society, and, by implication, within the discretion of society, to modify, alter, and even to subvert?"

I do not think that I am in the least degree exaggerating the language used by those who express their discontent at modern rents, or parodying the arguments by which they support their criticism on it. The number of such persons, and the urgency of their dissatisfaction, is increasing, and I cannot allow that the force of their attack is very satisfactorily met by the ordinary arguments alleged in favour of the existing system. I do not think that much can be made out of the implied guarantees of government, a favourite defence for a number of indefensible interests, nor is there much more truth in the allegation that landowners have been the improvers of their estates. In the great majority of cases, and in the most conspicuous examples of exalted rents, the very reverse is the fact, for the initial and induced value has been entirely the work of the occupier. Besides, landowners and their ordinary advocates speak of improvements as though they were indestructible, or perennial at least. Nothing can be more inaccurate, for nothing is more fleeting, unless under the condition of constant repair and replacement, than an agricultural improvement. At the very moment that it is finished it begins to deteriorate, and constant vigilance is needed in order to prevent the deterioration from becoming rapid. One of the worst and most stubborn facts in the present doctrine of agricultural land, is the certainty that large outlay will be needed in order to restore it to a cultivable condition. When men are idle, nature, against which the agriculturist is always battling, whose co-operation he can only secure by constant checks, is increasing the difficulty which renewed industry will have to meet. It is better, I am persuaded, to rest the case of the rent received on its own merits, not on his merits, for an exploded defence is worse than no defence at all.

The case against the rent receiver is heightened by the popular Ricardian doctrine. I have been sometimes puzzled as to whether this very considerable writer and thinker intended by the promulgation of his theory to frighten men into curtailing rent, by pointing out that, like the Cyclops, it would devour even Ulysses at last, or whether he intended to give a sound and philosophical exposition of its origin. If the former was his motive it certainly succeeded, for the compulsory appropriation of the unearned increment, which was Mr. Mill's project, and the wholesale confiscation of rent, which is the proposal of Mr. George, are avowedly based on the Ricardian doctrine, and, I must confess, if it were true, that it is very difficult, on principle, to refute either one or the other of these extreme suggestions. But let us take the other side of the question, and see whether it is true.

We may conveniently dismiss that part of the Ricardian theory which discovers the different fertility of soils, and that which assumes the enforced application of capital to inferior soils, under the pressure of population. The former was known in the days of Sesostris and Nebuchadnezzar, both of whom understood the difference between the irrigated valleys of the Nile and the Euphrates on the one hand, and the waterless sands on the border of the fertile district. The latter is historically false, and for a reason which I hope to make easily clear. Fertility is not only a relative term, but in many cases a progressive discovery. In agriculture, as in other arts, the waste of one generation, of one condition of experience, is the wealth of another condition, another generation. The history of the industrial arts is full of instances of the utilization of waste products, sometimes so considerable that the principal end of an earlier process becomes subsidiary, and even unimportant, in another state. No better illustration can be given than what can be gathered from the manufacture of gas and coal tar on the one hand, and soda ash on the other.

Again, no one begins a new undertaking with the prospect, nay, as Ricardo says, with the certainty, of scantier remuneration. He always does it in the hope, perhaps the assured prospect, of a higher remuneration. This is the rule of practice in manufacture; it has been the rule in agriculture. The so-called inferior soil in relation to its produce has been found less costly to work, or has had some other attractions than other land which has been longer in cultivation, and has thus, in an economical sense, become, experimentally at least, more fertile. Now that this has been the history of occupancy, I can say with confidence, perhaps with authority, for I have studied the annals of agriculture with no little care, and have come to the conclusion not only that facts are more valuable than theories, but that all true economical theories are, have been, and must be, inductions from facts. It was from facts that Ricardo derived his most valuable inductions as to the financial consequences of an inconvertible paper, and it was on baseless and extravagant theories that two silly people, Vansittart and Lord Stanhope, attempted to assail him, and, if parliamentary majorities are to be considered of any worth, assailed him successfully.

The cardinal error in Ricardo's theory is that rent is derived from the price of agricultural products. One quotation from his theory is conclusive as to this being his view. He alleges that the only check to progressively increasing rents is improvements in the process of agriculture; and in this he is followed by Mill. Now, as a matter of fact, the only cause of improved rent is improvement in agricultural processes. All the increase in agricultural rent from 3s. 6d. an acre, at which the Belvoir estates stood in 1689, to 36s. 8d., at which they stood in 1853, is due to improvements in agriculture, or, to put the matter into economical phrase, to more profit at less cost. Rent is the outcome of profits, not prices. In the days of 3s. 6d. an acre wheat was, on an average, dearer than it now is. In the days when £40 a year was given for the Cockspur Street site, business profits could bear no higher rent. Now they have increased so much that the new lessee sees it to his advantage to give £800 a year. And just the same cause is operative in the rents paid for places of business in Central London. I do not, indeed, allege that all rents have so harmless an origin. I must, as I have said, postpone this part of my subject to another lecture, when I deal with the regulation of rent. At present I am only concerned with its scientific origin. And though I cannot just yet point out to you how great is the difference and how grave are the consequences which are involved in the acceptance of either theory, I may at least claim that the distinction I make is neither merely antiquarian nor merely philosophical. It is of the highest significance in the practice of life. If rent is the outcome of price only, the rent receiver may be looked on, naturally, as a public enemy; if it be the outcome of profit only, it is the interest of the rent receiver to be as anxious about the occupier's profit as he is about his own rent, for with that profit, as he has latterly learned, his rent will rise, and without that profit his rent will tend to zero. I know that he has not learned more than the fact, for he still prates about the unearned increment, and sometimes dreams that he can reclaim protection, and, more foolish still, that his rents would rise if he could get protection.

Fully convinced that the Ricardian hypothesis as to the origin of rent was correct, Mr. Mill strove to secure it for the public, or at least all its future increment. Now he was far too just a man, and far too scrupulous about the rights of property, to counsel the confiscation of that which he believed was the product of scarcity. He certainly held that population had pressed on the means of subsistence, and that in this matter at least the gain of the few was derived from the stint of the many. He also believed, as was natural from his principles, that the growth of rent was inevitable and progressive, and, as is usual with economists who do not study facts, he concluded that the present conditions of human industry and supply were permanent, that it was idle to anticipate that the cost of freight would be materially reduced, and that foreign and distant places would ever come into competition with the home producer. For, as I have often stated, one of the most inveterate vices in merely speculative political economy, is that of believing that the present is the limit of the future, and that in dealing with human industry you may predict existing restraints as enduring hindrances. But they who study the facts contained in the history of human industry are much less confident about what he has named the elastic band.

There was more reason on Mr. Mill's side, in his sinister anticipations as to future supply, than in many other, but similar, predictions. For assuredly there are no commodities which have more of that natural protection which is implied in cost of freight and the use of intermediaries than agricultural produce of all kinds has. Mr. Atkinson gives the cost of freight from the Western States of the Union to Liverpool at 11s. a quarter, even under present conditions of exceedingly, some say ruinously, low freights. Mr. David Wells, one of the acutest of American economists, and for that reason ostracised by his protectionist fellow-countrymen, puts it at 9s. from Chicago. Now fairly good wheat-growing land in England, under proper cultivation, ought to produce four quarters, or thirty-two bushels, an acre. Every acre, then, of such land has in natural protection from 44s. to 36s. an acre, an indirect assistance to farmer and landowner which no other producer enjoys to anything like the same amount. There must be some deeper reason than mere prices to account for the declaration constantly made by British farmers that they cannot cultivate land to advantage, when the American producer is so heavily handicapped in the competition of supply. Perhaps in the course of our analysis we shall be able to come on the cause. You will see at a glance that the remedy is not artificial protection. Those of us who are old enough, now not many, to remember the days of the old Corn Laws, can well recall how incessant, during the existence of the system, was the cry of agricultural distress. It is not found in the end, depend on it, that exceptional profits come from robbing one's neighbours, or indeed that economical intolerance is economical wisdom.

Mr. Mill proposed to buy out the landowners, and so secure the unearned increment to the nation. I did not at that time indeed anticipate that the unearned increment might turn out to be an unexpected decrement, but I had a strong opinion that it was an hypothesis which might very well be baseless. Of course, if I pretended to be wise after the event, I could show how grave an error would have been committed if, fifteen or twenty years ago, the state had been induced to give consols value for the existing interests of the landowners, and how certain it is that the intolerable, the ruinous bargain would have been repudiated, especially if Parliament, as is its wont, had added 10 per cent. to the price as compensation for disturbance. But though I did not foresee what has happened, I should have anticipated its possibility had I known then as much about the history of agricultural rents as I know now.

My objection to the scheme was that, even if it could be proved to be economically advantageous, it would be politically unwise. Had it been carried out, and had the rent of land continued to rise so highly that the liabilities created by the legislation would have been met, with the probable compensation, and the official costs of managing the great national estate been annually cleared, I should still think, or have thought, that the experiment was a huge mistake. A landowner, even the most greedy and covetous of landowners, is, after all, a human being, who would rather be on good than on ill terms with his neighbours, is open in a hundred ways to pressure, and does not dare to outrage public opinion. But in the nature of things, an office has no such feelings. Clerks and surveyors would have far less scruple in selling a man up than the most resolute of landlords. I offer no opinion about the resistance made in Wales to the incidence of the tithe averages. Of course there is a radical difference between a tithe, even under the name of a rent-charge, and a rent. For the tithe rent-charge is leviable on produce, whereas, as I have said, ultimately, if not immediately, a rent is derivable from profits which are in excess of the ordinary rate of profit in agriculture, or in analogous callings. The extraordinary profits of the cultivator may disappear, he may even be working at less than the normal profit, though, if the conditions of agriculture are satisfied, this is unlikely, even if it be not impossible. If, however, it did occur, rent would ultimately disappear altogether. But the tithe rent-charge would not. If the destruction of profit were due to scarcity, *i.e.*, bad seasons, and prices rose without advantage to the cultivator, the tithe rent-charge would rise with them, and production which could not pay a rent would still be liable to tithe, and to an increased tithe. The incidence and the effect of tithe are not altered, though they were modified by the great commutation made more than fifty years ago.

Now in this struggle with the Welsh farmers the clergy and the lay impropriators have been infinitely more considerate than the Ecclesiastical Commissioners are. The loss to the former, especially to the clergy, was far more serious than it could be to the Commission, which possesses, in addition to vast estates in fee, an enormous accumulated fund in consols. But the Commissioners—I am not criticizing them, but only referring to the obvious animus of an official organization—have not only demanded the assistance of the police, and the forces, in order to effectually distrain; but have actually aggregated a further squadron of emergency men—in other words, have vindicated their rights of property by the levy of a private army. The process, I presume, is legal, but it is strangely novel, and, in my humble judgment, dangerous. But what the Ecclesiastical Commission has done with the Welsh tithe rent-charge, a land office would infallibly do with the tenants of the State. I would rather treat with the most greedy private owner than I would with the most considerate of officials. You may baffle the former, you may decline to treat with him if his claims are exorbitant; but with the State as the universal landowner, from whom you cannot escape, who can exact what terms he pleases from your necessities, and will exact them in order to justify the bargain and to get a reputation for shrewdness, the tyranny would be insupportable. I do not dwell on the enormous cost which would be involved in the establishment of an office with such universal duties.

Besides, all governments, even the strongest, are weak, corrupt, and incitably committed to favouritism. Owning but a very limited estate, the Woods and Forests have from time to time perpetrated enormous jobs. Governments depend on influence, and somehow or other, even under the most jealous scrutiny, influence is paid for. What shall we say of the economical prescience which would, in pursuit of a hypothetical and doubtful advantage, create a central monopoly, turn the landowner, who, after all, knows he has duties, however unwise he may be in the performance of them, into the recipient of a quarterly payment at the Bank of England, with the full freedom of transferring his claim to all and sundry, and substituting in his place a government office. An economist and a politician may have very strong opinions about landowners, but for my part I should think an economist worthy of the order of the strait jacket if he gravely wished to substitute a government office for them.

So much for the proposal of Mr. Mill. Mr. George, as you know, goes far beyond him. He would not, indeed, substitute a government office for the landowner, but he would appropriate any scrap of value in the soil, other than that which labour has provably induced upon it, without mercy, without compensation, by the simple operation of taxing it up to its full value, or, as economists say, its fertility. It is no matter to him that one man has invested the savings of a life in agricultural or building land, another in houses put on land, or in any form of labour produced wealth. With Mr. George the former should be confiscated, the latter should be respected. Everything, he alleges, which the individual makes, is, and should be, his own; everything which is due to the bounty of nature is common property, or rather the property of the taxpayers. Mr. George sweeps away all difficulties of detail, neither good or easily soluble. It is enough to say that we do not claim bygone receipts from these anomalous and undeserving owners. The whole of taxation is to be derived from the fertility of land. Then will come, he tells us, the millenium of labour.

The social philosophy of Mr. George differs greatly from that sour and malignant talk which characterizes most of those writings of continental socialists with which I have felt bound to be more or less familiar. I have read the book with not a little pleasure. It is very human. It is very possible that the author has more disciples and devoted followers on this side the Atlantic than he has in his own country. I have met hundreds of people to whom it is a complete economic gospel.

The great charm of "Progress and Poverty" is in the author's profound sympathy with the sorrows of labour and the dominant sincerity of his convictions. Most American economists are cowardly and dishonest. They discuss the labour question and invariably decline to examine into the effects of the American tariff on wages.

From these vices Mr. George is free. He is full of courage, and he never disparages; indeed, so convinced is he, he never thinks of an opponent. He appears to have counted the cost of his social heterodoxy, and to be resigned to it. He is not, when his pen is out of his hand, a competent controversialist. In conversation—I speak from meeting him—he can no more reason than the founder of a modern religion does. He can be baffled by the shallowest sophistries, as I have seen him baffled, when he happened to be in the right. The fact is, his political economy is a creed. He learned it in the struggle with the furious climate and the malignant soil of New England. He believed in it all the more when he cast his lot among the Californian miners. He was convinced of it when he saw the dens in which the workmen of American cities pay for less than the decencies of life. But the kernel of his theory is to be found in the generalities of two English economists, Malthus and Ricardo. The conclusions of the former are crude, and those of the latter—I am speaking of the rent theory only—false. Mr. George repudiates all that Malthus wrote, the germ of birth in his population theory, and is not, I think, very far wrong in the disparaging estimate which he makes of that person's abilities. But he accepts Mr. Ricardo's theory, concludes that the writer has discovered in it the key to all human misery, and credits parliaments and governments, either ignorantly or intentionally, with the machinery by which labour is degraded and beggared. I need hardly say that a man who has a warm and sturdy sympathy with the class from which he sprang is not likely to be nice about remedies when he is convinced of the origin of disease. Opinion, like action, I need hardly tell you, owes much to its surroundings. Of course, even so honest a man as Mr. George is, is not to be excused by his character when he is in the wrong.

Mr. George believes that " rent is the result of price. A number of men, no matter how, have gained possession of the soil in civilized countries, and exact a merciless toll from industry. As long as this system continues the tolls obtained from the monopoly grow, and inevitably absorb all but the bare subsistence of the labourer. Soon they will grind down the legitimate profit of capital to the same beggarly condition, and the favoured idler will appropriate all wealth to himself. There is, to be sure, a remedy. No human authority has a right to give away, in perpetuity, what belongs to society itself, and is essential to the existence of society. The property which the people possess is the mere creation of law. It is not necessary that the law should have been dishonest; it is enough that it is mistaken. The wisdom of the American constitution has declared that even the laws which Congress passes may be revised and annulled by the Supreme Court. The analysis of the social economist proves that the recognition by the State of the sacredness of rent was a mistake. The law of rent, formulated by Ricardo, proves that it is a danger. It is the sole and sufficient cause why the only producers of wealth, the capitalist and the labourer, toil all night and take nothing. Away with it." And Mr. George gets as angry, and I may say as loftily angry, as a Hebrew prophet. He has his followers, and as long as people err about rent he will find his following become a faith, perhaps a crusade.

It seems but a little change to-day. You are wholly wrong. Rent is not the outcome of price, but of profit. I was told the other day that this dictum of mine strengthened George's position, and made it almost unassailable. Let us see.

If rents are the outcome of prices it is difficult to avoid the conclusion that the landowner is, potentially at least, the public enemy, who is to thrive on the misery of his fellow-countrymen, whose gains are to be curtailed by sharp legislation, who is to be reduced from mischief-making to impotence, in pursuance of the inalienable right of every society to protect itself from ruin. If circumstances lend, or seem to lend, themselves to such a result, if landowners have, under a mistaken interpretation of their rights and powers, acted as though they could take all from the occupier beyond the bare means of life, it is clear that intervention is inevitable, as it has recently been asserted to be, on principles, for errors in judgment, fostered by mistaken conceptions of economical relations, may as much need correction by law as deliberate wrongdoing. If, in short, rent is the outcome of prices, the landowner need consider no person's interest but his own, and claim from the State, till the State becomes enlightened and indignant, the literal fulfilment of all contracts which he has imposed upon the unprotected and helpless occupier. Now I am well aware that there is a widespread opinion to the effect that this power of unlimited inaction exists, and that nothing but generosity or fear checks its exercise. I have often been told that no change in our system of local taxation, under which all charges are put on occupiers, will lighten the lot of such persons at all, for that the landowner can at once levy an increased rent fully up to the remission. The statement, indeed, betrays a total ignorance as to the principles which govern the incidence and shifting of taxation, but the opinion on which it is founded is dangerous, because it infers that the position of the landowner is inevitably anti-social and out of harmony with all other interests.

But if it be true that rent is the outcome of profits, and the history of agricultural rent, and even of ground or building rent, is absolutely conclusive on this point, when the economic basis of rent is examined, and irregularities of individual or collective action are checked, as I hope to show that they must be checked, the whole aspect of the situation changes. The landowner takes his place in the general harmony of social interests. If his present and future interests are to be and remain unimpaired, he is profoundly interested in the prosperity of the occupier, because in the success of those who occupy the soil, in which he has ownership, lies the continuity of present, and the prospect of future, rent. He has to consider the advantage of others if he has a care for his own advantage. The sufficiency of his tenant's capital, and vigilant care that that capital may be undiminished by any act of the rent receiver, are subjects on which, in his true interest, he should be nearly as anxious as the tenant himself; for if the landlord's rent absorbs the tenant's capital, the rent verges, as we now know, to extinction. And, beyond doubt, the present condition of British agriculture is due to the absorption of agricultural capital by exorbitant or exhaustive rents, rents which no profits would bear.

The process by which this result has been brought about is perfectly familiar to those who have studied modern agriculture, and has been expounded by such authorities as Sir James Caird, Mr. James Howard, and Mr. Bear, among others. Nor will a revival of agriculture be possible until landowners as a body reverse their policy, and study how to assist the accumulation of agricultural capital by honest contracts with their tenants, as assiduously as too many of them in time past have been induced, to their own ultimate ruin, to reduce and appropriate it.

Rent, then, is all that remains over the average rate of profit derivable from various industries when every other claim is satisfied. Exceptional rates of profit derived from exceptional abilities employed in various industries cannot, until they are diffused (and some of them never can be) among all the competitors in each industry, are not and cannot be, attacked by rent. This is true of agriculture, as it is of manufacture, of trade, of professional capacity. The ingenuity of no landowner can tax the abilities of exceptional inventive power, of exceptional business intelligence, of exceptional professional skill, fertilities as real, as solid, as substantial as any unearned increment or national fertility. To be more correct, we should call it discovered and utilized fertility in land. And, for my part, if one exceptional advantage, discovered and appropriated by an individual, is to be made the subject of legal confiscation, I cannot see why the fertilities of human invention and perseverance should not be subjected logically to the same absorption. Where, indeed, the capacity is so diffused as to be universally acquired, it is possible, under favourable conditions, that the rent receiver may come in for his share. He can obtain it with safety only when every other interest is satisfied.

I do not think rents are more sacred than any other kind of property. If a buyer has made a bad speculation in land, I do not see that he has any more claim to the consideration of society than the purchaser of railway stock, which pays no dividend, or of canal shares and turnpike trusts, obsolete or nearly obsolete forms of property. The State is no more called on to guarantee rents than it is to guarantee dividends. On the contrary, it is perfectly justified in regulating the price demanded for the use of a natural or artificial monopoly. It is no answer to the statement that land is a natural monopoly to say that abundance of it is always in the market, any more than it is an answer to the demand that the monopoly of transit practically enjoyed by railways is, due regard being had to existing and indeed permanent interests to be regulated by law, met by saying that railway stock is freely and abundantly sold on the Stock Exchange. When Selden attacked the theory that tithes were a divine institution, the clergy had him put in prison for his pains. A few years later the Long Parliament began to attack the human institution of tithes, and the clergy took to quoting Selden's book as an authority on behalf of their interests.

But though I do not believe that rent is more sacred than any other kind of property, and hold that it is, and must be, more peculiarly under State control, unless good sense obviates the necessity of State control, a result greatly to be desired, I cannot see how it is less real and less entitled to the protection of the State than any other kind of income-yielding investment is. Let us assume, and this is a large assumption, that the growth of rent has been entirely spontaneous. I happen to know that much is due to the untiring energies of the landowners in the eighteenth century, not as some foolish people say, to their outlay on permanent improvements, but to their diligent study of the art of agriculture, and to the proofs which they afforded to the tenant farmer that the new system was profitable. But let us admit that it is spontaneous, as it must be conceded that the rent of most building sites unquestionably is.

To whom should it go? It cannot, by the general law which governs profits, that other conditions being equal, the tendency of profits is to an equality, remain with the occupier. His profit satisfied, the residual value of what he produces is property. If this is to be treated as his own he becomes, *pro tanto*, a second landlord, and has that which he can sell, still retaining his business profits. I cannot see how it can be made out to belong to him. He has no more created it than the landowner has. Had he created it, a strong case of ownership could be made out on his behalf. But by the terms of the hypothesis he has been in no sense its author. It should belong to the State say Mr. Mill and Mr. George. But is all exceptional fertility to be appropriated by the

State? If so, how can you separate the capacity of land, the discovery and adaptation of which is the result of human intelligence, from any other capacity which gives a new utility and a new value to matter? Is it likely that human intelligence and invention will be stimulated, nay, even continued, if over every effort after industrial improvement the State is to step in and claim the ownership of the resultant value. I have never been able to discover any one who has a better title than the existing owner, of course under equitable and intelligible conditions.

Perhaps some of you have read the story of Frankenstein. The style of the narrative belongs to a past age, and to one of the most unpleasing periods of English writing. But the obvious inference of this story is highly instructive. It describes the results which ensue to those who undertake the reconstruction of society.

III.

CONTRACTS FOR THE USE OF LAND.

The excessive rise in agricultural rents—Two bad arguments—Consolidation of farms—Decline in agricultural enterprise—Irish rackrents—Comparison of English and Irish land systems—Judicial rents —Tenant right—Recent legislation for the United Kingdom—Lord Leicester's lease.

I HAVE, I trust, pointed out to you, in my last lecture, what is the true theory of economic rent; that it is the resultant of an excess of profits over that which satisfies the industrial agent in agriculture, and that it has been, when natural and spontaneous, developed entirely from the progress of improvement in the art of agriculture. So far is it from being the case, as Mr. Ricardo and Mr. Mill have alleged, that improvements in the art arrest rent, that the fact is, these improvements have been the sole cause of natural or economic rent. That this is the truth will be manifest to those who have given themselves any trouble to analyse the causes which have, historically, developed rent. I can discover, beyond the inevitable errors which ensue from the metaphysical treatment of economical topics, nothing which could have led these eminent writers into so mischievous and delusive a theory except the fact that, as long as an agricultural improvement is the sole property of an individual, the exceptional profits which he derives from his exceptional skill cannot, except under an operation which I shall presently describe, and then perhaps only to a limited extent, be appropriated by the landowner under whom he holds. When, in the eighteenth century, Smith and Bakewell made the capital discovery, in the herds of cattle and sheep, that the selection of such stock as laid on meat rapidly, and at the least cost, which came to maturity early, and in the hands of the dealer had the least possible amount of bone and offal, was, or would be, of great profit to the farmer, no landlord, till their skill and system of selection became the common property of all farmers, could appropriate a penny of their exceptional profits. Similarly, though in a less degree, purely agricultural improvements remain the advantage of agriculturists till the knowledge or skill is diffused. When they do become diffused they are the subject, sooner or later, of economic rent, and economic rent is that excess of value over average profit, which comes and always has come from solid agricultural improvement. As I have several times told you, this rent, entirely legitimate as I take it, was in the eighteenth century almost wholly the outcome of the energy and success with which many English landowners adopted the new agriculture, which had been long practised in Holland and Flanders, and instructed the tenants by the fortunate results of the landowners' experiments.

You will not, however, be slow to anticipate that the settlement, by the action of the landowner, of a genuine economic rent demands, on the part of such a landowner or his agent, a thorough acquaintance with the conditions under which alone agriculture can be successfully and permanently carried on. Every man who has anything to hire out, or lend, must understand the business of those who become tenants or borrow. There is an adage that excessive interest implies a bad security, and similarly the offer of a rent from a perfectly free agent, which every well-informed husbandman should know to be impossible without trenching on profits, and ultimately on capital, should be treated as suspicious and declined. It is no use for a landowner to say, "My tenant offered me a rent which I knew the land could not bear, but that is his lookout"; just as it is no use for a banker to say, "My customer offered me interest on a loan, which I know will leave him loss instead of profit in his business." A banker who makes reckless loans at high interest has no one but himself to blame if his advances are lost. A landowner who lets land at impossible rents will have no one but himself to thank if his land is at last thrown on his hands in bad condition, if he finds it ultimately impossible, the process of unwise letting having gone on extensively, to let his land at all, except on ruinous terms, and even if he drags down all rent, that of the prudent and foolish landowner alike, by his unwise acceptance of impossible rents. It is not always prudent to accept an attractive offer in the letting of land, any more than in the investment of savings.

But, it may be asked, why has this widespread misconception of the situation arisen? You evidently intend to imply that, up till recently, landowners have accepted rents which a proper experience or knowledge of the facts would have led them to decline. If they have been lacking in such experience or knowledge, they have employed agents or surveyors, whose business it is to interpret what land could bear, or what tenants with adequate capital could reasonably offer. In the most defensible cases, that is, in those where the extra rent has been pressed on the owner or his agent by competing tenants, there was one natural cause for an error in judgment. It is that, up to about 1874, the rent of agricultural land has been steadily rising. In the twenty years which preceded 1874, as we know from the income-tax returns of farmers' rents, the increase was actually $26\frac{1}{2}$ per cent., and there is reason to believe that, during this period, the area of purely agricultural land has diminished rather than increased, partly owing to the extension of market gardening, partly owing to the growth of towns. Now, such an increase explains, perhaps justifies, the acceptance of rents which in the end the tenant has found it impossible to pay. The calamities which have overtaken the tenant and the landowner might be well disguised under such a competitive increase, which is, after all, in accord, to a very great extent, with economic history. But this statement neither explains the real origin of the situation, nor the causes which have led to the present crisis. Too much rent has been paid, and has been paid, not out of profits, but out of capital ; and this absorption of capital by rent must have been either the outcome of ignorance or of compulsion, or of both. An examination of the circumstances will prove that both these agencies, if one can call ignorance an agent, have been at work with rents, and that these have been far more powerful factors in the result than foreign competition and low prices, and even than the disasters of 1879, which merely gave the final blow to the old system.

A man who carries on any business, especially one like agriculture, which is open to peculiar risks of climate and market, and does not keep accurate accounts, invites ruin. The risk is no doubt lessened when he is to a considerable extent the consumer of his own products. But the British farmer, as a rule, does not in these latter days keep accounts. In the thirteenth and fourteenth centuries such accounts were kept with the most scrupulous accuracy and minuteness, and the consumption of produce on the farm was debited as exactly to the gross receipts of agriculture as the purchases were. So much for the agriculture of England five or six centuries ago. In the eighteenth century, Arthur Young's tours are full of illustrations as to how landowners and farmers could and did take stock annually of their position, and carefully interpreted the gains and losses of the year, or the special crop. But in the present day, a bankrupt farmer is rarely found to have kept an intelligent account of his income and his outgoings. Under such circumstances, it is not wonderful that his capital slowly and insensibly melted away, that his personal expenditure was unreasonable, that he neglected small economies and small profits, that he wasted his substance without knowing it, and that his scale of expense was out of all proportion to his capital and its reasonable profits. For a man may be an excellent and accomplished agriculturist, but be a very bad man of business, and no man can be a worse man of business than he is who utterly neglects a balance sheet of income and expenditure, of profits and losses.

Perhaps the imprudence of the British farmer was greatly stimulated by a fashion which grew up thirty or forty years ago, of consolidating small farms, and building homesteads, which were out of all proportion to the possible capital and income of the occupying tenant. It used, before the agricultural trouble came on, to be commonly said that land was a luxury which none but rich people could indulge in, that it only paid 2, or, at best, 3 per cent. as an investment, and so on. Land was, and, to a great extent, is still, an investment which gives more social consideration and influence than any other kind of property does, and such advantages tend to heighten the price of that to which they are attached. Land in England, too, is peculiarly free from burdens. It pays no probate duty, and a modified succession duty. It is, unlike land in other European countries, liable to only a nominal tax for revenue purposes. The charges which are essential to its having anything but a prairie value are paid by occupiers, and not by owners. Even the tithe, which was commuted fifty years ago at a reduction of 25 per cent to the titheowner, in consideration of the benefits which this personage would obtain by the substitution of a rent-charge in place of feudal tithe, was shifted from the landlord to the occupier. In recent years, too, ancient charges on land have received subventions from imperial taxation. Now, it stands to reason that a property which is so peculiarly favoured should under ordinary circumstances bear an exalted price in the market.

The second argument, confidently and, it seems to me, ignorantly or sophistically alleged, that land pays a low rate of interest on the outlay or purchase money, is easily disposed of. People, indeed, do not say so now. But it will be plain that a security which, till recently, has steadily risen in value, and might probably be reasonably expected to continually rise in value, will bear a price in which the expectations of the future are included. If one capitalist in the days of Queen Anne, invested his savings, amounting to £100,000, in the public funds, and another purchased to the same amount land, each would probably have received some £6,000 a year by his investment. But if the same property is held at the present day, each by the descendant of those ancestors, the former would be receiving £2,500 a year, the other £60,000. It is true that in Anne's age so great a rise in the rent was not anticipated. Had it been, it would have appeared in the price, as the vendor or purchaser anticipated the character and period of the rise. But it was in the knowledge of men at that time that in little more than a hundred years rents had risen twelve times, and it was quite reasonable to conclude that they would continue to rise, however uncertain the process and the period might be to which they would owe their rise, at which the rise could be realized. Now, that such a rise was, till recently, anticipated is plain from Mr. Mill's theory of the unearned increment, and more plain from the passionateness with which this expectation was avowed when the English and Irish Agricultural Holdings Acts were being discussed in Committee. I am disposed to believe that not a few persons regret that they adhered so vehemently to what is, after all, a doubtful hypothesis.

The consolidation of small farms into one or a few of large size was an act of very doubtful wisdom. In the nature of things there is always more competition for moderate-sized holdings than for large ones, for there are always more agricultural capitalists of moderate than of large means. But the temptation to reduce the cost of repairs on many homesteads, after the obligation of these repairs, consequent on the practice of rackrenting became general, by substituting a few new ones in their place, was very strong, and there was a fashion for large farms, not very prudently encouraged by agents. But much more injudicious was the erection of farm buildings, which were out of all proportion to the capital and income of the tenant. There is no greater temptation to extravagance than the occupation of a house whose dimensions, quite apart from the rent, are beyond the means of the tenant. I have known many five-hundred-acre farms on which, at the best of times, the tenant has no more than £5,000 of capital, from which he could not expect a profit of more than 10 per cent. at the best, who has had a house built for him which suggests, encourages, induces an expenditure of £1,000 a year. My friend Lord Ducie informed me a few years ago that one of the greatest troubles which he had with his Oxfordshire estate was in the sumptuous homesteads which his father-in-law had built to five-hundred-acre farms. Unless I am strangely misinformed, the principal cause of the trouble into which one of our colleges has recently fallen, a trouble which induced it to solicit a temporary relief from Convocation, was due to a similar error in judgment. It may be also affecting others, but I have reason to believe that I am quite accurate in this case, for when the consolidation and rebuilding was going on, I expressed my doubts to the Bursar of the time, as to whether his course of action was politic. And I am pretty confident that at the present time—and I could cite many facts in support of my statement—small farmers have done better, and will do better than large ones, and, if for no other reason, because the supervision and personal labour which the former have given to their holdings, are still a considerable part of the capital outlay which they make on the land.

I am far from exonerating the farmer from his share in the catastrophe which has happened. Had he kept proper accounts, he could never have offered such competitive rents as he did offer, he never could have endured the process which I am about to describe. Had he duly informed himself of his position, he never would have lived in the lavish style which was too customary with his class fifteen or twenty years ago, and would never have neglected certain branches of his calling which he has most unwisely dropped. Above all, he could never have been gulled by imaginary remedies or have striven after vain expedients. In many cases, the men who have ruined him have fooled him. At one time they bid him dream that the Legislature will provide for his distresses, by taxing everybody else's food; at another, they encourage him in his demand that the local taxation, which should in part at least be borne by the landlord, must be put on the shoulders of the general public, and that he is to be eased at every one else's cost. But such men, undertaking to advise the farmer, never have the candour to say what is the truth. "We have ruined, have beggared you by impossible rents; we have practised on your ignorance and want of arithmetical knowledge and method, to slily extort from you what you could not possibly pay without trenching on your capital. We have, in our own persons, put before you an example of wanton extravagance of mischievous, and not over-honest waste; and we have bidden you, on one pretext or the other, to imitate us as far as you can in our follies and our vices." They do not say this, but they constantly allege that they are the farmers' friends, when they are, and have been, his most secret and persistent enemies.

The process by which this mischief has been induced is very simple and intelligible. I have mentioned it already in an earlier lecture, but I must recapitulate, perhaps expand, my statement here, because it is the key to the topic which I am handling to-day—the Regulation of Rents. Under the ordinary tenure of agricultural land, the dispossession of a tenant involves an inevitable loss of capital. I have been accustomed to put this at 10 per cent. Sir J. Caird states that it is 15 per cent. Now, if a tenant has the full capital which is needed for adequate cultivation, he will have £10 an acre on or in the land. Let his tenancy be one of 500 acres, and his rent £500, the figures being merely hypothetical. Now, in this case dispossession would mean a loss, however negligent or however careful he may be in keeping accounts, of £500 on my figures, of £750 on Sir James Caird's. Two shillings and sixpence an acre more rent, though it is an increase of 12½ per cent., and might eventually be more ruinous than the loss I have referred to, does not, to men who are slovenly or negligent in keeping accounts, seem so considerable as a 10 per cent. loss at once and at a stroke. Now, I never met any fair or honest person, who knew what the relations of landlord and tenant have been, till the recent breakdown of the system, who hesitated to admit that the single and sufficient cause why the tenant's capital has been extinguished, is the payment of rent out of capital under the process which I have described, and the threat of dispossession if the advance was not conceded, though the practice has been defended on the ground that till recently others would take the land, if the tenant gave it up; and that the owner was justified in exacting a competition rent to the full. But many things are justified which in practice turn out to be exceedingly foolish, and of the follies none is worse than the permanent ruin of an interest for the sake of a temporary gain.

Of course, if the tenant has made beyond the ordinary outlay of a skilful farmer, an outlay which involves irrecoverable loss on dispossession, a further expenditure on improvements of a more or less permanent character, he is still more open to aggression, and still more open to serious loss by the compulsory and penal exaltation of his rent during the period of his tenancy. Now they who study the accounts which Arthur Young gives of the new agriculture in England, just at the close of the third quarter of the eighteenth century, will find that he constantly comments on the courage and enterprise of certain tenant farmers in his day, who, relying on the equity of their landlords, ventured on heavy and serious charges for the improvement of their tenancies. But up to the last quarter of the eighteenth century, landowners knew their business, and would no more have thought of curtailing their tenants' capital by a penal rise of rent than they would of plundering his barn, carrying off his haystacks, or appropriating his sheep. Towards the conclusion of the century, when a worse and a more ignorant spirit sprang up, one hears a very different story. The agricultural reports sent to Young's Board of Agriculture from the various counties are full of complaints as to arbitrary rent-raising on the part of landlords, and the serious detriment which the practice was to the tenant-farmers' capital, and the adequate cultivation of the soil. Now, I am convinced that if the true doctrine of rent had thus been inculcated, viz., that rent is the outcome of agricultural profit, and not of agricultural prices, the unfair and suicidal practice which I have described would never have become customary among landlords.

I have stated before, and I repeat it, that for skill in manipulating land, the British farmer has no compeer. In parts of Normandy, in Belgium, and in the Rhenish Palatinate, there are agriculturists who nearly rival him, but their agriculture suffers from the capital defect of live stock as a rule. But the British agriculturist hardly goes beyond the *cultura annua*. The soil of New England is exceedingly sterile as a rule, but the hedges are full of peach trees. The fruit trees on the Bavarian and Norman farms and by the Belgian homesteads are abundant. But you do not see them in the United Kingdom, for the farmer fears that if he plants he will have to pay an enhanced rent on his own improvements. Fruit culture in England would soon dispense with the nine millions or thereabouts which we are annually paying for the imported fruit which we could easily grow ourselves, if the farmers were protected against uncertain rent. And what may be noticed in England, is still more marked in Ireland. When I was examining last autumn (1887) the agricultural condition of Ulster, and I did so with no common care, I was struck with the all but total absence of all fruit trees about the homesteads, and the exceeding badness of the few apples which appeared in the markets. They dared not cultivate what would be instantly made a plea for exalted rents, and though to some extent the Irish tenant is protected by the law against arbitrary rent raising, bad and timid habits have been formed, and cannot be easily shaken off. I was struck in reading one or two of the excellent handbooks put out by the Irish Education Board, works which would be well in the hands of some of our smaller farmers, how uniformly silent these manuals are about fruit raising. But I shall have a little to say about Ulster land presently.

Now I mentioned above that the rise of farmers' rents during the twenty years 1854–73, was 26½ per cent., and that this figure is arrived at by comparing the assessment of agricultural tenancies, in this case the rents returned at the two dates, and it should be noticed that this return does not include market gardens and nurseries. But it must not be imagined that this increase of rent has been identical in amount under all landlords. I know many considerable landowners who have assured me that the rent of their estates has never been raised during the whole of the above-mentioned term. There are I am glad to say many landowners, especially in England, who have recognized the principle that the tenant must make a reasonable profit before he can pay rent at all, and have steadily worked on this principle, in all their relations with their tenants. They have also been proof against the temptation to accept an impossible rent from an unwise competing tenant, being well assured that such a policy is suicidal in the end. But the people who have taken advantage of the situation, and have unduly and disastrously raised their rents, have not only ruined themselves, but have seriously crippled their innocent neighbours. When the catastrophe and crash came in 1879 and 1880, over 14 per cent. of the farmers became bankrupt, and all were panic-stricken. Now, under such circumstances, the competition for farms was suddenly arrested, and of course farmers are like other men, they offer less and less, as the turn of the market is in their favour. I do not doubt, if the British farmer could have escaped from the loss to which I referred above, and if he had the same facility of turning his capacity and his capital to other callings, the surrender of holdings would have been far more considerable. As it is, the wise and just landowner is punished for the vices of the unjust and unwise landlord, and some of the former have been unmeasured in their condemnation of some among the latter.

A short time ago, a very able, but uncertain, statesman, after warning the British landowners that they would have at an early date to ransom their estates, compared them to the lilies of Scripture, "which toil not, neither do they spin." The word "ransom" no doubt has an ugly sound, for it suggests successful brigandage, and the recovery of liberty and goods only under duress and compulsory payments. But the word may have a harmless sense. Every one who pays taxes may, by no violent stretch of imagination, be said to ransom the residue by surrendering a part of his substance. Now there should be no objection to a landowner paying his legitimate share of taxation, and there is good reason to allege that at present he escapes from this contribution, and that he has used his exceptional position, not only to evade his just liabilities, but to put not a few of his admitted liabilities on the shoulders of other people. To speak of ransom, then, may be an unpleasant form of giving a warning, that at some time or other, perhaps at no remote time, there will be a readjustment of these permanent liabilities.

But I entirely demur to the exactness of the scriptural metaphor. There has been a pretty mischievous activity in many quarters during those fatal twenty years to which I have alluded, the outcome of which has been wholly disastrous. Agents and surveyors have taught some landowners how to appropriate their tenants' capital, by insidious and gradual elevations of what were at the best of times full rack-rents, and the landowners have eagerly applied the lesson. The lilies of the field do not, I believe, appropriate more than can be extracted from intelligent and careful husbandry. The proper metaphor should have been some noxious and spreading weed, which cannot be eradicated, and finally starve the useful plants. There are persons to be found, and to be found in plenty, unhappily, for whom the lilies of the field is far too exaggerated a compliment.

And on the other hand, there are landowners, who labour in the management of their estates as sedulously and as wisely as a merchant or a manufacturer, who give unremitting attention to business, and in their own line are as well informed as any of those whom Mr. George allows to have made out a claim to the property which they have superintended and developed. There are too few such persons, but they do exist, and are not only a boon to those with whom they have to deal, but an example, unhappily not followed, to their more mischievous fellows. I could quote instances which are within my own knowledge, but the selection, like that of their contraries, would be invidious. But this I can say, that were all their fellows like them, the legislative regulation of rents would have been, and would remain, unnecessary, the depression of agriculture would never have occurred, the present sacrifices of rent receivers would never have been had to be made, and the inevitable consequences which ensue, from the stagnation of the most widespread, the most ancient, the most highly perfected, and the most valuable of our home industries would not have been the painful experience which it is at the present time.

The evil of which I complain in Great Britain, the arbitrary and constant exaltation of rack-rents without any consideration of the farmer's profits, has been exhibited with even greater plainness in Ireland, and has demanded a still more searching control from the legislature, a control which has been, owing to the ignorance of the British Parliament as to the Irish situation, too often capricious and unreal. I took myself, as a private member, a very active interest in the Land Act of 1881, but though I had travelled much in Ireland, and had studied its agriculture, particularly in the middle and south of the island, many things escaped my notice, with which I have since become familiar. Now I have been, from my youth up, familiar with land and agriculture. I have studied it since, by ocular survey over no little part of the civilized world. I venture on asserting that, if I viewed it at the proper time, any honest surveyor and I should not differ materially as to the letting value of a farm. With this kind of experience, in 1887, I went through the greater part of Ulster, excepting the County of Donegal, which is practically the same, with some disadvantages of its own, as the barren and congested west of the whole island. I came to the conclusion that average arable land in Ulster was worth about two-thirds of average arable land in England, that for every pound an English farmer should pay, an Irish tenant should pay 13s. 4d.

But I found the Irish rent, even after the Commissioners' reductions, was double the average English rent. I arrived independently at this conclusion, and I found it is confirmed by other observers.

Now I am willing enough to admit that it is a serious thing to interfere in contracts between persons who are *prima facie* competent to enter into them. The satisfaction of contracts, like the creation of them, is an early, difficult, and necessary part of that education which civilization seeks to achieve. So all important is it, that in the early codes of civilized peoples, the fulfilment of contracts was guaranteed with extreme severity, with such severity, that the working of the law was found to imperil the very society which it was intended to conserve. In course of time, it became necessary to affirm that as the forces of society were invited to enforce contracts, it was competent for society, speaking through its laws, to determine what contracts it would enforce, and to what extent it would enforce those contracts which it recognized. I should weary you with the details of this rule of practice. It is sufficient to say that what I have stated is fundamental to the laws of debt and bankruptcy in our own and in all civilized countries.

Now if every landowner was ready to recognize that the cultivator of the soil had a right not only to his existence from that on which he bestows his labour and capital, but to reasonable profits from his calling, and if the policy of all landowners had been that of those wise and just men whose names I might quote, whom I always refer to with the sincerest admiration, there would be no need for the legal regulation of rents. But the practice of many has been different and has been disastrous. If the consequences of this practice had been that of ordinary trade, we might leave the parties alone to the maxim of *caveat emptor*. But it is in the essence of all contracts, that the parties should be on equal terms, and in the tenancy of agricultural land, however numerous other callings are, and however wide is the choice offered to industrial agents, the tenant is from the very beginning of his holding particularly exposed to a compulsory exaltation of his rent, with the alternative of a severe pecuniary loss, unless he yields. Nor is this a complaint of yesterday. You will find it alleged, always with indignation, and frequently with a demand for remedial legislation from the days of Fitzherbert in the beginning of the sixteenth century, to our own time, late in the nineteenth. And besides, apart from the wrong done to the individual, the injury done to society by the appropriation and destruction of agricultural capital is so serious, that nothing but a powerful interest, and a widespread delusion as to the real nature of rent, could have prevented, long since, inquiry into the true relations of landlord and tenant, and a radical change in them, consequent on the interference of law. Nor am I dealing with a mere economical or political abstraction. What I have said was essential has been recognized and acted on in most civilized countries, and must be in all at last. The settlement by law of the relations of landlord and tenant has been adopted in the Scandinavian kingdoms, in Germany, in Holland, in France, though in the latter, I admit, with much suddenness and violence, as you may read, if you come across the volume, with much vividness of description, in Arthur Young's French and Italian tours in the year 1789. A similar reform or modification of long-standing rights was effected in Russia by the late emperor, perhaps, was too long delayed. Now wherever the reform was thorough, and coupled with certain intelligible conditions, it has proved eminently successful.

The legislation of the British Parliament has been of one kind in Ireland, of another in Great Britain. It must be admitted that the cases of the two countries are very different. In Ireland agriculture is almost the sole occupation of the people, and the cultivation of Irish land, as a rule, is by small holdings. The circumstances which have led, and that in comparatively recent times, to the consolidation of farms, have not been present in Ireland. In Great Britain, at least in that part of the island to the south of the Caledonian Canal, there have been infinite varieties of occupation and industry, though these began to be developed after the middle of the eighteenth century, when the country commenced that remarkable, but long delayed, industrial career which has since characterized it. Such new callings depleted the agricultural population by attracting its members into these enterprises. Besides, the experimental agriculture of the eighteenth century needed, or seemed to need, a considerable area for its development. It was, or seemed to be, wise to put farms together in order that the new system should have full play. It must be remembered, too, that the improvement in the art was in its beginning entirely, and in its progress mainly the work of the landowners themselves. It is not, indeed, true, as some persons have confidently alleged, that the permanent improvements of land, as homestead building, systematic drainage, and the like, was entirely the work of the landowners. What they did was to prove by their own example that a bold and experimental agriculture was possible. The agricultural reports returned to Arthur Young at the end of the eighteenth century, and the work of Sir John Sinclair, prove conclusively that in many, very many cases, these permanent improvements were the work of tenants on terms of years, and at moderate rents, and even under annual tenancies, with an honourable understanding. In course of time, when the first great elevation of rents had been effected, *i.e.*, between 1780 and 1810, the principle that the landowner should be answerable for permanent improvements, and the tenant only for good husbandry, the latter often very absurdly restricted, prevailed, and so rapidly does the memory of an earlier state of things pass away, that the division of capital investment in land is now always spoken of as though it was an ancient and traditional arrangement. In point of fact, at various times in English agricultural history, the relations of landlord and tenant have been very different. After the great convulsion of the fourteenth century, as I have more than once mentioned, the policy of the landowners was to induce the tenant to accept a land-and-stock lease, a fact which I first discovered; and in order to encourage the practice, the landowner insured his tenant against excessive losses of stock by disease, and as I have also discovered and shown, the guarantee very often proved to be a very serious loss. In the eighteenth century, the form which the stimulus to the new agriculture took, and the outlay of the tenant's capital on permanent improvements was a long lease on easy terms, and practical guarantees given to an improving tenant, against dispossession, and the inordinate raising of rent. Of course, when the dear times of the thirty years to which I have alluded came, the improvement had been effected, and the exaltation of rents ensued as a thing of course.

Now no such thing happened in Ireland. The English system of agriculture, as it was practised in the thirteenth and fourteenth centuries, was introduced into the early English Pale, for Roger Bigod of Edward I.'s time married one of the co-heiresses of Strongbow, and cultivated his Irish estates on the English model. These estates were principally in Wexford—Mr. Bagnall, in his early history of Ireland, has given what appears to me to be an accurate map of Bigod's estate in Wexford and elsewhere—and the bailiff's accounts are preserved among the rest of the Bigod Rolls in the Record Office. But, as every one knows, the Irish encroached on the Pale, and the early Anglo-Irish settlers readily imitated Irish customs and habits, so readily that the English Parliament denounced capital penalties against the adoption of the Irish dress and customs by the English settlers. I have no doubt that by the time that Henry VIII. attempted the reconquest of Ireland, the greater part of the English Pale had practically become Irish again.

Now you are probably aware that the ancient Irish land license was a peculiar holding in which several estates were only of a temporary character, a change in the occupancy occurring with every change in the numbers of the sept which constituted the joint settlement. Much such a system, according to Mr. Mackenzie Wallace, prevails in the Russian mir, where the headman of the village undertakes to distribute the common land, and has to meet a good deal of resistance and remonstrance from those who are invited to take more of this land than they feel disposed to accept, and with it some definite responsibilities. The system of Irish gavelkind had been denounced as hostile to all improvement, but at the time in which it was formally pronounced to be invalid and illegal by the Irish Bench in 1610, and at the instance of Sir John Davis, no agricultural improvement had been made, not in Ireland only, but in England, for centuries. The motive which induced the decision of law, to which I have referred, was unquestionably that of securing to the new grantees after O'Neill's and Tyrone's rebellion, a more profitable lordship than the ancient custom could have afforded them. During the seventeenth century these grantees put on the Irish tenants as far as possible the severest exactions which the law could enforce, and their position would suggest. The condition to which the Irish tenant was reduced explains the ferocious, but abortive, uprisings of 1642 and 1689.

The improving English landowner of the eighteenth century never appeared in Ireland. He never appeared in Scotland till long after he had finished his beneficent work in England. Swift described the condition of the Irish farmer in the first half of the eighteenth century with considerable plainness, and I well remember quoting passages from his works in the House of Commons during the passage of the Irish Act of 1881, which my audience imagined were taken from some recent writer. Towards the end of the same century, Arthur Young uttered a similarly indignant protest against the condition of the Irish tenant, the oppression and servitude under which he lived, and the extortion to which he was subjected. He was under none of that influence of which his English fellow-subject had experience. He had always been a peasant farmer, or cottier, and towards the close of the eighteenth century, he was encouraged in subdividing his holding, because in this way votes were multiplied for the landlord. The congestion of the Irish mountain districts was the deliberate work of the landowners, and was not due to the recklessness and improvidence of the Irish peasant, as some ill-informed or malignant writers have said. Added to this, every local industry, except the linen-weaving of Ulster, was carefully uprooted by the English Parliament. The system began with the evil days which followed on the Restoration, and was pursued steadily up to the period of Grattan's Parliament, by which time almost the memory of these local industries had disappeared. At the time of the Union, Sir Robert Peel, father of the great minister, and a prosperous cotton-spinner at Bury, expressed his alarm that the inestimable blessings of the Union might have a drawback, in the possible rivalry of the Irish with the Lancashire cotton-spinners.

Now the extinction of every industry in a country, except agriculture (and the English Parliament intended to make the Irish farmer dependent on English manufacturers for everything he needed), puts a precarious tenant into the worst possible position as against his landlord. He is tied to a calling from which there is no escape, and to which there is no alternative. He must take land on any terms, or starve. The situation was so intolerable to the Scotch settlers of Ulster, that they not only began the Irish exodus to the New World, but furnished the most stubborn and resolute of the volunteers to whom the English Government yielded in 1782. But the Union added to the troubles of the Irish farmer in that he was thereafter constrained to pay rent in increasing quantities to increasingly absentee landowners. These people saw in England how English rents had grown. They did not see how thoroughly the English landowners had deserved the increase, and they very naturally, though with no deserts, claimed to be equally fortunate. Now the late Mr. MacCulloch, who I do not remember to have written anything wise, defended the rents of absentee proprietors. He did not see, perhaps could not see, how such a system operates. Its effect is exactly that of a tribute. Now if a victorious general or state can impose a tribute, and the subject country can pay it, it can do so only by offering more of its produce at a less price or profit, in order to cover the balance of its indebtedness, in short, do just as I have described to you in the position of a country whose debt is extensively held out of its own borders. It may be constrained to trench on its capital, in order to meet its liabilities, and become impoverished, without the satisfaction of feeling that it has the smallest equivalent for its fragments, or the poor consolation that it has resisted, and been forced to succumb.

A custom, however, sprang up in Ulster, and in the first place on the estates of the London Companies, whose property had been gradually, and by no means suddenly acquired in consideration of advances which those companies had made in order to meet the pressing wants of the first two Stuart kings. It may have been policy, it may have been generosity, which induced these companies to permit the growth of tenant right, and to set the fashion in Ulster. I am disposed to think, from what I know of these companies in the seventeenth and eighteenth centuries, when they were what they professed to be, organizations of trade, that the latter motive was dominant, though they might have also thought that they were strengthening the Protestant interest. This tenant right, as you are probably aware, became a marketable commodity, and was the subject of much wonder, owing to its being sold at such high rates, even though under rack-rents, which were constantly increased. But, in fact, the tenant right was the price of security against external competition, and the growing feeling that it was morally due to the sitting or present tenant explains in great measure the tenacity with which the Irish cottier has resented any attempt to make his holding the subject of competition among strangers. I have been recently informed that the value of tenant right under the judicial rents is declining.

Now Parliament attempted, though in no serious fashion, to deal with this subject, Irish rack-rents, in the Parliament of 1868. It is a curious illustration of the imperfect acquaintance which English politicians have of the Irish land system, that under the Encumbered Estates Act, a Parliamentary title was actually given to purchasers of the traditional tenant right of Ulster. The legislation of 1881 recognized the joint ownership of landlord and tenant, and created a body of commissioners whose duty it should be to fix judicial rents. In the nature of things, as I ventured on pointing out, these rents would inevitably be, like the fee-farm rents of the Middle Ages, incapable of future exaltation, and in order to obviate the risk of their future depression—a contingency which, in spite of my very imperfect acquaintance at that time with the actual rents paid before the Act, and to be paid after the judicial rent was settled, I saw to be highly probable—I suggested that the principle of the rent-charge should be adopted, and that rents should rise and fall with the price of produce, the averages being taken over short periods. But at that time, and perhaps still, the mischievous belief that rent was due to the price of products irrespective of profits, and that the unearned increment which had been experienced so long was destined to be continuous was still too strong for my proposal that the share of the landlord should be adjusted by the money value of the peasant's produce. Now precisely what I foresaw is come. The rent was made an inelastic money quantity, and, justly or unjustly, the tenants asserted that the valuation was fixed at too high a rate, and that they could not pay it.

I do not here pretend to enter into the very vexed and thorny question of these valuations, still less into the expedients by which

Irish tenants have recently combined to defeat, or at least to lower them. But I may state, and I think with entire accuracy, that a peasant holding will, proportionately to its magnitude, always pay a higher rent to the acre than a large farm. The reason is twofold. In the first place, assuming that the occupier does his best, he is more alive to small economies in cultivation than the larger tenant is, and therefore acre for acre, gets a larger produce, to say nothing of the fact that the actual amount of capital which the tenant expends in labour as well as dressing is proportionately greater than that laid out by the larger farmer. In the next place, the proportion of produce which the small tenant consumes from his holding is much greater than that which the larger one does. On this he saves all the intermediate expenses of carriage, markets, and agents. I shall try to form an estimate of these savings in my next lecture, and I think that I shall be able to give you some striking and conclusive evidence on the subject. Now whether the valuation is too high or not, it cannot be denied that Parliament in regulating the relations of landlord and tenant in Ireland, and to some extent in the Scottish highlands, has made a new departure of a most significant kind, and by implication has condemned in a most emphatic way the principle of competitive rents. One cannot infer that such legislation is final and will not be extended.

In regard to English and Scottish holdings, the Legislature has been far less thorough. It has to a limited extent modified as regards land under the plough the ancient legal maxim *cujus est solum, ejus est usque ad cœlum*, for it has recognized the tenants' property in a limited number of improvements of a more or less permanent kind, and decreed compensation for them, in the event of dispossession. By an Act of Parliament of 1874, the right was recognized in form, but the landlord was allowed to contract himself out of his liabilities, a permissive clause which led, in my opinion, to the most disastrous results. It would have been better to have offered nothing at all than to have offered an illusory guarantee, especially as well-nigh every landowner availed himself of the permissive clause. But during the passage of the second Act, there were many of us who thought that the most deserving kind of tenant, whom we agreed to call the sitting tenant, that is the person whose occupation was continuous and continued, and who was therefore presumably the most competent agriculturist, was entirely unprotected by legislation, since the compensation for an exhausted improvement was claimable only when the tenancy was determined, while no security was given against a penal rise of rent, in the case of a tenant who improved and held on; that, in short, such a tenant might still be compellable to pay an enhanced rent on his own improvements. But our contention was too novel, perhaps too premature, to secure consideration, and since that time very serious and very unexpected incidents have occurred. There has been a panic among landowners and tenants, and unless very marked and substantial concessions are made as to the form of occupancy, I cannot foresee any amendment in the situation.

Of course it is difficult to revive confidence, especially in a class which is very backward and suspicious. It is difficult to recall capital to an industry in which it has been destroyed. It is difficult to suggest with any hope of success, to a class which is peculiarly tenacious of traditional practices, any new departure, even within their own industry. Thus we are told that farmers are unwilling to take leases, even on favourable terms, and with great licenses of cultivation. Again, it is too clear that in the rapid accumulation of English capital there is very little inclination to embark any of this capital in husbandry. Again, we cannot get farmers to adopt the Swiss, Danish, and American system of co-operative cheese and butter making, to attempt fruit culture and market gardening on a sufficiently extended scale, or even to resort to careful poultry breeding and feeding. For example, one of my friends, Lord Sudely, has with singular success undertaken fruit culture and fruit preserving on a very extensive scale. But I do not hear from him that his success has stimulated imitation, even in those counties where no extraordinary tithe is alleged to be a fatal bar to horticultural experiment.

I must, however, bring this lecture to a close. In conclusion, I may invite your attention to Lord Leicester's lease, as I have heard it described. The family of Coke has been distinguished for more than a century and a half for the zeal and perseverance with which it has followed up agricultural improvements, and for the entirely successful and satisfactory relations which it has established between the landlord and his tenants. Now I am told that the principles of Lord Leicester's lease are as follows. The tenant takes a lease for, say, twenty-one years, entire discretion being given him as to the course of cultivation, and as to sales from the land. At the conclusion of a part of the term, the duration of the lease is extended at the pleasure of the tenant, the basis of the new rent being taken from an average of agricultural prices at or about the time of the renewal, so that the rent is continually adjusted, for though prices do not determine profits, they aid usefully in interpreting them. As I have been told, during the term the tenant is allowed a discretion in cultivating his land and selling his produce, but if he elects to run his lease out he is very properly put under restrictions during the last three years of his holding. I am told that the system has operated to the satisfaction of all parties, nor do I doubt that Lord Leicester deals very generously and wisely with his tenants when they undertake permanent improvements of an obvious kind. Now this lease, the particulars of which, as far as my memory goes, I heard from my friend, Mr. James Howard, embodies everything which, in concert with some of my colleagues in the House of Commons, I strove in vain to urge upon Parliament, when the Agricultural Holdings Act was in Committee. But the failures of some people are the successes of others, and I do not doubt that in course of time its natural complement will be added to English and Scotch legislation. But even then, I fear, for reasons already given, the recovery will be slow. The British farmer is more given to illusions than any of his countrymen. Next to him is the ordinary landowner. But this may be confidently alleged, that in matters of high public interest the obligation on Parliament to revise and regulate contracts is measured by the stupidity and wrongdoing of those who enter into and make them.

IV.

LARGE AND SMALL HOLDINGS.

Latifundia Italiæ—Bigod's estate—The enclosures of the sixteenth century—The introduction of the new agriculture—Arthur Young—Scottish farming—The Allotments Act of 1589—The energy of small landholders—Foreign experience—Poor Law and allotments—The Conacre—Modern experiments in allotments and co-operative farming—Summing up.

I KNOW no expression in the whole range of economic history and economic criticism, which has been more misunderstood and misapplied than the famous utterance of Pliny ("Nat. Hist." xviii. 7. 3), "Latifundia perdidere Italiam, jam rus et provincias." This statement has been interpreted to mean that the wreck of ancient agriculture in Italy, to those who admitted the truth, "verum confitentibus," was due to the great estates of the Roman nobles, and that the evil was spreading to the provinces. To be sure, Pliny gives some colour to the popular interpretation by saying that six persons " possessed " half the province of Africa, when Nero put them to death. But in fact, Pliny is not thinking of ownership here, but of occupancies in which the free cultivator of antiquity is crowded out, and agriculture on a large scale was carried on by slaves, of which he justly says, " Coli rura ab ergastulis pessimum est." Pliny was advocating a system of small farms, and even of what we should call peasant proprietors, for he rightly saw that large holdings were ill-cultivated, that agriculture on a large scale is wasteful, and that the expatriation or extinction of an agricultural population is a national loss. And he goes on to tell a story that in old days one C. Furius Cresinus, a freedman, obtained such great crops from his small farm in contrast with those reaped by those of his neighbours, who had very large ones, that he was charged with bewitching their fields, before the ædile. Put on his trial, he could think of no better defence before the tribes than bringing into court his labourers, strong, well-fed, and well-clothed, his stout oxen, his improved implements of husbandry. Then we are told that he said, "This is the witchcraft I use, Romans; but I cannot bring into court and show you my careful study, my pains, my toils." As might have been expected, he was unanimously acquitted. And Pliny observes, agriculture consists not in expenditure, but in judicious labour. And hence the ancients said that the master's eye was the best dressing a farm can get, or, as another alleged, "Agrum fronte oportat colere, non occipitio." You must till your ground with your forehead, not with the back of your head, in which nature puts no eyes, and no useful brains. In dealing with the question as to the distribution of land, one must distinguish between what people are exceedingly apt to confuse—large ownership and large occupancy.

Now England has always been a country of large owners. The consideration under which the ownership was acquired will not in many cases, bear examination. It was often dishonest, violent, discreditable. Estates have been obtained and accumulated from the days of the Conqueror to the days of the Georges—often in Great Britain, oftener in Ireland—by expedients which deserved a very different recompense. They have been extended and protected by artifices which any respectable lawyer would declare to be nefarious and contrary to public policy. They have been encumbered with charges, till the nominal owner is not only disabled from performing his natural duty by his estate, but is become a mere annuitant, who postures as a great proprietor. Now, I believe that there is nothing more demoralizing than for a person to be driven into an affectation of wealth, when he is in secret driven into the mean and furtive tricks of poverty. I am convinced that not a little of the trouble into which British agriculture has been brought, the process of which I described in my last lecture, is due to the devices which bankrupt landowners have adopted to keep up the semblance of wealth when they were reduced to dire shifts, sometimes by their own misconduct, sometimes by the misconduct of those whose debts they have inherited along with a nominal property. A man who is reputed to have £100,000 in consols but has pledged £90,000 of it to his creditors and has spent the proceeds, is possessed in reality of only a modest competence. But the person who has the same nominal estate in land, but whose debts and mortgages have absorbed ninety per cent. of the capital value of his estate, is in a worse condition, especially if he fancies himself bound to air the pretence of being unencumbered.

It is probable that in the thirteenth century great estates were fewer, and were even larger than they now are. With some exceptions, where accumulation has been the policy of a family, a policy which has very often proved disastrous, I think it as likely that in the eighteenth century they were generally as large as they now are. In one year, 1292, I have counted on Roger Bigod's Norfolk and Suffolk estates, thirty-four manors on which this Earl of Norfolk was cultivating land. Besides these he had most likely other properties where he was not carrying on agriculture on his own account, and he also had a considerable Irish estate, which he was cultivating in the English fashion to a great extent. But it by no means follows that the mere fragments of his numerous accounts, which have survived the risks of six centuries and are now safe in the Record Office, represent the whole of the great estate which he surrendered to the king after his quarrel with his brother John, and thereby defeated his brother's title to his estate and dignity. Similar facts might be alleged as to the estates of the Earl of Gloucester, although at that time the machinery for direct alienation was by no means easy to work. There was, however, a very effective process of indirect alienation, in the practice of subinfeudation, which was possible after the statute of *Quia emptores* provided certain forms and conditions were carefully observed.

Now the ownership of land is one thing, its distribution is a totally different thing; and if we take into account the number of persons who had an absolute fixity of tenure under various kinds of rent in the thirteenth century, there never was a time in English history in which land was practically so subdivided, or, in an economical sense so distributed, as in that period and onwards. And the reason is not far to seek. Agriculture in England then, as is the case with agriculture in Ireland now, was the principal occupation of the whole nation. The landless man was a dangerous character then, one on whom his neighbours had no hold, a probable outlaw and brigand. He was as much suspected by the landowners and occupiers as a weaver in the fourteenth century was by the clergy, when a weaver was deemed to be a synonym for a Lollard or a heretic. Every one held land, not the peasant farmer only, but the day labourer; and far into the eighteenth century when landlord cultivation revived, the great proprietor relied largely for his labour on the small farmers about him. Even the artisans held land, as I have found from such building accounts of those early ages as have been preserved. I very much doubt, indeed, whether out of the great towns, any artisan, or for the matter of that, any trader could have safely calculated on continuous business in his calling.

Now, as I have stated more than once, at two well-defined periods of English economical history, the great landowners conferred incalculable benefits on English industry. These periods are from about 1260 to 1350, and from about 1730 to 1780. I do not say that the process was entirely lost after those dates, but it was seriously interrupted, in the first case by the great plague, in the second by the enormous exaltation of agricultural prices at the conclusion of the eighteenth century. But during each epoch as much of the lesson as could be taught was taught. The English farmer learned from the experimental landlord, as for example, Bigod, how to cultivate his land according to the best lights of the time. He applied the teaching thoroughly, he was exceedingly thriving during the great war of succession in the fifteenth century, and out of his prosperity arose that great body of moderate freeholders who were so strangely numerous in the beginning of the seventeenth century, and were absorbed so strangely at its conclusion.

The fourteenth and fifteenth centuries, though the rate of production from land was small, were eminently a period of small occupiers and owners. It was a common practice, at a time when currency was scarce, to pay workmen with occupancies more or less permanent, just as it was common up to the potato famine of 1846 to pay Irish labourers by conacre, *i.e.*, a plot of prepared potato ground. I do not, indeed, mean to imply that the Irish labourer was as well treated in the nineteenth as the English labourer was in the fifteenth century, but merely to point out that a similar cause led to a similar expedient. To be sure the small holding of these by-gone times differed in one particular of great importance from the small holding of later experience. The peasant farmer of the earlier age had the advantage of abundant common pasture. It would have been impossible, in the existing state of the art of agriculture, for short farming to have been practised, except under the condition of abundant common of pasture. Hence any attempt to curtail this right, and to enclose common of pasture gave rise to the most violent discontents. We are expressly told that the formidable insurrection of Ket in Edward VI.'s reign, the turbulence of which cost Norwich its prosperity, the suppression of which, on mild terms, cost Somerset his life, was expressly due to an authorized and arbitrary enclosures. You may read how a fifteenth-century farm was managed in Latimer's sermons, where he describes his father's tenancy, and the occupations of those who were engaged on the land. You may find it in the thirty-first sermon. It is most delightfully bucolic.

It must not be believed that landlord cultivation quite died out, and with it the example of enterprise and educated intelligence. I have found sufficient evidence to prove its continuity, not sufficient, unluckily, to infer as to its character. Thus Battle Abbey, up to the Dissolution, kept the farms in its own hands. Sion kept one. It seems, too, till the home farm of Westminster Abbey (now known as the Covent Garden Estate) was wrested from it by Henry, in order to endow the newly bestowed rank of the Earl of Bedford, was similarly cultivated. But after the Reformation I have found some examples of landlord cultivation. Cranfield, afterwards Earl of Middlesex, and Financial Minister of James I., cultivated his Essex estate. So did D'Ewes, the

Parliamentary Puritan, his in Suffolk. It may be that records of such practice are still existent in old muniment rooms. But in the nature of things, the interest in such old accounts was very transient. "Etiam perierunt ruinæ." After the chaos and orgie of the Restoration, all agricultural industry becomes obscure. Even the literature of the art retrogrades. Worlidge, the authority of the time, is not such a valuable authority as Hartlib.

Gregory King estimates that in his time there were 310,000 small freeholders and farmers. He gives a little under sixty-eight acres of arable and pasture to each family, or a little over twenty-nine acres arable. It would appear, then, that at the close of the seventeenth century, the average size of a holding did not differ materially from that which I have found it stand at in the fifteenth century, and that England was, and remained, a country of small occupiers well into the eighteenth century. The proportion of pasture to arable in this estimate is entirely in accordance with the state of agriculture at the time, for winter roots were practically unknown, and artificial grasses very exceptionally cultivated. Hence there was no real rotation of crops, and little winter feed beyond hay and straw. Nor could a beneficial change, I truly admit, have been expected from these small occupiers. Low as the rents were, they were severe rack-rents, paid with difficulty and the subject of incessant complaint. As I have mentioned before, Gregory King credits the English farmer with the least possible power of saving from his meagre income. I suspect, however, that as he was the principal consumer of his own produce, his condition was more comfortable than King makes out.

I do not as yet know, perhaps I shall never exactly find out, where the new agriculture was first seriously taken up and by whom. It was certainly not known in 1721, the date of Mortimer's Essays on Agriculture, for he knows nothing of it. It certainly was known in 1730, for Lord Lovell, subsequently the first Lord Leicester of the Coke family, practised it. It was known to Tull in 1731, for he describes it, and dwells on its advantages. But, again, it is not clear whether he or Lord Townshend of Raynham, began it. At any rate it was adopted on a large scale in Norfolk, the original home of many a great economical development in England, and of many other developments besides, for it is impossible to limit the direction in which an active intelligence runs when it once takes root. Unfortunately it is possible to destroy a local intelligence, and to blot out the memory of its existence. I could illustrate this extinction of local spirit and local character by many instances. There are foolish and shallow people who talk of their fellow creatures as though they were in a process of continual progress. But this may be in one of as marked retrogression. The theory of continual progress is, I believe, a Teutonic fancy; I trust for the sake of the race that it is a Teutonic reality. The German people has not yet recovered from the Thirty Years' War. They had a great leeway to make up after it, and have not been always wisely guided in the path of progress which has been laid out for them.

The chief feature of the new agriculture was the change which it made in the rotation of crops, in the substitution of roots, especially the turnip for bare fallows, in the careful hoeing and weeding of the root crop, and in the fertilization of the soil by the feeding the root crop by sheep. Not a single stage of this process had to be omitted. There were unhoed and unweeded turnip crops in Lord Lovell's time, and fifty years after, during the travels of Arthur Young. These rubbishy crops were fed by sheep, who got little good from them, and the land less. In Young's days the system of bare fallows was not extinct, and over and over again he denounces the folly of the farmer in language which is not philosophic. But after a few years, and in his later works, for this excellent person had, fortunately, a long period of literary activity and of practical usefulness, the changes which he desired came, not indeed always as he would have wished them, and the English farmer became the model, perhaps the envy of other nations. I know nothing fresher and more genuine than the way in which this honest and serviceable man, wherever he may be, in Irish country houses or Irish hovels, among English squires or English farmers, in the hotels of Paris, in the country seats, in the roturier's homestead, among the nobles of Italy and the meteyer, after listening to Italian operas, and growing fervid over the genius of the dramatist, Alfieri, who ran away with the wife of the young Pretender, loses no opportunity, and carefully chronicles his opportunity of proposing the British toast of "Speed the Plough."

Now it is certain that this passion for experimental agriculture, of which Young was the annalist and the economist, did great, incalculable service to the art. It is satisfactory to note that Young was everywhere recognized as the pioneer of the new system, a praise which, though he was by no means a braggart, he does not disclaim. And though I believe that a great variety of motives induced the landowners of the day to take this new departure, and that all their motives were not of the highest, as indeed a very slight study of eighteenth-century literature would prove, it would be invidious to disparage or vilify the public good which they effected. They certainly doubled the produce from the same area of corn-growing crops, they kept the land in constant activity and in constant heart, and this without pressing unduly on their tenants. They gave the farmers time to learn, and they did learn. In point of fact, the indisposition of these experimental and improving landlords to raise the rents of their sluggish tenants, rouses the wrath of Young, who constantly avers in his tomes, that the new agriculture will never make due progress till it was stimulated by a genuine rack-rent, by which he means a rack-rent which will force the farmer to make the profit which can be made by agriculture. The process by which the tenant farmers' capital is drained away by successive and invidious additions to a rent which is already full, would have roused his sharpest wrath. The man who looked with a forgiving eye on the events which occurred in France during the autumn of 1789 was not likely to have looked favourably on a grasping English landowner, who has striven to save himself from the consequences of his own extravagance and profligacy by slily and surreptitiously appropriating his tenant's capital. But the process of improvement, even under these favourable conditions, went on slowly. Haste, who wrote on agriculture just after the peace of Paris, busies himself with discussing the motives which make the English farmer so unaccountably slow in accepting these demonstrable improvements. But great progress was made between 1763 and 1800.

The progress of Scottish agriculture was much slower and much later. For an agricultural tenant to camp on a landowner's estate for eighteen years, to bring his stock and labourers with him, to build for this term his homestead and shelters, and at the end of the term to entirely clear out, with all his belongings and all his followers, and migrate to some other locality, does not appear to me to promise good husbandry. On the contrary, it seems to account for the exceeding prevalence of gipsy hordes among an otherwise shrewd population, and to explain the sympathy with which these wanderers were viewed. In fact, the system worked detestably. You can read of its worst forms in Hugh Miller's reminiscences, especially when he speaks of the obstinacy with which the Scottish farmers would tie the ploughs to the tails of their horses, and in the despairing efforts of Mr. Triptolemus Yellowby in Scott's "Pirate." The real author of Scottish agriculture was Sir John Sinclair.

That the small occupier profited by the experiences which he gathered from experimental agriculture on the new system, is, I think, clear by the cessation of their complaints against rack-renting, common and bitter enough in the seventeenth century, when, as I have told you, the average rent of arable land was 4s. 6d. an acre at most, and the rise of rents, within seventy years, without, I repeat, these complaints, to more than double the rate at which they previously stood. For the first seventy years too of the eighteenth century the price of some kinds of farm produce, *e.g.*, meat, was stationary, that of butter and cheese rose very slightly, that of wool sensibly, even greatly declined, while the average price of grain was considerably below that at which it stood in the previous century. On the other hand, the price of agricultural labour rose, a proof, if any were needed, that the rate of wages rises and falls with the price of food, only when the labourer is getting the wages of a slave, as indeed he did after these latter days were over. The rents of the eighteenth century, for at least the first three quarters of it, were genuine economic rents, *i.e.*, they were paid by the excess of agricultural profits over normal or average rates of profit.

There were two facts, however, connected with the agricultural system of the eighteenth century on which I must dwell for a short time. In the year 1589 Elizabeth's government passed an Act, under which four acres of land were to be annexed to every new labourer's cottage which was built, and crowding in cottages was prohibited, by inflicting very substantial penalties on owners who permitted more than one family to inhabit the same tenement. This statute, I am persuaded, was one of the many expedients which Elizabeth or her advisers adopted with the hope of staving off what at last became inevitable, the Poor Law of 1601. The Act did not annex these plots to existing cottages, and the preamble of the Act, like the preambles of most Acts of which I have had experience, is misleading, for I assure you that these preambles contain more of what I will venture on describing as Parliamentary hypocrisy than any documents extant, even the most florid circulars of a new gold mine. But as time went on, the Act was operative. As population increased it became a substantial obligation, and at last, for a reason which I shall immediately give, a substantial grievance, which Parliament removed by abrogating the Act early in George III.'s reign. But while it lasted it was a palliative, and, I have little doubt, a substantial palliative to pauperism, especially during the cheap times and higher wages which prevailed for nearly three-quarters of the eighteenth century.

The grievance which was felt arose from the custom of enclosures. As I have stated, enclosures of land were practised early. There is a justification for some of them in very ancient statutes, with which I need not trouble you. But in the reign of Anne enclosures began by private Acts of Parliament, and the volumes of these private Acts, of which we possess a large, but I believe not an exhaustive series in the Bodleian, are crowded with these Acts. Now, under what became a stereotyped system of enclosure, it was not difficult to enclose common fields and common of pasture, as some said at the time, to "steal the common from the goose," but it was difficult to deal with these small holdings annexed to cottages. They were often added by independent owners, who would stand out for their terms before they yielded. Arthur Young complains bitterly of the hindrance which these cottage holdings put in the way of his favourite enclosures, and, sympathetic as he generally is with everybody who cultivates land, great and small, I think that he is a little hard on the peasant, who enjoyed this substantial addition to his wages. So the Act of Elizabeth was repealed. Perhaps it is new to some of you, that the doctrine of three acres and a cow—for near two centuries four—attached to the labourer's cottage, has so respectable an antiquity as an Act of Elizabeth, a date which precedes the creation of any existing dukedom and most peerages.

The consolidation of small farms and the creation of large holdings is comparatively recent. It had scarcely begun a century ago It began with the entire concurrence of the tenant farmer. For a period the time was passed away in which the farmer, in his bitterness at rack-rents and their discouraging effect on him, if he ventured on bold cultivation, used to mutter :

"He that havocks may sit,
He that improves must flit,"

a saying which was current up to the middle of the eighteenth century, and meant that a man who racked his land could stay, while he who cultivated it well would have his rent raised upon him, and be made to pay interest on his improvements, or go. In those days they went. Their descendants have stayed, and have been ruined. Rents were raised on prices, and agricultural distress, even when the artificial famine was created during the great Continental War, was an incessant complaint.

The excuse or defence of consolidation was the opportunity which it gave of developing improvements on a large scale. It was alleged, and with considerable show of reason, that experimental agriculture could not be carried on, except on a large scale and with abundant capital, that labour-saving machines could not be purchased and applied, and that the economies of invention could not be adapted to agriculture, unless an adequate area were given for their use. Another reason, not generally avowed, but certainly effectual, aided in bringing about the change. It was plain that the regular and permanent charges put on the landlord by custom, and generally borne by him, would be lessened. It stands to reason, that if three farms of one hundred acres each could be turned into one of three hundred, far less outlay would be required in buildings and repairs, and this was felt more sensibly, when, under the miserable fiscal system of the United Kingdom, any article which could be used in any of the industrial arts was, visited by heavy excises. But there was another motive. The custom which had hitherto been so common among large landowners, of carrying on experimental agriculture on part of their own estates, and with their own capital, was beginning to decline. This becomes clear from Young's reports, and the condensation of their results with the addition of more recent experience given by Sir John Sinclair.

I cannot see that the possession of land in very large quantities by very few persons is in itself injurious to agriculture, or to agricultural progress. The balance of evidence, gathered from the experiences of the thirteenth and eighteenth centuries, would induce one to believe that in England, at least, it has not been harmful, but the reverse. I cannot, then, merely considering the condition of agriculture, share those alarms and echo that indignation which are customary with many who have analysed the New Domesday. It may be, and in some particulars is, I think, a bad thing, that comparatively few people have an interest in the land of the country, for reasons which I hope to give. I am sure that it is a bad thing that families are protected from the consequence of their own vices by settlements of land, and that it is a worse thing, when profligacy has brought ruin, that such persons as have put themselves into so evil a plight should be further assisted by Private Acts of Parliament settling their estates, and thus invoking the aid of the Legislature to do that which every sound lawyer, every rational economist, and every practical statesman knows to be intrinsically indefensible under the best circumstances, and is wholly without apology in the worst. It is very injurious to the public interest again that a man should have the nominal ownership of land when, by reason of his embarrassments, he cannot possibly do his duty by it, and satisfy Mr. Drummond's famous dictum, that property has its duties as well as its rights. We want a short and thorough remedy for the grave inconvenience of bankrupt landowners, to whose practices much of the trouble which has overtaken agriculture may be traced, by whose attitude the Legislature has had forced upon it the odious but inevitable duty of arbitrating between landlord and tenant, and revising contracts for the use of land. But a wise and prudent landowner, who understands his own duties, and recognizes the right of his tenants, is in my judgment one of the most useful of Englishmen, and I do not grudge if he be the owner of half a million acres, or rejoice if he be reduced to not a hundredth part of that quantity. If all landowners had been like him we should have had no agricultural trouble, no waste of agricultural capital, and none of that widespread distrust which incontestably at this time paralyses the efforts of those who would reconstruct the system of a bitter past. Undoubtedly, too, it is easier to deal, when remedial measures are urgent, with a few than it is with many, and it will be easier still, when some of the nonsense which the worst landowners habitually utter is exposed and repudiated ; and I reiterate, without fear of contradiction, that there is no person who gives more honest and intelligent labour to his calling, and his livelihood which is his rent, than a wise and prudent landowner does. And whatever my opinion may be worth it is, at least, disinterested, for my ownership of English land amounts to less than an acre of it.

That it would be well for social reasons if land were distributed among a larger number of persons I readily allow. In the first place, the present system is invidious. In the next, it is very extensively abused. Now, I believe that the principal strength of communism, the danger which is menacing all society, is in the badness or unwisdom of governments, in the maintenance of unfair and irritating privileges, and the use of the force of legislation in order to confer exceptional advantages on certain classes. Men who are dissatisfied with the machinery which they think they have created, or could at least control, are very apt to become anarchical. They are still more apt when they despair of its justice. Now the particular form of injustice which is at present most keenly felt is that the English law and, till recently in a still more marked degree, the Irish law, allows the landlord to confiscate his tenant's property, under an antiquated maxim of law, which was not just when it was enunciated, and is now flagrantly unfair. Thus it seems to me that a system of perpetual ground rents, such as under the name of chief prevails in the North of England, and of feu in Scotland, should become the only legal lease. I am persuaded that the hope of agricultural restoration in England and Scotland is vain until a similar security is afforded to the agriculturist. Now a qualified or limited ownership, in which the capital rule is preserved, that the limited owner is secure in his own outlay, effects all the good results of a greater distribution of property, the most satisfactory result being that the more people there are in a country who are interested in its prosperity, the more solid and substantial is the resistance which they make to those, who with the best intentions, perhaps, would reconstruct society.

"The magic of property," says Arthur Young, "turns sand into gold. Put a man into a precarious possession," he continues, "and he will turn a garden into a desert; put him into a state in which he can securely anticipate the fruit of his own labours, and he will turn a desert into a garden." The only powers of the soil, as he saw, which are of any value, are eminently destructible, and can be destroyed in a very short time. The indestructible qualities of land are those which make it infertile. If they are wholly indestructible, the land is absolutely barren. A granite rock, a mountain moor, a peasant's holding in Donegal or Galway possess, I regret to say, the indestructible powers of the soil, while the hop lands of Farnham and Kent, the corn of Gowrie and the Lothians have qualities which have been induced by intelligence, and may be extinguished by the absence of that quality, even though the modern Banquo smiles on them, and points to them as his. What Young was thinking of was the improved and guaranteed lease of Flanders, a system of tenure which more than two centuries ago English writers on husbandry pointed to as the model for imitation. By this lease the barren heather of Brabant has been turned into a fertile garden. The process was exceedingly simple. The tenant took a holding say of a hundred acres at a rent for twenty years. The rent was no doubt higher than that which was procurable for the land before he entered on it, for hope raises rent, just as despair at fair dealing depresses it. The tenant was to cultivate it as he pleased, and as he could, and was guaranteed the difference at the conclusion of the term between the developed value of the land and its original rent. In other words, the unearned increment, which is really the tenant's property, was secured to him, instead of being appropriated by the person who has in equity no colourable right to it. The Brabant farmers and the Brabant landowners had too much sense to be gulled by the nonsense which socialists have talked about indestructible fertility. Of course, at the end of the term, if the owner saw proper he resumed possession, and either cultivated the improved holding himself, or made terms with the old tenant, or procured a new one. And I repeat there was a value in the term, analogous to that which the tenant farmer acquired in Ulster, a value which I have been accustomed to call the price of security.

Now, setting aside the personal reasons which may have suggested and brought about the consolidation or aggregation of farms, it may be worth while to inquire whether the benefits which are ordinarily alleged to come from large holdings are not unreal, exaggerated, and unduly claimed for them? In the first place, it is not infrequently the case that in past times, perhaps in present, tenants have been disposed to apply for holdings, to the adequate cultivation of which their capital was entirely insufficient. In my youth, and in my own native place, where there was not for a long time a single tenant farmer, I have seen an analogous evil, with its natural results. I mean the purchase of land with borrowed money, and its cultivation with insufficient means. I well remember one of these yeomen, the nominal owner of near a thousand acres, who was, according to the lights of the time, a capable agriculturist, who was thrifty, almost penurious, but who died a poorer man than he was when he inherited a more modest estate. He had bought, borrowed the greater part of the purchase money, and carried on his agriculture with a stinted and insufficient capital. I imagine that this has been markedly the characteristic during the last twenty years with the tenants who have taken land at competition rents. But I should have thought that if there was one thing which a prudent landowner might insist on knowing, and on which he would be affirmatively advised by an honest agent or surveyor, it would be the amount of capital which an intending tenant proposed expending on his holding. That this knowledge was not obtained, or if obtained was not communicated by the agents to the owners, is plain from the information which I received from one of the largest agents in this district, ten or twelve years ago, that the average capital to the acre, possessed by the tenants of the estates which he administered, was not more than £4, when efficient agriculture requires £10.

It is by no means certain, even if the tenants of large holdings can purchase improved machinery, that smaller ones, as is presumed, will do without them. More than twenty years ago, in my first Irish agricultural tour, I met my friend Mr., now Sir Bernhard Samuelson, at a Limerick hotel. Some of you may know that he is, among other things, an agricultural implement maker. Now he told me that on that day he had learned from his Limerick agent that between forty and fifty of the Limerick farmers, not one of whom held over forty acres of arable land, had bought reaping machines. The arable land in the valley of the Shannon is rich, and yields great crops to good cultivation, but I should think it probable that few English tenant farmers on such holdings would have purchased such expensive machinery. Besides, it is quite possible for small tenants, when they are clearly convinced that the new process is an economy, to hire machines or to purchase them on co-operative principles. When the practice of drilling had by no means superseded that of broad-cast sowing, it was common, as I know, for persons to own drills, and let them out, or do the work for farmers. And drilling is an operation now near two centuries old.

It should always be remembered, too, that, acre for acre, a small occupier, if one considers only his labour and that of his family, expends more capital on his holding than a large one does. The tenant of a ten-acre farm in the better parts of Ireland constantly gives his own labour and that of his family for the whole or the greater part of the year to his land, with the effect that the cultivation is almost that of a garden. Beyond the manure which he collects from his stock, he constantly puts many loads to the acre of peat and lime, or, in some parts, limestone, and with the best effects. It is true, that most of his capital is in his labour, and there are persons who, believing that the economy of labour is the end of agriculture, censure such unremitting toil as he bestows. But I cannot believe that the true end of agriculture is to get a scanty crop at a cheap rate. If I did, a western wheat farm in Iowa, where the cultivator, never appearing except at seed time and harvest, gets some twelve bushels an acre from the prairie, would be the perfection of agriculture. No doubt it is an economical benefit to get any result with the least possible expenditure, but we must not forget that the result is to be the largest possible. Now, if we can trust the agricultural education books put out by the Irish Society, it is possible for a peasant and his family to live plentifully from the produce of, not only a ten-acre farm, but from one of five only. To judge from the columns of questions and answers on agricultural topics, which are found in every Irish paper, even those which popular opinion in England conceives to be entirely and strongly political, the Irish peasant is exceedingly anxious to get the best and most recent agricultural information supplied to him.

The policy which has consolidated farms is by no means an unmixed advantage. The object of a landlord is, I presume, to let his land. But it seems obvious that the competition for large farms, even in the most stirring times, must be less than the competition for those of more moderate size. Some years ago the bursar of one of our colleges began the system of consolidation. I put the question to him whether he could be quite so sure of his tenants under the large-farm system. He was confident, and I was incredulous. It would have been well, as I have been told, for the corporation whose affairs he administered, if he had partaken of my doubts, for I am assured that the experiment has been a costly, almost a ruinous, failure.

There is one feature in moderate farming which is often lost sight of. This is the value of a farmer's own labour. When it is given, and the farmer's own hands are always busy with the work of his farm, I reckon that his own labour on a hundred-acre, or a hundred-and-fifty-acre tenancy is worth at least £100 a year. That of his hands may not be worth to him more than a third as much, but there is all the difference between working for one's own profit, and for that of another. I have been informed by several considerable landowners that there is far less distress and depression among small farmers than there has been among those who cultivate large holdings, and far less reduction of rent. I have already stated, and I must repeat it, that some part of this is due to the fact that the proportion of produce which a small farmer consumes for himself and his family is far greater than that which a large holder consumes, and that this portion of his earnings is hardly mulcted at all by the middle-man. Besides he has a more practical knowledge of what land is worth and capable of than a large farmer has, to say nothing of a multitude of small economies which his neighbour is too negligent or slothful to take advantage of—in the dairy, the poultry yard, and the garden.

There is a good deal of literature about small farming, by which I do not mean labourers' allotments, on which I shall have a word to say presently. A good many years ago, Mr. Samuel Laing gave an exceedingly instructive account about peasant farming in Norway. Mr. Thornton, in his plea for peasant proprietors, incorporated with his own notes of Channel Island farming, what had been written on the subject at the date of his publication, some thirty years ago. Mr. Mill discovered and expatiated on some of the indirect advantages which accrued from the system, and gave the weight of his authority in favour of it. Many persons have commented on the remarkable efficiency of peasant farming in Belgium, from which country, as I was recently informed, the longest and finest flax fibre is regularly imported, to be manipulated at Belfast, and re-exported as yarn. The small farming of Holland and Denmark has also been favourably noticed. I have drawn similar conclusions from the Rhenish Palatinate and Bavaria. Very recently, Mr. Samuel Hoare has examined and reported on the small farms of Denmark. But, on the other hand, M. le Play, and recently Lady Verney, have commented adversely on French peasant farming, mostly as I think from the supposed moral effect which small estates held by poor and struggling cultivators have on their owners and occupiers. The evidence, differences of race, or as I prefer to conclude, differences in the history of their calling, appears to be on the whole conclusive as to the social and economical value of the small system. It is difficult to say what would be its effect if induced on English agricultural life, for of course I am thinking of farms no larger than twenty or thirty acres, mainly, if not entirely, cultivated by the labour of the occupier or owner. They who have commented on the system in England have always insisted that it is more advisable to sell land and rent, than to buy and work it, and point to the gradual extinction of small owners, the low rate of interest on land, and sometimes unwisely enough insist that land is the luxury of the rich. But if the land of the small owners, when bought, goes into a settlement, the gradual extinction is explained. The reasoning invariably compares land as an investment, and land as an instrument, two widely different things; and as regards the low rate of interest on land, that I have already disposed of. For the rest, at the present time, very many people find that land is anything but a luxury.

In some of these countries which have been referred to, what is called peasant proprietorship is in reality market gardening. This is particularly the case in the Channel and the Scilly Islands, where the mildness of the climate brings the produce into an early market, where it can be disposed of at high prices. To some extent this is the case in Belgium, to a larger in parts of France. But this is not peasant agriculture in our sense of the word. But I think that, on the whole, Mr. Mill has not exaggerated the moral education of peasant agriculture, especially when it has the constant experience of larger holdings, and the way in which they are cultivated, though I think he has set too much store on the Malthusian checks which he has detected in them.

In recent times considerable interest, a little action, and not a little unreasonable, perhaps interested, ridicule has been expended on agricultural labourers' allotments. A couple of generations ago, allotments formed part of the regular system of Poor Law relief and management, and just as with the Irish conacre, these allotments were given in lieu of wages, were a kind of agricultural truck system. After the old Poor Law was modified, every part of the older system was attacked almost with ferocity, and the new system was administered with almost brutal severity. Perhaps there has been no lesson which Guardians and the Central Board in London were so slow to learn, as that it was possible to carry out the law with humanity, in deserving cases even with generosity, and even to effect a reduction in the cost of parochial maintenance. The allotments soon went. The philosophers denounced them, sometimes because they were cultivated with the spade, and the farmers were glad to get rid of what they thought was apt to make the poor too independent. Recently the practice has been revived on entirely practical, and by no means on sentimental grounds, by such highly-intelligent and well-informed landowners as Lord Tollemache, and a little legislation of a timid and tentative character has been enacted.

The principal advantages of a decently sized allotment—I should prefer myself the Elizabethan four-acre plot — are twofold. In the first case, it gives the peasant an interest in that form of property which he best understands, and tends to keep alive in him that very various knowledge which a good farm hand always used to possess. In this way it discourages that restlessness and discontent which is now driving him into towns, to swell the numbers of the unemployed. If he held such a plot as I have indicated, and was guaranteed his improvements in it, as the larger farmer is, or should be, I do not doubt that he would not only cultivate it with assiduity and care, but that he would rapidly develop that respect for other people's property which his forefathers had, and he is reputed to have lost. The other reason is, that his labour is of singular value to him. I have often been told by labouring men, who have owned two or three acres or more of land, and have cultivated it with their own hands, that the produce of every day's work which they gave has been worth 10s. to them, not to sell, but for the maintenance of their families. My friend Mr. Tuckwell, who has carried out the system with the greatest success and acceptance on his own living of Stockton near Rugby, makes the more modest estimate of 7s. 6d. a day. In point of fact, these allotments of a reasonable size are the best form of savings bank to an agricultural labourer, and in my opinion should be as warmly encouraged as the benefit society and the clothing club are. Nor does such a small tenure indispose the occupier from working for hire on other people's land. Many of Mr. Tuckwell's tenants are labourers at the gasworks in the neighbourhood, and are certainly not irregular in attending to their normal calling. I understand, too, that the farmers are no longer alarmed at the probable independence of the labourers, for they find that being better fed, they are more worth their wages, and are by no means averse to improving their incomes. But there are and always will be, I presume, prophets of evil, who predict all sorts of mischief when a little generosity and practical good sense are allowed their way. Now I, for my part, never cared much for uninspired prophecy, and in what I have been able to do, never allowed myself to be deterred by it.

More ambitious than the modest system of allotments, the benefits of which would, I am sure, be great, is the attempt to introduce the principles of co-operation into agriculture. One of these co-operative farms has been, I believe, in existence for some time at Arsington; another owed its existence a very few years ago to Mr. Bolton King, and is not far from Leamington; a third is being carried on on an estate in the Berkshire hills, which is the generous gift of Lord Wantage. A few years ago—I believe in 1885—I was invited to attend a meeting in the Westminster Palace Hotel, at which the policy of co-operative farming was advocated, and the gift of Lord Wantage was announced. I have not had the opportunity of examining any of these farms, and of forming a judgment on the character of the undertaking in each or in any case. I see indeed no reason why co-operative production in agriculture with what it involves, should not be even more successful than co-operative production in cotton-spinning and stocking-weaving, though of course reasonable proximity to a market is very important for the sale of agricultural products, and the enterprise may be unduly weighted at its inception by the bad condition of the estate on which the experiment is made; for, as Young says, you cannot give too much for good land, and too little for bad, and of all kinds of bad land, that land has the worst reputation, the cultivation of which has been abandoned because it has been badly cultivated. This, some of you may remember, is Virgil's agricultural desert and despair.

I should conclude, however, that the greatest benefit derivable from a tenancy like this, at least till the land has been thoroughly and efficiently cultivated, would lie in the extent to which the labourers on it can be maintained on the spot from their own produce. The workmen on such a farm should obtain to the full the benefits which come from a well-tilled allotment, and the profit which the farmer secures by his own labour, the banquet of Horace's Sabine husbandman, whom Appius of the Roman Stock Exchange envied, but declined to imitate, professing perhaps to instruct him in the indestructible powers of the soil. I do not indeed doubt that such farmers may in the end do well as dealers, do better than the ordinary tenant farmer has done; but in the beginning it seems to me that it is more important for them to subsist on the land, than to be too eager in selling its produce. But I must venture no farther in discussing an experiment, the process of which I have not witnessed.

To sum up. While I am entirely indifferent as an economist to extended and extensive ownership, when the estate is unencumbered and is judiciously managed, I am quite persuaded that a greatly divided occupancy, under which the tenant, whether flitting or sitting, is secured in his improvements and protected against any rise of rent whatever on his own outlay, is the best hope for the revival of British agriculture. This country is overflowing with capital. Never in its history has it witnessed so low a rate of interest on investments. The outflow is in every direction, colonies, where one can obtain 6 or 7 per cent. on first-class mortgages, and banking overdrafts are charged at the rate of 9 or 10 per cent., as a normal and natural interests, are borrowing on their Government securities at as low a rate as the British Government could raise consols. The annual waste of improvident investments is, I am sure, equal to the revenue of many a European state. But agriculture languishes. We are importing more and more every day, not only of grain, but of minor agricultural products—eggs, poultry, fruit. The natural protection afforded to the products of British agriculture by the cost of ocean freight and land transit, is greater than it is to any product whatever except coal and some mineral ores. The soil has been in past times cultivated to perfection. The skilled British agriculturist has no rival in the civilized world. But the agricultural capital has vanished, and no part of the great store flows in to fill up the void. For this state of things there is and can be but one reason: and that reason is distrust.

V.

MOVEMENTS OF LABOUR.

1. EMIGRATION.

The migration of barbarians—English emigration to Ireland—Virginia—New England—Emigration of the Scotch Highlanders to Canada—Irish emigration—The convict colonies—Australia—The economic aspect of emigration—Emigration of the "unemployed"—American troubles—Colonial loans—Emigration of skilled workmen.

I AM using the words Emigration and Immigration in the two lectures which I design to deliver on the Movements of Labour, in a limited, perhaps in an arbitrary sense. Even if the newcomers settle in a perfectly uninhabited district, such as were the islands of Mauritius and St. Helena, emigration and immigration are only two aspects of the same process, and involve certain results. I intend, therefore, to imply in the former of these words the efflux of population into more or less settled countries, as for instance that from Great Britain into the northern part of the American continent, limiting myself on the present occasion to movements on the part of our own countrymen in the United Kingdom; and by the latter movements on the part of foreigners, in the first place, and to some extent of British and Irish subjects to divers districts of the United Kingdom. You will anticipate that these movements, in so far as they are historically traceable, have had marked economic effects. Again I have used the word "labour" designedly. I am not at present concerned with piratical movements, such as those of Saxons, Danes, or Normans. Nor do I intend to refer, except slightly, to those few colonies of conquest which the British nation has acquired and possesses, meaning by colonies of conquest those in which the ascendency of an earlier civilized occupancy has been superseded, as in Lower Canada, in the state of New York, and at the Cape; nor again to that slight and entirely superficial occupancy by officials and a few capitalists, which has been established in tropical regions, notably the so-called Indian Empire. I say slight and superficial; for I am informed by those who study the origins of the Aryan race, and assign a different, primeval seat nearly every six months, that the present favourite is the shores of the Baltic. It may be the case that in those ancient times on which this instructive speculation is expended, the inhabitants of those almost Arctic regions were able to accommodate themselves to the Indian climate. But the immigrants of a more favourable zone are not capable of such adaptations. It is said, and is not, I believe, contradicted, that in those days at least, the children of Anglo-Indian parents, such children being brought up in India to puberty, are, if married, invariably childless. If this be the fact, and it is capable of every disproof and verification, British India cannot be colonized by persons of British descent.

Nor do I deal with the tempting subject of those great movements of populations which followed on the decline of the military Empire of the West, the occupation of Spain by the Goths, of Gaul by the Franks, of Roman Britain by divers Teutonic tribes, of Italy by the numerous races which descended on it, of the Eastern Empire by the Slavs in what was once Northern Turkey, and now, happily, rent from it, or of the later movements of the Turkish hordes in Asia Minor, Syria, and Eastern Europe. The economical consequences of these movements were prodigious. They entirely changed the face of that part of the world in which they occurred. In Western and Central Europe these events have, though very slowly, led to the formation of powerful states, possessing a high degree of civilization, in the south-east and in the basin of the Mediterranean, they have substituted a revolting savagery for diffused opulence, great intellectual progress, and a remarkable, but peculiar civilization. There were, as you are probably aware, great and prosperous kingdoms in the plains of Mesopotamia, and in Central Asia from prehistoric antiquity till the days of Mohammedan conquests, and even afterwards. In the time of the earlier Roman Empire the three principal seats of learning or education were—I give them in the contemporary writer's order of excellence—Tarsus, Alexandria, and Athens. Northern Africa, from the border of Egypt to the Straits of Gibraltar, was studded with numerous cities, whose record has perished, whose palaces are now for the most part tenanted by savages.

Many of these movements, though comparatively late in recorded history, are really prehistoric. We know more about the invasion of the Cimri and Teutones, about a century before our era, than we do of the battle of Soissons and the defeat of Syagrius, in the fifth century after that era. We know a little, but only a little, from the work of Bede as to the Teutonic conquest of Britain. The settlement of Northern France by Scandinavian rovers is very imperfectly narrated. I conclude that, where it was possible, the movements of the tribes was very like what Cæsar describes in the case of the Helvetii, and what occurred in the centre of Asia Minor at the early immigration of the Gallic tribes, into what was afterwards Galatia. In more modern times we learn something about the movements of Tamerlane, of Ginghis Khan, of the conquest of Northern Hindostan, and of the Tartar or Mongol empire in Russia. I refer to these facts briefly, in order to show that there were movements of races, the effect of which has had a vast and enduring influence on the communities which have been subject to them, an influence which might justly claim the attention of the economist. For the genuine student of economics as well as of political history must search into the past for the interpretation of the present, if he is to save himself from barren logomachies. It would be of great interest and value to dwell on the economical consequences to Europe of these great movements, and on the results which have, in so far as they are traceable, been brought about by this fusion of races.

People predict that in a century hence the English tongue will be the language of the civilized world, an English-speaking race, how collected is very conjectural, will be the dominant force of the future. For the English is by no means assimilative. We have taken our colours from immigrants, but we have only, except within the limits of administrative law and language, given a colour to those with whom we have associated ourselves. No nation in Europe has ever had such power in assimilating foreign elements to itself as the French has. Its occupation of the district about Metz dates from the early part of the sixteenth century, of the part of the Flemish frontier from the later half of the seventeenth, its acquisition of Alsace, Lorraine, and the Strasburg district from the conclusion of the same century. But whatever may be said about the economical loss which has followed on the restoration of Alsace and Lorraine to Germany, in many minds of the inhabitants there is, I think, no doubt, though it is well known that these Teutonic parts of later France were perpetually ridiculed by France proper, and not very generously used in French wars, that they were very completely assimilated. The provinces were, I believe, sincerely attached to the French connection, and were greatly discontented at their severance from what they had come to consider their country. But our efforts in this direction have been exceedingly unsuccessful. We had to make a complete, and under the circumstances a far from creditable, surrender to the Canadian-French some half century ago; our relations with the Dutch inhabitants of the Cape have been strained, and by no means indicative of hopeful statesmanship; and there is a country ever nearer to us, in which the dominant or superior race has had to console itself with the subjective conviction of its own superiority. I should be led into the domain of practical politics if I gave you my reasons for this conspicuous failure, in which, I regret, we stand almost alone among those nations which may be fairly called progressive. There is, indeed, one race kindred to us, which is even more incapable of assimilation than ourselves. This is the North German people, and perhaps you may discover in their characteristics what makes our work, with far larger opportunities and far wider experiences, so difficult and disappointing to us.

With one exception, English emigration is very late. The

exception is that of Ireland. I trust that in time Mr. Bagwell will find it to the purpose to continue his inquiry into the relations of the English pale to the Irish race, for I have rarely read any work which casts more light on the early English settlement in Ireland than Mr. Bagwell's history does. To me it came with peculiar interest, as I had already discovered and briefly commented on, more than a quarter of a century ago, what was the condition of the Anglo-Irish pale, in my examination of the Bigod accounts. Bigod, Earl of Norfolk, had married one of the co-heiresses of Stongbow, had acquired a considerable estate by this marriage in South-east Ireland, and had evidently introduced into his part of the island the English system of land tenure, with its grants on fixed and invariable rents, and its practice of assisting manufactures, fairs, and markets by relieving them of arbitrary exactions. I am convinced, from what I gathered from Bigod's system, that if the action of the English pale had been traditional with the successors of those earlier settlers, Irish trouble would not have been perennial. But the prospect was soon clouded. The most unfortunate invasion of Edward Bruce, the more unfortunate trust which the Irish reposed in this adventurer, his defeat and death, and the final destruction of the Irish levies at Athenry were the beginnings of a new and disastrous epoch. You many remember that the Battle of Athenry, a place some ten or a dozen miles from Galway, occurred in the same year as the Scottish victory at Bannockburn. The late Dr. Arnold was wont to say that Bannockburn was the making of Scotland and Athenry the ruin of Ireland. Like most generalities, neither statement was correct. But Athenry was the beginning of a new Irish policy, the mischief of which the Plantagenet sovereigns foresaw, though owing to the passion which filled them for the conquest of France, they were impotent to check.

I do not intend to lead you through the history of English emigration to Ireland. It was almost extirpated at the end of the fourteenth century, when Richard II. tried to restore the English pale, and gave occasion thereby to a successful revolt against him in England. It might perhaps have been restored, and with the goodwill of the Irish, by Richard, Duke of York, in the middle of the fifteenth century, had not the danger in which Richard stood, or thought he stood, compelled him to return to England, and to make a final struggle against Margaret of Anjou. It was one of the greatest faults in the reign of Edward IV. that he did not make use of his father's popularity for the settlement of Ireland. How attached the Irish were to his family is seen in the assistance which they gave to pretenders in the reign of Henry VII. The situation determined Henry on adopting a special policy in Ireland, the type of which was Poynings Act. Thenceforward the emigration of Englishmen to Ireland was the settlement of adventurers on confiscated estates. The rebellion of the Geraldines and the revolt of O'Neill in the sixteenth century, with the consequent attainders, in which the rights of the proscribed nobles were treated as identical with those of an English traitor, led to enormous changes of property and the extinction of the tribesmen's interests. James distributed Ulster, the forfeiture of O'Neills, mainly among Scotchmen, though he sold much to the wealthier City Companies. Then came the uprising of 1641, its suppression by Cromwell, all the more harsh, because the Parliament had discovered the negotiations of Charles through Glamorgan; the uneasy period of the Restoration; the uprising of 1689, its Parliament, and its retaliatory confiscations; the Battle of the Boyne; the capture of Limerick by Ginkell; the fresh confiscations and the Penal Code, drawn up from beginning to end, by Chancellor Brodrick, who was made a peer for his pains. There is, I believe, no country in Europe, the confiscation of the land in which has been so often repeated as in Ireland. There is none in which the memory of these transactions is so lasting, none in which the assimilation of races has been rendered so hopeless. The earliest experiences of emigration by the English have been by no means encouraging. The emigration from Ireland is by no means to be dissociated from this policy and those events, and is part of economical history, and that of no little significance.

An attempt was made by Raleigh to found a colony in North America. But Raleigh never conceived anything higher than a buccaneering expedition, in which an empire like those of Cortes and Pizarro were to be discovered and conquered. He did not discover in Virginia, as he named his settlement, in honour of the great Queen, the El Dorado of his expectations; but tribes of cunning and ferocious savages, from whom a conquest would extort nothing. Here there was neither Mexico nor Peru. So Raleigh's settlement came to naught, to be revived at a far later period, and his failure was remembered against him at a subsequent part of his career.

The first genuine emigration of Englishmen was that of the Puritans to New England. It was the emigration of discontent at the institutions of the home country, as not a little of our emigration has regularly been. The British constitution and our social institutions are probably very noble; but, oddly enough, despite the assurances of De Lolme and Mr. Justice Blackstone, the English race has been by no means satisfied with them. In old days, they used to rebel and depose unpopular sovereigns; in latter days, they have fled from unappreciated benefits. They failed to recognize the comprehension of Elizabeth, and they entirely resented the change of front, when James abandoned the tenets of the Synod of Dort, and surrendered himself to those of Laud, Andrews, Overall, and the Divine right of kings party. Now, whatever may be thought of the wisdom of Laud and his supporters, I am inclined to think that the new school was more genial and easy than the old discipline of the Episcopal Calvinists. But the Puritans of Laud's time, while they were indignant at being coerced into conformity, and persecuted, were even more indignant at the fact that those who differed from them were not coerced into conformity, and severely put down, or even extirpated. Dissent from the manifest will of God, as announced in the Scriptures, was the most heinous of crimes. This was their major premiss, even more emphatically than it was with their opponents. They then supplied the minor premiss, that they alone were in the right in affirming, what was the manifest will of God, and the syllogism was complete; and what was more important when the opportunity came, it supplied an infallible guide in practical politics.

Some of these men fled to the New World, and founded the New England colonies. The Dutch with similar tenets, but with greater latitude of toleration, had founded there colonies too, in immediate proximity to New England, and no doubt sympathized with the voluntary exiles. Some stayed behind, and in due course manipulated the situation. Some of them, it is said, wished to go, but were prevented. If the story is true, that the intended emigration of Hampden and Cromwell was prevented by an Order in Council at the instance of Laud, the king and his adviser were creating their own Nemesis. The early history of the Puritan colonies is by no means encouraging. They had their bickerings even in the midst of their dangers. They had by no means cast off the persecuting spirit. They shudderingly believed in witchcraft, and they abhorred Anabaptists and Quakers, visiting all with severe, even with capital, penalties. No doubt the Quakers of Fox's day were very offensive and intrusive people. When men are not content in believing in their superior sanctity, but take every opportunity they can to affront the religious convictions of others, to call them men of sin, dumb dogs, and heap on them similar compliments, offence is naturally taken. The Anabaptists, too, were supposed to have immoral proclivities, and to be prone to Communism. So there was a justification, at least in minds of most New Englanders, for the severities with which these sectaries were treated.

The whole of the New World, from the Pacific to the Atlantic, from the territory of Alaska to Cape Horn, was included in Borgia's Bull and Borgia's Grant. It is true that, in ancient times, the Scandinavians had in some fashion settled Greenland; for we are told that the ruin of that region was due to an Arctic cataclysm, which was contemporaneous with the Black Death. But though nominally the overlords of the whole continent, the Spaniards contented themselves with Central America, especially on its western side. Here they found weak races, plentiful plunder, rich mines, and a docile people who could be worked to death in those mines. How bitterly and energetically they resented all intrusion on their conquests is seen in the issue of the unfortunate Darien expedition in 1698, and the war of 1739 undertaken in the interests of the South Sea trade, and the excesses of the Guarda Costas. But Spain never seriously attempted to colonize the eastern coast of North America, nor indeed that of South America; it was not attractive. The district which lies between the St. Lawrence and the Hudson was not favourable to buccaneers. It contains noble harbours and great rivers; but the soil, on the whole, is barren, and the climate extreme, both in winter and summer. The inhabitants were active, treacherous, and bloodthirsty savages, from whom the victor could get no spoils, the vanquished could expect no mercy. The last echoes of the theory of Rousseau, that the savage was more commendable than the civilized man, are I suppose to be found in Cooper's Red Indian novels. The grave of Uncas, the chief of the Mohegans, is still shown at Norwich in Connecticut, for the meeting-place of the Six Nations was in the meadows which lie by the river of that American town. But Uncas, though he was on good terms with the Puritan settlers, was a savage. I was shown the monument which marks the place where this noble of the woods slew the chief of the Nassagansets and devoured him afterwards, as far as he could.

New York, originally New Amsterdam, was settled by the Dutch; New Jersey by the Dutch and Swedes. They fell to England in the first Dutch war after the Restoration. But before and after this event, colonies were planted on the eastern coast in a fashion characteristic of the time, when regulated and joint-stock companies were the fashion. Charters were granted to wealthy adventurers, who found the means for settling the district which they selected. Thus the Calserts, themselves Roman Catholics, founded the Catholic state of Baltimore—though, to the credit of the founder, toleration became the law of that state, or, rather, religious equality from the first. Similarly, Penn was the founder of Philadelphia, and of the great state which goes by his name. This form of colony led to the system of proprietary rights, under which considerable administrative power was secured to the representatives of the founders. Early in the eighteenth century an attempt was twice made in Parliament to extinguish these rights, and twice failed. At last, when the Colonial system was developed, and the regulation of the Colonial trade was deemed to be of the highest importance to British trade, Parliament purchased these rights at the expense of the British taxpayer, and vested the family appointments in the Crown. We are still paying a large annual sum to the heirs of William Penn, of the Duke of Schomberg, and Pulteney Earl of Bath. It is surprising to see how singularly vital those families are who are possessed of perpetual pensions. I have no doubt that, had Parliament granted a perpetual pension to the heirs general of Melchizedec or Sennacherib, claimants on the nation's bounty would still be forthcoming. One would like to know what is the evidence that satisfies the Treasury that its liabilities are enduring.

During the eighteenth century there were two sources of voluntary immigration, if one can call the process by so honest a name. The first was from the Scottish Highlands, the other was from the Irish Protestants. When, after the events of 1745-6, the British Parliament determined to abolish the heritable jurisdictions in Scotland, and so put an end to the system which constantly menaced the peace, Parliament paid these savage chiefs compensation for the loss of that which they ought not in any civilized community to have possessed at all. I know nothing in social history to match the ingratitude with which these chieftains rewarded the clansmen over whom they had ruled. As soon as the men were free they were found to be superfluous, and the Highland clearings began, to be continued to our time. The practice has been defended on the double ground of the rights of property and *laissez faire*. The Scotch judges decided that the clansmen had no rights, and certainly up to the end of the eighteenth century a Scotch judge was a veritable successor to Jefferies and Scroggs, for there was hardly a lord of session whom we should not call infamous, and with perfect propriety. But I have yet to learn that property in land is to be measured by rights only, or that *laissez faire* can be allowed to be dominant in every relation of life, even when the relation is voluntary and necessary.

Many of these Highlanders emigrated to Canada. When I was in the Dominion, I came across, in the neighbourhood of Montreal, villages, all the inhabitants of which had Highland names. But they all spoke French, and no other tongue, and were all sturdy Roman Catholics. On inquiry I found that they were emigrant clansmen, who got their wives among the French Canadians, their descendants adopting the speech and religion of their mothers. I believe that, after the later clearings, Canada was the region to which the expatriated clansmen went. It is a commonplace to say that England is not popular with the Celtic populations of the New World. The people would have been preternaturally forgiving if it had been. For, in the nature of things, the dislike which those feel who think themselves wronged by persons and institutions towards those who have injured them gets transferred to the people who are supposed in a vague way to be responsible for the vices of governments and the maladministration of law.

The Irish emigration of the last century was of a different kind. It was from one point of view as voluntary as that of the Puritan settlers of New England. After the capture of Limerick in 1690, and the total rout of the Irish party, the policy of the victors was to extirpate the Irish religion, or at least to confine it to the peasantry, and to transfer all the power of government which the Irish executive had to the Protestant minority, and even to a section of this, the adherents of the Episcopal Church. Now so keen was the hatred and dread which the whole Protestant population of Ireland entertained towards the Catholics that the Protestant dissenters acquiesced in their own entire exclusion from all political power and the disabilities which the policy of what was called by its authors Protestant ascendency put on them. But in course of time, when the alarm had died away, the disability was felt to be galling, and thousands of the Protestant Irish emigrated to the English Plantations in America, where religious opinion had ceased to be a bar to civil rights. At last, as is well known, the most strenuous advocates of the constitution of 1782 were the disabled Protestants of Ulster, who were the founders of the volunteer movement.

The British Government has only founded colonies of convicts. In the first instance, it is true, these convicts were merely of political origin, though they were none the less reduced to slavery. Cromwell sold hundreds or thousands of his baffled political enemies into the plantations of the New World. I do not know whether any genealogist has traced the descendants of these involuntary exiles and settlers. After the Restoration and Revolution capital penalties inflicted by the sanguinary criminal code of the time were constantly commuted, even at the pleasure of the offender, into exile, the destination of the criminal being the plantations, whither apparently they went as free settlers. I have not found any evidence that the American plantations resented the intrusion of these emigrants. But after the discoveries of Captain Cook, synchronous with the progress of the American War of Independence, Australia was settled, and made the more or less permanent abode of those offenders whom it became intolerable to allow at home. In course of time voluntary emigrants began to settle in that great island, and very speedily, with very good reason, expressed the loudest discontent at the intrusion of this undesirable element into colonial life. In the end, though within living memory, the practice was abandoned, and the English Government has engaged to deal with its own criminal population at home. Some of you may remember the very lively alarm with which the inhabitants of Queensland met a project of the French Government, by which it was proposed that offenders of a certain class, and that the worst, should be transported to a penal settlement which the Australian population considered to be too near their borders.

By far the largest part of the emigrants from the United Kingdom make straight for the United States. This country is the nearest, the widest, and, on the whole, the most attractive. It is said that many of those who emigrate to Canada ultimately settle in the States, for Canada, owing to the length and severity of the winter, can never be densely peopled. In the United States the emigrant finds institutions near enough in character to his own, perhaps with the most objectionable parts of the earlier experience taken away from these institutions. The Government of the Union interposes a considerable time, too, between the immigration of the new-comer and his admission to political rights, so that he is not in the first instance distracted by unfamiliar cries. The United States, too, have an attraction on which I shall have to comment later on, in the civil equality of all its citizens. The American Union recognizes no hereditary rank. It does not even allow its citizens to accept a personal decoration. It has no knights of St. Michael and St. George. The only distinctions which it recognizes are those of military or militia rank, and sensible people who have seen real service, unless they are in the army and navy of the Union, generally drop these distinctions. It also allows the courtesy title of honourable not only to those who are actual members of the legislatures state and federal, and to the principal state officials, but recognizes the retention of the title after the person who has been entitled to it by service goes out of Congress or out of office. My experience of the United States induces me to conclude that Americans, though they do not abuse it, value this equality. You never see a servile American, and rarely meet one who is insolent.

The occupation of Australasia by voluntary emigration has been comparatively slow. Distance no doubt counts for something as a check. Nor do the Colonial governments hold out the same attractions to individual settlers as the United States and Canada do, or did, to agriculturists. There is a tendency, to which these districts lend themselves, towards cattle and sheep farming on a large scale rather than to corn growing and small occupancy. And, though I am aware that the Colonial governments give only a limited usufruct of pasture, yet it is not very easy to reverse a policy and eject an occupant after he has been long in possession; and, if I am not misinformed in the accounts which reach me, there is not a little discontent expressed at the privileges of the squatters. Now I do not understand how this discontent can arise, unless some alarm or dissatisfaction was felt at the duration of the holding. Cattle and sheep farmers, too, who have written on their experiences after their return to the United Kingdom, have expressed themselves very contemptuously about the townsfolk and the colonial democracy. The tone, moreover, of those who have returned, and have settled in the old country, in reference to social questions at home, suggests that they are by no means in sympathy with the institutions under which their wealth has been accumulated. But, on the whole, the vast majority of the emigrants have selected a permanent home for themselves and their descendants, and constantly have relatives and friends in the old country, whom they attract to the new. Perhaps, too, the British colonies of voluntary settlement contain a far larger proportion of colonists of British origin than the United States have, who have attracted a vast number of Germans and Scandinavians, so large a number indeed that Mr. Walker, who had undertaken the census once or twice, told me that the German settlers were rapidly outnumbering the Irish.

But it is time that I should quit the historical, and deal with the present economical aspect of British emigration. And first, what is the principal factor which stimulates emigration? Is it discontent, or is it a spontaneous enterprise? Or is it due to the excessive growth of population? The latter, I think, needs only to be mentioned in order to be dismissed. No doubt if all the British emigrants who have left were still here with us, the country would be, to use a modern phrase, congested. But, in the first place, voluntary emigration is not of the really surplus population, except in the most superficial sense, and in the next the growth of the resident population is far greater in amount than the most liberal estimates of emigration are. The population, in brief, which has grown and not emigrated, is far larger than that which has adopted this expedient.

Discontent is felt at the social or political institutions of the country from which the emigration proceeds. It appears that the earlier movements from England were not stimulated by the former cause of discontent. There is no reason to believe that the settlement of New England was due to dissatisfaction entertained towards the social system of the mother country. The Puritan fathers were not by way of being levellers. That they treated all those who were associated for the purpose of the new settlement with consideration, and recognized the equality of all conditions with greater fulness than could be expected in the old country, is obvious, and must be explained on the ground that the necessity of common defence constrained the acknowledgment of fairly equal rights. In the original settlement of Connecticut the organization of the colony contemplated and practised the assignment of an adequate occupation to all those families who threw in their lot with the colony. I mention this because the Connecticut settlement contrived to keep on good terms with the native tribes, whose headquarters were in the neighbourhood of Norwich, the principal town in the early history of the state, and were therefore more secure against Indian raids than some others were. But the settlers were neither disloyal to the home government, nor disposed to modify the social laws which then ruled in England. The English constitution, as they understood it at the time, was not distasteful to them. The Lords were a powerless body, and remained powerless till the Restoration, when they made attempts, and with considerable success, to vindicate an authority for themselves which their ancestors in the days of the Tudors and early Stuarts would never have dared to claim. The House of Commons was in their eyes the perpetual check to arbitrary power, and a proper model for imitation, not as they afterwards found it, or believed that they found it, a selfish and oppressive oligarchy.

Their discontent was with the administration. They believed that the ecclesiastical favourites of the Crown were bent on reversing the tenets on which the true Reformation was founded. The administration of Elizabeth, though it was harsh and oppressive, inclined to the discipline of Geneva, and whatever it might do at home, by no means repudiated fellowship with the numerous sects of the Reformation. For a time the Stuart policy was in accord with the Synod of Dort and the discipline of Abbot. But a new party made itself acceptable in the end to James, not so much it appears by reason of its ecclesiastical theories, as by its profound deference to the royal authority and prerogative. The school of Andrews and Laud exalted the royal office above all criticism, and in return James and Charles permitted the representatives of the school to put their theories of Church government into practice. It was against these theories that the Puritans revolted, from this administration that some of them fled. And as might be expected, when they emigrated and settled in Massachusetts Bay, they claimed authority for themselves and their organization, and denied it to those who dissented from them. But in the nature of things they did not detect danger to their political system in nonconformity, as the English administrations did, but an affront to their religious organization. New England became, therefore, a place of refuge to those Englishmen to whom the repressive legislation of the Stuarts, helped by the hatred of the country party towards the memories of the Protectorate, became intolerable. For it is noteworthy that hostility to the principles of the Great Rebellion, as it was called, long survived the existence of the political and ecclesiastical tenets which gave occasion to it.

The eighteenth century was an age of scepticism, for in it principles of government in Church and State were freely discussed, and, as is generally the case, the most strenuous advocates of administrative authority were most contemptuous towards ecclesiastical pretensions. I do not know that the situation has been better described by any one than by Swift. "I have observed," he says, " with what insolence and haughtiness some lords of the High Church party treated all clergymen, whatsoever, though this was sufficiently recompensed by their professions of zeal to the Church, and I had likewise observed how the Whig lords took an entirely contrary measure ; treated the persons of particular clergymen with great courtesy, but showed much ill-will and contempt for the order in general." Now what Swift had noted at the time when Anne, in 1710, made the changes in her ministry which seemed so ominously dangerous, characterized the policy of those two historical parties during the whole century, and may be even noted now. But during this century the rights of property, especially of landed property, were strained to the uttermost, and the former cause of discontent, and with it of emigration, became dominant, being especially powerful, as might be expected, in Ireland, where it operated first on the Protestant population of Ulster, and later on, in a still more marked manner, on the Catholic population of the other three provinces. I shall attempt to point out later on in this lecture what are the consequences of this emigration of discontent in the relations of the colony to the country of its origin, provided the memory of the causes is kept alive.

The voluntary emigration of colonists who are merely anxious to better themselves in their own way of life is of far more recent date. It has been in the largest degree to the United States. Men who are resolved to trying whether they can mend their fortunes by emigration, are troubled by no scruples of loyalty towards their place of birth, and as we all know, the judge-made dictum, " Nemo potest exerere patriam," broke down hopelessly in practice before it was repealed in fact. Now nearness to places which are equally desirable as settlements in other respects is naturally a determining cause of choice. But the readiness with which political and social institutions accommodate themselves as conditions to the intending emigrant is even more attractive. The settler in the American Union at once, and permanently, escapes from the range of privileged classes and privileged institutions. I will not assert that he gains more social freedom. I am disposed to believe that he finds that the authority of custom is quite as rigorous and inquisitorial as that of privilege is, especially when privilege being challenged and criticized, is constrained to content itself with protests against these innovations, and predictions as to their consequences. But he is liberated from all appearance of them, and becomes a more ardent advocate of the system which he has adopted than they are who have been born to the situation.

The emigration to our colonies of occupation, as opposed to the colonies of conquest was seriously crippled in the early days of the colony, by the support which the home government gave to land jobbing by privileged companies or associations on a large scale. The rights claimed in Upper Canada by these adventurers were not only a hindrance to emigration, but a powerful cause of that discontent which found its issue in the rebellion of Lower Canada. Similar associations were formed in Australia and New Zealand, and men otherwise respectable, practised expedients for their personal advantage which were highly injurious to emigration. In course of time the system entirely broke down. The Colony declined to submit its fortunes to these non-resident proprietors, or permit its energies to be cramped by them. After a struggle, the Colonial Office surrendered the whole disposition of Colonial land to Colonial administration, and with it all dependence on the central government, or mother country, and association with it for any practical purpose. With much more reason, Colonial governments have resented or resisted any attempt to make them the receptacle of the criminal, or even of the pauper classes of the Old World. ¡The United States Government searches very effectually into the motives and the resources of those who design to settle within its borders, and apparently designs an emigration tax of $5. It cannot to be sure exclude all undesirable immigrants, though it has adopted very successful restraints on Mongol immigration, for some reasons among others, which cannot be very conveniently explained. But it has, or professes to have, not a little trouble with some of those whose coming it does not check. It used to be said that the Irish emigration was distasteful to it. Latterly it has had to deal somewhat rigorously with German Socialism. And perhaps there is no little political difficulty created for every possible administration which may be formed in the American Union from the antipathies which

European emigrants feel towards the governments which they have abandoned.

Irishmen fly from the Irish land system ; Germans from the conscription and from the incessant meddlesomeness of the German Government. They carry with them an intense and wrathful animosity, which seeks its own occasions of vexing the institutions which they have repudiated. Now these facts have of course their political causes, and are open to political criticism. With these, as an economist, I have nothing to do. But it would be idle to doubt that the sentiments to which I refer have their effect on the economical relations which subsist between the emigrant and the countries which he has repudiated and has adopted. It is, of course, too, that trade is but little affected by international enmities. The dealer is indifferent to the origin of that in which he trades. But the politician is not so indifferent, even if, as is not invariably the case, he does not condescend to the common tricks of his calling. Now it cannot, I think, be doubted that much of the appeal to American patriotism which is notoriously uttered on behalf of American protection is founded on the enduring animosities which have been nurtured for a century in the minds of Americans, and are readily caught at by emigrants, who have grievances of their own to avenge or to ventilate. Men who have experience of affairs know that international trade smooths away asperities, and with equal clearness, they who wish to keep up international asperities know that the vitality of such sentiments is assisted by hindrances put on international trade.

In most of our Colonies, as I have shown to you before, the administration has borrowed largely from the savings of British wealth. To borrow in the colony would have been ruinous and slow. In order to develop the country, as the process is called, it has been found expedient to appeal to British capitalists, and to offer a Government guarantee for advances on public works. The appeal has been greatly successful. The Colonies have borrowed at low rates, sometimes over-hastily and unwisely, and have given an emphatic negative to the dictum of that past generation of economists, which alleged that there is a close relation between the interest of public securities and the discount on mercantile securities, a rule which is true only when the loans are made in the same market and substantially from the same fund; and not even always true, under these conditions, as is plain from the price of American Government securities, and the ordinary rate of bankers' discounts and loans on mortgage in the union. But it is probable that British capitalists have lent more money to American projectors than they have to Colonial Governments, and that, not only without the shadow of a guarantee, but under the worst system conceivable. Of this system, our Canadian colonists have shown themselves accomplished imitators, and I doubt whether the most thoroughly watered of the American railways has been manipulated more scandalously than the Grand Trunk of Canada has been, or been supported by British investors more unwisely.

I am ready enough to admit, then, that most of our Colonies have entered into obligations which require on their part the continuance of friendly, even of deferential relations, on the part of the settlers, for they may be trusted to see how all-important is the maintenance of their public credit. They wish, as recent experience informs us, to give these securities so high a sanction, as to allow the investment of trusts in them, the trustee being indemnified I presume, if, by any untoward accident, the value of the security should seriously decline. But I very much doubt whether this enforced amity and deference would be strong enough to resist an antipathy. The refusal of the Queensland Government, one which more than any other Australian colony, relies on the Colonial Office for the support of its foreign policy, and its relations to the Colonial experiments of Germany and France, to accept as its governor a nominee of the Colonial Office is sufficiently ominous. It is perfectly well known that this refusal was based on a dislike to the antecedents of the nominee, expressed pretty loudly to the government in possession, and the Opposition in expectancy. It is also plain from which of the nationalities contained in the Colony that opposition sprang, and the whole facts show that the social system, and the domestic policy of the mother country, are examined with a keen, perhaps an unfriendly interest, by those who are able to make an administration reflect their views. Now I have referred to this case, not to utter any judgment on either social system or policy, but to illustrate what I said before. But in the interpretation of the relations which subsist between emigrants and the country of their origin, an important element in the anticipation of economical harmony exists, and has to be duly estimated in the emigration of discontent.

It seems at first sight that all emigration must relieve the excess of population. It is plain that they who remain are all the fewer by reason of those who go. But the facts do not admit of so easy a solution. It is necessary first to determine in what direction the excess of population is to be discovered and relieved. In the next, it is a question of great importance to decide whether, however much the individual is benefited by emigration, the community is not weakened. But the interpretation of the first question is one which requires a knowledge as to what are and what are not the industrial forces of society ; of the second, what is the proportion in which the various industrial agents in a community must stand to each other, in order to bring about a due harmony of interests ? Now it would not be possible, except after a very exhaustive search into the facts of each case, to arrive at definite conclusions on the subject. The most which we can do at present is to enunciate some general principles and to examine a few crucial instances.

We shall not now need to be told that the industrial progress of a country depends upon an adequate supply of competent labour, and upon a similarly adequate supply of industrial capital. In each, especially in the latter, there is always a margin over, on which a draft can be made for occasions of extraordinary demand. Hence all accumulations of capital employed for foreign investment are not, except very indirectly, and as subsidiary to exchange, elements of national wealth. Again, the industry which strengthens and remunerates all is that which leaves the narrowest margin of idlers or parasites, or, in economic language, of waste producers in the economic census. Nations are not richer, as Mr. Mill insists, by what they spend, but by what they save, meaning by spend, what is consumed without any addition, direct or indirect, to the productive resources of a community. Furthermore, as these non-industrial classes increase, and the share which they appropriate from the annual produce of capital and labour becomes greater, the more unsatisfactory does the condition of the bulk of really industrial agents become. I have thought it necessary indeed to protest against the narrow metaphysics which seeks to define unproductive labour and its inevitable concomitant consumption, and have included under productive labourers all who contribute direct or indirectly, but provably to the industrial energies of economic existence. It may be, for instance, ignorance on my part, but I cannot discover the slightest or smallest economic advantage from horse racing, and its indirect mischiefs are of the gravest and most menacing kind. It will not therefore be difficult to discover in what quarters we should seek for the excess of population, which emigration would conveniently carry off. But this excess is what other communities, who might welcome emigrants, would not have at any price, or could not maintain, even if such persons were willing to go. In new, progressive, and, as far as individuals are concerned, wealthy communities, there is no place for any unproductive persons, and only for certain productive ones. They who encourage emigration to our colonies tell us very plainly whom they want, and whom they do not want ; and it is plain, they do not want those whom we could well spare, and they do want those whom we can ill afford to spare. In effect, they do no want to obtain the unemployed, but the employed, at least, in certain well-defined directions. The more precise they are, the more exactly do they claim from the countries of emigration the very persons who are most useful to the country of their origin.

A community, then, is none the better for losing its ablest, most energetic, and most enterprising workers, however much they may be bettered by the change. Our forefathers saw this when under the old labour statutes, repealed in 1825, they sternly prohibited the emigration of artisans and skilled workmen. In these times of course they cannot be detained against their will. But there is no small reason in detaining them with their will. It is impossible that any rational and thinking person should conclude that an emigration which carries all the best stocks and all the best workmen off, and leaves the idler, the tramp, the pauper, the shiftless, the worthless, and the criminal behind, is a benefit to a community which is continually depleted of its best hands, and is compelled to witness and put up with an increasingly valueless residuum. I have never pretended to look with satisfaction on the emigration of the best British workmen, and the retention of the least valuable element in our social system. I do not know whether the wisdom of Parliament will hereafter strive to make their native country the most attractive home to the best hands which we possess; but I am quite sure that it would be worth while to try the experiment, and equally sure that it has not been attempted as yet.

There is, however, yet another consideration. The material progress of a country depends on the harmony, and, if I may use the expression, the equation of all interests, the most obvious test of the success being found in the prosperity of the home trade. If obstacles are removed, the harmony and equation are developed spontaneously. If a great injury, owing to selfishness, folly, and indifference on the part of a government, is inflicted on a capital industry, the effect will be manifested in a depression of the home trade. I do not doubt that nine-tenths of the trouble which has been endemic in Great Britain during the last nine years or thereabouts, is due to the calamities which have overtaken British agriculture, calamities which will not be cured by the attempt to establish artificial prices, but by an entire remodelling of the mischievous law of landlord and tenant, under which the owner is enabled to appropriate the occupiers' property or improvements. If contracts had been entered into wisely and justly, the state would have no need to interfere. But until we repudiate the judge-made dictum, "cujus est solum, ejus est usque ad cœlum," and according to the latest gloss, "usque ad centrum terræ," there is no hope of agricultural restoration. Sooner or later, the *bonâ fide*, manifest, and accessible improvements of an occupier will have to be recognized as his property, the reality and permanence of which no contract, other than that of bargain and sale, should be allowed to negative. All civil communities have recognized that there are contracts which must not be enforced, and the contract for the occupancy of land, in which the owner of the soil is empowered to plunder the tenant at the completion of his occupancy, is one of those contracts. It is, I submit, expedient to render the country of their birth attractive to the best elements in British industry, and I can conceive nothing which renders it more unattractive than to inform, in the most practical way, these people that they are tenants at will, under an arrangement in which they are sure to lose.

To all appearance the most obvious case in which emigration would be a benefit is the relief of those congested agricultural districts of Ireland, in which the holdings are so small, that even on the smallest rent the occupier finds it difficult, with the most unsparing industry, to get an adequate subsistence from his tenancy. I have seen such tenancies by hundreds, and I can allege, that there is no more baseless calumny than that which charges the Irish cottier with laziness or unwillingness to work. But it is not a light thing to expatriate a man, especially in a country where the passionate devotion of the inhabitant to his native soil is as real as it is inexplicable to the ordinary observer. It is not a wise thing to expatriate him, when he nourishes, even in the midst of an infinitely better condition of things, a deep and abiding animosity against the government which has exiled him, and the race which has condoned the injury. His feeling may be irrational, but it is very clear and very lasting. Now the true statesman does not seek to force his remedies on the unwilling ; he studies their case, and soothes them instead of irritating them. Hence it has been suggested, and as I think with wisdom, that a system of migration cautiously encouraged, and, under the circumstances, safeguarded in Ireland, would be a better remedy than emigration. No one can say that, with a population which is not more than half what it was forty years ago, Ireland is over densely peopled. Nor do I doubt that in time, and under conditions of hope, and perhaps of consideration, the industries which were violently suppressed in Ireland more than a century ago will be revived and flourished. It was noted, at the time of the union, that Ireland was singularly well adapted by nature for the cloth industry. I know that it is far easier to destroy than to renew, but of all the silly calumnies which can be uttered, none is more silly than that of denying to a race, which has contrived to maintain its vitality, the power of recuperating its industries.

VI.

MOVEMENTS OF LABOUR.

II. IMMIGRATION.

"The true-born Englishman"—The foreign merchant—The preservation of peace on the highway—Speaker Tresham—Immigration of the Flemings in the fourteenth and sixteenth centuries—Immigration of the Huguenots—Alien laws—Naturalization Act—Pauper immigration from Russia and Germany—Movement of agricultural labour to the towns.

DEFOE, a pamphleteer, who was ready to take a brief, properly marked, from any side, was, I believe, the first person who called attention to the particularly mixed origin of what we call the English race. He referred, it is true, to the immigration of Roman, Saxon, Dane, and Norman, and hinted that it be very difficult to find that true-born Englishman, after whom certain so-called patriots were said to be in search. But I am not concerned to-day with the immigration of military adventurers, such as were the several races who dominated more or less entirely over weaker races. As might be expected, the most inviting parts of the British Isles, or, to be more exact, the three kingdoms, were the most liable to these raids. The purest aboriginal blood, I presume is that of the mountainous districts of England, Scotland, and Ireland, and in each case, the western district. But the pedigree of the more attractive regions is made up from many successive arrivals. Of those parts of the kingdoms where early settlements were made, Southern and Eastern Scotland is, I conclude, most free from later admixtures. The Scottish Lowlands appear to be inhabited by a Teutonic race, which has been little affected by foreign immigration. It was in this part of the island that the Saxon element made a resolute stand, and in spite of the efforts made by the Norman and Angevin kings, assured itself of its independence at Bannockburn. In the same year the Irish suffered the final and fatal defeat of Athenry. When last summer I was at this little town no one knew the place where that battle was fought which extinguished Irish independence.

I am concerned with what I may call economic immigration, *i.e.*, the arrival of strangers, either as artisans or merchants, for industrial purposes. But we should understand that the attractiveness of a region to settlers depends on conditions which may vary as time goes on. There is no doubt that in early times the eastern district of England, *i.e.*, the counties which lie between the Thames on the south and the Wash on the north, were very speedily, after the Conquest, the part which foreign immigrants chiefly sought. At this time extensive forests occupied a large part of Central England. But apart from the insecurity which nearness to these forests involved, it is well known that wooded districts are liable to rainfalls which are often heavy and inconvenient. Even now the lowest rainfall in England is on the south-eastern side, and excessive rain was the principal peril of agriculture in the Middle Ages, as indeed it now is.

They who write about the life of Mediæval England are exceedingly apt to confuse the peace as kept in parish and manor, and the peace as kept on the king's highway. I have no doubt that the former was very effectively maintained, the latter most precariously enforced. Everything was done to secure an efficient discipline in the place of a man's own home. The inhabitants were registered and the presence of strangers was suspicious, and in the householder who harboured them, culpable. Of course, an English village in the Middle Ages, before the magistrates superseded the parish authorities, was not an Elysium. There were people who broke the peace, there were alehouse keepers who cheated their customers, millers who took excessive toll, traders who had false weights and measures, common carriers, who strove to avoid their liability as bailees under an implied or special contract. But it is certain that very effectual means were taken for discovering, presenting, and chastising these offences. The manor courts did not, as a rule, take cognisance of other than petty misconduct. But the inhabitants were interested in the peace being kept. The lord, who acted through his steward, was willing to improve his income by the fines levied on ill-doers. But if the fine were excessive, its object would be defeated ; and it does not seem that the police of the manor court would or could lend itself to private spite. Moreover in the many thousands of accounts which I have read for my researches, it has been very rarely the case that I have noted thefts of farm produce, though the bailiffs' rolls register and account for every gallon of corn, every chicken, every egg.

But the case was quite different outside the boundaries of parish and manor, and on the king's highway. Laws, as any student of the historical life of Englishmen knows, were enacted indeed, but very imperfectly enforced. Even the great jurist Coke, as late as the seventeenth century, affirms that statute law is of no significance, unless it expound, enforce, or supplement the common law. Statutes were broken or neglected, and there was no adequate security for chastising offenders, no police organization whatever beyond that of the parish. Then there were men and women, too, who were made outlaws. The natural resource of such persons was brigandage, and as long as they preyed on the high-road, and did not harry the villagers, their depredations excited no anger in the minds of the villagers, if indeed they did not evoke active sympathy. Travelling merchants, especially foreigners, were plundered occasionally, and little heed was taken of their losses. When the monasteries became unpopular, the fact that a rich abbot or prior was captured, and held to ransom, excited no indignation. Robin Hood and his followers were objects of popular admiration, the heroes of ballads which, though modernized in their present shape, are of old tradition. But I conceive that if these freebooters had quitted the king's forest and highway, and made raids on the farmers, every one's hand would have been against them.

Matthew Paris tells a characteristic story of the robbers of Alton, of how they made raids on the Flemish merchants, who, landing their goods at Southampton, made their way through the Hampshire forests, of the international troubles which were foreseen, if these practices went unpunished, of the entire sympathy of the population with these offenders, of the refusal of juries to give evidence, notwithstanding the king's rage and the bishop's excommunication, of how the proof was extorted by imprisonment in the lowest dungeon, and of the discovery at last that the chief of the gang were found to be servants in the king's household, whose wages were indifferently paid, and who thereupon adopted this alternative of highway robbery, in order to supplement the inadequacy of their resources. Henry III. was, I believe, on the whole an amiable personage, who had, as amiable people sometimes have, an over-sanguine estimate of his own abilities, and who had, as many amiable people have, a habit of unduly procrastinating the payment of his debts. Now I do not doubt that much of this kind of freebooting went on. It did to a far larger extent, and with greater impartiality in the time of the Georges, as any one can see if one glances at the newspapers of the period. The convictions of highwaymen too were very frequent, but we may be sure that the convictions were not so numerous as to make the calling desperate. Smollett's hero, Mat. Bramble, whom he intended, and I think successfully, to represent as the type of a well-bred, honest, and kind-hearted English gentleman, takes compassion on a highwayman, who seems disposed to abandon his calling owing to his coming into some money, assists him with his credit, points out a way how he may escape justice, and assures him of his countenance and recommendations, if he can contrive to escape to one of the British plantations. I very much doubt whether the king's highway during the epoch of the Plantagenets was more unsafe than it was in those brave times when George III. was king.

But with all this, there was much internal trade. Common carriers, from a very early date, traversed the roads between Oxford and Southampton, even between Oxford and Newcastle-on-Tyne. They undertook to deliver money, of course under a special contract, and they who employ their services pay less for the convoy than the king does, perhaps naturally, for the king's messenger would be credited with spoil worth securing, and the king had put the freebooter out of his peace. The great fairs of the country, notably that of Stourbridge, near the town of Cambridge, were frequented by thousands, for there is hardly an account of expenditure extant which does not make note of purchases at this fair. Now, not to dwell on the fact that the accounts to which I refer make no note of losses, it is clear that if the roads had been as insecure as some of our writers on the Middle Ages allege, traffic would have been impossible, and travelling most insane. I printed some years ago an account of a progress made by the Warden and two fellows of Merton College to the North of England. They do not carry arms, nor do their servants, to all appearance. But bursars of colleges after the Restoration, when the king was enjoying his own again, as the loyal songs said, carried firearms on progress.

M. Jusserand, who has written a very readable book on the Wayfarers of Mediæval England, and has collected a great deal of accurate information on the subject, has cited certain instances in which outrages were committed by persons of some social standing, and seems to suggest that these perils of the road were ubiquitous. But he quotes from the Rolls of Parliament, and the narrative of the outrages in such a place convinces me that the event was exceptional. And though I am far from alleging that travelling was not perilous, I feel certain that a direct appeal to the king through a parliamentary petition, to the effect that the sheriff was deterred by *force majeure* from doing his duty, could hardly have represented a recurrent or common risk.

This author, who has made considerable use of the Rolls of Parliament, has not noted what is perhaps the most tragic story, certainly the most graphic, in those volumes. I allude to the murder of Speaker Tresham, in the summer of 1450, not far from Northampton, the story being told by his widow. But 1450 was the beginning of those atrocious feuds which caused and marked the thirty years' civil war of the royal succession. It is not to be wondered at that the time had its victims. I may only say, that from what I have seen, travellers varied their route, in going and returning, and took care to make the route which they determined on a secret. Both were precautions taken, I make no doubt, in the eighteenth as much as in the fourteenth century. One of the best touches in the petition of Isabel Tresham is the narrative which she gives of the manner in which a servant of Lord Grey de Ruthin, Tresham's murderer, wormed out of him the secret of his intended journey. I do not think that such precautions are needed now, but I think that any man would be unwise who allowed a suspicion that he had money or valuables about him to be entertained at the time when highwaymen by profession are travelling about.

The eastern counties, and especially Norfolk and Suffolk, were on the whole open country, protected on the western side by fens. They were a good deal under the administration of the Dukes of Norfolk, the Bigods, and the Mowbrays—the latter family, for sufficient reasons, nourishing an enduring hostility towards the Lancastrian kings, and apparently protecting to the utmost of their powers, those whom the house of Lancaster, perhaps in the first instance from motives of policy, persecuted. Norfolk was the special home of the Lollards, and when the feud broke out, became persistently Yorkist, as a couple of centuries later it was as emphatically on the side of Parliament. Besides it was near to Flanders. The eastern sea is always safer than the western, and maritime enterprise on this quarter long preceded similar efforts from the west. The English sovereigns were willing enough to encourage the settlement of weavers in that part of England which was most convenient and attractive to them, and it is clear that immigration into these counties and some contiguous to them, as for example Cambridge, took place at an early date. There was also a considerable export of grain from these counties, notably of barley and malt, to Flanders. Fastolfe, the captain in the French war, who was said to have shown the white feather at Patay, and was in the end an unintentional benefactor of Magdalene College, traded largely with the Low Countries. The wool of the eastern counties was the worst which bore a price, but its barley was excellent, and highly appreciated by the Flemings, who had a high opinion of the merits of beer.

I long ago suspected that this immigration of Flemings or Germans from the Baltic was considerable in the eastern counties, from the remarkable number of Teutonic names which I have found in certain accounts and papers which I have read. I do not doubt that if the taxing rolls of Norfolk, which are almost certain to exist in the Record Office, were consulted, what I have found in Cambridgeshire would be abundantly illustrated in what were the manufacturing counties of the Middle Ages. Now the history of Norfolk is peculiarly interesting. It has twice been made the seat of a weaving industry, and on both occasions by immigration from the same race, the Flemings, in the first instance by a kind of voluntary outflow, encouraged beyond question by the Plantagenet sovereigns, in the second by the compulsory exile of the Flemish Calvinists, during the time that Alva's Council of Blood, Grandville, and Titelmann were engaged in extirpating or expatriating the Flemish Protestants. On the consequences which ensued from these immigrations, social and political, I shall make a few comments further on. For the weavers of the Middle Ages, and for a long while after the Middle Ages, were and remained its heretics.

There were, however, some previous immigrations of this race into England, and at an early time, the origin of the migration being obscure. Colonies of Flemings were established in Glamorganshire, in the district of Gower, and in Pembrokeshire, as early, it is said, as the reign of Henry II. South Wales was, as you are aware, an acquisition of the English Crown, at a far earlier date than the northern part of the principality, and the principal noble of this district was the Earl of Clare. How important a personage this was may be illustrated by two facts, both, I do not doubt, known to you. The expedition for the conquest of Ireland was undertaken by one member of this family. A century or so later, the head of this house associated himself for a time with Simon de Montfort, and as long as this relation subsisted, the party which that remarkable man led was in the ascendant. But the defection of the Earl of Clare brought about the catastrophe of Evesham. Now I think it most probable that this settlement of Flemings in South Wales was intended to be a check on the native population. It is said that these districts not only still retain certain marked peculiarities, but that they are by no means friendly to their Welsh neighbours.

There was also an immigration of merchants into the city of London, in the shape of the representatives of the Hanse towns and the Flemish settlement in and about Fleet Street. Under the name of the Aldermen and Merchants of the Steelyard (a description which will suggest to you that they used measures which were different from those which Roman influences had made familiar), both in business and in currency, the Hanse towns, though comparatively speaking in their decline, were gladly accorded a settlement in London. If it could be worked out, I am sure that the origin and history of the early days in which the Hanseatic League was formed, would be shown to have been exceedingly significant in the civilization of Europe. It is clear that the association was formed in order to put down the Norse freebooters, whom a foolish habit of seeing courage and spirit in piracy and brigandage has whitewashed. In this object they succeeded; they became a power, had a treasury, and the fatal gift of property which could be plundered; and plundered they were, first by the Teutonic Knights—a gang of thieves whose history is not more respectable than the freebooters is—then by the Margrave of Brandenburg, who became in the later days Elector and King of Prussia, and in our own time Emperor of Germany, in which last capacity he has devoured the last of the free cities—Hamburg.

The Hanse towns and their League are the object of many charters. But besides them there were, in London at least, colonies of Lombards, Flemings, and other foreigners. Edward I. expelled the Jews, in consequence it appears of their inveterate attachment to usury. But it may be doubted whether the Lombards were more merciful creditors, and they were certainly less open to arbitrary plunder than the Jews were. These Italians practised usury, in defiance of English and Papal law. But English kings borrowed of them, and for the matter of that popes too. There is no doubt a strong inclination on the part of those who habitually adopt a social practice to denounce the imitation of the practice. In old days it was an unheard-of iniquity for heretics to retaliate on the Inquisition. In our own, it is a crime in the eyes of the Pope, as we are told, to adopt the practice of exclusive dealing, and its complement social proscription. And yet the Pope bases his authority on excommunication and his literary criticism on the *Index prohibitus*. These inconsistencies make us wonder, as long at least as we do not take account of human inconsistency.

The English Statute Book, especially on its financial side, is full of legislation about denizens and aliens. This is sufficient to show, if we had no other evidence, how largely the trade of London and other considerable towns was in the hands of immigrant foreigners. They were not, it seems, popular, and were constantly the incidental objects of popular disfavour, when outbreaks occurred. During the period of Tyler's insurrection the Flemish merchants were harshly treated. I cannot but think that the sympathy which the London citizens exhibited towards this great uprising was coupled with the expectation that the Londoners might find occasion to harry the detested foreigner. At any rate during the occupation of London by Tyler's followers, the Flemings were very severely handled.

The immigration of Teutonic weavers from the Netherlands into the eastern counties led to marked social consequences. When handicraftsmen are aggregated into a district, there is sure to arise a habit of criticizing on, and of dissenting from, established authority. A weaver, as I have told you, was for a long time a synonym for a heretic. Now I believe, that except among philosophers, who are bound to no rule whatever, scepticism as to ecclesiastical is closely followed by scepticism as to secular authority. Wiklif began by applying his maxiom, that dominion, *i.e.*, authority, is founded on grace, that is, on graced worthiness, to the Pope. He did not teach long after this avowal and its application before he extended it to temporal lords. I admit that the process was inconvenient and in a sense unpopular, but I contend that it was inevitable. Now it is certain that his doctrine took deep and abiding root among the Norfolk and Suffolk weavers. Even the beneficed clergy of the day, as the attainder roll of Tyler's adherents proves, were not proof against the general tendency, for several rectors and vicars of Suffolk parishes are proscribed among the adherents to the king's rebel. There is good reason to believe that in early days the Flemings were not severely orthodox, as their descendants are now. The immigrants into the eastern counties had a great deal more to do with political changes than the ordinary historian knows and recognizes. In the present day Dr. Jessopp, from the point of view of a parochial clergyman, finds that he has rather stubborn elements to deal with in Arcady. To understand the facts, one must go a long way back into the local history of the race, for it cannot be too constantly insisted on, in the solution or interpretation of economic problems, that the present situation must be carried back to the past, and that unless one does do this, we may wonder at facts, but be at a loss to know what they really mean.

In course of time the industries of Eastern England decayed. Norfolk was very severely visited by the fourteenth-century plague. Soon afterwards, perhaps owing to trade regulations, many of which were Acts of the Legislature, the peculiar industries of Norfolk began to migrate southwards and westwards, and the counties lost their dominant industries, though they retained many of their peculiar characteristics. Considering the time at which it occurred, and the special character of the Norfolk peasants, Ket's rebellion is a very significant fact in the sixteenth century. That Somerset was greatly alarmed when he gave such lenient terms to the insurgents is plain, I should conclude, to all who know anything of the subject. Equally suggestive to my mind is the fact that a short time afterwards the Norfolk heretics secured the throne to Mary Tudor. She repaid them for their loyalty, so useful at the crisis and so unexpected, in a characteristic fashion.

From the Statute Book of Henry VIII.'s reign there is evidence that the population of the country towns decreased considerably during the reign of Mr. Froude's patriot king; for there are several laws enacted, in which an attempt is made to check depopulation by penalties. The attempt was of course fruitless and foolish, but it is one which people called statesmen have in our day attempted to revive or practice. The void was filled up by the great immigration of the Flemings to England, as soon as ever Alva's blood council was in full operation. We are expressly informed of this immigration. It is possible that most of the immigrants went to London. But they certainly spread into other districts, for we are informed as exactly, that the say industry of

Norwich and the baize, or as our forefathers called it, the bay industry of Colchester, were the work of the expatriated Flemings. The latter of these industries was evidently considered of great importance, for the price of Colchester baize by the ell was, and long remained, the type of the woollen industry, giving, I conclude, by its invariable quotation, the price for other kinds of woollen fabrics. Many of the principal London merchants, at the Revolution of 1688, were of Flemish origin.

To these immigrants we owe the skill with which in later times we have been able to develop the arts of life. I have stated here already, and not without some shame, that we English were the most backward among the nations of Western Europe, and that we were indebted to immigrant foreigners for our first start in the industrial competition of modern times. That we have improved on our teaching I am ready enough to admit, but there still lingers I think a trace of the old temper, in a readiness with which we defer to Teutonic bounce. We have a habit of disparaging our own work and our own workmen in many departments of life, and are apt to allow that foreigners, especially Germans, know more of English literature, philology, and history than Englishmen do themselves. I am at a loss, I confess, to understand how this modesty is justified. Of course it is unlikely that the great race will hesitate to accept the surrender.

After the Union of the Crowns, the population of the counties north of the Trent rapidly filled up. It was here, I feel sure, that the great increase in the population of England which was so characteristic of the seventeenth century was effected. But it is probable that the greater part of this increase was an English migration. I have found no trace—I will not say that so negative a statement is conclusive—of foreign immigration into the new home of the textile industries. That the northern counties became early in the seventeenth century the seat of these manufactures is proved by many Acts of Parliament, regulating the woollen trade, the particulars of which are referred to in my "History of Prices." But the new industry required the protection of the police, such as then existed. Bleaching and drying after fulling was completed, as it still is in the Irish linen weaving districts, by exposure to the air; and goods out of doors attracted thieves. Now in these vast northern parishes, and their bigness is a proof of how sparse the population was in early times, the new industry could not be carried on except sharp remedies were employed against robbers. The maiden of Halifax—a kind of guillotine—is an example of early discipline exercised on pilferers.

More significant, however, than the immigration of the Flemish weavers, was that of the French Huguenots after the revocation of the Edict of Nantes. It appears that nearly all the manufactures of France, and not a little of its business was in the hands of these sectaries. Till the epoch began in which conversion was chiefly due to Court influence, and the desire to achieve a career which was barred to the heretic, a large proportion of the nobles in Southern France, from the east to the west, had embraced the Calvinist type of the Reformed creed. Now from the first it was seen that Calvinism was certain to be in opposition to the monarchical position, and, one must add, was believed to be inimical to that union of France under a strong government, which had been the policy of French monarchs, from the reign of Philip Augustus in the twelfth, to that of Louis XIV. in the seventeenth century. Of course, long before the Reformation, the French nobles had striven to depress the power of the Crown. The English gained their entries into France in the Hundred Years' War, and owed some of their successes to the invitation and co-operation of discontented French nobles. It is no wonder then that the French king was not on good terms with the nobility till he had routed them. But when, in addition to this hereditary tendency, they added the stimulants of a republican religion, the movement was more distasteful than ever. We hardly require any other explanation of the hatred of the reigning powers to the Huguenots, and the repeated massacres that took place. The Calvinist nobility had, it is true, put Henry IV. on the throne, though the new king did not think himself strong enough to do without conformity, being convinced that his old comrades would not desert him. But he gave them security by his celebrated edict of toleration, and they were on the whole, worthy of the trust which was put in them. But after the affair of Rochelle, at the beginning of our Charles I.'s reign, and the foolish expedition of Buckingham, Richelieu thought it necessary to gradually disarm them. Neither Richelieu or Mazarin had any religion, but they had a good deal of policy, and their policy was the union and strengthening of France. But if the policy of those able and unscrupulous men had been followed, I do not believe that violence would have been done to the French Calvinists, whom the schemes of Colbert were making the most useful instruments of French wealth, disastrous as those schemes were to the general interests of the country.

I mention these facts, because there is an explanation, from an administrative point of view, of the policy which was adopted towards the French Calvinists during the first three quarters of the seventeenth century. There is an explanation, but no apology, for the action of the French Government in the last quarter. The Huguenot aristocracy had generally conformed to the State religion, and there was no reason why the king and his counsellors should be alarmed at Calvinist preachers, merchants, and artisans. But after the peace of Nimeguen, Louis became utterly intolerant of any divergence from his views on any subject whatever. The French king was not a moral man, for his illegitimate children were exceedingly numerous, and very efficiently acknowledged. Nor was he a loyal Catholic, for he quarrelled with the Pope, and gave a precedent for despoiling him of his temporal power. But in his eyes the man who presumed to differ from his sovereign's religion was to be coerced into uniformity, or expelled. He was very like our own Henry VIII. in temper, though vastly the superior to that monarch in intelligence and real force of purpose. So Louis decided on expelling the most wealthy, capable, and enterprising of his subjects.

They came to England by thousands. Our people never took kindly to foreigners, least of all to Calvinists, particularly after the Commonwealth and the Restoration, but they welcomed the French exiles. They gave a practical proof of their goodwill in the great subscription which they raised, considering the times, for their relief; quite a third, and not far from half of the yearly revenue of the Crown. It came from all quarters. The subscriptions of the Oxford Colleges, at that time the advocates of non-resistance and divine right in its most grotesque and absurd form, were great and unexpected. Some of the colleges, as I have seen from their accounts, undertook to pay handsome yearly allowances to dispossessed Calvinist ministers. The King (James) was puzzled at the zeal. But his indignation was more powerful than his anxiety to explain so unexpected a liberality. It would have been better for him if he had worked out the problem, and desisted from his purposes.

Many of the French Huguenots emigrated to Holland. But a very large colony settled in England. The artisans set up the silk industry in London, occupying a considerable district in Spitalfields, and extended the say industry in Norwich. There is good reason to believe that they were great promoters and improvers of pottery in many parts of the kingdom. Many families, some of them early ennobled, trace their origin to Huguenot immigrants. To pass by the career of military men, like Schomberg and Ruvigny, many persons eminent in letters, in the public service, and in the learned professions were the descendants of these exiles. Several names, presumably French, are found in the first directorate of the Bank of England. I do not pretend to have studied the pedigrees of these exiles. I do not even know whether an attempt has been made to trace them. But one remembers certain names. Perhaps few persons did greater services to the English people than Sir Samuel Romilly, the reformer of our atrocious criminal law. He was of Huguenot descent. Nor do I doubt that much of the loyalty to the Act of Settlement, needed for a long time after the Revolution, is to be traced to the English of Huguenot origin. They had been received generously in England, and they were at once grateful to the country of their adoption, and to the principles which secured them in their new abode.

England has not been generally disposed to welcome aliens to the privileges of English subjects. Even when the union of the two crowns was effected, Scotchmen remained under divers disabilities, which were not removed except by negotiation at the time of the Union. It appears that by the common law it was even out of the power of the king to naturalize an alien. The utmost the Crown could do was to make him a denizen. When during the Commonwealth children were born to some of the Royalist exiles, it was held that an Act of Parliament was absolutely necessary, in order to give them the rights of British subjects, and such an Act was passed (29 Car. II. sec. 6). To this rule it seems that there were originally only two exceptions, the children of ambassadors and those of the reigning monarch. But it is to be noted that an Act of Parliament (25 Ed. III. stat. 2) declares the latter to be "the law of the Crown of England." There was reason in this, for the second and third surviving sons of Edward were born in Flanders.

The first general relaxation of the old law was made by an Act of William III. (12 cap. 2). Since that time naturalization Acts were passed on behalf of individuals, by virtue of which they became, certain reservations being made, or conditions generally specified, to all purposes British subjects. More recently, and at the instance of the United States Government, which admits vast numbers of immigrant settlers, and was disposed to resent the ancient law under which, according to the maxim, *nemo potest exerere patriam*, a subject could not throw off his allegiance, the acquisition of the rights of subjects by foreigners is made exceedingly easy and inexpensive. Parliament, in short, has acted as Parliament is accustomed to act, was unreasonably tenacious of an untenable position, and made an almost complete surrender when it yielded at last. There is nothing to prevent Great Britain from becoming a *sentina gentium*, and there are persons who are of opinion that we have gone too far. There are already symptoms that in some of our large towns, and notably London, native-born artisans and labourers are beginning to resent the wholesale immigration of foreigners, and that some of this jealousy is felt in other quarters.

The United States, though decidedly wishful to encourage immigration, exercise a very energetic police over their visitors, though Professor Bryce says that it is occasionally relaxed. They insist on knowing what their antecedents are. They cannot, perhaps, entirely prevent the settlement of criminals, especially if they are what I may perhaps call capitalist criminals, but they would emphatically resent any impulse being given to such undesirable arrivals. They have excluded the whole Mongol race from settlement, even a temporary sojourn in the States; and, if I can accept the reason alleged by my friend, Mr. Francis

Walker, who for some time managed the American census, for a sufficient cause. They will not have paupers. They will not accept foreigners who have been expelled for reasons of government, as the Russian Jews. At New York a very effective inquiry about emigrants is held at Castle Gardens, and none but likely persons are allowed to proceed into the interior. Even when they are permitted to settle, the States, liberal in the highest degree to useful foreigners, put temporary disabilities on the political privileges of the immigrant. The settler must be of some standing before he can vote, and then must make a declaration of his intending to be a citizen of the States. And even after he is qualified, certain offices are reserved for native-born citizens.

These precautions, then, are taken against undesirable immigrants in a country whose sea-board is some 3,000 miles distant at least from the immigrants' place of origin, and in many cases is much more remote. One would think that the helpless and useless would hardly find the means to undertake so distant a voyage. The Americans therefore conclude that when such persons arrive they are sent out by some administration, and the States are in no humour for being made the victims of an experiment, of a social difficulty, of a social prejudice, of a social inconvenience. They are charged with deferring to the immigrant Irish, but unless all my informants are mistaken, they resent being the recipients of those whom they conceive, rightly or wrongly, to be the victims of a vicious political and social system. When the evil, whatever it may be, is, in their opinion, of measurable magnitude, they have a way of jesting on the fact that it is their destiny to cure the evils of European Governments, and to bear the vexation and costs of the process. But they can be tired of the experiment, and the outbreak of the German anarchists at Chicago, sharply and rapidly suppressed, tried, as I am informed, their patience to the utmost. With the conceit which, in one form or another, seems to affect all communities who have a belief in their destiny and the excellence of their own institutions—I do not find that we are free of it—they conclude that many immigrants import the vices of the Old World into the States, and that they give a great deal of trouble before they are rid of old and bad habits. And it must be admitted that almost alone among settlers of British descent, the United States have an extraordinary power of assimilating the very varied peoples who settle among them. Out of the sea-bound towns English, Irish, German, Italian, Scandinavian settlers acquire in a very short time all the characteristics and all the political utterances of the native American.

Now we are not to expect, especially as we exercise no supervision over those who come hither to settle, that a distance which is not more than a hundredth of that space which separates the Old World from North America will guarantee us immigrants even of the average quality which the American Union procures. The immigrant from a distant country may be fairly considered to have weighed the circumstances well before he made the venture; to be possessed of those qualities which are likely to secure him success in the country of his adoption; to be enterprising, competent, satisfied with the field of his future operations; and to be possessed of means sufficient to maintain him with while he looks about him, or with friends in the country who will welcome, shelter, and assist for a time till he settles. Spontaneous emigration to a distant country is generally of the best and most hopeful states among the working classes, whose departure is a loss to the country of their birth and bringing up, a gain to that of their adoption. If you take men who are always wanted in a new country, of which character most of the immigrants into the States and the British Colonies are, the exportation of wealth in skilled and competent labour, ready at once to assist the productive energies of the country to which they go, amounts annually to an enormous sum. It is no marvel that, despite their atrocious and demoralizing financial system, the wealth of the American Union grows at so rapid a rate. The character and purposes of the immigrants is sufficient to account for the result. The Union takes a tribute from the Old World, being at the pains to regulate it by the best machinery which it can devise, in the shape of skilled labour, which, if the true balance of exports and imports were given, would very materially modify some conclusions as to these matters which foolish people have arrived at. We export annually an enormous amount of national wealth, without any equivalent in return for it.

On the other hand, the immigrants whom we receive crowd hither for totally different reasons. Coming to a near country, they are unenterprising, shiftless, often sunk in poverty, and an instant burden to those among whom they come. There are sentiments, some honourable to our humanity, some, it would appear, which are far from creditable, which induce people to look complacently on this ever-increasing tide of foreign beggary and foreign pauperism which flow into this country and especially into London. It is honourable to the English race that they are willing to see this country an asylum for the persecuted and miserable in other governments. There have been periods in our economic history when the shelter which we have given immigrants has been abundantly repaid in moral and industrial return. We have learnt more from these people than we have taught them. But it is quite conceivable, and, according to some careful experiences, real, that our shelter may be too liberal, may be even suicidal. It is quite possible that such persons are encouraged here, because they form a perennial supply of cheap labour, and become the ready victims of the farmer of labour, now called a sweater. It is probable that they may seriously depress the wages of born English men and women, and be answerable for the lack of employment and poverty whose reappearance is becoming periodic in London, is a very serious social difficulty, and threatens to become a still greater one. It may be that a community, through its administration, should find employment and accommodation for those who can find neither, though this is a very arguable question, but it certainly cannot be the duty of those who work for their living, *i.e.*, the persons who repair the annual consumption of wealth, that they should find work and house-room for all the waifs and strays of Europe, for all the failures of the paternal governments of the Continent. It may be doubted whether there can be an excess of a healthy, vigorous, industrious population, but every addition we may chance to get from the vagabondage of Europe is an excess of population with a witness.

I am well aware that it is unpopular to suggest a restraint on these immigrants. They fly from persecution as the Russian and German Jews do, and the appeal is to our humanity. They fly from an all-devouring military conscription, and it seems to be a homage to our more generous and free institutions. They avoid by their voluntary exile the incessant meddlesomeness, the mischievous and pauperising effects of the financial system with which financiers in the several European states are enamoured or besotted, get better prospects of employment as they think, more goods for their money, more freedom for their life than they did at home. It is a compliment to us, it seems, that they prefer Great Britain to the place of their birth. But one may buy compliments too dearly. There is nothing as far as I can see to prevent European governments from shovelling their paupers, their lunatics, or even their criminals on us, without any check whatsoever on our part. There is no great advantage as far as I can see in exchanging the best of our peasants and labourers for the squalid offscourings of continental cities. Perhaps one of the most formidable facts in modern social life is the increasing burden of pauper lunacy. It is not to be wondered at, if we are annually depleted of our strongest, most resolute, and most enterprising stocks, and have to put up with a residuum, reinforced, if one can use such a verb, with a further European residuum. Some time ago I was struck with the reports sent to me from the metropolitan asylums as to the great and growing increase of lunatic foreigners in those necessary places of refuge. I am quite certain that every country but our own would take steps to check so undesirable an element to the population.

Hitherto the working-classes in the large towns have shown but little hostility to this intrusive foreign element. But it would be a mistake to think that they are not dissatisfied with it. As yet, however, workmen are very imperfectly organized, have very little *esprit de corps*, and where they are organized are strangely indifferent to the miseries of unskilled labour. There are callings to be sure in which the union is almost complete. But I should be surprised if I found that more than 8 per cent. of the working-classes are united into trade unions or labour partnerships, and I should be exceedingly gratified if I learned that the trade unions were seriously taking up with a view to reporting on, as they could do very effectually, the number of the unemployed, and the causes of their condition. If they did, I am convinced that foreign immigration of the poorest, most helpless, least serviceable classes would be dwelt on with peculiar emphasis. A few years ago one of the London papers requested the opinion of known politicians and economists on the question of the unemployed, and consulted me among others. I told the editor that in my opinion there was only one process by which the facts could be arrived at, the action of the trade unions, who could report on the actual situation and the causes of it. It has not been undertaken by those organizations. Meanwhile imperfect and spasmodic attempts have been made to remedy some of the worst features in the system, and very crude nostrums have been promulgated, as the regulation of the hours of adult labour by the State, the establishment of national workshops, the supply at the public expense, *i.e.*, at the expense of honest and successful labour, of adequate house-accommodation for the poor. I venture on predicting that if any of these expedients were seriously adopted, the stream of immigrant continental pauperism would become a torrent, and that the latter end would be worse than the beginning. After all, perhaps, our old laws, discouraging the settlement of aliens, except for very sufficient reasons, were not so very ungenerous and inhospitable.

Under conditions which are not quite so unsatisfactory and, I may add, unsavoury as one can take account of in Eastern London, Great Britain has considerable attractions to the natives of certain European countries. We have a great and an increasing German population in England, for I do not hear that they migrate in considerable numbers north of the Tweed. They are not, with certain exceptions, much devoted to manufacturing industry, but swell the ranks of the middleman, of agents and traders. It may be the case, as some allege, that the trading Englishman has become so well off that he is content to make room for the more needy and more active settlers of immediate Teutonic descent. But there are many motives for this immigration. The youth escapes barrack life. Sharply as they compete against young Englishmen, the wages which they earn are better than those which they can get in the deliberately restricted markets of their own country. They are said to be better educated, more versatile, and less insatiate after amusement than our own young people. It is stated too that they are more observant and imitative, sometimes inconveniently observant and imitative. To many of them a temporary residence in England is an exceedingly practical apprenticeship which they can put to good use either here or abroad. To such people England offers many attractions. If they prosper, they have a far wider field than they would have at home, and the opportunities of a far pleasanter life. The social system of England is far more generous and far less inquisitive as to the sources of wealth than that of Germany is. We have no noble class, and many of those who belong to our limited nobility are not unwilling to associate with wealth, however obtained and accumulated. Now if a rich man is snubbed in the country of his birth, but welcomed and even respected in that of his adoption, the latter has irresistible attractions for him.

There yet remains in connection with the immigrant movements of population a question of great gravity. I mean the growth of towns and the character of the elements from which they grow. A century ago England was eminently a country of rural life; at present it is as emphatically one of town life. The rural population is decreasing, to the satisfaction of some people, to the alarm of others. There are facts in connection with this very marked change which justify to a considerable extent the alarm.

I am by no means convinced that the art of agriculture has made less progress than manufacture has, but I am sure that manufacturing ability is more diffused than agricultural skill or ability is. Where an Englishman or a Scotchman is a really competent agriculturist, he has no rival in any country whatever. But to be successful he must not only understand his craft, but must measure his expenditure by his profits, keep accurate accounts, and know how best to dispose of his produce. I do not villify a calling, in which for many reasons I have the warmest interests, when I say that such conditions are rarely co-existent. The absence of them is the primary, I might almost say, the sufficient, explanation of what is called agricultural distress. When Arthur Young wrote his Tours, agricultural produce was not more than half its present price, taking all things together, the cost of labour, more efficient then than now, was, excepting for two months of the hay and corn harvest, not more than a shilling a day, and the price of such tools and implements as the agriculturist needed were cheaper than they are at present. But over and over again Young insists that adequate cultivation requires a capital of at least £5 an acre. Now more than a dozen years ago, I learnt to my surprise that in Oxfordshire the average capital on land was less than £4, and I had no difficulty in predicting a catastrophe. It came like a cataract in the first bad harvest.

Now the rural population has decreased, the number of farmers, owing especially to the pernicious and short-sighted custom of consolidating farms has decreased, and the skilled farm-hand has to a great extent vanished. Near a quarter of a century ago, I foresaw the exodus of the peasantry, and I forecast, to the distaste and wrath of those who took note of my utterances, the evils which would ensue from the change. It is I am sure in the last degree unwise to utterly alienate the peasant from the occupation of land, and I am an ardent advocate, for very sufficient and entirely economical reasons, of that recall of the agricultural labourer to the land which has been parodied into the three-acres-and-a-cow cry. I am quite certain, for reasons which I have given before, that peasant-farming would greatly elevate the condition of farm labourers, would give a better class of workmen to the farmer, and under adequate guarantees, would greatly lessen the dependence of consumers in this country on foreign supply.

Now what has become of these hands? Many of them are no doubt cultivating the soil in the United States and the Colonies, *i.e.*, the most enterprising among them, those I repeat whom we can least of all afford to lose. As I was returning from my first visit to the States, I came across a specimen of this class. He was a cabin passenger, of about sixty years of age, whose face and hands bore evidence of hard work and exposure in the extremes of the American climate. When his shyness wore off, he told me that he had emigrated thirty years before from the town of Nottingham, that he had been brought up as a farm-hand, that he had saved a little money, and had resolved to emigrate. His history was that of thousands in the States. He had worked at first, and for good wages; had purchased and enlarged his homestead, and was now the possessor, beyond house and farm, of several thousand dollars. He had never returned to the old country since his exodus; but his sons had grown up, had followed his calling, and they too had prospered, so that he could safely leave the conduct of his affairs in their hands. He had an object in returning to see two sisters of his, whom he had long supported, on whose old age he proposed settling a part of his wealth. Then he would return. He asked me then what was his route from Liverpool to Nottingham. I should have liked to see that meeting. I do not wonder that America has its attractions for the peasant.

But a very large number has gone to swell the ranks of unskilled labour in the towns. No doubt many of these have, in time, though after many hardships, accommodated themselves to manufacturing employment. There are of course certain handicrafts in manufacture in which, to gain the requisite skill, eye and hand must be educated from childhood. But many can be learned by adults. In other callings such persons remain labourers, with less content than the Irish hodman had, who said that his calling was to run up and down a ladder, with hods full of bricks and mortar, while another fellow at the top did all the work. They are fortunate if they get work. Many of them get nothing or little to do. Some three or four years ago some friends of mine, in the borough which I represented, got up a society for the relief of the deserving poor in the winter. One Saturday night they got together about a hundred, more or less, of these unwilling waifs. They had had no midday meal, and no money for a night's lodging; and my friends, as their object was, fed and housed them. Over 90 per cent. were agricultural labourers.

Labour has not been exiled from the country because machinery has been substituted for the work of the hands. On the larger Ulster farms, as I found when I was there, double the number of labourers are employed than used to be in England at the best epoch, *i.e.*, one skilled labourer to twenty acres, for I found that the rate was one to ten, not, observe, Irish, but statute. There was every kind of new and expensive machine too employed. The decline of British agriculture is due to the waste of capital. Who has got it and spent it, I know only too well, and have stated the facts, before a more august assembly than this.

The immigration of the industrial population into the towns, for that of idlers has no interest, is the most formidable phenomenon of modern experience. In so far as it is due to economic causes, it is not only intelligible, but desirable. In so far as it is a result of anti-social and mischievous practices, it is deplorable, and calls loudly for remedies. Meanwhile there is an increasing cry on the part of those who have lost hope, that the remedy should be subversive of the existing order of things. I can only foresee that people who have committed more wrong than is bearable, will hereafter run a serious risk of receiving less than is rightly their due.

[N.B.—Since these Lectures were written a great deal of information has been collected on the subject of the influx of foreign labour and native agricultural labour into the large towns. Charles Booth's " Life and Labour in London," vol. i., has a chapter by H. Llewellyn Smith, especially devoted to the subject, in which many figures and much excellent argument are given to show that some of the statements contained in the above Lecture must be modified, as far as East London is concerned; and there is no reason for thinking that that district differs materially from other large centres of industry in this respect. I have, however, adhered to the rule given in the preface of only altering the text where the continuity of the Lecture will not be interfered with.   A.G.L.R.]

VII.

MOVEMENTS OF CURRENCY.

BIMETALLISM.

Attempts of governments to regulate trade—Unpopularity of the excise—The exportation of English silver—Variations of the mintage of coins in England—The proportion of silver to gold—Free mintage—Eight principles for the regulation of coinage by the State—The Bimetallic movement of 1825—Three causes which diminish prices—Effect of the discoveries in Australia and California—The adoption of a gold standard in Europe—Bimetalism and the rupee.

AMONG the errors which governments make about their powers, none is more inveterate and disappointing than that which they commit when they are under the impression that they can regulate the course of trade. They can, it is true, prohibit trade altogether, as was done, though not with complete success, by some Mongol monarchies, notably China and Japan. They can destroy industries, almost, it would seem, beyond hope of revival, when a wiser or more generous policy is adopted, as the English Parliament did by the industries of Ireland, and would have done, had it dared, by the industries of Scotland. It is even possible for the policy of government to ruin that which they design to foster. This, unless we are misinformed by all experts, is the effect of the protective policy of the United States on the mercantile marine of the Republic. It is indeed a question which may well be argued, whether a protective system does not in the end always injure the very industries which it designs to foster. For we should never forget that when government travels out of its proper sphere, which is to arbitrate between contending interests, to decide what is the equitable settlement of their relations, and even their contracts, and if inveterate stupidity and selfishness is doing mischief, or even inflicting private wrong, to give the force of law to its conclusions, and to coerce the obstinate illdoer. If, I say, it travels out of this sphere, it instantly enters on dangerous and at the best highly debatable ground. It runs the risk of becoming a partisan instead of a judge in equity, in giving the force of law to importunate and indefensible claims, and of subscribing to the most mischievous heresy which a government can fall into, that of admitting that the sustentation of private interests is a public good. I could occupy the whole of my time this morning with illustrations of the evil which has been done when governments have listened to, and been beguiled by, this plausible theory, and I could trace with exactness and conclusiveness the worst disasters which have befallen civilization and society to this fatal doctrine. In short, however plausible the arguments may seem, by which this doctrine is supported or defended, however cogent seems the case which is made out by the applicant for government favour, the more vigilant should be the scrutiny into the merits of the case, and the more thorough should be the proof, that this instance at least, is an exception to the general law. I do not deny that there have been exceptions, though even in most of these cases the evil in the end has overweighed the good. There was a defence for the East India Company, there was a defence for the exclusive privileges of the Bank of England. But I very much doubt whether in the long run the privileges which these two remarkable corporations acquired and exercise were not injurious rather than beneficial, certainly to the public, and not obscurely to the corporation.

The restraining power of governments in respect of trade, where the sympathies of the public whose affairs they administer are against their policy, will bear but little strain. During the Wars of the English and Spanish Succesion, *i.e.*, from 1689 to 1697, and again from 1702 to 1714, it was the policy of Parliament to prohibit trade with France, and in particular to shut out French produce from the country. But the attempt was a failure. The public took the part of the smugglers, and the tax was for a brief time an impost on the ordinary trader. Very speedily the trader, say in London, made common cause with the smuggler ; the revenue of the customs was diminished, and the ends of the government revenue and policy were defeated. I have recently made it my business to collect the prices of French goods in London and elsewhere during the prohibition, and the Methuen treaty. Nearly all historians and economists are under the impression that these restraints and prohibitions were effectual. An examination of price lists proves that they were nugatory. French wine and brandy is no dearer, and the prices are freely quoted in trade lists, in newspapers, in advertisements. And the same is true of French silks. The prohibition of these articles did not save the Lutestring Company from a complete and ruinous collapse. In Scotland after the Union, our Northern fellow-countrymen were rightly and wisely admitted to all the trade privileges of their Southern neighbours. But they abhorred and would have none of our revenue laws. In vain did the judges admonish the magistrates, that these laws must be obeyed, and the customs collected. In vain did the most eminent of Scottish statesmen, Duncan Forbes, reprove his countrymen for their habitual breach of law and order, and becoming indignant, ask the Scottish country gentlemen, whether any one of them could lay his hand upon his heart, and declare that he was not a scoundrel. In vain the most eminent men of letters were appointed to well-paid offices in connection with the revenue. David Hume, who repaid his handsome sinecure with incessant abuse of the English taxpayers who gave him his wealth ; Adam Smith, who had a similarly lucrative office, but was more courteous. Does not Macpherson inform us that the costs of collecting the Scottish customs was in excess of the receipts ? It is true that towards the end of the century, the government of the day endowed the services of Burns with a pitiful place in the excise. But it may be very well doubted whether the Scottish poet really earned his salary, if receipts are to exceed expenses. It is quite certain that this author joined in the outcry against his own calling, and proffered his thanks in most amusing verse, to "the little black devil, who carried away the exciseman." A preventive service we may depend upon it, on behalf of the customs duties, is rarely effective if the population sides with those who make it their business to break the law.

But of all the articles which make up trade, none is more difficult for a government to regulate than that of the precious metals, or for many centuries the movements of silver bullion and coins. For as I have told you, when a man takes money, he takes that kind of merchandise—I am speaking of traders only—which is of the least value to him, unless he can get rid of it in the shortest possible time, and with the least possible hindrance. If he imports foreign articles, his object is to trade with them at a profit. If he imports foreign money, he wishes at once to exchange it for trade commodities in order that he may make his profits continuous. No trader from the days of the Plantagenets to those of the house of Hanover, ever has wished or could wish to retain more money in his hands than was sufficient for his trade and his liabilities, and his instincts and experience would lead him to resist or baffle any expedient of policy which would compel him to retain what he knew it was his interest to get rid of. The king strove to limit trade in certain staple produce of England to certain markets, notably wool and hides. It is certain that the regulations were evaded, and that trade in these articles was carried on in a hundred ports. He strove in the same way to secure a balance of bargain on such trade as he thought he could regulate, and he complains that the country is denuded of its treasure, when probably the expedients which he had adopted were the very means by which the disappearance of treasure was simulated. There is nothing more absurd, in the economical history of this and other countries, than the regulations adopted for the control of the trade in the precious metals. And yet these regulations and restraints were continued up to 1819, when they were swept away at the final resumption of cash payments, and the trade in the precious metals was made free. The fact is, of all articles, the precious metals are the most mobile or fluid.

Up to comparatively modern times the currency of Europe was silver. It was so during the Middle Ages; it was so long after the discovery of the great American mines at the conclusion of the sixteenth century, for the principal supply of the New World was silver. This was partly due to custom, partly to the fact that except in one district in Europe, silver was the only metal which could be procured in any abundance. There were, it is true, superficial deposits of native gold. Such was the case in ancient Gaul, Britain, and Spain. But these casual sources of this precious metal has been collected and absorbed in ancient and even in prehistoric times. In the fifteenth century it is said that gold of the finest quality was still procurable in Ireland. It seems to have been mainly used for personal ornament, though there was a British gold coinage before the invasion of Cæsar, for many specimens, even of prehistoric kings have been found. But the supply of gold in Eastern Europe and Western Asia seems to have been far more copious in early times. Perhaps as a succession from the Western Empire, the Byzantine coinage was largely gold. When there was close commercial intercourse with the Eastern Empire, Asia Minor, Syria, and Egypt, the Italian cities at the end of the thirteenth century began a gold coinage. It became to some extent at least the currency of the Papal Court at Rome, and afterwards at Avignon. It was imitated, though the Mint issues must have been very small, by the Plantagenet kings. Practically, however, till near the close of the seventeenth century, the currency was mainly silver.

In an earlier lecture, I pointed out to you that the source of silver, up to the time in which the New World, and especially the mines of Potosi were discovered, was particularly England. Sulphuret of lead (not indeed in the wide veins recently discovered in the range of the Rocky Mountains) has been from time immemorial worked in several parts of England. Now this ore always contains silver, sometimes in considerable quantities. I think that I am entirely right in saying that those countries with which early English trade was generally carried on, are destitute of lead ores. I am nearly as convinced that at the time of which I am speaking, perhaps in all cases, silver is produced almost exclusively from the lead ore to which I have referred. There was a considerable export trade in lead, and I have never found in all my researches, a trace of its import from foreign countries. And though the arts of roasting galena, and subsequently oxidizing the metallic lead, with a view to the separation of the silver were made, they were certainly obvious, easy, and traditional. The search after the more valuable metal was not exhaustive as it is under the modern process with which refiners are familiar, that by spelter. But it is not impossible that processes were lost after the cost of reducing English ores was too great for competition with the new American silver. Now I am persuaded that, in England at least, the principal source of supply was the lead mines. But lead during the whole time before the rise in prices, due I am certain to changes in the currency after 1563, is not dearer, nor is silver cheaper, and I therefore conclude that, as long as it lasted, the process and the prices were equally *in equilibrio*. But English lead was cheap, and was largely exported, for it was used extensively in France and Flanders, at any rate for church building.

There were two articles then—one exclusively of English produce, the other mainly—wool and silver. The process by which the former was distributed is well known, and its peculiarities as a financial instrument, it being solidly taxed on exportation. The financial annals of this country, not indeed perfectly preserved, but very fully, and very characteristically, show us how the export of wool was used for revenue purposes. But there is no record of the export of silver, and for the sufficient reason, that it was illegal to export it, as far as paper or parchment Acts of Parliament could make it illegal. But as every student of early English history knows, a law was one thing and its efficiency quite a different thing. The king's exchanger was personally, or by deputy, present at all the great marts; his control over trade transactions was another matter.

There were two great outlets of English wealth, in the form of currency. The one was the foreign policy of the Plantagenets, a policy which was continued at intervals from the middle of the thirteenth to the middle of the sixteenth centuries. The king who wished to control the export of his subjects' specie, had no objection to exporting it himself in order to serve the purposes of his ambition. Considering the times, the drain of treasure for the military chests of the Edwards and the Henrys must have been enormous. The English army you will remember was not collected by conscription as the foreign militias were, but by enlistment. It was drilled well, and handsomely paid. It was small, but singularly efficient. The daily pay of an archer was as high as that of an artisan, and he was equipped, very probably provisioned to boot. I do not believe that a single continental nation could have kept an army on foot like that which the Edwards had at Crecy and Poictiers, Henry at Agincourt, and elsewhere. Now the maintenance of these forces came, I am sure, from my investigations into the facts, out of home-grown wool and home-produced silver.

The other source of the drain was the payments to the Papal Court and its nominees. We are constantly told—it may be exaggeration due to discontent—that the drain on England was equal to the Royal Revenue. The statute of Provisors was the subject of heartfelt and sincere indignation at Avignon and Rome. The contemporary writer in the first half of the fifteenth century, while though a good Catholic he is sincere in his devotion to the Roman faith, has no language too strong for his indignation of the Papal Court, at its plunder of English benefices, and at the intrigues and threats it used in order to get rid of the hateful statute of Provisors, inadequately as it was obeyed. Martin V. threatened to put England under an interdict if it were not repealed, and would have acted on his resolve, if death had not prevented him; though he owed his election, according to the same well-informed authority, to Cardinal Beaufort.

English wool and English silver were not such dominant forces as they had been after the New World and its plunder were discovered. But the treasures of New Spain were insufficient for the projects of Charles V., and even less sufficient for those of Philip II. Charles was always in pecuniary straits, and Philip at last became bankrupt. But in the interval, the power of England shrank to that of a third-rate power, more respectable I conclude for its memories than for its actual power. But it is to my mind very doubtful, whether England received any notable part of the new treasure till the beginning of the seventeenth century, and when it did, it procured it of course by foreign trade, this being the trade of the old East India Company, whose career was very prosperous in the first half of the seventeenth century, and still more prosperous in the second half.

But I must now call your attention to the relations of gold and silver as currency. For all practical purposes, gold was not a currency in England till the seventeenth century. There is said to have been a coinage in 1257, but no specimen has been found of it. There was one in 1344, and so onwards ; but it was almost certainly for foreign use, and the exportation of it was permitted. Now, I pointed out long ago, that the price of gold bullion weight for weight with silver, at the period of this first reported coinage, was as $9\frac{1}{2}$ and 10 to 1 ; that towards the end of the century the ratio rose to 12 and $12\frac{1}{2}$ to 1, and that gradually gold became relatively dearer, till at last, when the two metals were in circulation together, the ratio was at from 15 to $15\frac{1}{2}$ to 1. By this I mean that different weights of silver were required at different times, in order to purchase a given weight of gold. I pointed out, too, in my lectures last year, that the cause of this rise was the gradually increased use of gold as currency, commenced as far as the Western World was concerned, by the adoption of gold currencies in the Italian trading cities. The evidence of these relative prices is not very abundant, but is, I am sure, conclusive. No doubt, if one could discover information as to frequent purchases of gold, the information would be more copious, and would give us an insight into changes in the relative value of the rarer metal. But it would not be more decisive. I am perfectly satisfied with the proof as to the change in the value of gold between the reign of Henry III. and that of his son, an interval of about forty years.

Beyond the fact that all recorded information as to the relation of social instruments to each other has a value in the history of all social relations, the principal and important inference which one can draw, and with absolute confidence as to these early prices of gold, is that the fundamental cause of value in the precious metals is their use as currency. This conclusion is not so obvious as it might appear. Up to recently, ordinary political economists have been accustomed to accept Mr. Senior's dictum, that the measure of value in the precious metals is their use in the Arts. It is very possible that this view is still accepted, notwithstanding the experiences of the last fifteen years, during which events have occurred which would, one might think, induce these people to reconsider their conclusion.

I make no doubt that the managers of the English Mint had this knowledge before them, in what seems to be the capricious coinage of the seventeenth and eighteenth centuries. Taking its value as given in the records of the Mint, Elizabeth coined six times as much silver as she did gold; James more than twice as much gold as he did silver. Charles, however, coined nearly three times as much silver as he did gold, and the Commonwealth, whose issues were not large, more than six times. Charles II. coined silver and gold in approximately equal quantities, his brother four times as much gold as he did silver. In William's reign the coinage of silver was nearly three times as much as that of gold. Now during this period there were two recoinages on a large scale. That of Elizabeth, in order to extinguish the base money of her father and brother; that of William, in 1696, to restore the worn and clipped money. In the former case, the new issues are known to have been derived from the base money; in the latter, the metal must have been purchased to at least half the extent of the new issue. Besides during the reign of Charles, there was a considerable coinage of plate, mainly, I presume, by the king's party. Hence, in three of these reigns, there were distinctly disturbing causes which should be held to explain the great excess of silver money which was issued by the three sovereigns.

Now, to credit these sovereigns with an intelligent appreciation of the wants of commerce and a wish to relieve the currency from all but the most obvious strains, is to infer that which reason and experience could not warrant, but would be an absurd anachronism. The Mint was looked on as a department of the exchequer, and as subordinated to the Royal Revenue. It received money in payment of taxes and dues; it coined what it needed for the expenses of government; and it coined, we cannot doubt, that metal which it could procure at the cheapest rate, in preference to that which cost more. Thus, between 1701 and 1724, according to Erasmus Philips, value for value, fourteen times as much gold was coined as there was of silver. The writers of the time explained this fact by the over-valuation of gold in England, and its consequent importation in exchange for silver. The same excess of gold coinage marks the first seven years of George II.'s reign. It cannot be doubted that the Mint coined the cheapest metal and strove to give it circulation. It is true that early in the eighteenth century it reduced the guinea from 21s. 6d. to 21s.

but there is good reason to believe that even at this rate the gold currency was over-valued, and that while the profit of the Mint consisted in the coinage of gold, the profit of the bullion dealers lay in the exportation of silver and the importation of gold.[1] The exportation of British coin was prohibited. I have already stated that for sufficient reasons this prohibition was sure to be inoperative. But the government of the day, by putting a mint charge on the coinage of gold and silver, *i.e.*, by exacting a seignorage, had recourse to a far more effective check, for it will be plain to you that the coin when out of the kingdom was worth less in bullion than its nominal value. Besides, the silver currency was that which was generally in circulation, and nothing but a very small denomination of paper money can extract metallic money from those who must needs have and use it. The operations of money-dealers were therefore limited to the silver in the market, and this was no doubt procured by the trade with Spain and its transatlantic colonies.

Two propositions are very commonly and confidently laid down by some modern theorists on metallic currencies. One is that the ratio of $15\frac{1}{2}$ to 1 between gold and silver has been, or was, undisturbed for a century and a half, and that during this time there was a free coinage of gold and silver. Both of these statements are out of harmony with the facts. For the first half of the eighteenth century, at least, you will not take up a newspaper which busied itself with commerce, without finding in it quotations of the price of gold and silver bullion and foreign money, both gold and silver. Now if the ratio had been immutable, what was the use of publishing this intelligence. But an examination of the returns proves that no such immutable ratio existed, but that even in time of peace considerable fluctuation occurred in the relative value of the metals, fluctuations which are far in excess of those needed in order to give motion to the metals themselves, and stimulate a trade in them. The margin necessary for such a stimulus is very small. Mr. Tooke, whose authority on this subject is not only of the highest, but is indisputable, states

[1] According to Ruding, the average annual coinage of gold and silver from the accession of Anne to the death of George IV. (128 years) was £1,050,645 of the former, £90,457 of the latter metal.

that in 1826, when a project, similar to that which I shall comment on presently, was being ventilated, as a matter of experience, a fall of one penny an ounce in the value of silver, equivalent to an advantage of 1½ per cent. to a debtor, would lead to the payment of all debts in silver, and an extinction of the gold circulation, or the establishment of a premium on gold and gold payments. The same author also alleges that the restricted statement as to the concurrent circulation of silver and gold in France at a fixed ratio (of 15½ to 1) is more of an apparent than a real fact, that silver was the only actual standard there, and that gold constantly fetched a premium varying from one-tenth to 1 per cent. He adds, further, that remittances in silver as compared with gold, on the hypothesis that the former mode of settlement is under the circumstances to be preferred, can always be effected, and are effected at a sacrifice of one-half to one-quarter per cent. These facts and figures, taken from indisputable experience are, as I shall show, of the highest significance and conclusiveness.

There never was, and there never will be, except under a distinct understanding, which I shall presently explain, a free mintage of gold and silver in any country whatever. Let us see what a free mintage must mean. It must not include seignorage, agio, or premium, *i.e.*, the Mint must deliver to the person who brings standard gold or silver to an establishment for minting exactly the same weight of coined money without delay. Now, in this country, whose gold currency circulates freely all over Europe, because its currency value is almost exactly the same as its bullion value, a slight seignorage, too trivial I admit, to disturb the operation, but significant enough in large transactions, is charged. The Bank of England, really the only person who coins at the Mint, buys gold under the Act of 1844, at £3 17s. 9d. and issues sovereigns at £3 17s. 10½d. an ounce. The percentage is small, little over 1½ per mille, or, to be exact, 1s. 6d. per pound on the coinage of gold. But on an issue of half a million sovereigns, containing nearly 9,760 lbs. troy of gold, the difference is £732. I do not know whether this seignorage tempts the Bank to coin gold alone, for no one has ever heard, except as a whim, of any private person approaching the Mint with bullion, or whether, as I suspect, deposits of bullion made by the Bank at the Mint are treated in the weekly issues as still in the Bank cellar, and therefore are available for issues of notes. I have asked the question of Bank directors, and they make a mystery of the subject. The Bank of England, like any other mercantile concern, has its secrets. I believe that the secrets are after all transparent, and that they can be revealed by the knowledge of the prices of Bank Stock and the rates of discount.

A private individual has no such advantage. He is not possessed of the Bank of England privilege of buying at one price and selling at another. If he chooses to take gold to the Mint, the Mint will, I presume, appropriate the difference. But it will do more. He must wait till his bullion is coined. How long that will be I cannot guess. But the proceedings of a government office are measured, not to say slow. It is fortunate if they are marked with intelligence and even with integrity. That the Mint issues nothing but genuine coin I can readily believe. If it committed the crimes of the ordnance department, it would speedily find out how differently playing with the lives of soldiers and playing with the interests of money-dealers are criticized. But I think that it would not prefer the demands of the individual to those of a department of the State which the mechanism of the Bank of England assuredly is, in relation to the currency, and I may add, is most wisely considered to be. Let us put the delay at six months. During this period, the applicant's bullion would be dead capital, yielding no profit, and not even any interest. Now bullion dealers are not absolute fools, and I do not suppose that any of them, if the question were put to them in a practical shape, would admit that there ever was, or could be, a free coinage.

Nor has there ever been an unlimited coinage. The State always has controlled the mint, and always must do so. The Federal Government of the American Union in an evil hour, and in deference to those detestable private interests which have always masqueraded in the Union as forms of the public good, passed the Bland Silver Bill, and committed itself to the yearly mintage of a large quantity of silver. It does not, of course, buy bullion at the mint, but at the market price, and is therefore not committed to free coinage in any sort or shape. In every community, most of all in France, and subsequently in the Latin Union, long before the modern trouble came, the principle of the Government's policy and of the Latin Convention was the limitation, the restraint of coining. I well remember the indignation with which the French peasant, who had been taught, as I heard, that the Pope was lying on straw in the dungeon of the Vatican, while devout divines, advocates of the temporal power, were selling the relics of his uncomfortable couch to those peasants, at last exploded the pious fiction, when they found that Pio Nono had been issuing more silver than the Convention of the Latin Union allowed him, and had even minted large coins of an alloy which was inferior in purity to the conventional standard. You know, perhaps, that men of high religious pretensions are sometimes apt to take advantage of their reputation, and to perpetrate what in more secular individuals would be called frauds, not to say swindles. Now I am entirely convinced that under no circumstances could the State allow individuals the right of free coinage in any form whatsoever. Whether, after experience, it would be possible for a convention to agree on, and enforce, an engagement between states is a question to which I shall advert presently.

It is time, however, that I should lay down certain principles in connection with the regulation of currencies by the State, in order that I may be able to deal in a general way with the topic which I have connected with this lecture, a topic which has excited recently a good deal of attention. I will throw what I have to say at this stage into the form of a series of propositions.

1. It is the province and the duty of the State to elect which of the precious metals it pleases to take as a legal tender for satisfying obligations or contracts. If it enters into obligations or contracts itself it must abide by its choice until those obligations are satisfied.

2. Subject to its maintaining its own standard in full weight and purity, it can limit its obligations and those of its subjects or citizens to one coin only, as well as to one metal, and may make all other coins in the same metal or of other metals, tokens only, provided it guarantees that such subsidiary coins shall be capable of exchange at their nominal value.

3. The value of each of the precious metals depends remotely on the cost of production and acquisition, immediately on the use which civilized communities make of them as legal tender.

4. The State, under the foregoing conditions, can, within its own jurisdiction, confer an arbitrary value at its discretion on a subsidiary currency, whether it be a token currency or paper money. But if it makes such a token currency or paper money (the issues of them being uncontrolled or indefinite) a legal tender, the undervalued currency will inevitably disappear, for it cannot be the interest of any one to liquidate obligations in a currency which is more costly to purchase, if the State gives him a discretion of discharging them in an easier and cheaper medium.

5. It is theoretically possible to establish a convention between civilized communities, under which an artificial value may be given to a subsidiary or token currency, which shall circulate at conventional rates between the consenting parties to such an agreement. But the issues of such a supplementary currency must not only be regulated in quantity by a distinct understanding, and the machinery must be provided, by which any state which violates the conditions of the convention shall be chastised or coerced. In other words, the sovereign rights of states must be suspended, in so far as the necessary police of such a convention may be found requisite. The restraint must include (*a*) the amount of the issue, and (*b*) the fineness of the standard.

6. It is possible under these circumstances to give a value to coin which is totally different from that which the bullion from which it is manufactured possesses. But this arbitrary value is an act of government, and will exist, even under the most stringent conditions, only as long as the convention is in force. Nothing but the power of government can give such an artificial value, and nothing but the unanimous co-operation of governments can maintain or secure such an artificial value.

7. The excessive over-valuation of any metal used as currency may be met by the practice of private coining. It is not known whether the present over-valuation of token silver in the United Kingdom has not led to this result, though as yet the probabilities are against it.

8. The difficulties of the situation are enhanced or increased,

if the over-valued metal is subject to considerable fluctuations, *e.g.*, silver in relation to gold. For if the ratio should happen to be pitched too low, there is risk, if not certainty, that the under-valued metal may disappear, and if it be pitched too high, the whole machinery of the convention will eventuate in a mere waste of strength, for it may be concluded that though the convention would prohibit an excess of issue in an over-valued currency, it would hardly constrain a proportionate issue of an under-valued currency.

These are, I think, the general principles which would regulate the issues of metallic currencies, and those which must be adopted and enforced in an international bimetallic system. *Prima facie* it is as absurd and irrational for a government to determine what shall be the relative value of gold and silver as it would be to do so in the case of iron and copper, barley and wheat, cotton and wool. It needs that a very strong case indeed should be made out in favour of a government assigning an arbitrary value to any product of human industry and of human demand, even if the product is one of its own manufacture. The bimetallists demand that government should so act, and I conclude not only that they must prove the necessity of the situation fully, but that they must explain what are to be the means by which the stipulations of the international convention shall be enforced. For you must expect, even in so vital and delicate an instrument as currency is, that attempts will be made to prove that private interests are public benefits, and that all the force of government, and in this case, of all civilized governments, must be invoked, in order to obviate what may, after all, turn out to be nothing worse than a trade difficulty affecting a very limited class of persons, or even in the case of some people, what Adam Smith calls the passionate confidence of interested falsehood. Attempts to tamper with the currency were made in 1696 and in 1816, in both cases plausibly. And in just the same way the bimetallic theory was launched in 1825, under circumstances which were similar to those which prevail now, though the phenomena were not exhibited on so gigantic a scale.

The history of the modern movement is as follows. Up to nearly forty years ago, the production of gold and silver appears to have been so evenly proportioned that no very serious variation arose in the traditional ratio which had been established among them. It is absurd and false to say that no variation arose, but it was easy, within the comparatively narrow limits of the fluctuation for the governments of countries which used—I must say, more nominally than really—a double currency, to check the depreciation of either by limiting the issues of their respective mints, the operation affecting, of course, the circulation of that country only which adopted such limitations.

The United Kingdom was the only civilized community which had adopted a gold standard. It was said in the eighteenth century that this change was primarily brought about by the trade of the East India Company, and that this was owing to the fact that gold was under-valued in Hindoostan. It became, therefore, a profitable trade to export silver to the East, and import gold. I have pointed out how the mints of the Georgian era lent themselves to this tendency. But silver and gold coin were, for a long time, equally legal tenders, gold at £3 17s. 10d. the oz., silver at 5s. 2d., when the two were supposed to be *in equilibrio, i.e.*, at a small fraction over 15 to 1.[1] In 1774, when the Government was about to recoin worn and light money at the public cost, a restraint was put on the legal tender of silver coin by tale, to a maximum of £25, and after the resumption of cash payments, when silver money was made a mere token, the limit was permanently put at 40s.

Now shortly after this resumption, the Spanish colonies of Mexico, Chili, Peru, and some other Equatorial settlements in America, revolted against the authority of Spain, and after a short struggle achieved their independence. Great hopes were entertained that a new and most important field of British trade would be opened to the United Kingdom. It was on this occasion that Canning uttered his celebrated vaunt, that he had called in the New World, to redress the balance of the Old. Canning had

---

[1] According to Ruding, "Annals of the Mint," from Henry I. to Edward I., the ratio was 1 to 9. From Edward III. to Mary Tudor, between 1 to 12 and 1 to 11. During the seventeenth century, from 1 to 12¼ to 1 to 13. In the eighteenth century, 1 to $15\frac{2450}{13010}$; the rise from the seventeenth century being $39\frac{32}{167}$ per cent.

a hearty, and entirely honest hatred of the Holy Alliance, an arrangement entered into between certain European sovereigns, in which, under the hypocritical pretence of carrying out the principles of the New Testament, they resolved to crush out all political liberty in their several dominions. The last thing, I assure you, which they thought of was the New Testament, even the preface to it, though they might have inscribed their policy on the blank leaf for all I know. But Canning's vaunt was premature. The Spanish Government had effectually destroyed for two generations the possibility of an orderly system, and the history of the Central and South American republics was marked only by domestic revolutions. But Englishmen at the time were nearly as mad after the new trade as they had been more than a century before, when the South Sea Scheme attracted the attention, and enticed the co-operation of the shrewdest. The mercantile classes ventured much and lost much. The bankers joined in the race, and lost even more.

Now these South and Central American republics were silver currency countries. The British merchant who had overestimated the trade, and therefore suffered from trade losses, had to negotiate the metal in which he was paid in a gold currency market, and very speedily depressed the price of that which he took as currency, and had to exchange. There was an instant call for a bimetallic standard, and arguments recently put forward were insisted on with all that fervency with which trades demand that the public should save them not only from loss, but from the contingency of loss, and even of trouble. So loud was the demand that the Chancellor of the Exchequer promised legislation, not, probably, with any serious intention of satisfying his pledge, but with that of conciliating hostility. They who are familiar with the attitude and action of governments are perfectly prepared for promises of legislation, and scarce ever feel surprise when these promises remain unfulfilled, generally under the plea that other public business is too pressing to be postponed.

The peculiarity in the situation of 1825 was that it was accompanied by a formidable collapse of banking credit. Now you will find whenever persons are put to straits, that they will always discover that the cause of the trouble is not due to their own miscalculations, mismanagement, or recklessness, but to some cause to which they have not contributed in any degree whatever, and is the result of some universal law, or some occult and sinister influence. I find, for example, that at the present time, men otherwise sensible and rational, are prepared to explain all the phenomena of low prices, such as have prevailed for some years past, to the appreciation as they call it, of gold only. Now I have stated before now that there are three causes, which in a healthy state of things diminish prices. They are cheapening of the cost of production, cheapening of the cost of freight, and increased scarcity of the precious metals; but that, while the first two causes are stimulated to the utmost by the interests of those who are engaged in trade, that of the latter was retarded to the utmost by every motive which can influence a vendor or purchaser. When the precious metals are presumably scarce, there is every motive to economise their use, or as economists say, to increase the efficiency of the currency; when they are inconveniently abundant, every effort is made to get rid of them. It is very possible that during the years in which new gold was being poured abundantly into Europe, prices were heightened. But it would be a very hasty conclusion to allege, as many people did, and do still, that this was due to the new plenty which was created. It may have been entirely the result of the fact that demand was ahead of supply, that a new industry was created on a gigantic scale, which pinched on existing stocks of goods and existing facilities of continuous supply, and it is quite certain that, however much people may welcome high prices of everything, they are by no means willing to see money depreciated, and they will strive against it, with no little energy and acuteness.

You will see that I stated that the three causes to which I have referred produce their effect in a healthy state of things. But cost of production and cost of freight, whether they be slow or rapid in their diminution, always postulate the equilibrium or the progressive increase of supply. The cost of production is economised in the hope of a wider market, and so is the cost of freight. Blight or narrow the market, and you effectually check economies, or at least discourage them, except in so far as existing industrial agents strive to postpone loss. But it is certain that the result of such a phenomenon is to lower price. Now it cannot be doubted that one, and that a most important branch of British industry, has suffered from a very severe depression of profits. I refer, of course, to agriculture. Nor is there the least doubt as to the cause of this depression. It has been the payment of excessive rent under a precarious tenure, and this cause has been entirely sufficient for all the phenomena. I find that, according to an exceedingly intelligent paper, read at the Farmers' Club recently, that on the whole, excluding machinery and cattle labour, the labour bill of the farmer on arable land is less than 20s. an acre, and on pasture about 9s., the wages of the farm-hand having fallen to what they were in 1860. With this labour the British farmer produces more than twice as much grain as the American farmer does 5,000 miles or more off, who has to pay relatively a far higher rate for labour, and must clear the cost of freight, from 9s. to 11s. a quarter, before he can touch a cent of profit. I must consent to surrender all my faculties before I allow that foreign competition has depressed the British farmer. He has paid too much for the land he uses, he has been made to pay rent on his own outlay, and he has insensibly, but assuredly, lost his capital in the one certain appreciation, the appreciation of rent.

I do not on this occasion pursue this aspect of the subject further. But it will be plain to every one, whatever may be the cause, the effect of stinting or extinguishing the demand of a large number of consumers of home manufactures must have a very damaging effect on prices. Their expenditure may have been in old times ill-advised, abnormal, profuse. In general, however, there is no great harm done in the curtailment of needless, unbecoming, and mischievous luxuries. But the stint in the consumption of staple products, of clothing, and decent comforts, is another matter. And be it remembered this not only affects the farmer, but all who live on land, and most certainly those who used to supply him. And when you have these necessary and obvious causes before you, it is mere poltroonery to ascribe them to an appreciation of gold, and sheer folly to imagine that any remedy whatever can be found in the adoption of bimetallism. But I have met people, who, in a desperate resolve to find an explanation of the facts in anything but their own shortsightedness and folly, will believe that a bimetallic standard will bring back old prices and old rents. As well expect that the abandonment of Newton's astronomy and the adoption anew of Ptolemy's will produce the same highly gratifying results. Not a scintilla of evidence is adduced in support of this hypothesis.

When the gold products of Australia and California were thrown on the European market, and a great stimulus owing to the demands of the mining population was given to manufacture and trade, great alarm was expressed at the inevitable consequences of depreciation. Prices, I allow, rose, and for reasons to which, for all I can find, the addition to the gold currency contributed little or nothing ; for, on the whole, it cost no less to produce and acquire gold than it did before. But M. Chevalier gave utterance to an alarm in a work which he wrote on the subject, a work on which my friend, Mr. Cobden, lavished the superfluous labour of translation. The Dutch, a shrewd people, were actually so far carried away by the panic as to demonetise gold. The French and those members of the Latin Union which could follow their example, began to coin gold in increasing quantities, wisely, as I do not doubt, because, at the old rate of $15\frac{1}{2}$, it was the cheaper metal to manipulate at the Mint. During the reign of Louis Philippe from 1830 to 1848, the French Mint issued near 216 million francs in gold, and nearly 1,737 million francs in silver, according to M. Roswag. But from the commencement of the Second Empire in November 1852 to December 31, 1863, a little more than eleven years, near 4,523 millions of gold were coined, and only 199 millions of silver, according to the same authority. It is difficult to doubt that, for all which may be said about free mintage in France, and the invariable ratio of $15\frac{1}{4}$ to 1, the Government put into circulation that form of currency which was cheapest to get in the raw form of bullion. The difference may not have been much, but it was sufficient to determine the choice. So anxious was the Government to supersede silver for gold, perhaps with some convenience to the public, that they issued spangles called five-franc gold pieces, which, by the way, were very easily lost.

After the Franco-German war, Germany resolved to adopt a

gold standard. It had a mass of rubbish to get rid of which had been in circulation for more than a century. The means for the purchase was partly obtained from the indemnity paid by France, partly from the sale of silver which it resolved on superseding. In a short time the price of silver began to fall. The fall was aggravated by the suspension of silver minting in the Latin Union. Soon afterwards Italy retired her paper money and established a gold standard. The same process was adopted in Scandinavia and Denmark. As a consequence, the rest of the Latin Union was constrained to virtually accept a gold standard, and gold may be actually said to be standard throughout Europe, except in Austria and Russia, where a forced paper currency is in circulation. At present silver, as estimated in gold, has fallen from 5s.6d. an ounce to 3s. 6d. The fall is entirely due to the cessation of silver minting and the abandonment of a silver standard, according to the law which I laid down in an earlier part of this lecture, that the dominant factor in any one of the precious metals which determines its value is its use as currency. Had European communities abandoned the mintage of gold, and had held only to silver, gold, whether supplied plentifully or scantily, would have fallen to the ratio in which it stood in England up to the reign of Edward I. Even now, if Austria and Russia were to retire their paper, and issue metallic florins and roubles instead of it, there would be an immediate rise in the gold price of silver; and if, furthermore, the vast Chinese Empire were to establish a silver currency for the whole population, it is more than probable that the old ratio would be nearly, if not quite, restored.

There is, then, undoubtedly, as measured by the wants of European communities, or as interpreted by their governments, an excess of silver capable of being employed as currency in the world. But the curious thing is that in silver-currency countries prices have not risen. The rupee of the Indian Government used, on an average, to be worth 2s. on the English Exchange; is now worth little more than two-thirds that sum, or about 1s. 4d. But in the purchase of commodities and labour in India, the rupee goes just as far as it formerly did. We have been told so on the highest authority. Of course there is one explanation of this. The Indian Mint does not allow its issues to exceed the ascertained wants of its Indian subjects. The issues of the Mint are regulated, not free. There is a difference of nearly 30 per cent. between the Mint and the bullion price of silver, and that difference represents or measures the power of the Government to give an artificial value to a manufactured article, the use of which is requisite to the business of life.

The recent bimetallic movement began in France—that country of logical inferences from imperfect and erroneous premises. Its earliest advocates were Cornuschi and Walowski, and years ago I used to receive numerous pamphlets and even larger schemes from these writers. It has more recently formed a headquarters in England, and its advocates have been influential enough to procure a Royal Commission. This commission has recently issued a report, in which the allegations of the several partisans are very carefully and very fairly marshalled, and has expressed an opinion that if the wishes of the bimetallic advocates could be met, it would be very desirable to meet them. Now, this is not the place in which to analyze a report of this magnitude. I can only allow myself to say thus much: the advocates of the change are confident and aggressive; the defence of the present system does not appear to me thorough and hearty. But the latter are in possession; and were the acceptance of the theory brought within the range of practical politics, I think that a great deal more emphasis and cogency could be given to the defence. For my own part, having read the report, I think I may confidently say that every argument alleged by the bimetallists has been alleged and dealt with more than sixty years ago, when a similar project was put forward.

I do not mean an invidious statement when I say that the principal and the most vigorous advocates of the change are eminent merchants of high character and undoubted worth, but whose principal business is with silver-currency countries. Now, these gentlemen have, in addition to a fluctuating standard in which they buy, the necessity of performing a second operation in the process of their trade, for they have to trade on the standard of the country—now treated as bullion—as well as on the goods in which they deal. If I buy in a gold standard, the profit of my business lies in the goods which I purchase only; if I buy in a silver standard, my risks extend over the standard and the goods.

It is inconvenient, but as the trade goes on and even increases, it would appear that the additional risk is calculable. Now, to some extent this case is stated, though with not a little irrelevance, for it is difficult to see how the price of Indian wheat is lowered in England by the silver currency of that currency, if the grain is bought with goods produced under a gold currency *régime*, or in respect to which the Indian Government has given a fictitious Mint value. The Mint authorities in Calcutta must be very much asleep, if they have given coined rupees for uncoined bullion. The latter they, of course, buy at its gold price.

Bimetallism would become practicable if every civilized government would agree to give the same artificial value to their silver coins, and all would guarantee an international currency. But they must make a fixed ratio, and they must enter into an international agreement to regulate their issues. They must next devise penalties and the means of enforcing these penalties on those who violate the convention, by the agency of a powerful and respected international police. If they do not, governments will do as they always have done, when circumstances almost established a ratio, coin in the cheapest metal. I confess I cannot tell how the convention is to agree, and how the police is to be established.

Now, let us suppose this done, and the silver coins by the act of government, or, rather, of all the governments in unison, dragged up to gold prices. What would be the result? You would have two currencies of equal Mint value circulating instead of one. If I am to receive a debt, my debtor can pay it in silver coins or in silver currency notes at my pleasure, and I can do the same with my creditor. But by the very terms of the hypothesis money would be none the more plentiful, none the cheaper, and prices would remain unaffected. There would, it is true, be an exceedingly difficult machine to work—the international convention; and it would be fortunate if suspicion as to irregular practices did not ripen into conviction, and a very violent strain be put on the international agreement. One thing might, perhaps, be gained—a certain class of traders would be relieved of some trouble and a little risk. But to this I answer that private interests are not necessarily the public good.

VIII.

PEASANT AGRICULTURE AND MANUFACTURE.

The dangers of large farms—Arthur Young on small holdings—Servile tenure compared with knight service—Early date of leasehold system —The stock and land lease—The enclosures of the sixteenth century— Repeated in the eighteenth century—Young's cure for unimproving tenants—Emigration of the skilled labourer—Mistaken policy of the Oxford colleges—Economic influence of allotments.

THERE is no economic subject on which opinion has been more thoroughly contrasted than on that of peasant agriculture. There has been less variety of views with regard to peasant manufacture, for the sentiment has generally been one of regret at the inevitable extinction of the small handicraftsmen by the capitalist manufacturer, armed as the latter is with indefinite power and multiplicative machinery. In fact, by no means such large issues are involved in the question of manufacture. It may be doubted whether machinery can ever supersede the use of the human hand, except in those particulars where automatic uniformity is required. Here indeed there is only one limit to supply, *i.e.*, demand. But the case is very different with agricultural industries. You may supplement human labour to a great extent by cultivating the soil, by gathering, cleansing, and storing its products; but infinitely the greatest work, and the most significant, is the application of intelligence, foresight, and perseverance to the very varied routine of a husbandman's calling. And though no one can tell what is the limit of agricultural production, though nothing has been more childish and ignorant than the chatter about the margin of cultivation, and similarly indefinite and incommensurable contingencies; yet it is true that one cannot at any given time turn out, as a manufacturer can, an unlimited quantity of agricultural products, as one can practically supplies of iron, of cotton cloth, of woollen stuffs, and of hosiery.

Nor is the question of production on a large and on a small scale, to be measured by the cost of production only. Cost of production may be a matter of very obscure and difficult analysis. In the case of a manufacturer or an agriculturist on a large scale, whose outgoings are sales, it can be, or ought to be, exhibited on a balance-sheet, containing assets and liabilities with a profit and loss account, and the whole process may be given with arithmetical precision. The producer buys plant and stock, builds or hires the necessary buildings for his calling, hires and pays labour, collects produce, and, if he be shrewd and successful, waits for the market. The cost of production can be given with absolute accuracy. The regular element of risk in the calling is whether the produce, apart from other risks, plentifully strewed over the process, will command the expected price. Yet there is no calling, I am persuaded, under the sun in which there are more risks than in that of a tenant farmer on a large scale, who produces almost entirely in expectation of the market; and no man, who in contracts for the use of the land which he cultivates, ought to have a wider margin, or, if you please, a greater contingency of profit, in order to cover the risks of his enterprise. He needs on his own account so to distribute his husbandry as to make, as far as possible, the gains of one crop counterbalance what I may call the weather losses of the other. If the seasons are propitious on the whole, and he is not, therefore, as he rarely would be in these days, overwhelmed with a cheapness which brings the prices of his produce perilously near the cost of production—a risk quite as recurrent under protection—he has the risk of disease among his stock and blight on his corn. I cannot better illustrate the risks of agriculture than by stating that in which every practical farmer would agree with me, that no one but a lunatic would invest the whole of his substance in the contingency of one crop, *e.g.*, of hop growing. Nor need I at this particular point dwell on the necessity which there is of making contracts for the use of land liberal, equitable, and elastic, unless one wishes, as in recent years, to see ruin overtake both interests, that of the landowner and that of the farmer.

But when you come to production on a small scale you cannot exhibit the same balance-sheet. What is the cost of production is a question which you may ask without getting an answer. In the case which I have just now described, the capital invested in plant, stock, buildings, rent and labour, may, hypothetically at least, be conceived of as invested in some other calling, some other premises, some other farm. Though economists have talked absurdly, that is, metaphysically, about capitals invested in business as essentially mobile, when they could not be realized and changed from their present object without serious loss, and probably ruin, there has been a time when the individual possessor could have exercised a fairly free discretion in the investment of his property. I will admit that the discretion is not absolute. Men cannot change from calling to calling with facility. An unsuccessful tradesman cannot turn himself into a successful physician, unless he practices homœopathy, where I have heard that such a mutation has been, advantageously for the individual, effected, for the law steps in to prevent it. Men in carrying on an occupation are very much tied by their early training and its associations. Economists have written as unwisely about changes of industry as they have about wage funds, with an ignorance which is almost sublime as to the invariable and manifest facts of human life. I say this that I may not be misunderstood. There is a freedom in production on a large scale, but the freedom is limited by conditions in the first instance, and soon becomes curtailed when the choice is made.

But in the case of a producer on a small scale the cost of production may be almost intangible and incapable of estimate. This has been noted long since in what economists call by-industries, that is callings which do not constitute the regular labour and livelihood of those who practice them. Generally it must be allowed this by-industry, when its produce comes to be sold, is very poorly remunerated. But what if it be used in the family?

It is possible to conceive that the whole clothing of a household may be supplied by industry carried on in the spare hours of those who are generally occupied in a different calling. Such a result was exceedingly common in those old days when the spinning wheel was in every home, and the hand loom in many. It is said that there are many districts in the civilized world in which all the household linen in a new home, all the bedding, and the greater part of the clothing, if not the whole, which the bride possesses are the work of her own hands. Or what if the workman be also an occupier of land, which he cultivates in his spare hours, the produce of which to a very considerable extent maintains his family? In both these cases the cost of production cannot be estimated, because if the labour had not been employed as I have described, it would have been lost, let alone the chance that the enforced idleness would have involved waste and expense. I have heard some rigid economists talk of agricultural allotments and spade husbandry as a return to barbarism, a deliberate contempt for the progress of science. But the best economic condition is not that in which the greatest amount of produce is obtained at the cheapest rate, the greatest amount of capitalists pick up the greatest amount of profits; but one in which the greatest amount of workmen can live in the greatest possible comfort and security. I do not profess to admire the condition of the Scottish crofters; but I am certain that it is better for the country that they should live in content and hope, than that thousands of them should be cleared off, in order to provide a desert for a Yankee speculator to shoot over, and an aggregate rent for a Scotch tradesman to collect. He must be a very sturdy advocate of *laissez faire* who affirms that it is better to create a solitude for twenty square miles than have it peopled by human beings. And yet so amazing is the insolence of some landowners, that I have had to listen in my time to an angry, perhaps an uneasy, defence of Scotch deer forests.

To Arthur Young, whose notes on agriculture in the latter part of the eighteenth century are of such paramount importance to the students of agricultural history, small holdings were an abomination. When they were in the occupancy of labourers they hindered enclosures, and ensured the continuance of the villainous three-course system, viz., two white crops and a fallow. In the hands of the small farmers they were only a little less obnoxious. They were centres of stupidity, ignorance, and prejudice, and Young can devise no better means of improving them than that of adding 50 per cent. to the rent of the holding. Not that Young wished to see the creation of enormous farms, still less occupancies with insufficient capital. His typical farmer, Bakewell of Dishley, the real founder of pedigree stock in cattle and sheep, had only 440 acres of land in his holding, of which 110 only were arable. He performed, says Young, "great and expensive works on the property of another," though, Young also tells us that " he was fortunate in a generous and considerate landlord," a phenomena which was not so rare a century ago as it now is. But for unimproving tenants, as he considers most small farmers to be, he has no mercy. "A bad tenant," he says, "cannot have his rent raised too high." In Young's time this was the only obvious means of getting rid of such people, and it was not exceedingly effectual then, for farmers were not much more disposed to migrate in England than they are in Ireland now. The economist is apt to ignore association and sentiment; but they who have to interpret facts are constrained to take them into account. Besides the legislature has established a price for them in the Committee rooms.

In more recent times the tide of opinion has turned the other way. It must be forty years ago since my late friend, Mr. Thornton, published his plea for peasant proprietorship, a work most of the details of which were derived from the author's experiences in the Channel Islands. It must be nearly as long since Mr. Laing published his book on the Norwegian land system, a far better illustration of peasant holdings than the market gardens of Guernsey and Jersey. Then the passionate devotion of the French peasant to his holding, and the very varied character of his industry, were commented on, in his characteristic way, by Michelet; and Mr. Mill, though with some cautions and alarms, derived from the experiences he had or had heard of the allotment system under the old Poor Law, and the conacre holdings in Ireland, under which labourers were paid in strips of potato ground, generally endorsed the sentiment, and saw in it, duly guarded, a remedy against the risks of over-population. The same has been said of the Belgian holdings, in which industry is traditional, agriculture on the whole excellent, and the peasantry fairly secured against extortion. My own observations of continental agriculture, especially in Southern Germany, confirm most of these conclusions. But, on the other hand, Lady Verney has lately drawn a deplorable picture of the peasant holdings in Auvergne, and of the sordid struggle for existence in that region. But France, especially rural France, is not the country in which to trust to first impressions about the peasantry. I drew hasty, and, as I found afterwards, erroneous conclusions about the Breton peasantry, conclusions which further experience disabused me of. But there is no part of the economic question in which it is more necessary to have recourse to agricultural history than it is on agricultural tenancies, and I must, in order to substantiate the conclusions which I shall have to draw further on in this lecture, give you a sketch of agricultural tenancies from remote to recent times.

The earliest evidence which we have of a conclusive and general character as to the division of land and its occupancy dates from the middle of Henry III.'s reign, or a little later, *i.e.*, from about 1240. At this time it became the custom, the practice being uniform from Northumberland to Cornwall, for rentals to be drawn up, in which the number of holdings on each manor, with the extent of each, was carefully defined in carucates, virgates, and sometimes in acres, the subdivisions in the northern counties being generally bovates. The plots of an acre or more are, I am pretty sure, pieces held in severalty, the ordinary holding being so many strips in a common-field. The system of common-fields was universal, and no doubt ancient. It may have been an outcome of Roman civilization or peasant life, and possibly the common-fields, which I remember seeing in my youth, in Warwickshire, may have been the form in which Sulla's veterans were planted on the soil dangerously for the fortunes of the Roman Republic in the days of Catiline's rebellion, and even to those of Virgil, when the Corycian old man, rescued from piracy to all appearance, was quartered, an involuntary guest, on the rural holdings of the Mantuan peasants. It is not at all improbable that the serfs of the English manor were in the first place the subject British, and that their numbers were recruited from those

Saxon offenders who could not pay their wite, and so fell into bondage.

There were always three classes of persons to be found in a manor, and sometimes four. They were the lord, who generally had about one half of the area in his own hands, including closes in severalty, who shared with the tenants in the use of the common, and possessed the woods. Then there were the freeholders, or socage tenants, who held of the lord at a fixed rent, generally in money, but not infrequently in produce; and the serfs, or villains, some of whom held under their peculiar tenure estates as large as the freeholders, sometimes merely a cottage and curtilage. In the law books these serfs had no right as against the lord; in historical agriculture they had as secure a holding as the freeholders possessed as long as they satisfied its conditions, having, as events proved, a more secured holding, as the evidence of their title was found in the Court Roll. Their due was generally labour, but it was commutable for a money payment of a very moderate amount, and on the whole, as I have proved by hundreds of instances, their permanent obligations were not more onerous than those of the freeholder. Those were the regular, I may say the invariable, elements of the manor. But there were almost as constantly tenants for a term of years and other franchises, and there were not infrequently tenants for terms at a rent. I have found tenants on a temporary holding in the very earliest accounts, for it might well happen, especially when an estate was remote, that it was more prudent for the owner to let it than to be at the trouble of cultivating it himself.

On the whole, except for the dignified character of his holding, I am disposed to think that the lord, supposing, for the sake of illustration, he held of the king, as all ultimately did, was in no particular better off, and in some was worse off, than the serf. He had to serve in war, at his own expense, for a longer time than the serf had to labour on the fields for him. This liability, grievous enough when the field of operations was the Welsh or the Scottish marches, was all but intolerable when the service was on the king's continental possessions. An attempt was made to commute it in the middle of the twelfth century, and every one knows the quarrel of Edward I. and his two great earls when he wished to revive the duty in their case. During the nonage of his heir his estate was wasted, his son and daughters might be disposed of in marriage, and could escape from this obligation only by a smart fine, and his heirs succeeded only after a payment which was very similar to the fine on entry exacted from the serf. The tenure was no doubt an exalted one, but its incidents to my mind were as onerous as those of the villain. In one particular he was worse off than the serf. The serf could not maintain an action against his lord, nor could the lord against the king. But the courts of law interposed, we are told, to protect the serf against atrocious injuries at the hand of his lord. The lord's only remedy against the king was insurrection, and I must allow that he used this pretty freely. It is a most remarkable fact in English economic history that, while in France the position of the roturier, and in Teutonic countries of the bauer or bonder, became progressively worse, it became in the end the object of those who held land under the honoured form of knight service, to level their estates down to that of the socages, and to emancipate themselves at once from their dignity and their liabilities, by occupying what is historically the far humbler position of socage tenants.

I have given this brief sketch of the occupants or owners in an ancient manor, because it seems to me that we must discover in the liabilities of the lord the motive for protecting the rights of the humbler tenants. The king and the lord were equally interested in making or conciliating a party among the less dignified classes in society, the former as a counterpoise to the lords, the latter as a protection against arbitrary acts by the king. And on the whole the latter had, I do not doubt, the advantage. The fidelity of the retainers to their lords during the long war of the royal succession is an illustration of what I mean, and the contempt and disgust at the conduct of Banister, the servant of Buckingham, who betrayed his master to Richard III. towards the conclusion of this savage strife, is a proof how completely this fidelity was expected, and how generally the breach of it was condemned.

I have stated that tenancies for a term existed, these being the exemplars of the modern tenant farmer on a lease. The terms were of different duration. I have found them as short as five and as long as thirty years. But they were comparatively rare. In early times, then, the system of double ownership was universal and familiar. I know from these tenancies on lease that the liabilities of a socager, or a serf were quite up to those which were put on a tenant for a term, with this additional disadvantage, that the permanent occupiers had to do all their own improvements, while the landlord was expected to do all this and more for his temporary tenant. The position, then, of a landlord to a tenant on a ;term] was not so advantageous as that of a person who cultivated his own estate with his own capital and to his own profit, and hence landlord cultivation was so universal that the exceptions to it are rare, and can be explained by very intelligible reasons. From the king to the serf all cultivated land. Even artisans and citizens were agriculturists, and the England of the Middle Ages was a country in which half the soil was in the hands of peasant occupiers, or agriculturists on a small scale.

Now I must at once admit that all records of this industry have perished. I do not suppose that there exists a single account of a socager's husbandry during the whole epoch of the old agriculture. It is possible that such people did not keep accounts, or at best kept them by tallies. If they did keep them there was no motive for preserving them, as there was with the lords, to whom they formed collateral and valuable evidence of title. But though the accounts of the tenants are lost, those of the lords and their bailiffs exist by thousands. I have examined all that I could come across, and from them I have been able to construct an exact description of English agriculture through the Middle Ages. I know very much more of that agriculture, its process, its prospects, and its profits, than I do of the agriculture of England after the Reformation. But it is, as I have said, of the lords alone. I know of only one description of peasant husbandry during the whole of the period, and that is the picture which Latimer gives of his father's homestead at the end of the fifteenth century. But though I suspect the worthy bishop of having a little exaggerated the subsequent fortunes of his father's successor, I am ready to admit that he gives a precise picture of his youthful experiences in the house of a moderate occupation by an

English yeoman. His husbandry, in brief, was that of his superiors in rank.

Besides, the landlord's cultivation was in the open. Beyond his closes of pasture, his own estate, like that of the freeholders and serfs, was in the common fields, as Fitzherbert describes them in his treatise of surveying at the commencement of the sixteenth century, and Langdon displays them in those exact and beautiful surveys in the possession of All Souls and Merton Colleges. His bailiff was a native of the village, a freeholder, or even a tenant in villenage himself. The best and most continuous accounts of the thirteenth and first half of the fourteenth century which I have ever read are those of Cuxham, an Oxfordshire village. But the bailiff's father and son were serfs of the manor, for I find them so described in the rentals; and when the great plague swept the whole family away, its estate, real and personal, passed by escheat to the lord, and is duly recorded. Whatever the lord did by his bailiff the peasant cultivator saw and could do himself, and though the progress of agriculture was checked by the excessive dearness of necessary materials, and the inevitable backwardness of all agriculture in common fields, some improvements were made, and some experiments were tried. There is evidence, for example, of an attempt to improve the breed of sheep, of draining and the marling of land. If the lord undertook this there was no reason why the tenant should not follow his example. Subject to his fixed liabilities, his land was his own, and every improvement which he made on it was free from the risks of his lord's rapacity. Even if an attempt was indirectly made to raise rents by exacting and excessive fines for admittance by descent or purchase from copyholders, the law was at hand to protect the latter by limiting its amount; and Fitzherbert expressly tells us that with the extension of tenancies on terms or at will, the custom of marling lands had died out. And he says significantly, men will not improve if they run a risk of losing the fruit of their improvements. It may therefore be reasonably concluded that peasant husbandry closely imitated landlord husbandry, about which there is overwhelming evidence.

I am therefore, I think, justified in concluding that the landowners of the thirteenth and fourteenth centuries did a great service to English agriculture by the habit they had of cultivating their estates themselves. It is true that the husbandry of the time was not scientific; but I am sure that in England it was better than it was anywhere else. The landowners had a very solid stake in the country, the stake of stock, which might be easily stolen by a plunderer. But though it might be easy, as I said in a late lecture, to discover acts of violence on the king's highway, property was respected and protected in the parish. The possession of removable property by all classes created a very effective police against marauders; and the picture which Latimer gives of the plenty and security of his father's house is certainly historical. It is all very well to rake up scraps and fragments about mediæval life, of its petty cares, its sordid habits, its poor aspirations. I do not think that England has ever been an Elysium, but I am sure that in the old days of peasant ownership and cultivation there never existed, five or six centuries ago, such abject misery, such sullen apathy, such hopeless penury as may be found in our day, not in the slums of London only, but in country villages.

The old system of landlord cultivation broke down from the effects of the great plague of 1348–9. The rise of wages was very great, the demand for produce, even when the produce was scanty, was low. I have been able to discover and have published the evidence of what profits were made in agriculture before and after that prodigious calamity. Not that the old system was abandoned at once. Some landowners struggled on for fifty or even seventy years. Some, particularly the great monasteries, kept home farms in their own hands, and did so up to the Dissolution, because the system was convenient if not profitable. But of the rest, all or most of them betook themselves to a new system, which I was the first to discover, the land-and-stock lease, under which the tenant held for a term, rented the stock under penalties if it were not intact at the conclusion of the term, the landowner generally insuring the flock from losses beyond a certain percentage. Such a system was more advantageous to the lord than it would be to have let the land without the stock, as I have proved by comparing the rental of the same estate under this system with the rent paid after the system was abandoned. It lasted generally for about seventy years after its commencement on the estate. It is a curious fact that in these leases the tenant often had several plots or plough-lands for terms, the commencement of which greatly varied. He may have been beginning the term for one parcel, and be nearly at the end of it with another. This seems to prove that the peasant cultivators gradually extended their holdings, and that it was easier to occupy land than to find tenants. The custom of stock-and-land leasing was continued by the monasteries up to the Dissolution, and commonly on very easy terms. Hence, when the king entered on the chattels of the monasteries, not a little of the famous stock was found to be alienated during the continuance of a long lease. During the sixteenth century it was not found possible to raise rents, for the competing farmer from a distance was all but unknown, and it was not popular, perhaps not safe, to offer a higher rent for land than a sitting tenant was willing to pay, or was in the habit of paying. Dislike to what is called in modern times, and in particular localities, a land-grabber, is by no means a feeling of recent growth. I shall hope to show you hereafter upon what conditions it has arisen. But the system of fines on the renewal of leases, with the alternative, was developed during the sixteenth century. We have literary and contemporaneous evidence of the fact, of the discontent it caused, and of the evictions which followed on refusal to pay. Then, perhaps, the landlord could command a somewhat enhanced rent. But I am persuaded that it would have been unsafe to have done this on a large scale, or to an exorbitant amount. Till very recent times the English tenant has not been patient under exactions, and some very ominous events, failures to be sure, but alarming for all that, were found in the Pilgrimage of grace, in Ket's rebellion, and in the insurrection of the northern earls. When Mary Tudor in 1544 procured the repeal of all her father's statutes since the rupture with Rome, she felt herself constrained to allow the alienation of the abbey lands. The nobles of the day, as the Spanish proverb goes, stole the sheep and kept it, but gave God the trotters. I felt convinced years ago that rents up to the end of the sixteenth century could not have been raised, except indirectly; and I found that a theory which I had worked out by facts was confirmed by the evidence of rent actually paid.

The seventeenth century developed the system of rack-renting. To modern notions the rent of arable land was not high, for from the facts which I have collected it is plainly not more than from 4s. 6d. to 5s. an acre. But agriculture made no progress, and the new system was an effectual bar to its progress, as is asserted by nearly every writer on agriculture throughout the century. Tenancies remained small, for the farmers were too poor to increase their holdings. Gregory King allows the farming class no greater saving power than 25s. a year, the lowest among all orders of society, whom he whimsically enough calls the saving classes. For as I must inform you, no notable or general improvement was made in agriculture during the seventeenth century. I do not say that no one introduced the new system from Holland, but no persons did it sufficiently to leaven the mass of agriculturists. The fields remained unenclosed, the old three-course system of two white crops and a fallow continued, and the agriculture of the last Stuart reign did not differ materially either in method or in productiveness, from the agriculture of the Early Plantagenets. It was only when the enclosure, or rather the rational partition, of the common fields was seriously taken in hand, and this was towards the end of Anne's reign, that turnip culture, the sowing of artificial grasses with a white crop, barley, or oats, began, and the four-course system, so characteristic of British agriculture, was fairly set on foot. But it took a long time to extend it. Farmers were slow, prejudiced, and suspicious. They detected the contingency of more stringent rack-rents under the new agriculture, and their experiences did not tend to disabuse them of their fears. By the end of the first quarter of the eighteenth century, though prices were generally low, and remained exceedingly low for many years, rack-rents rose from 4s. 6d. and 5s. to 7s. an acre, and distress, for so the fashion of the age called plenty, prevailed. Now it must be allowed, and should always be stated, that the new agriculture and its success was the work of many untiring, energetic, and enlightened landowners throughout the kingdom. In the thirteenth and fourteenth centuries, and again in the eighteenth, the action of the landowners, due most likely to an enlightened self-interest, but, in the eyes of the economist, none the worse for that, bestowed great and lasting benefits on British agriculture. Even in these days, when the noble art has fallen on bad times, due to intelligible causes and to mischievous agencies, the British agriculturist is far beyond any in the world.

Upon the relics of the bad old system, Arthur Young directed his observation and uttered his indignant comments. He was in no sense a critic of historical causes; all his wisdom lay in the interpretation of the existing situation, and in this he was a master. No Englishman has dealt with agriculture, either before or since his time, who has shown more practical knowledge, more untiring zeal, and more zealous devotion. A gentleman by birth and breeding, Young has great tact and great self-respect. His admiration for Mr. Bakewell and Colonel St. Leger, though graduated according to their social rank, is profound and hearty. His political economy is not worth much, for he preferred Stewart to Adam Smith, and believed that the bounty and the Corn Laws were the buttresses of British agriculture, or I must say English, for he did not think Scotland worthy of notice, though it was then enjoying the blessings of the nineteen-years lease, and fastening the plough not to the necks, but to the tails of the horses.

Even if Young had been a better historian and a better economist than he was, his agricultural zeal would have made him abhor the occupier of forty acres in a common field with less than twenty of enclosed land, who was wedded to the old arrangement and the three-course system. Some special knowledge, and a very wide experience of men in all ranks of life and in all callings has made me, I trust, very tolerant of fools, even when I am quite aware that their folly is hereditary or self-induced. But I think if I had observed agriculture with Arthur Young I should have denounced peasant occupancy, even though I might have known the causes of its downfall. But you cannot ruin men and then claim from them the gift of enterprise. I should have seen that these relics of the old system were incompatible with progress, and should have demanded full play for that competition which results in the survival of the fittest. So much for Arthur Young's time. In own our I should demand the exhibition of the same political cathartic, and though I cannot here illustrate my opinion of men and things by name, I should desire, with much fervency, the expulsion of the unfittest. The incompetent, if incurable should be cleared off, provided always that they hindered the development of true knowledge and progress, as unimproving and invincibly ignorant tenant farmers do. For this purpose, Young had but one remedy—a penal rise in rents. This, he believed, and he could quote numerous cases on his side of the question, was the cure for sloth and prejudice. And yet it is singular that a writer who saw more clearly in my opinion than any one who has written on agriculture, that adequate security to a tenant's capital is a *sine qua non* with the mass of men who risk their money in a calling that you never can expect more than a few Bakewells, and that these men by an unerring instinct turn their attention to the improvement of stock, in which process they cannot easily be plundered, instead of to the improvement of land in which they can easily be plundered, did not at once detect the origin of bad farming, and concurrently with his penal remedy, insist that the genuine improvement of land, due to the tenant's capital and intelligence are, and should be, his property. Of all the unjust and mischievous rules which pedantic lawyers have foisted into law, the maxim, "Cujus est solum, ejus est usque ad cœlum," is the most disastrous. It is the primary cause of the distressful condition of agriculture. It is a serious bar to productiveness in a hundred ways. It is the principal reason why the poor in large towns are huddled into filthy and unwholesome dens. It should be swept away, and the reverse principle established. That whatever value the capital and labour of an occupier has induced on the soil shall be deemed and be his own property, and that no clause or condition in any lease or tenancy at will should be recognized in law, which strives to defeat this rule. If the tenant farmers of the eighteenth century had been like the small freeholders of the fourteenth and fifteenth, whatever agriculture was possible would have been imitated and carried out perfectly by them.

So enamoured is Young of his drastic remedy, that he even welcomes the common and increasing vices of his day, reckless and ruinous gambling at the hazard table, as the means by which tenants paying too little for their holdings could be made to pay adequate rents. He endorsed the villainous maxim of Mandeville, that private vices were public benefits. As time went on, he began to doubt whether he had not been as the proverb says, "holding a candle to the devil," for Young lived on to 1820, and had experience of the horrible calamities which came upon England, upon all, indeed, but landowners during the great Continental War—the wanton, sordid, selfish work of the heaven-born Pitt. During this period, though it cannot be said that rents did not rise—they went from an average of 10s. an acre to more than 35s. —agricultural skill was diffused rather than progressive, the weaker tenants were squeezed out owing to those unnatural fluctuations in price, which these tenants could neither anticipate nor interpret, and the condition of the agricultural labourer was deplorably degraded. Nor was there any escape from the depression of wages, for emigration was unknown to them, and even transportation, which a vigorous and brave government, resolved on maintaining law and order, freely practised, was not copious enough to relieve population of the unemployed and starving.

Now let us look at what has happened since 1820, the year of Young's death. Within five years the old labour laws were abolished, and with them the emigration of artisans was permitted. A dozen years more and the old Poor Law came to an end, and with it the doctrine that the peasant was to be compensated out of the rates for the loss he had sustained by the enclosure of commons. These enclosures, from the reign of Anne to about thirty-five years ago, amounted in area to nine million acres, and the compensation once given for the loss of interest in this was now taken away. A few years later and free trade in food was accorded. The effect of this was to put an end to the desire of extracting profit and rent from the misery and stint of the poor, or at least to check the hope of it, and not less markedly to offer the energetic stimulant of a free market to food-producing countries. Now this led to a great increase in the mercantile marine, for the open market was soon aided by the removal of all restraints on navigation. But as soon as ever countries inhabited by persons of British descent entered into the new market, the necessity for hands to undertake agricultural operations was rapidly felt, and emigration on a large scale ensued. Offers under the homestead law of land at nominal prices became known to men who were grudgingly paid ten shillings a week, with the new workhouse in prospect at the end of their career. The construction of railways, part of the new freight system, and as yet a force in the future whose significance was ill understood even by the acutest minds, drew mainly from rural places the strongest, sturdiest, and most enterprising men to new fields of labour and settlement. There were attractive prospects held out before the agricultural hand, and the best of them, as I foresaw and said a quarter of a century ago, to the vehement indignation of some people here, were leaving and would leave the country. Now, no one but a demented Malthusian would believe and allege that a community was all the better off for losing its best hands. I see that my old acquaintance, Mr. Clare Read, at a recent meeting of the Farmers' Club, complained that the agricultural labourer wants in these days to get the maximum of pay with the minimum of labour, and I was pleased to notice that one, at least, of the farmers present replied that this was human nature, and that no doubt it was as keenly entertained by Mr. Clare Read himself as it was by any workman in his employment. But Mr. Read was in one sense right. Twenty or thirty years ago there was no opportunity for the farm-hand, even in his most sanguine visions, to entertain the hope that wages would follow demand, or that resignation to hopeless hardship was ever to be exchanged for the discontent which discovers an escape from bondage. We economists, when we are in our senses, look on discontent as the basis of most economical virtues and welcome its manifestations.

And now about agriculture. The skill has not gone. Any one who takes up those periodicals which deal principally with agricultural products will see, as before, that the British farmer is the most competent husbandman in the world. A well-tilled farm is to me the most pleasant sight which I can view, and I will not hold myself up to the execration of artists and authors, or their intractable, but sometimes friendly, associates, the professional critics, by comparing the husbandman's craft to the exhibition of pictures, and the choicest products of the paradise of publishers, the historic row. The British farmer supplies pedigree stock to the civilized world. The American manufacturer, who, with all his bounce, looks anxiously at the wages of the immigrant factory hand, and stints him to the utmost of his power, does not care what he gives for a herd of Jersey cows. I have heard him talk of how he manipulates his workmen, and what he gives for pedigree stock. He is as proud of his parsimony to the former as he is of his profusion for the latter. I shall begin to fear for British agriculture when I see its rivals outstripping it in produce and in quality.

But there is another side of the shield. The skill is present, the capital is gone. The English landowner has followed only too faithfully a part of Young's advice. He has rack-rented his tenant mercilessly, and with rare, and those most honourable, exceptions, has done nothing useful besides. He can very likely ride well to hounds, shoot as successfully as his gamekeepers, waste his substance as the prodigal devoured his, ruin his farmers, plunge on the turf, rely on his stud for an income, and supplement it by being a rook where he used to be a pigeon, qualify himself as a farmer's friend, after behaving as his bitterest enemy, and in rare cases, even talk about bimetallism, and laud his nostrum as the one cure for agricultural depression. But the race of the St. Legers and the Bakewells, with whom Young made acquaintance, is, I regret to say, almost passed away.

Some landowners have no doubt unconsciously encouraged their tenants in recklessness. Some years ago a landowner of my acquaintance in this country, who had an ample fortune from other sources than land, began the process of amalgamating farms on his estate. He told me that his experiments had been so thorough that he did not expect to get more than $1\frac{1}{2}$ per cent. on his outlay. Like the rich man in the parable, he pulled down his barns and built bigger. He supplied his tenants with houses to four-hundred-acre farms, his general rule of size, which would suggest the expenditure of £1,000 a year. The farm buildings, I grant, were excellent, and entirely fitted for their purposes. But the farmhouse was a comfortable mansion. Now in Young's time, when stock was not half the price it now is, and wages much lower, £4 an acre was the minimum for a farm of which one-third was arable and two-thirds pasture. At the present time the minimum should be £10. But on the average times, and after making due allowance for the risks of his calling, a farmer cannot expect to make more than 10 per cent. on his capital. It may be doubted whether he made so much, for his calling was attractive, and, as we all know, was open to active competition. Now for a man to live in a house which invites an expenditure that is two and a half times more than the tenant can possibly earn by his calling is a very dangerous matter. And when his capital has slowly leaked away, and owing to his unfortunate habit of not keeping a good and full balance sheet, without his knowledge, the danger is increased, and ruin is still more imminent. I am glad to see that farmers are beginning to take stock of their position, at least those who are spokesmen at the Farmers' Club, and to allege that a new departure had to be made, and has been made. But I know well enough how disappointing has been the experience of those who have inherited these fancy farmhouses.

It was not to be wondered at that the worst errors of the old system were faithfully imitated among others, and there were added to them the peculiar irregularities of the locality. The head and fellows of a college are in the strictest sense of the word limited owners. They have in equity less rights and more duties than the owner of a life estate under a strict settlement. They are debarred from waste, and if any one is at the pains of looking after them they can be restrained from appropriating the proceeds of mines and minerals. They are like all limited owners, under the obligation of keeping their tenements in repair, and of effecting these repairs from income only. On this head they ought not to owe a sixpence of borrowed money. But I should be very much surprised if it was certified to me that the interest on their liabilities on this score did not amount to a sensible part of their income, and their outlay to several years' income. It is more than probable that they have amalgamated farms, and find it difficult to get tenants. It is likely that they have listened to perfidious agents, and have rack-rented their tenants till they find it hard to get half the rent which they used to get. It is not difficult to get at the facts, for under the Act of 1877 the Colleges are bound to supply an annual balance sheet of their income and expenditure. But we all know that matters are at a deadlock. The University Commission put certain obligations on the Colleges in the interest of the University. Those obligations are not satisfied, and, from all that can be learned, they are not likely to be satisfied. One College has been formally allowed to repudiate its duties, and when the action was sanctioned we were instructed that the repudiation was likely to be permanent. Meanwhile the apparatus of prize fellowships has been suspended. In plain English, the future has been sacrificed to the present and the past. From what I hear, Cambridge is by no means in so awkward a condition as Oxford. But in that University, as I am told, it has not been the practice for limited owners to transfer their proper burdens to posterity.

In dealing with the Wealth of Nations, Adam Smith thought it germane to the matter to treat of the effect of endowments on education and learning, and to illustrate what he said very plentifully, and with no compliments to the place of his education, from his Oxford experiences. And, in fact, an honest economist cannot well do otherwise. I have no doubt that learning flourishes here exceedingly, and that our home-bred savants have a European reputation. The great Teutonic race, I make no question, acknowledges our contributions to letters, as heartily and as guilelessly as we do theirs. But the economist is justified in examining the machinery of endowments, from which these great results of learning and research are quickened and strengthened, and in disarming the question of the probability of their continuance. Whatever men do, as Juvenal says, is the stuff from which we draw our inferences. And to speak truth, the present outlook is not encouraging. It seems that the future generation is to live on memories, a diet as unpalatable as the east wind.

The question as to how a true economic rent is to be restored is of vital importance. That rents of agricultural land have fallen below their economic value is, I submit, indisputable. If these rents were too high between 1860 and 1879 inclusive, they have fallen unreasonably, though not perhaps unnaturally, since. Now in dealing with the situation, as Johnson said, we must rid ourselves of cant, and cant is irrational optimism, or unjustifiable pretence. Scottish farming was not promoted, but rather hindered, by the nineteen-years lease. It was due in the main to the energy of Sir John Sinclair, and to the perseverance and ability of the

Scottish farmers, who did for Scotland what Arthur Young and the Board of Agriculture did for England. It is no use to suggest to the farmer that he will increase his profits and pay his rent out of Protection. It is no use to tell him that the same two-sided benefit will accrue to him from the acceptance of bimetallism. *Non tali auxilio, nec defensoribus istis*, he has learned in his rational moments to utter in honest English. I am disposed to believe that the scales have fallen from his eyes, and that he has recovered his economic vision.

The first thing which the tenant farmer needs, be he large, moderate, or small, is security. To offer a man a lease for five years at a nominal rental, and reserve to the owner the right to pounce on his tenant's outlay at the end of the term is a mockery. If he has put value into land it ought to be secured to him, and it is not difficult to appraise the value. If he has taken value out of the land he should pay for it, and it is as easy to appraise the damage, for crops tell tales. The principal cause why agriculture has suffered in England and Scotland, and rents have sunk ruinously, has been the insecurity of the sitting tenant. It is perfectly true that the law as laid down and administered has created that insecurity, and has even emphasized it. Now the law as it stands at present gives compensation for certain agricultural improvements, for some absolutely, for others if the owner agrees to them, for some not at all. But instead of taking the effect of the improvement on the tenement, it takes the cost of the outlay, and attempts to give it a diminishing value. In my judgment, and I stated that judgment very freely while the existing law was under discussion, the theory of agricultural compensation was radically vicious, vexatious, and delusive. There is a very simple test. What is the measurable value of the service which the tenant has done to the fertility of land? But one reasoned in vain. The landowners were still besotted by the doctrine of the unearned increment. To be just, they alleged that the system of valuation would disable the valuer from discerning what part of the increase was due to the unearned increment. And the unearned increment is gone with Breitmann's party.

Besides, under the system which was ultimately adopted, no security was given to the sitting tenant. If the occupier, from despair, or weariness, or incapacity, or from merely changing his mind, gave up his holding, the value of his permitted improvements was secured to him, if he struggled on, if he met bad times with parsimony, with enterprise, with diligence, with activity, he can still be rack-rented on his own outlay. But to imagine that people will deliberately, with their eyes open, when they are fully informed as to the state of the law, and while they are still able to exercise their discretion, invest their capital on what is so precarious as the abstinence of a landowner, whose wants may be pressing, whose devices are boundless, and who hankers after the unearned increment, is a remedy for agricultural difficulty which might be imagined in Laputa, but is, to use an expressive vulgarism, played out here. The dream of the unearned increment, was the hindrance to justice being done the sitting tenant. And I assure you the dreams of stupid people are often very solid obstacles. If security were accorded, I have no doubt that capital would flow back to land, and a rational competition become the order of the day. I cannot indeed predict that the rents of 1879 would be recovered, but I make no question that there would be a speedy increase on the rents of 1889. I hold with Young, that people ought to pay for their holdings what they are worth. But the question as to what a thing is worth involves a great many considerations, on which people's attention has been recently quickened. One of them is, what is the extent of their risks?

The size of tenancies will always vary in countries where there is a great variety of employments over which a choice can be exercised. In such a country agriculture has its own peculiar attractions, and in many cases high profits are not incentives. But it is plain that fewer persons will compete for large than will for small farms, for the people that possess moderate incomes are more numerous than those who have large means. But in countries where the agricultural population greatly exceeds those who are engaged in other callings, farms will always be small. France is emphatically a country of small holdings, not because land is compulsorily divided after the death of an owner between his descending or ascending heirs; but because France is, has been, and must be, a country where rural pursuits are in the ascendency. In Ireland occupancies will remain small. If this part of the United Kingdom recovered the industries which the British Parliament destroyed, the epoch of large farms would begin and progress. No doubt Irish tenancies were rendered more diminutive than was natural from the practice which prevailed up to 1829 of creating freeholds in order to manufacture votes, and the mischief once done, it could not be recalled. But Ireland is, and will remain, a country of peasant farming, and, as I can affirm, however uncouth the surroundings of the farmer are, of minute and careful cultivation, to which, by the way, the publications of the Irish Society have greatly contributed. And in proof of what I say, one may note the columns of replies to correspondents on agricultural topics, which is so marked a feature of the Irish press. And in the same way the Channel Islands will always be a centre of peasant farming. Beyond this, and the keeping of lodging-houses, with the necessary shops, there is no choice of occupation.

The policy of granting allotments at economic rents, and with the same conditions of security to agricultural labourers, and for the matter of that to village artisans, and even to small shopkeepers, is recommended in my judgment by many considerations. I have often referred to the Act of Elizabeth in 1589, under which four acres of land were to be allotted to every new cottage, and overcrowding was forbidden in all cottages. The motive of this measure was undoubtedly to stop pauperism. But the remedy was not retrospective, and was therefore partial, and it probably came too late. But it was the law for nearly two centuries, and I am sure that its repeal, and not the practice of tea drinking, as Young thinks, was the cause of that increase of pauperism which Young notes and deplores. Its revival in some form or other would, I am certain, be a greater check to rural pauperism than anything else. It would, at least, make it more manageable.

It is, I am convinced, of great importance to fix the rural population to the soil by the tie of their own advantage. Some of the best hands have no doubt fled from a calling which held them out no hope in England. It is not expedient on grounds of the barest utility to drive the peasantry out of country places. A three- or four-acre holding would not indeed afford a very inviting prospect to a resolute and enterprising young man, but it is plainly very attractive to the mass of workmen. Where allotments can be obtained, even in much smaller patches, they are eagerly sought after and carefully cultivated. Nor is it difficult even for agricultural labourers to find the necessary capital for spade husbandry, and even for the plough, if need be. It is clear, too, that the village would be a good deal the better for the voluntary scavenging of these small occupiers. In peasant cultivation the chief outlay is labour ; the chief requisite, manure.

It is greatly to the purpose to develop the sense of property in the rural classes. It will always be found that in countries where peasant holdings are the rule, that crimes against property and robbery with violence are rare. Ireland is a remarkable illustration of the fact. Take away agrarian outrages—and however you may be disposed to view them, no one can doubt that there are special causes for them—however you may condemn them, and there is not a twentieth part of the committals for crime that there is in England. The assizes are constantly a blank. I do not affirm that under the most favourable circumstances peasant agriculture developes a lofty and heroic spirit. But it is singularly free from common crime. In Norway, in Belgium, in Switzerland, crimes against person and property are rare, almost unknown. The Channel Islanders say that all their criminals are imports. Even in rural France, where the hardness of temper which comes from poverty and parsimony sometimes leads to brutality, there is not a tenth the violence and theft recorded which marks a year's work in any London police court.

Allotments to workmen are a most valuable supplement to money wages. The reason is that the producer is also the consumer. If he works for what he gets from the land, he consumes his produce directly or indirectly on his family. Working men who occupy these little holdings have told me over and over again, at distant localities and with a frequency that left no doubt of their conviction, that every day's work which they gave to their allotment was worth ten shillings to them. And then, seeing my surprise, they volunteered their explanation, that this is what it would have cost them, if they bought the produce. There was indeed no other process by which they could estimate its value. Of course the labour of a farm-hand is worth nothing like that to his employer, and however hearty it may be is not, as a rule, paid at more than a fifth the rate. But the farmer has to live from his labourer's work, to pay rent from it, and, most important of all, to pay market charges from it. One should compare the profits of an allotment with the profits of a small farmer who holds fifty acres, who employs at most a man and a boy, and works as hard as both of them himself if one would realize the facts.

I have attempted to give you in this sketch of English agriculture, some evidence by which to interpret the present situation. The question is a large one, and is assuredly of supreme importance. Unless the relations of landlord and tenant are laid for the future on new lines, I can only foresee more serious consequences than have yet happened, to say nothing of a growth of subversive ideas, which is already inconveniently rapid. My earliest interests and experiences were in English agriculture, and my desire for its prosperity has not been lessened during the long years in which I have been its historian.

IX.

HOME TRADE AND DOMESTIC COMPETITION.

The development of wants—Economic importance of secondary wants—Immutability of prices in the Middle Ages—The guild system—Exceptions to the general rule—The Common Law on Rings—The reaction to the principles of "laissez faire"—The monopolies of the present century—Competition of capitals—The middleman—Shops and co-operative stores.

COMPETITION is an effect induced on those who are engaged in production or trade, by the interpretation which they make of demand and supply. The various persons who constitute a social unit have certain wants. Some of these, as of food, clothing, and house-room or shelter, are primary and imperative, some are secondary, or voluntary, and can remain unsatisfied without injury to the individual. The tendency of human societies is always towards the multiplication of these secondary wants, the primary having been necessarily, and, as the name implies, previously satisfied. Of course as long as there are persons who depend absolutely on others for the supply of primary wants, it is always possible to draw the line between the two classes of objects, though even here, habit may elevate that into a primary want, which may in other places be secondary. Thus in England generally, no one would doubt that stockings and leathern shoes would be a primary want with which they who are the objects of compulsory charity must be supplied. But in the north of England, where clogs or wooden shoes are worn, such articles would be deemed good enough for the inmates of workhouses, and the recipients of Poor Law relief. Farther north in Scotland, the use of shoes and stockings are or may be dispersed with altogether. In brief, the relief of those who live on the rates which are collected from those who have more than enough for their necessary wants, always tends towards what custom declares to be the minimum required for subsistence, in the three items of food, clothing, and shelter.

Now a sensible economist is by no means dissatisfied by the extension of certain secondary wants, and by their gradually becoming in a certain sense primary wants. In the first place, it is greatly to be desired that habits of refinement should be extended to all classes of society. It would be well if all the labouring classes—I use a convenient expression with the distinct knowledge that all persons who have any value in society whatever, labour—were able to satisfy secondary wants. One would rejoice if all the workers were well-fed, well-clad, and well-housed. There are few persons nowadays, who are so malignant and so silly as to wish to deprive such people of enjoyments, to tie them down to a mere routine of labour and of existence, to grudge them anything beyond the barest subsistence, and to deny them comforts and culture. From the narrowest view, one does not better the character of a man's work by refusing to allow him any relaxation and any learning. We have wisely concluded, however unwisely we may carry out the process, that an educated race is worth more, even as a mere machine of production, than one which is devoid of all training beyond that which gives him the requisite skill in his calling. Our educational system is open, I grant, to a good deal of destructive criticism. It is, in my judgment, a vicious and foolish compromise, superintended and manipulated under a ludicrously pedantic method. But it is so far sound, that it recognizes the necessity that the human being should be trained to something which is not mere work, and that this educational training should be universal, compulsory, and precedent to special or technical training. And what applies to the life of the young, and their preparation, applies to the education of people, as Adam Smith says, of all ages. The saying of the ancient sage, that men should keep learning as long as they live, is true of all classes. Every kind of education from the highest to the lowest, which is ostensibly completed in youth, is if properly understood, and wisely used, but the supply of instruments, by which knowledge is constantly collected, accumulated, and utilized. Now to most adults, this growth of knowledge comes out of books, and one's personal observations.

Again the multiplication of innocuous secondary wants acts as a barrier against imprudence and misconduct. Once induce on the individual a feeling of self-respect, and he will not lightly sacrifice his position. This is that part of the Malthusian doctrine which is true, that self-restraint in lightly undertaking responsibilities, however natural and innocent they may seem, and under circumstances are, is a check to imprudent marriage. The rest of the theory, as I have told you before, is false. Vice and misery are not checks to population, but stimulants of it. When the vice and misery are the inevitable consequences of legislation, as they were when Malthus wrote, the same agency is the cause of overpopulation. It would not I grant have been palatable, if Malthus had told the truth, and it is highly probable that his work would have failed of acceptance, had he traced certain economical results to their true causes. For men are reckless when they have nothing to lose, and in the days of Malthus, the quarter-sessions assessment of wages had effectually cut away all margin from the peasant and the artisan beyond a bare subsistence. But when secondary wants have become habitual and customary, there is a margin which its professor is unwilling to forego, which is, so to speak, a reserve of power on which he can reckon, can act, or can forbear acting. A community which subsists habitually on comparatively dear food is always more removed from the risks of famine, than another is, which lives on the cheapest which it can procure. If we could extirpate vice and misery from amongst us, and could instil into all minds a dread of falling from an existing position, it would be possible to deal with the most serious problems of modern society. Now I do not here discuss the means by which one could grapple with these evils. But I am sure that no action which diminishes the sum of them, fails of helping towards a solution of the graver difficulties, that such action is worth a trial, and that all success brings us within measurable distance of the incorrigible residuum, and the acquisition of powers for dealing with that too. The extension therefore of secondary wants is no small factor in the moral progress of society. I had therefore good reason in urging that the economic doctrine of waste, of unproductive labour, and of unproductive consumption should be revised, that it should be stripped of barren metaphysics, and should be examined in the light of facts.

The competition which I am thinking of is of production or acquisition under the conditions of trade, and of supply on the interpretation of demand. It is therefore of the highest interest to know what the demand will be, and to this result nothing contributes more than the freedom of the market. In a sense this is acknowledged by every one. The people of the United States have adopted and maintain a protective system. But within the boundaries of the union the trade which is carried on is, by a fundamental rule of the constitution, free. We had not adopted such a rule with Scotland, little more than a century after it had been ruled over by the same king whom England had. We did not adopt this rule in Ireland little less than a century ago. The case was far worse in France. Trade was prohibited or hampered between the several provinces of which that country was composed, and in consequence, while there was famine in one province, there was unmanageable plenty in another. Nor, again, do I understand by competition the bare struggle for existence. To this perpetual struggle against the contingencies of famine, when man is not emerged from the savage stage, we owe the main of those curious customs among uncivilized tribes, which have attracted so much attention among anthropologists, and have been made, almost too hastily, the key by which certain practices, still surviving among civilized communities, are confidently expounded and accounted for. I can assure you, that what people boldly call scientific inferences are very apt to be reckless, perhaps unfounded. There are fallacies too in scepticism just as there are fallacies in superstition.

It was much more easy to interpret demand up to a century and a half ago, than it is in these later times. In studying the history of prices, I have often been struck with their uniformity during long periods, and with the fulness of the interpretation which definite historical events give of mutations in prices. When no such event occurs, hardly any fluctuations occur, and it would seem that the equation of demand and supply was habitually achieved. A powerful contributor to this result was the entire absence of speculation, a tendency to which is necessarily heightened by any obscurity as to possible demand and possible supply. Another cause was the great slowness with which the cost of production was lessened. I will take an instance from the eighteenth century. During the greater part of the first half of this century, the price of lead and iron hardly changed. They were nearly identical, viz., £16 the ton. The cost of production I conclude remained the same, the demand almost invariable and quite intelligible, the supply equally certain. Of course corn prices varied from year to year, although England rarely suffered from famine. But over a considerable number of years, the same uniformity is discoverable. From 1261 to 1400, the average price by the quarter is 5s. 10¾d., from 1401 to 1540, it is 5s. 11¼d. I could multiply cases of the kind, and exhibit to you in detail how unchanged prices are. Of course great events changed the ordinary uniformity. The Great Plague affected the price of labour, and of commodities, most of the value of which depends on labour. The conquest of Egypt by Selim I. trebled the price of Indian produce. The dissolution of the monasteries affected the value of what was the more permanent spoil of them. The issue of base money and the imperfect restoration under Elizabeth produced their effects on general prices—most of all on labour. The severance of England from Guienne, the last possession of the house of Anjou, had its effect on wine and salt imports, while the ruin of the Flemings under the rule of Alva had its proper result in the decay of the woollen trade.

The policy of town government and the guild system was unfriendly to competition, as understood ordinarily in economical theories. It, no doubt, assisted another form of competition, that not for indefinite demand, but for known customers. The essence of the guild system was the limitation of producers and traders. In early English life, to use Mr. Edwin Chadwick's phrase, the competition was not in the field, but for the field, a form of competition, which, as I shall show you, is by no means extinct now. It was considered to be a legitimate act of authority for the rulers of a guild to fine a member who had offered a higher rent for a tenement than the sitting tenant was paying. It is clear that the proffer of a competition rent for arable land by a stranger was difficult, and would be resented if successful. The system of apprenticeship was a very effectual attempt to limit competition. The subsequent enrolment of the craftsman or trader in a guild, with fines for admission, and the strict limitation of occupancy to such persons as had been formally admitted, was another means of controlling competition. In this University, the restraint in certain callings by guild rules was vexatious, and the authorities easily obtained rights of matriculating persons whose callings were conceived peculiarly necessary or convenient to the University, and so of shielding them from the control of the town guilds. Booksellers, stationers, chemists, and barbers, were thus admitted, and the practice was continued up to living memory. For though the guilds were stripped of their property by Somerset, it still remained a rule of law that no person should carry on a trade or mystery in a town, where such persons existed by charter, who was not a freeman of the city or borough, *i.e.*, had paid for the privilege of corporate membership, or been admitted to the privilege through the ordinary road of apprenticeship. Now competition is either of producers or in the thing produced. In modern times, the double operation that producers compete against each other for custom, and profess superior quality or cheapness in the goods which they offer is familiar and customary. But up to recent times, *i.e.*, to the Corporation Act, the competition of producers was restrained, a practical limit being put on their number.

Subject to this restraint, which was, indeed, of the very essence of a corporation, and seemed to be not only practically defensible, but actually necessary for the development of trade, the policy of this country favoured competition, and the practice of the law courts enforced it. I do not doubt that any attempt on the part of these producers and dealers to form a syndicate or pool, with the view of regulating prices, would have been resented, and have brought the producers of such a scheme within the perils of the legal definition of conspiracy. The doctrine of the restraint of trade was a very substantial check to attempted monopolies. Parliament was much more keen in its attacks on those who attempted by royal license to secure a sole trade, than it was against those other violations of private liberty, of which the prerogative was guilty. The custom of selling goods at fairs, all but universal a generation or two ago, must have given full play to competition under such circumstances. What Adam Smith calls the higgling of the market must have been all but universal. As far as regards producers in these days, the old practice is almost limited to farm produce, for the shop, with its arbitrary or discretionary, and fixed charges has superseded the market bargain. But the law went further. It created certain trade offences, and these in the interest of the consumer. These were badgering, forestalling, regrating, and engrossing. A badger, said to be derived from the French *baggage*, was a dealer in food, who purchased in one place and sold in another. These traders appear to have been liable to prosecution at common law, but were exempted from the penalties of 5 and 6 Ed. VI. cap. 14, under which the other offences were defined, and their punishment secured. But by 5 Eliz. cap. 12, badgers had to be licensed for a year only, and under recognisances against forestalling, engrossing, and regrating, a penalty of £5 being exacted, half to go to the Crown, half to the prosecutor, for any badger who dealt without a license. The offence of forestalling was that of purchasing food on the way to market, with the intent to sell the same at a higher or dearer price. Engrossing is an attempt to control the market, by purchasing the stock of food in existence, with the intention of exacting a higher price. Regrating is the re-sale of articles which had been previously purchased in the same market. The statute of Edward VI., which defines and punishes these reputed offences, was repealed by 12 Geo. III. cap. 71, apparently because the remedy seemed worse than the disease, though the repealing statute still recognizes certain acts of traders as offences, such, for example, as spreading rumours with intent to enhance the price of hops. The repeal of the Act of Edward left these offenders to the common law, and there were prosecutions and convictions under the common law after the repeal of the statute referred to. The law was undoubtedly intended to protect the poor consumer against attempts on the part of the wealthy dealer to create an artificial price which should be inimical to him, and this was the plea for the several actions at common law which were taken. It was held by the courts that the doctrine on this subject applied to food only, and to such articles as custom or habit made equivalent to food, as for example, hops.

These offences, even at common law, have become obsolete. But in 1799, a period of great dearth, even of famine, one, Rusby, was indicted for having bought 90 quarters of oats at 41s. the quarter, and selling 30 of them at 43s. on the same day, the offence of regrating. Lord Kenyon, who presided in the court, dealt severely with Rusby's crime, denounced the repealing Act of 1772, congratulated the jury on the continued existence of the common law, assured the jurymen that forestalling was an offence under the laws of the Anglo-Saxons, regretted that Adam Smith was not alive in order that he might have sensible proof of how absurd his doctrine was, procured the conviction of Rusby, and fined him heavily. The sentence was not carried out, for a court of appeal was equally divided on the question whether regrating was, or was not, an offence at common law. In 1844 (7 and 8 Vict. cap. 24) the whole of the statutes, English, Scotch, and Irish, 36 in number, defining these offences, were cited and repealed, and with them the supposed common-law foundation for the repressive measures.

In England, then, these restraints on the action of traders are abrogated. But all the states of the American Union, with the exception of Louisiana, are under the English common law, the decisions of which law are of authority in the American courts. It is a principle, too, contained in the constitution, that laws cannot be passed, either by the State or Federal legislature, except under certain solemnities, without incurring the risk of being set aside as unconstitutional, by the Supreme Court of the State, or of the Federation, a check on legislation, which is decidedly popular in the Union. Hence, according to Dr. Dwight, the common-law doctrine of the English courts, before 1844, is the doctrine of the American courts at this time. Since Dr. Dwight has written his essay on trusts and their legality in the

December number (1888) of the "Political Science Quarterly," the facts have received a practical illustration in a decision of the New York Supreme Court, which has declared the illegality of the Sugar Trust, the very syndicate or pool which Dr. Dwight adduces and defends. It seems, also, that the reasons which induced the Federal Congress in its inter-state commerce law, to declare railway pools illegal, was founded on the same principle which has ruled in the more recent case. A pool is an arrangement between divers competing railways, under which they agree to regulate the traffic, avoid cutting rates of carriage, and divide the receipts on a mutual or reciprocal understanding. In point of fact, the concession of the principle of free competition among producers has been discovered to possibly involve elements of danger to the consumer. The comment of the younger Stephenson on railway enterprise, that where combination is possible, competition ceases to be operative, is quoted with much frequency and intensity by those who quarrel with present results, and it is not a little remarkable that in the country where domestic competition is declared to be a social law, this outcome of free action is criticised and repressed.

The English common law, as yet dominant in the United States, simply considers the case of food, or whatever may have been construed, or can be construed, as food, as the object or objects to which these reputedly illegal practices apply. But it is exceedingly difficult to draw the line. The services of a carrier can hardly, except by a strain of the facts, be included under this head, and yet an abnormal and excessive charge for carriage may paralyze a good market. The United States railway law, to which reference has been made, has put the conveyance of merchandise under what is practically the old law of forestalling and engrossing, the grievance being, so to speak, reversed. In the United Kingdom, we have adopted similar legislation, the ultimate effect of which must be tested by future experience. In theory, the legislation is intended for the benefit of the producer or trader; in point of fact, it plainly is in the interest of the consumer, since facilities of transit are really an indirect mode of cheapening the cost of production, unless, indeed, the advantage which producer and consumer anticipate from the process of cheapening freight are intercepted by the middle-man, a risk which I shall comment on in the course of this lecture.

The justification of the policy which puts an end to all restraints on the free action of the dealer is found in the writings of the founder of modern economic science, and in those of the latest great authority on the subject—Adam Smith and Mill. The reasonings of the former are to be found in Book iv. cap. 5, of the "Wealth of Nations." The policy of Europe, says Smith, was to force the husbandman to undertake simultaneously the functions of a producer and a dealer, while it discouraged the manufacturer of other goods from taking on himself the functions of a shopkeeper. But, says Smith, such a violation of natural liberty is impolitic as well as unjust; the latter, because it wastes the producer's means by multiplying his avocations, the former, because it diminishes the capital which may be employed in cultivating land; and he urges that the trade of the corn merchant in reality increases the means by which corn can be raised. And again, the corn merchant acts on his own judgment, and must bear the loss of an error, as well as expect the gain of a wise foresight. If he is in the right, he distributes the produce of the year, an important social fact in the days when the home market was almost the sole source of supply, and though he makes the consumer "feel the inconvenience of a dearth somewhat earlier than he otherwise might, he prevents them from feeling them afterwards so severely as they certainly would." He then compares the popular fear of forestalling and engrossing to the popular terrors and suspicions of witchcraft. Smith had written his book before 12 Geo. III. was enacted. He gives some praise to the Act 15 Car. II. cap. 7, which gave some liberty to the corn dealer. The reasoning which I have condensed was that which excited the anger of Lord Kenyon in Rusby's case. The arguments of Mr. Mill, Book iii. cap. ii. sec. 5, do not differ fundamentally from those of Smith, beyond this, "that the gains of a speculator in corn are not secured by the losses of the consumer, but by the losses of other speculators." This broad statement, under certain conditions entirely accurate, has a significance which I shall speedily refer to.

The acceptance of the principle of free competition was partly the reaction from the restraints imposed by the old system of guild and freeman production and trade. This system was by no means universal, for the great industries of the north were not shackled by these limitations, and very likely owed their rapid growth to the freedom under which they were carried on. It was partly due to reaction against the protective laws which prevailed almost universally in the United Kingdom up to 1820, and were only partially relaxed for the next quarter of a century. As industry after industry was relieved from its trammels, the progress which each made seemed to demonstrate how great, how wholesome a boon was *laissez faire* and unrestricted competition. When Mr. Mill wrote, the country was just enjoying unwonted liberty, and was invigorated by it. Hence, Mill speaks warmly of competition, justly alleging that prices are lessened by its operation, as trade is exalted by it. For the most successful competitor in supply is the producer who lowers the price of the article in which he deals, and at the same time improves its quality, the next is the person who lowers price and maintains quality. It is towards one or both of these results that all invention, or in other words, all diminished cost of production is directed, and conversely in the absence of competition, inventive skill is arrested or at least checked. To extinguish competition, therefore, is to extinguish enterprise, and perhaps the policy of production and trade which our forefathers accepted as judicious and just, may account for that singular backwardness in the arts of life which characterized most English industries up to the middle of the eighteenth century, and nearly all of them up to the beginning of the same epoch.

But these prosperous and progressive days are in the nature of things not perpetual. Mr. Mill is entirely accurate in saying that there is no competition of capitals, for though the distribution of capital is by no means as easy and spontaneous as most writers on political economy affect to consider it, it is distribution, operating by the greater or less attractiveness of the object, and the real or apparent security which the object affords to the person who employs or lends capital, which dominates the direction which it shall take. If all persons were absolutely well informed, if they could interpret every risk, and still more important if they had an absolute discretion, because they had an equal skill or opportunity over all the industrial processes for which capital is needed, the distribution of capital would be almost mechanical, and the apparent competition would be simply determined by the relative attractiveness of the pursuit. But, in fact, the fluidity of capital is very different in degree. In some cases it is entirely lost; in others it cannot be recovered without a loss. As I have often said that capital alone possesses the qualities which unthinking and inexperienced writers are apt to postulate of all forms of what they call floating capital, which is actually characteristic of a banker's balance. Even here the owner may be disabled by want of knowledge or skill from employing it advantageously on many objects which wider knowledge and greater skill would suggest. In brief, large masses of capital are being advanced, as large masses of capital have been advanced in callings which prove unremunerative, or scantily remunerative at best. The fluidity of capital taken generally, is as unreal as the wage fund. Much of the wealth which is accumulated with a view to production is virtually pledged by the owner to a special calling; much is waiting for opportunities. So with the capital which is destined to pay wages. Most of it is dedicated to special industries, and when more is wanted in any industry a draft is made on unemployed labour and unemployed capital.

There is, however, a very real competition of capitalists. This competition is sharpest in those countries where very few opportunities are given individuals to exchange from one industry to another, a state of things which is very characteristic of great industrial activity. The result of this competition is that profits are attenuated. The volume of business may be greater than ever; but the number of persons who design to share the profits may increase more rapidly than the trade does, and the resultant eagerness to get a share in the work of supply may force down profits, not only relatively as in the case of the increased number of competitors, but absolutely by the necessity of forcing trade. In other words, supply may be in excess of demand, and prices may fall below what is remunerative. Such a state of things, if we can believe the complaints which have been made, and were loud and persistent enough to secure a hearing from a Royal Commission, was characteristic of British production and trade pretty universally up to about a year ago (1888), and induced many persons to seriously doubt whether the speculative economists were after all in the right when they repudiated the possibility of a general glut. This state of things is, I conclude, what Mr. Mill means when he speaks of the tendency of profits to a minimum, and the stationary state, though as usual, he appears to have loanable capital in his mind only, and not that which is actually and permanently engaged in production. Or the competition derived from the manifest facts of a particular time may be directed to a particular class of objects, the production of which has been exceedingly in excess of demand, but the output of which can with difficulty, owing to the enormous loss due to the cessation of industry, be lessened or suspended. This was particularly the case with the coal and iron industries at or shortly after the events of 1874. The demand for these products was very great, and capital in the most inextricable form was heaped upon them. In a very short time prices became so low, owing to the enormous output and the inadequate, because discontinuous, demand, that if we are to credit producers, for years past there has been no appreciable profit obtained from hundreds of undertakings. It is said that the same fact is true of the salt trade, and that whatever were the gains of individuals a few years ago, the whole of those who are interested in this industry have hardly, for some time, earned interest on their capital. It seems that the beneficent operation of competition is at an end, and that if the existing body of producers is to exist, some other expedient is to be adopted by which a fair profit can be gained by a national industry.

The expedient which is being adopted in certain cases, notably the last named, is that of associating all undertakings, regulating the output, and regulating the price, compensation being made from the common fund of all sales effected on this heightened price, to those whose personal action is curtailed or suspended for the common good of producers. Attempts of this kind, under the names of ring and corner, have been frequently made, but hitherto by private speculators, generally with disaster at the end, a disaster which our lax bankruptcy law is apt to condone. But recently, under the name of trusts in the United States, or in the case of railways, pools, and syndicates in the United Kingdom, it has been sought to check cutting rates of competition by syndicates or agreements. As I have said, the Sugar Trust of New York State has been declared illegal, but no attempt has been made to test the legality of the British syndicate, and we are informed that it is expected that the syndicate system will be extended to coal and iron, or that at any rate, some binding understanding will be entered into by which prices will be regulated and profits secured.

These efforts do not appear as yet to create any alarm or hostility. There is a feeling which is natural and generous, that a reasonable profit should be obtained in all industrial callings, and that if some small sacrifice is demanded from the public, it should be borne patiently. There is a stronger feeling still, that except the circumstances are as rare as those in which an export duty can be imposed, conditions which I have stated before, but may repeat: (1) That there is no other source of supply; (2) that there can be no substitute for the article; (3) that there can be no economy in its use; and (4) that the article is a necessary of life, such expedients are destined to failure, and even to a greater loss than the continuance of the industry under the old conditions, however unsatisfactory they may seem and are.

Attempts to secure prices to producers against competition have constantly been made and have constantly failed. The most profitable process hitherto known and employed is for strong men, or a combination of strong men, to ruin weak ones by low or unremunerative prices, and having secured a monopoly, to commence a legal pillage of the public. But though the expedient may enrich individuals it is essentially transitory. Sooner or later competition reappears, and extraordinary profits are arrested. I have heard of persons who, having acquired almost a monopoly of production, have bought out rivals at a price which is greatly in excess of the value which they have in the business. Such a proceeding, if it became known, would obviously be a stimulant to competition, and if it were extensively imitated would, it seems, prove ruinous to the purchaser of rival interests. Or an understanding is entered into by which some well-known firm publishes its prices, and suggests to others that they should follow the price, not compete by cheapness, but compete by custom. This is said to have been, for instance, the case in the iron trade, and that Dudley gave the price. It is also said to be practised in the yarn business. But it does not seem in either of these instances to have arrested a fall, or assisted a rise. Externally, the practice of the Bank of England of publishing its rate of discount, which has been its regular habit since the Act of 1844, appears to be of a similar character. But though the Bank rate suggests the charge for discounts in the open markets, it is well known that it does not regulate them. It is even said that the Bank is not consistent with its own declaration, and that it has different rates for different kinds of paper and different customers. But in reality, the Bank rate of discount is the interpretation given in the Parlour of the sufficiency of the reserve, that is of the amount of specie which the Bank holds in its cellars. Still less successful is the attempt to create a temporary monopoly by controlling the market of supply, a tradesman's device, to which I have already referred, and to which I may add the statement that if it fails, and the speculator loses other people's money by bankruptcy, he ought to be severely punished, as he is by the French law of bankruptcy and insolvency.

Recently an attempt has made to control the salt trade of Worcestershire and Cheshire. We are informed, and we hear it with some astonishment, after taking account of the great fortunes which some salt producers have made, who notoriously began with nothing, that competition has extinguished profits in this industry. At any rate, it appears that an inclusive syndicate of salt manufacturers has been passed, and that this organization has already materially enhanced the price of the article. Now the salt industry, which consists in drawing strong natural brine from the soil by pumping and evaporating the fluid, began, or was revived, in England at the end of the seventeenth century, as Houghton, a diligent observer of facts, informs us. The object of the industry at first was to supersede the old process—the evaporation of sea water by solar heat—a process which was successfully carried on in the south-west of Europe, and particularly on the French seaboard. So important was the supply from this source, that it constantly becomes an object of diplomatic negotiation and treaties, the English Government stipulating for the free export of French salt, of which you may find copious evidence in Dumont's collection of treaties. The next stage was due to the growth of chemical science. Easy and cheap processes were discovered, by which salt was successively transformed into sulphate and carbonate of soda, in which latter form it has a great economical use, as for instance, in the manufacture of hard soaps. The third stage was also the result of chemical discovery, and is due to the utilization of waste or bittern, which is always present in sea water, and generally in salt springs, and contains those important elements, iodine and bromine, though I have recently been informed by a well-known manufacturer, and promoter of the syndicate, that the Cheshire springs are almost devoid of these constituents; and therefore, if as is constantly the case, the profits of the manufacture depend on the bye-products, are in a less favourable position than other deposits, such as those of Eastern and Southern Germany, where they are far more plentiful.

Now let us grant, as evidence seems to prove, that the action of the syndicate has raised prices, and consequently profits. The question is, will the rise be permanent, or indeed anything but temporary? One of the first announcements after the combination had taken effect was that there are vast, and as yet unworked, salt deposits in the county of Durham, which an exaltation of price will assuredly bring into the market, that is, into competition with the syndicate. These deposits are said to be deep, but at present Artesian boring can be carried on at a quarter the expense which was necessary twenty or thirty years ago. Only a few days ago, I read that more accessible deposits exist in the Carnforth district of North-west Lancashire. Besides, these are the great salt mines of Cracow, and those from the Saltz Kammergut. An appreciable exaltation of prices would bring these into the market, and expedite the transit of them by new railways. Now, the consequences of this kind of competition are that if it be once taken in hand and carried into completion, the latter end of the existing production will be worse than the beginning, for it is a rule in production which speculative economists are apt to entirely lose sight of, that existing industries, however they may have originally come into existence, make desperate efforts to survive, and will endure a long period of depressive profits before those who are interested in them are willing to witness a total loss of the capital which they have invested in the undertaking. I should infer, therefore, that the power of combination as a check to the reputed evils of competition is precarious, temporary, and liable to a ruinous reversal. Nor do I feel entirely convinced that the legislature would, if the consequences became serious, permit the rule which it still lays down, as to practices which are reputed to be "in restraint of trade," to be covertly or openly evaded.

We have, it is true, got rid of the statute of Edward VI., first by the Act of 1772, which referred what were conceived to be obnoxious practices to the common law, and next by the Act of 1844, which negatived even the common-law doctrine. It is possible that the courts of law in those days would require abundant proofs before they ruled that a practice was in restraint of trade. But no such conditions bind the British legislature, and it is quite possible that unwisdom and the charge of rapacity might induce the Parliament to interfere with this new development of *laissez faire*. The object of *laissez faire* is to favour individualism, as people call it, not to favour combination, still less what might be held with more or less show of reason to be a conspiracy against the consumer, and that an unequal conspiracy, in which the profit, if any, accrues for a time to the combination, while the loss falls first on the public, and only subsequently on the projectors and their creditors. And though it is highly probable that the British legislature and the courts of law would consider these economic checks quite sufficient to prevent serious mischief to industry, it is, if we can judge from the practice of legislature, and especially from a recent act of legislation, by no means the intention of Parliament to allow *laissez faire* in combination, or even in the individual, when it is believed that such a course of action would lead to public or even to grave private inconvenience. Thus the legislature has fixed a tariff of its own for the hire of certain public conveyance, in others it trusts so far to competition that it will allow the trader to fix his price, but constrains him under penalties to publish and abide by it, and by a recent act of legislation has put all railways, especially as conveyers of goods under a Commission, which possesses very energetic powers of discipline. The State in the United Kingdom is quite willing enough to act when combination against the presumed interests of the public is proved to exist; it declines to act, or is indifferent to the action, when it believes, as it generally believes with reason, that the expedient adopted carries its own remedy with it. At the same time, I am entirely persuaded that if the practice, of which we have seen a few experiments lately, and of which more are threatened, became general, and was believed to be mischievous, that Parliament would not hesitate to intervene.

The natural check to excessive and ruinous competition is the likelihood that the weaker combatants in the struggle will succumb, that in a rough way the survival of the fittest will be the result, and that the industry will ultimately right itself. Anybody who studies the history of manufacture and trade will find that competition has been effectually operative against classes of workers and against localities. For example, hand-loom weaving has been practically extirpated by machinery, wood-cutting machines have greatly curtailed the work of the joiner, machines for the manufacture of nails and screws, and, as far as I can judge of a recent case, chains, have extinguished the trade of the nail smith, the hand screw-maker, and the chain maker. It is idle to think that the successes of mechanical science have been a universal gain to all sections of the community. Every invention which shortens labour in the aggregate, impoverishes labour in detail, and it is foolish and impertinent to dwell exclusively on the optimist side of industrial progress. The palliative is that it comes slowly, that if the change is made, it takes a generation before it becomes universal, always provided that no unfair action is taken. Thus, for example, the Nottingham Frame-breakers Act (52 Geo. III. cap. 16, 1812), inflicting the penalty of death on this offence, apart from the atrocity of the penalties, was an outrageous act of injustice. The legislature, under the Quarter Sessions Assessment Act, had driven the wages of workmen forcibly down to starvation point, and was now inflicting the punishment of death on those who refused to take starvation patiently.

So, again, industry under domestic competition may be transferred from one locality to another. In early days the county of

Norfolk was peculiarly fitted for woollen and linen weaving. Under the agriculture of the time the soil was easily worked, and there was close commercial intercourse between this county and Flanders. But the climate, Norfolk being the driest county in England, was unfavourable to the production of the best yarns, and the manufacture gradually drifted away to the more congenial west, and especially when steam power came into use, to the neighbourhood of the Somersetshire coal field. Simultaneously, at first for coarse fabrics, and subsequently for the best kinds of goods, Lancashire and Yorkshire and the southern Scottish counties distanced the western manufacturer. Here the downward process was accelerated by the foolish ruling of a particularly foolish judge, Lord Kenyon, who granted the farmers and landowners the power of rating machinery, a permission of which the Yorkshire spinners declined to avail themselves. Still, in accordance with a law or practice, which I have several times commented on, that people will make prolonged struggles in order to obviate the loss of fixed capital, some of these ancient centres of the cloth trade continued to exist. Their existence has been helped in some instances by railway communications. Thus there is a thriving cloth manufactory at Chipping Norton in this county, where the industry has been carried on for centuries, and though the industries of Frome, Taunton, and a hundred other localities have been extinguished, I heard last summer that the weavers of Bradford-on-Avon in Wilts, are as satisfied with their industry as the weavers of Bradford in Yorkshire are with theirs.

Again, in early times, nearly the whole shipping industry of England was centred in the southern ports. When Edward III. collected his fleet for the engagement at Sluys, and, as the custom was then, impressed the merchant vessels, the little town of Fowey in Cornwall supplied him with the largest contingent. So active was the trade of King's Lynn, that in the Middle Ages it went by the name of "Villa Mercatorum." The port of Bristol was in its infancy, that of Hull was being begun, that of Liverpool in the distant future, even that of London was unequal and uncertain. The reason is not far to seek. The vessels of the time were of light tonnage and draught, and for such vessels the southern ports were numerous and accessible. The mariners of Fowey were perpetually engaged in private war with France, and memories still survive in that little port of reciprocal surprises and massacres on both coasts. The southern and eastern towns, too, were in close proximity to the Baltic trade, and to commerce with the wealthy towns of Flanders. The mercantile marine of England was therefore inevitably developed here. Besides, the German Ocean is generally calm, while we may be sure that the Atlantic was looked on, by the mariners of the time, with undisguised dread. In course of time, the New World and the Cape Passage were discovered, and though the English people, as usual, was exceedingly slow in using these discoveries, it did at last get a firm hold of the best regions in the New World of America, and the Old World of India, where it founded vast empires, one of which was entirely lost by the folly of a Hanoverian king, and the other only saved by a minister whom the same Hanoverian king most unwillingly employed.

In short, domestic competition, if one studies it historically, has wholly transposed the centres of industry during the last few centuries, a fact which the teachers of political, physical, and commercial geography would do well to study, instead of merely contenting themselves with present conditions. For, in short, though human folly, and especially the folly of government, may wreck the fairest opportunities and destroy by unwisdom or greed what it cannot recall or revive—as perhaps the English Parliament did permanently by Irish industries—much depends on natural conditions, and these conditions are worthy of constant and attentive study. I can quite conceive that the best prospects of commercial and political unity may be rendered impossible by mischievous political elements and selfish social aims, for the hardest, and on the whole the most unsuccessful efforts are made by shallow persons who try to reconcile the incongruous, and have not the intelligence to discern the incongruity, to say nothing of their ignorant impatience with those who show them the difficulties in their way. And the student of social history has often to mourn over the presumption which characterizes "men of light and leading," of "sovereigns and statesmen," or, as the latest phrase has it, "of persons who have the leisure and the means" to undertake affairs, and inflicts irreparable injury on what it undertakes.

Much complaint has been made of late years by those who study, perhaps perforce, the conditions of manufacture and trade, at the enormous difference between the price at which they sell, and that at which the consumer buys. The complaint comes from husbandmen and manufacturer alike, and the facts are in strange contrast with the experience of an earlier age, in which producer and consumer were brought more closely together than they are at present. There is, in brief, a considerable, it may be an unintelligent, outcry against the middle-man, and more reasonably against the large number of persons, all expecting a profit, and constantly a large profit, on an article which the producer would be glad if he knew the way to deal indirectly with the consumer. For this result, the indolence of the principal parties to the transaction is responsible in the main. More than a century ago Arthur Young complains that the staple produce of the farmer, wheat, passes through the hands of a dozen or half a dozen brigands. Recently Mr. Illingworth, of Bradford, has been calling attention that the staple industry of that town is charged 100 per cent. above the selling price when it reaches the consumer through the middle-man, and traces with much plausibility the depression of trade to the outrageous profits which the distributors appropriate. There must be some truth in the allegation, for one of my own personal friends, an eminent manufacturer in the district, assured me that he raised a decaying industry, to which he was brought up, into a prosperous one, by the elimination of useless and costly intermediaries.

Half a century or a little more ago, the consumer was brought into contact with the producer, in a manner which modern experience or habit has no conception of. I speak from personal memory. My father, a country physician, in extensive practice to be sure, but with an enormous family, brought up in the main under Pitt's income tax, and to quote the worst of the gang, Vansittart's finance, habitually purchased nearly all which his own estate did not produce for his household at the great fairs of the neighbourhood, clothing, leather, and certain agricultural produce, the two former being made up by local artisans working at piece. Except under this system I do not see how he and a hundred other of the poorer gentry could have lived through these evil times. People could not endure the charges of shops and the profits of retail trade, and therefore bought extensively and immediately from producers, with whom they bargained for what they purchased, under what Adam Smith calls the higgling of the market. Speaking generally, even when they purchased foreign produce, they bought in bulk — wine by the pipe, half pipe, butt, or half butt; tea by the chest. I am not quite sure that in the general stint which atrocious finance caused, they were entirely unmoved by the chance of procuring smuggled goods. It is certain that all the country-side sympathized with those bold traders who elected to avoid, if possible, customs charges, and did, I suspect, with much activity and success.

The epoch of shops is comparatively recent. It is true that nothing fades more rapidly from the memory of a later generation than the domestic expedients of an earlier epoch, and we are now further removed from the experiences of my youth in these matters, than our fathers were from the age of Elizabeth and the Stuarts. Now it will be plain that a shopkeeper must maintain himself and his family and pay rent and local charges out of the profit of his goods. If in a given town half a million of money is turned over every year in groceries, and there are two hundred and fifty grocers in the town, it is plain that each of these traders on an average will have a turnover of £2,000. Of course, some will have a turnover of ten or twenty times the amount, and therefore the business done by the others is so much the less. But two things are plain—(1) The profits of his business must be sufficient to supply the charges of the grocer, who, keeping his head above water, has the smallest amount of remunerative business; and (2) the man who does the largest business has no reason to regret or dispense with the initial charges of the least prosperous among his fellows. It is like what is said of land. If the least fertile land can be worked at a profit, or at least to cover all outlay whatsoever, all the better for the best land. And this is the case generally with retail trade. Its charges, under the name of gross profits, bear all the expenses incurred by all the traders. If the large trader sold at a price which could pay him say 10 per cent. only, and the public knew it, he would infallibly extinguish the less prosperous trader. As it is both compete, not at cutting prices, but in such a way as to secure the largest custom. It is the competition for custom, not by cheapness. To this all the fashions of modern social life lend themselves. The habit of bargaining has totally passed away from retail trade. The shopkeeper fixes prices, and strives to get custom. Of course if his goods are not perishable, and his sales are rapid, he can afford to make his gross profits moderate. But as long as demand remains the same, the multiplicity of dealers makes him to a great extent independent of market fluctuations, and relieves him from the inclination of giving his customers the benefit of a reduction. The farmer complains that he is constrained to sell his cattle and sheep at ruinously low prices, but the householder cannot trace the depression in his butcher's bill. Cotton, wool, and silk are cheap beyond experience, and the rivalry of manufacturers reduces the cost of production in even a greater ratio. But the depression is not exhibited in the draper's scale of prices or in the tailor's charges. And the same sort of thing is witnessed in those articles where the substitution of machinery for manual labour has greatly cheapened the cost of production. The working tailor and the seamstress earn a miserable pittance, but the charge to the consumer remains unchanged. There is, in short, it is alleged, an understanding among dealers, which ensures some profit to all, and the consumer has no appreciable advantage in lowered prices.

The habit of buying everything at shops, and nothing from the producer, is peculiar to this country, where marketing by private families is practically obsolete. It survives, as every one may see, in continental cities; if, for example, any one were to visit the Brussels market in any one day through its successive changes of merchandise. It is a good deal assisted in this country by the practice of producers who might, and to a small extent do, sell, by demanding and expecting shopkeepers' prices for what they bring round. Now no one can be expected to give as much for that which comes to him at a fixed price as he has to give for what he purchases at a shop at his own time and discretion. The same result is assisted by the fact that there is no understanding or association at all among producers, especially of agricultural products. In Switzerland the dairy farmers send their milk to a central association, where it is turned into butter and cheese, the contributors of the milk securing a rateable proportion from the price at which the product is sold. The same system is practised in the creameries and cheese factories of the United States. This is a step only in the direction of that return to ancient usage, which, according to those who have written about the grievances of the producer's trade, one may hope to see taken, always on the assumption that the grievances are real. They seem to be, when one considers how important to the small farmer is the profit, or rather the economy of loss on his own consumption.

An attempt has been made to economize the shopkeeper's charges in the so-called co-operative stores. These institutions are of great significance to artisans and labourers, for the charges of the retail shop are very heavy when the trade is precarious and the parcels are small. In this trading, owing to the practice which these associations have uniformly adopted, of taking ordinary retail price, and dividing what remains over the cost of distribution among the members, in proportion to their purchases, it is easy to discover what was the cost of retail trade to the poor. The system has been extended to other classes, and it is understood that a very large business is carried on in them, greatly to the discontent of London tradesmen, with whom dealing at stores is almost an inexpiable offence.

One disagreeable result has come from competition in domestic trade. I refer to the adulteration of goods. The customer as much purchases the reputed skill and experience of the trader in the purchase of what he needs as a patient does the acquirements of a physician, the client those of a solicitor. To make an implied trust the ground of a fraud, to use the skill which one plies in order to procure genuine goods as a cover to the sale of adulterated articles, is an offence which the law should punish severely. But there are persons whom one has been surprised to hear in defence of these practices, and it is plain that they who commit these frauds consider themselves ill used when they are detected, exposed, and punished. It is doubtful whether public opinion would endure the French practice, under which the malefactor is compelled to publish the evidence of his own offence. There is still a good deal of tenderness shown to the tricks of trade. It is said, with what truth I cannot discover, that even the co-operative shops, the fundamental position of which was that they would sell genuine goods at ready money only, have occasionally succumbed to this form of competition for cheapness, and that some of the reproaches which have been cast upon competition among working men are due to the fact that their own order has yielded to temptation.

The duty of legislature seems clear. There should be no truce with those who sell unwholesome food, for this is a common danger, induced by a very base appetite for fraud. But generally it is in the interests of honesty and fair dealing to chastise those who in trade sell, calling what they sell by a name which it is not. It has been found necessary to check malpractices in international trade, after loudly expressed complaints ; but it is certainly inconsistent to condone identical practices in domestic trade.

X.

HOME TRADE AND INTERNATIONAL COMPETITION.

Protective tariffs used to facilitate international competition—National monopolies—The colonial theory—Struggles of English statesmen to create a sole market—The South Sea Scheme—The American War of Independence—Free trade and competition—The unions with Scotland and Ireland—Reputations for commercial integrity.

WHATEVER may be said about competition for the home market among home producers, in which the home producer has two great natural advantages—saving in the cost of freight, and a more ready and rapid interpretation of demand—there is no question that competition rules absolutely in the foreign market. So great is the superiority conferred on the home producer by these advantages, that I am accustomed, and with justice, to call them a natural protection. They are in fact equivalent to a considerable duty imposed for protectionist purposes, and they cannot be annulled. In the colonial trade the manufacturers of Great Britain have also an advantage. They stand, to be sure, on the same natural level with the producers of other nations in the matter of freight, in those countries, at least, that can compete with Great Britain in the carrying trade. But the British trader has in some degree the second advantage. He is better able to interpret demand than his foreign rival is. He has another ad-

HOME TRADE AND INTERNATIONAL COMPETITION. 391

vantage as an extensive, and it may be believed, a sole creditor of the colonial purchaser, on which I shall have to comment presently. There are, to be sure, two processes, one unlimited in extent but temporary in duration, which some foreigners, especially Germans, have not scrupled to use. This is the forgery of trade marks, and the vending of worthless goods under creditable but assumed names. We have put an end to the practice, none too soon, in our imports, and it would be wise if our dependencies followed our example. The other process is limited in extent, but may be permanent. It is that by which the manufacturers and traders of a protectionist country put the costs of their competition on the consumers of their own country. It will be manifest that if the producers of any country induce the government of their country to impose protective duties, it must be on the plea that, notwithstanding the natural protection expounded just now, they cannot carry on the industry without it. If they could the tax would be a merely wanton exercise of power, and the reputed benefit would eventually be repudiated, and that without much delay, by the protected industry. But by the very terms of the case such a product would have no chance in competing in a country against identical goods produced by a community which repudiates protection, and in which the price generally conforms to the cost of production. The only means by which an entrance can be effected is by lowering what is sold below the cost of production in the country of its origin. But it must be allowed that people will not produce at a loss. There is only one process by which the loss can be made good. This is by charging the home consumer with the costs of the venture, a process facilitated by protective laws, which leave the consumer at the mercy of the producer. But the same circumstances make the experiment a limited one. If it grow to be a considerable trade, the additional charge to the consumer would be intolerable. And, in point of fact, the cases to which fair traders point are exceedingly trivial. I hear of Belgian and German iron being imported into England, but I do not find the entries even in the expanded returns of imports by the Board of Trade. If you hear of large shipments of foreign goods produced under protection competing against similar goods produced by free-trade countries in a neutral market, you may, before you assent to the assertion, ask two questions : 1. Is the fact as is stated ? 2. Are these goods fraudulently marked or not ? and nine cases out of ten it will be found that the first question will be answered in the negative and the second in the affirmative. There may be, indeed, an honest attempt made to procure information as to the market, and to establish a connection, for which traders are content to make temporary sacrifices. But in the long run the business cannot be maintained except at the expense of the consumers in the protection-ridden country.

In a neutral market, *i.e.*, one which, whatever be its fiscal system, shows no favour to any particular nation, competition is absolute, and combination, if not impossible, is in the highest degree hazardous. One reads, to be sure, in the United States, of corn and cotton rings, and such expedients ; but I do not remember to have heard of one which has not ultimately landed its projectors in a loss. It would be difficult, but perhaps not impossible, to rule the market, when the commodity is not only a sole product, but conforms to the conditions which I have stated in my last lecture. But such a commodity is of the rarest occurrence. Years ago, when I was preparing an edition of MacCulloch's "Dictionary of Commerce," I thought that I had discovered a sole product. This was emery powder from the Isle of Naxos. Emery is a kind of coarse corundum, its hardness being inferior to the diamond only. It is a necessary to the steel polisher. But since that time the article has been found elsewhere, and Naxos, and with it the Sultan's establishment, into the maintenance of which the greater part of the Turkish revenue goes, and the Turkish loans have gone, lost their monopoly. At the outbreak of the Civil War in America, cotton seemed to almost conform to the conditions which I have laid down, and certainly great distress ensued in Lancashire on the failure of the cotton supply. But the facts did not correspond with the theory, and perhaps one important, indirect advantage which ensued from that terrible war, was the extension of the area of cotton planting, and the consequent relief of the cotton industry from dependence on almost a single source of supply.

I am assuming that no favour is shown to any country in trade with a foreign market. Such favour has been shown in the history of international commerce. The Methuen treaty was a case in point, under which the English government gave exceptional advantages to Portuguese wines, and received exceptional advantages for English woollens. In practice it is found that the adoption of what is called the most-favoured-nation clause in commercial diplomacy becomes in time a general concession. Every community desires to increase its foreign trade, for success in this process stimulates industry, secures profits, and gives a wider choice of imports. The most protection-ridden country wishes to sell, however much selfishness, having acquired influence ; and folly, which is misled by sophistry, may curtail discretion in buying. Hence if one government sees that its rival in commerce has secured a trade advantage by treaty, it chafes at the favour, resents it if it be powerful enough, and is always on the look out to secure what benefits such trade possesses, or is reputed to possess, for its own citizens or subjects. The Methuen treaty with Portugal was, to be sure, very enduring. But there were political reasons for it. Philip the Second of Spain and his descendants were undoubtedly, according to the law of inheritance as recognized in the two countries, the heirs of the Portuguese monarchy after the death of Henry of Portugal in 1580, and Philip, after a brief struggle, annexed that kingdom to his dominions. Sixty years later, and the Portuguese re-asserted their independence, and after a long struggle secured it. But the old Spanish family never forgot its rights as it reckoned them, and assuredly they were as keenly entertained by the Bourbons. Hence when the Grand Alliance, designed to prevent the accession of Philip of France to the Spanish throne, was formed, the Portuguese, after some hesitation, joined it, and when, after the peace of Utrecht, and the European guarantee given to Portugal, the French and Spanish houses associated themselves in what is known as the family compact, the renewed danger strengthened the policy which had been adopted more than a generation before. In point of fact, for dynastic reasons, Portugal remained the ally of Great Britain in the Spanish peninsula.

In order to treat properly the subject which I have taken for this morning's lecture, the extension, namely, of the foreign trade of the United Kingdom by means of British manufacture, it will be necessary to give you a sketch of the origin and development of English, and subsequently of British, trade. Its progress was very deferred, and exceedingly slow, so late and so slow that we cannot account for the facts except by showing that some natural hindrances, and certainly some national backwardness, must be assumed. The former are not obvious, for England always was a powerful maritime nation, except for a time during the Stuart dynasty, and certainly very close to her shores, England must have been exceedingly familiar with a country of prosperous manufactures and great commercial wealth, first in Flanders, and later on in Holland. But it did not succeed in imitating and rivalling the latter of these communities till after a considerable interval, and they who study the history of Holland can easily see how incessant and how unfair were the intrigues with which the Stuart and the Hanoverian governments alike tried to pander to mercantile greed in depressing the trade, narrowing the manufactures, and lessening the credit of the Dutch. It was the policy of English public men from the days of Selden to the days of Canning, and in my judgment the policy was as unwise as it was discreditable.

The English, as I have said, were always a seafaring nation, though after the cessation of Norse piracy, due, as I believe, to the repressive action of the Hanseatic League, maritime battles, the inevitable accompaniment of maritime adventure, are not much heard of. But the fleet which conveyed Richard to Palestine in his crusade against Saladin was, according to contemporary writers, collected entirely from the English ports, and was remarkably large. The battle of Dover, in 1217, in which the vessels of the Cinque Ports totally defeated and captured the French fleet of Eustace the Monk, is perhaps the earliest English naval battle of which we have record. When war was being waged, it was the monarch's prerogative to impress merchant vessels into his service, and it was not till the reign of Henry VIII. that the king began to construct vessels in his own dockyards for purposes of war. It was to Henry that Portsmouth owes its rise as an arsenal and dockyard. But it is not necessary for me to follow the fortunes of the British navy. It declined greatly under the early Stuarts, was revived and rendered effective by Cromwell, and was the object of some attention from James Duke of York.

The export trade of England was trivial for centuries, except in its two staple articles, wool and hides; in the former of which it possessed an actual monopoly, and was rendered capable of exercising great diplomatic power by virtue of this important produce. A very considerable part of the military expenditure of the Edwards and Henrys, during what has latterly been called the Hundred Years' War, was derived from export duties on wool. So complete was the monopoly possessed by the English sheep-masters, that Parliament was able constantly to exact a duty of more than 100 per cent. on the sack of ordinary wool without checking the demand, lessening the price, or impoverishing the husbandman. In point of fact English wool satisfied the dreams of a financier. It bore an export duty, every penny of which the foreigner paid. But though the cloth which might have been manufactured from this wool was, weight for weight, five or six times the value of the wool—I have recorded the weights and prices of both the material and the goods, and, therefore, can speak with confidence—there was no manufacture of cloth in England which had any reasonable prospect of a foreign market. In the statutes of 4 Henry VIII. and 23 Henry VIII., regulating and defining the cost of freight from and to the various European ports which English vessels frequented, from the Hanse towns on the Baltic to Malaga, the range of English commerce, there is no evidence of exports from England other than of raw produce. So profitable was the growth of wool that it was deemed to be a discouragement to general agriculture, and several statutes were passed in the first half of the sixteenth century restraining the keeping of excessive numbers of sheep. In brief the price of wool remained very high till near the end of that century.

The fact that manufactures did not extend themselves in England was not for want of legislation on the subject. I should weary you with a profitless recital were I to enumerate and comment on the numerous statutes which were enacted for the encouragement of the woollen trade, the police which was established in order to ensure its quality, and the powers given to guilds with the same ends. The mass of the English people were no doubt clad in home-spun, but there appears to have been little or no exportation of English cloth. Even at the end of the seventeenth century, the broadcloth in which the wealthier classes were clad on certain occasions, for you must not imagine that on ordinary days the nobles were dressed as you see them in pictures, came from Spain and Holland, and is regularly so described in their private accounts. It was not till the eighteenth century that the English procured the best qualities of cloth from English factories, and the emulation of the Scotch, admitted after 1706 to all the advantages of English trade, was aroused.

There is no doubt that such progress as was made in the arts of life was mainly due to immigrant foreigners, from Flanders in the sixteenth century, from France in the seventeenth. Religious persecution drove away from their homes the Calvinists of these two countries. England, either as a cause of backwardness in the manufacturing arts, or as an effect of backwardness, was rural and agricultural, and up to the middle of the eighteenth century was exceedingly behindhand in its dominant industry. Now the country people were always intolerant of strange settlers, and would be very much more so of foreigners. I do not doubt that the severe and unjust law of parochial settlement was by no means unpopular. Easy and rapid communication between places has done much to modify a sentiment which one or two generations ago was well-nigh universal. A stranger, commonly called a foreigner in a parish, was a rare and unpleasing phenomenon. I can remember in my own youth the dislike with which a strange labourer or strange artisan was admitted into a country parish. Now with this feeling about, and it was undoubtedly stronger two centuries ago and more, foreign immigrants would be constrained to aggregate in towns, and to ply their craft where they would be under a less jealous scrutiny. Men might subscribe to maintain the refugees of persecution, and yet would be very unwilling to admit them to social equality and general acceptance. The towns then grew by the influx of foreigners, new industries were developed, and old ones were improved or perfected by the presence of these industrious exiles. But the process was very slow. I very much doubt whether a ton of English or Scotch iron was exported till after the first half of the eighteenth century. I am quite certain that the English manufacturer for home consumption depended, up to the time of which I am speaking, for this necessary product on the Biscayan and Swedish forges, for three kinds of iron alone are quoted in prices current. These tables are given generally in certain newspapers of the time and in the monthly magazines.

The Methuen treaty, to which allusion has been made above, contemplated and probably secured an export trade in some coarse woollen goods of English origin. But the pains taken in the treaty to procure a sole market, furnish to my mind a very convincing proof that without this advantage the market would have been small and doubtful. And, of course, the stipulation itself is evidence that the exports would be of a low quality, because the object was to supply the Portuguese peasantry with English goods. Nor is there reason to believe that the trade of the East India Company was a vent for English manufactures. The produce of India was chiefly procured by exports of silver, and the earliest efforts of the company were directed towards a relaxation of the English currency laws in their favour, and the permission was granted, on a plea, so characteristic of the theories which were popular at the time, that the resale of Indian produce would bring far more silver into the country than the purchase necessarily carried out. Besides, as soon as India began to pay tribute the exports and imports of silver began to balance each other.

The beginning of the trade in English manufactures is to be found in the trade relations between this country and the American Plantations, and it may be strange for you to hear that the most important factors in that trade were tobacco and rice, the former much more significant than the latter. The practice of smoking became very general in the seventeenth century. By a standing rule of the House of Commons, and one among the earliest, members are forbidden to smoke in the House or its lobbies, and the rule is reverently obeyed. I am not sure whether a similar rule has been enacted by the Lords. It certainly was not in that assembly at the beginning of the eighteenth century, if Hearne is to be trusted, when he tells us that on one of those recurrent occasions when the High Church Tories moved that the Church was in danger, Bishop Bull not only refused to vote, but sat smoking in the lobby while his brethren were asserting or denying the motion by their votes. Tobacco was generally cultivated in England during the time of Charles I. and the Commonwealth, but forbidden at the Restoration under heavy penalties.

Before the Virginia tobacco came into the English market, and after the prohibition, the source of supply was Spanish America. The first note which I have made of it was in 1652. It was dear, and grew dearer, rising from 7s. to 10s. a pound, of course including the customs duty. The first entry which I have made of Virginia tobacco is in 1684, when it was bought at 1s. and 1s. 8d. the lb. Pipes are often bought for guests in large quantities by the Oxford and Cambridge colleges and the Eton fellows. Now, not only was Virginia tobacco much cheaper, but, according to the taste of the time, much better than Spanish. In a short time it became an important part of colonial merchandize, and early in the eighteenth century the colony supplied nearly all smokers with the plant. You may see allusions to it in popular novels. There is, for example, a great deal of tobacco in "Robinson Crusoe." As time went on it becomes cheaper, and tobacco is constantly quoted in the price lists of the early eighteenth century at from 4d. to 8d. a pound, according to quality, all being plantation. The same facts in a minor degree apply to rice. It was believed that rice was the healthiest kind of grain that could be used on ship-board, and it was procured for that and other objects from Northern Italy, particularly along the valley of the Po. But a new supply, more copious, of better quality, and cheaper, came from Carolina, and the market for this was of course in English hands.

Even if the scanty and scattered inhabitants of the English Plantations in America had been informed of the abundant mineral treasures possessed by that continent, they were not in the condition to work them. The population of the Plantations was littoral, and the minerals of this American continent are some hundreds of miles inland. Besides, the inevitable occupation of a new body of settlers is agriculture, and when the climate of a country is peculiarily favourable to the prosecution of certain kinds of agriculture the impulse to such pursuits is made stronger. Manufactures cannot be easily carried on in a new country. The capital of such a country is scanty; its market narrow and precarious. To obtain such produce as it wants, it is cheaper, more obvious, more convenient, to procure them from another country; and when the colony was producing an agricultural article for which the demand was increasing, the readiest road to wealth was in the culture of that in which it possessed unquestionable advantages. The gentry of Virginia grew rich from their tobacco plantations, and were glad enough to confine their attentions to so lucrative a pursuit. Even if the colonial system, which Adam Smith attacked with such conclusive vigour, had not been in existence, Great Britain was the natural market for colonial produce, and the Plantations the natural purchasers of British goods. And a conclusive proof of what I say is furnished by the fact, that after the War of Independence, a war carried on with great bitterness, and in the most irritating manner, to the surprise of all, the volume of trade between Great Britain and her old colonies greatly increased.

The dream of the eighteenth century was a sole market for British goods and British trade. The fiscal policy of this country was dominated by this idea, so was its colonial policy, so as far as possible was its diplomacy. The wars we waged up to the peace of Ryswick and the treaty of Utrecht were dynastic in form, commercial in fact. That war of cross purposes and apparently motiveless campaigns, the war of the Austrian Succession, is intelligible only in the light of the motive of all British statesmen, the acquisition of a sole market. The South Sea Bubble was fed and swoln on the prospect of securing a sole market in the American continent from the St. Lawrence to the La Plata. The dream again occupied the minds of British traders more than a century later, and the disasters of 1825 were due to the belief that the liberation of the Spanish Colonies was the signal to an enormous trade with the states of Central and Southern America. So ignorant and so hopeful was mercantile adventure then, that I have read of the shipment of a cargo of hearthrugs to Central America. When the skipper found that the article, owing to the climate, was unsaleable, he assured his possible customers that a hearthrug under a saddle was the newest fashion with European equestrians, and so contrived to get rid of his goods. But such ready wit, such opportunities, and such credulity, are exceptional.

England had the field before it which Portugal and Spain occupied in part. It may be doubted, had England been enterprising enough, as it certainly was strong and skilful enough, to search after the New World, and to essay the Cape Passage, whether the Bulls of Borgia would have been strong enough to deter her merchants. Such at least was not her reputation before the Reformation, and after the rupture with the Pope no scruples would have held her back. But for a hundred years, from the battle of Bosworth to the days of Drake, a strange languor came over commercial England. The people who guess at history, especially that which can only be interpreted from economical facts, and their name is legion, set this down to the desolating wars of succession in the fifteenth century. I am persuaded, from a somewhat careful study of English social history during this period, that there is hardly a time in which industrial England was more prosperous than during the period when the partisans of the nobles and the disbanded soldiers of the French war were slaying each other. It was a long duel between the idlers and the adventurers of both sides, in which the partisans wore each other out, and the workers were entirely unconcerned and indifferent. During the mean and rapacious reign of Henry VII. the country still prospered; during the wanton and rapacious reign of his execrable son, it sank to a powerless state in Europe, though I do not find that any but a few, such as Latimer was, detected the cause of this deplorable retrogression. As soon however as England recovered in a measure from the injuries which Henry inflicted on her the old spirit revived, and Drake became the founder of a new school of mariners.

Nothing, I must inform you again, changed the face of Europe and the fortunes of the Mediterranean cities, including those of the Rhine, the Danube, and certain of the Flemish towns, so much as the conquest of Egypt did by Selim I. Historians are of course completely ignorant of anything but the fact. This event entirely destroyed commerce with the East, of which the centre was, and had been for two centuries at least, the city of Alexandria; and it was only in time, and that a time long deferred, that it was restored by means of the Cape Passage. But it was more than a century after the discovery of this route, that English traders essayed it, and then with infinitely less resources than the Dutch had. Englishmen still believed in the Levant and Turkey trade, which the Ottomans tried clumsily and unsuccessfully to restore. The trade was a failure from the beginning. Elizabeth patronized it, granted it privileges, and lost money over her well-meaning attempt. For it is much more easy to destroy a trade than to revive it, and the Turk has been good for little else than destruction. No doubt the early trade with Hindostan was lucrative. It yielded a considerable profit to those who took part in it, but its volume till the latter part of the seventeenth century was inconsiderable, and even then was trifling beside that of the New Company which Montague founded by Act of Parliament in 1698. A glance at the prices of the New Company's stock—I have printed the facts in the sixth volume of my "History of Prices"—will prove what I say.

The most prosperous trade which eighteenth-century England had was with the Plantations in North America. The South Sea trade turned out so ill, that at last the Company, founded in the first place to carry it on, and a successful scheme of Hastings in 1711, successful only because from the beginning a delusion was fostered, petitioned Parliament to be relieved of it. But the Plantation trade, although controlled to all appearance by the Colonial system, which is described by Adam Smith, was constantly and progressively prosperous. It was not in the hands of a company. The acquisitions of Great Britain in the New World, with the exception of New York, which was easily occupied, were colonies of settlement and not of conquest. Trade with them was therefore spontaneous and natural. It is true that the trade was regulated in the interest of the British producer and trader, and entirely from the point of view of a sole market. But the regulation was, I am persuaded, futile and superfluous. Had the Colonial system never existed, I do not believe that the volume of trade between England and her plantations would have been lessened. The restraint was on paper only. It is true that American manufactures were discouraged, or even prohibited in the interests of British industry. But it may be doubted whether they would have been undertaken, if the colonists had been allowed the freest action. The primary, and for the matter of that the enduring, industries on the Atlantic seaboard, are agriculture and the fisheries. I am aware that before the rupture with the Colonies in 1772, there were grievances arising out of the Colonial system. I cannot object to the criticism which Adam Smith utters about that system. But I am sure that the grievances were sentimental rather than solid, and foolish as the legislation was, it happened to lie for once on the lines of reciprocal self-interest, and would never by itself have been made the subject of quarrel.

But I must say a little more in detail about the theory of a sole market, which was not indeed a peculiarly English delusion. The Spaniards and Portuguese held to it tenaciously. Their rivals, the Dutch, willing as they were even to trade with their enemies, were exclusive in the narrowest sense in the countries where they had authority and influence. The French were as keen after it as any of their neighbours, for the Mississippi scheme and the attempt to create an Indian Empire, which was foiled by Clive and his successors, had this object before them. In the first half of the eighteenth century, even Austria attempted the same grand design by the Ostend Company. In our own days, the French are trying to achieve the result in Madagascar and Tonquin, the North Germans in Zanzibar, Samoa, and New Guinea, though with results which are far from encouraging. It was a universal opinion in the eighteenth century, and for no small part of the nineteenth, that trade could be effectually created by conquest ; and the foolish and disastrous fallacy, that private advantage is the public good, and should be sought for by public sacrifices and losses, was the general belief of those people who have been called, I would fain hope cynically, " men of light and leading," or " sovereigns and statesmen."

The war of the English Succession, which came to an end with the peace of Ryswick, is only slightly connected with the doctrine of the sole market. But it developed and rendered traditional the instrument by which that result could be best obtained, England's supremacy on sea. The uneasiness with which the treaty of

Utrecht was received, a treaty in which everything seemed to be sacrificed and nothing gained by England, was a little lightened by the concession of the Assiento treaty, and the extravagant hopes which it excited. During the long peace which followed, broken only and that briefly, by the strange war with Spain, the same object was before the public or at least before those who undertook public business. I have referred already to the war of the Austrian Succession. The policy of the Seven Years' War was to destroy France as a colonizing and a commercial country, and to transfer to British trade the markets of the New World and supremacy in India. As far as this object went, it was completely successful, and in accordance with the lights of the time put England entirely, and, as was fondly believed, permanently in possession of the great aim of commerce. The war of American Independence, unwise as was the commencement, and still more unwise as was the conduct of the war, was a desperate attempt to maintain that sole market which it was the interest and the purpose of every European state to invade, for which the armed neutrality was devised by Russia and adopted by other European powers. With the same object were connected the right of search, and the doctrine, passionately insisted on by English jurists and statesmen, that a maritime power had the right to follow enemies' goods in the vessels of neutral powers. The acquisition of a sole market was a much more enduring object with English public men in the eighteenth century than the maintenance of the balance of power, which was really a cloak for the ulterior end.

And yet the economist who studies the social and industrial history of the time is constrained to conclude, however mistaken and in the end disastrous this *ignis fatuus* was, that it had not a little to do with the development of commercial activity and manufacturing skill in England. The first result of movement was, that the Government was constrained to root out that spirit of buccaneering or piracy, which in the early days of maritime enterprise was almost considered heroism, and if one can judge from novels, remained an object of interest long after the practice had been put down. The next was, that apparently under restrictive laws, passed and adapted to these ends, a real trade of mutual benefit was carried on with the Plantations. The Colonial system may not have contributed to this trade at all. It was developed, continued, enlarged in spite of it. But I believe that it gave confidence to the initiative, no small matter in commercial and manufacturing ventures, however little the system deserved the confidence. Enterprise is naturally aided by the conviction that a market is secured, and it seemed that the policy of England had secured the market. All along the seaboard from the St. Lawrence to the borders of Florida, after the Seven Years' War there was a rapidly growing people whose duty it was to take English goods, whose interest it was to ship colonial produce to English markets. They would perhaps have taken them without the Colonial system, but by this system the reciprocity of trade was guaranteed. The market was extended by the prosperity of the sugar colonies, whose produce became very soon nearly as important as the tobacco plantations were, and from which, as you should be told, Europe was supplied till the utilization of beet products during the Continental War. Nor will you probably be slow to realize that the semblance of a force is nearly as efficient to most minds as the reality of a force.

That the Colonial and sole-market theory was after all an economical delusion, and was proved to be by the remarkably rapid extension of English manufactures and commerce after the system was entirely exploded, is not in my opinion inconsistent with what I have said as to the force of these stimulants in the initiative. It is not given to every one to detect an economic fallacy. During the eighteenth century agriculture was assisted, as far as the intentions of Parliament went, with a bounty, and protective laws against imports. But the protective laws were entirely inoperative. Except for the two years 1709, 1710, the price of wheat during the first sixty years of the century was 30 per cent. below the average of what it had been in the seventeenth century, in many years not half the price. The bounty really stimulated the production of grain, for it was a premium on its export, and many more people thought they would get it than did get it; for it was a genuine lottery, in which as you know every one is apt to conclude that his good luck will be better than that of his neighbour, just as shrewd bookmakers know that men who back their favourites invariably overrate their own judgment, and mistake their fancies for realities. But Arthur Young, shrewd observer and competent agriculturist as he was, imagined that the bounty and the Corn Laws were the mainstay of British agriculture. Now it is quite possible that the bounty, which was probably an unmixed evil, did act in some degree as a stimulus to invention. But what gave its character to the agriculture of the eighteenth century was the general spirit of enterprise among landowners. It was by no means easy to increase rents, for the farmers as a rule were not inclined to venture on new and doubtful experiments. But it was easy to increase profits by undertaking the cultivation of land with abundant capital, with a sturdy resolution to be deterred from no reasonable experiment, and, it must be added, by the spectacle of the marked success which had attended the new husbandry in Belgium and Holland. Men do and will mistake concomitants for causes, say what one may, especially when the legislature avers that what it does are and must be causes.

When the English manufacturer and merchant had once got into the world's markets, he was certain not to relinquish his hold without a struggle, and as certain to assist his energies by labour-saving inventions. He rapidly found out when in his case the old theory was overthrown, that the only way to keep what he had acquired, was by quality, cheapness, and convenience. The popularity of British goods, even during the Continental War, and the continuance of the Berlin and Milan decrees was maintained, and to a considerable extent assisted by the fact that the supremacy of this country by sea made the United Kingdom in reality the only source of supply. But it is also certain that from the third quarter of the eighteenth century onwards, the inventiveness of British mechanicians and manufactures was in singular contrast to their characteristics in a previous age. They were threatened with rivalry in a field which they had created, no matter how, and they retained their superiority by incessant improvements in the process of production. I have my own opinion about the policy of Pitt in rushing into the Continental War. I cannot but condemn in the strongest way, the fiscal expedient which he adopted in order to provide the charges of the war; but I am strongly convinced that the war which raged during that terrible period from Gibraltar to Moscow, precluded all competition against

England throughout the Continent. It was in possession of the market, and everything conspired together to make that market secure. At last, shortly after peace was proclaimed, the tardy wisdom of Parliament liberated the industries of this country from taxes on raw material, and its staple manufactures from excises on the produce. But in my next lecture, I shall have to point out to you how serious were the difficulties which the fiscal policy of Pitt and his successors put on British industry, and how vigorous were the efforts made to compensate for their inevitable consequences.

There is no period in European history, certainly none within the last three hundred years in which Europe was in a state of more complete prostration than it was after the final defeat of Napoleon and the French in 1815. It is true that Germany was more wasted at the peace of Westphalia, near two centuries before, than it was during the great Continental War. But Germany suffered more than any other part of Europe during this war, for it was the design of the first Napoleon to permanently weaken the whole Teutonic race. Now it is very difficult for a country which has been entirely impoverished by war, to make progress in the arts of peace. Even under the most entire reversal of the old system, the process would be slow and disappointing, but the memories of that terrible time lie deep in German minds, and the only escape from their repetition appeared to be militarism. More recent events have not reassured European countries. The utterly unprovoked war of 1870, in which whatever may be said for past events in her history, Prussia and Northern Germany were entirely on the defensive, has not mended the situation. The energies of the country are wasted on gigantic armaments. It is possible that no price can be dear for security, but the price may extinguish industrial progress. And added to this Germany is every year more involved in protective schemes. Every interest which can succeed in imposing on German Parliaments and statesmen is engaged in plundering the public. It is very possible that the exigencies of the national defence may make the Government the ready recipients of whatever fiscal revenues may be offered them. The same facts apply to other European countries. Industry is cramped, distorted, and made ignorant. The masses of the people are impoverished and turn angrily on the Government, because they are led to consider that as everything is done by Government, it is responsible for the evil as well as for the good. Practical wisdom induces prudent men to circumscribe the forces of government as far as possible, to invoke them as rarely as possible, and it is marvellous to see how slow Governments are in arriving at the same conclusion.

We English people are now ostensibly at least engaged in an <u>industrial competition</u> with the whole civilized world, for, as I have told you, however hampered a community may be in its power of purchase, it is always allowed to sell if it can, and is always desirous of selling. I am quite aware that some countries are much given to creating and selling securities or public debts, and that we in the United Kingdom have greatly assisted them, though not always wisely, in the distribution of these debts. I mention this because some peculiarly ignorant or deceitful people are trying to persuade our countrymen that they are going to ruin, because our debtors are paying the interest on their debts. But beyond doubt, all European nations, and some in other parts of the world, are willing to compete against us if they can only get the chance. Now it may be worth while to take stock, as merchants say, of our present position, to see what it depends on, and to what extent it has the elements of continuance and progress.

First for our fiscal policy. We have put ourselves, and all those of our colonies and dependencies in which the central government has authority, on the same level with our neighbours, however hostile their tariff may be to us, on which subject I shall have to speak presently. We therefore submit our trade, as far as foreign competition is concerned, to the entirely unimpeded rivalry of the foreign producer and trader. Every effort is made by most European and some Transatlantic Governments to exclude British goods from the use of the people whose affairs these Governments administer, and except for the purpose of fraudulent imitation (a vice which is peculiarly characteristic of the North German race), the administration of these several communities would gladly effect their wholesale prohibition ; we allow (except recently under the Act which prohibits imports which have false marks of origin and forgeries of the signatures and trade marks of British manufacturers) the German, French, American, or any other people to freely import their goods into Great Britain, subject only to certain fiscal charges, to countervail which we levy identical excises on similar British manufactures. We do the same in India and the Crown Colonies. We ask for no favour from those of our Colonies which are possessed of the power of arranging their own taxation, and we get no favour, though certain of the Colonies have pressed us for differential duties on their own products. Some of our people have affected a virtuous indignation at bounties given on certain products, and are foolishly or ignorantly trying to discover some process by which they can prevent foreigners selling us goods at lower rates than we believe some of these people believe that they can afford to make them. But it could easily be shown, as indeed might be expected, that the bounty-fed producer abroad is a good deal worse off than the bounty-threatened producer at home. Our allegiance to our principles is so absolute, that even they who dispute this wisdom and success are perpetually appealing to these principles in support of their desire to deviate from them. We have almost, if not quite, succeeded in making Great Britain a free port for the civilized world, and as a consequence, no trivial or unimportant result, we fix the market price for nearly every product of human industry, for we have excluded every element of cost from imports, except that of warehouse room, which is of course a universal necessity.

Our contention is that our free-trade policy enables us to arrive at the most accurate estimate possible of our own powers. We do not plant olive or orange groves or vineyards in our climate, for we know that they will not thrive or will not live. No doubt they might be grown in greenhouses. But we are not so foolish as to put such a duty on the foreign produce of olives, oranges, and grapes, as to encourage native industry in growing them under these adverse and costly conditions, as a consistent protectionist or fair trader would have us do. For it is only a matter of degree between the most plausible protection and the most grotesque illustration of the practice. We do not think it right that the people should starve in order that a stupid and servile farmer may pay a rent which he has not the wit to see that his land will not bear, or the manliness to resist if he does happen to see it. The consequence of our fiscal policy is that we see what we can do best, and having found out what we can do best, we are at the pains to add improvements to it according to our ability. For it stands to reason that if the State secures a market and a price for the producer of an article in universal demand—it is no use protecting what people will take or leave as they like—the State at once takes away all motive for improvement. Thirty years ago and more, the American people were noted for the invention of labour-saving machines. The faculty is by no means extinct, but it has been notoriously discouraged, and is no way so prolific as it used to be. Nor do we retaliate, for we know that though other nations may harm our trade we shall do ourselves no good by harming theirs. We have come to the conclusion that a State does not become a better neighbour by being impoverished, it may be by its own act, still less by ours, because people may be blinded by ignorance or be made the dupes of sophistry, but every one understands and resents an international wrong, however much his own conduct may have provoked it. If we were to prohibit the goods of those countries which refuse to admit ours, or put serious hindrances on their importation, we should very likely be doing what is entirely futile in the same class of goods, for it would be very absurd to think that goods which require protection in the home market could come into rivalry with the same goods in a foreign market, and it would be mischievous in the case of materials for manufacture, because it is to be presumed that we go to a particular country, because we get these materials at a cheaper rate or of better quality, while the adoption of the precious policy of retaliation would supply us with materials at a dearer rate or of an inferior quality. And the proof of what I have said is to be found in the fact that the import of articles in which Great Britain is admitted to be well in advance, is too trivial for enumeration or classification. The British Government has, I believe, imported Teutonic swords and Teutonic bayonets, which have been found to be rather less valuable than Teutonic metaphysics. But though it seems that our soldiers have lost their lives out of this luckless venture, it does not seem possible to bring the offence home to the official culprits who have speculated in the rubbish.

I am convinced that the only condition under which foreign trade may be successfully carried on is that of working on free-trade principles. Before the tariff reforms of Sir Robert Peel were carried out, the volume of exports and imports did not equal or exceed a month's present business, British shipping was not a tenth of what it now is, business was stationary, and the revenue inelastic or declining. We have now the simplest tariff in the civilized world. The volume of our trade is larger in extent and more varied in character than that of any other nation; the shipping of Great Britain carries two-thirds of all the goods sent out from various countries, and grows, it may be presumed, because we can perform the service better and more cheaply than other nations can. We are withal able, constantly, to overleap the boundaries of national and artificial protection; the former being the cost of freight, and the power of interpreting the market which comes from proximity to it; the other, the present which Government makes out of the pockets of consumers, to persistent and greedy clamour, to interested sophists, or to some scheme of grandmotherly assistance.

I do not deny that British manufacture and trade are hindered by the protective tariffs of other countries. The law allows the subject of it to buy one pair of boots where he might buy two pairs, and stints him in many ways. He is not, therefore, so good a customer as he could be if he were left to his own discretion. Besides, the advantages of trade are to the mass of people, and the disadvantage of a protective tariff also fall on the mass. It may not signify to the rich man that he is called upon to pay 50 per cent more for his sugar or his clothing than he would be if the markets were open. But it signifies a good deal to a poor man, whose margin over necessaries is narrow, and is likely to get narrower as population increases and demand becomes wider. Besides, as every one knows, it is much more easy to smuggle broadcloth goods than it is to smuggle frieze goods, and the weavers of broadcloth knowing it, act upon it with alacrity and confidence. But though it is true that the fiscal regulations of foreign and colonial states do harm to British manufacture and trade because they stint demand, and though it is certain that a relaxation of existing laws would give an impulse to British industry and commerce, it does not follow that the advantage would be lasting. It is quite possible that many of them, if they resolved on relying on natural protection only, might speedily find that they could supply the greater part of their own home-market themselves. As it is the great difficulties in the way of this consummation is self-imposed protection. Many of my American friends have alleged that we English people are free traders for ourselves, and much more for them, because we want to get a wider market for our goods ; and I have always answered that I very much doubt whether the market would be more than temporary, a consideration in the policy of nations, however little it may be in that of individuals : whereas, the intention of protection may narrow our market in the States a little, but renders that market permanent, since it inflicts a permanent disability on their rivalry.

I am quite alive to the geographical and climatical advantages which Great Britain possesses, in its equable climate, in its varied mineral resources, and in its singular accessibility for all products. I have mentioned before that, two centuries ago, Bishop Burnett declared that it would become and remain the best country in the world for textile fabrics, and what was then confidently said, when the collection of observed physical facts was scanty, is true now that the collection of these facts has become almost overwhelmingly abundant. But I need hardly remind you of what you will find in the manuals of geography which form an elementary study in physics, though it is singular that even in a progressive country great local advantages may be neglected. Nothing has struck me more than the merits of the harbour at Milford Haven. It is capable of taking, and seems destined to take, the traffic of the world, just as the harbour of Brest, not unlike it in formation, seems capable. Now what I say now, was said four and a half centuries ago by the author of the "Libel of English Policy." But incomparably inferior harbours, such as those of Bristol and Liverpool, inferior because they are tidal, have become the sources and centres of great commercial prosperity.

More remarkable and more noteworthy, however, is the decline of cities and localities. In the last quarter of the fourteenth century, Bristol had become the second port in England after London. The next was Plymouth, and both these ports are still flourishing. But the third was King's Lynn. I am drawing my estimate from the taxable population in 1377. Next came Colchester; but Hull and Southampton were quite small. No doubt the changes are to be explained by the character of the trade then carried on. There is not a single port besides Bristol which is named on the western coast. More notable still is the effect induced by bad government. In 1657, when Cromwell ordered an assessment for Scotland and Ireland, the assessment of Dublin city was more than twice as high as that of Edinburgh, the only Scotch town which paid as much as three figures. Glasgow, now the second city in the United Kingdom, was then less wealthy than Dundee, and the taxation of each was not much more than a hundredth part of the London payment. But even after the union of the two crowns, Scotland made progress. The progress was rapid indeed after the union of 1706, for the Scottish Parliament laid the basis of their negotiations in the absolute equality of the two nations, and in the maintenance of Scottish nationality in the Church and the Courts of Law. Scotland claimed and obtained entire freedom of manufacture and trade. But from the Restoration onwards, much more after the Revolution and the Treaty of Limerick, it was the policy of the British Parliament to destroy the manufactures and trade of Ireland with the exception of the Ulster linen factories, which owed their existence or first development to Strafford. Now what has been destroyed has never been revived, though the natural advantages of Ireland as a home for textile industries are as great as those of England. In point of fact, the fitness of Ireland for competition with England in the woollen manufacture and trade was made the plea for destroying its industry.

I once asked a friend of mine, the late Mr. Samuel Morley—my intimacy with him justified so personal a question—to what he ascribed the remarkable commercial success which attended the business of which he was the head, in its competition with other traders. I was a good deal struck with his answer. He said that apart from attention to his calling and the necessary method in so vast a business, which he said were shared to the full by others who were engaged in the same trade, he could think of nothing beyond the fact that any bale of goods which went from his house, and was duly identified as packed in his warehouses, would be taken all the world over without opening and sampling. This illustrates another important condition of successful competition, the reputation of unblemished and irreproachable good faith. Competence in determining the value of goods is, I presume, a common acquirements of merchants. It would be well if one were convinced that commercial integrity were as common and unquestionable, if it were not necessary to build up a reputation for honesty by a process as laborious and as prolonged as that of founding a business. For the temptation to impose on the unwary may be there, and persons may flatter themselves that for a time they may escape detection; but the discovery of malpractices is dangerous. Some years ago, I heard that a fraud in the manufacture of brass rods for the African trade—my informant could only guess at the uses to which the rods were put—was detected in the case of one manufacturer, and that the discovery led to the destruction of his trade and that of all others who were engaged in it, and had committed no fraud. Illustrations of the kind may be multiplied. I once heard of a Birmingham quaker who manufactured guns for the African trade. As there was no proof made of cheap guns at that time, this adventurous manufacturer made the barrels of inferior metal, in fact, I was told, of gas-piping, and when remonstrance was made to him of the dangerous character of his wares, he defended himself on the ground that he put no touch-holes to them. I do not know whether he ever effected two shipments of such rubbish, but the Government very properly interposed, and ordered that all barrels, without exception, should be proved.

Some persons have defended adulteration on the ground that the public likes cheap goods. It may be they do, but I am convinced that the public likes genuine goods more. But, in fact, fraud and adulteration are the bane of honest competition. The cheapness which comes from improvement in the product, and the result of economy in the process, is not only legitimate, but in the end beneficent, if good faith is kept. If it is not kept, innocent persons are injured by the action of the guilty. It is said that at one time the genuine trade of Manchester was seriously imperilled in consequence of a practice adopted by some firms of heavily sizing cotton goods with flour and whiting. Silk will bear an enormous amount of adulteration and, its fabric remaining to all appearance the same, be weighted with adventitious substances to sixfold its original quantity. It is alleged, and I have not heard it contradicted, that this seductive process has seriously injured the silk manufacture of Lyons. The Sheffield cutlers insisted on a remedy against German imitations of their goods, and the fraudulent marking of eminent manufacturer's names on the articles, with the addition of Sheffield make, not because of the loss which fell upon them by being supplanted, but because the reputation of the whole district was endangered by the action.

In brief, then, if industrial communities first learn, by the only way in which they can learn, in what they can excel, if they resolutely resist every insidious proposal which, affecting to assist, will really cramp their energies and damp their enterprise, if ever they make it their business to discover where demand and supply may be best adjusted ; if they do as much of their work themselves as they can, and avoid the multiplication of intermediaries, and if they are resolved, cost what it may in delay, to maintain their reputation for probity, the home trade of every country need fear no disaster in international competition. Errors may be made, no doubt, but the obvious palliative of an error is to correct it for the future. It is by these plain rules of action that British manufacture and trade has been extended and is extending, and it is by the maintenance of these rules that it will be secured and enlarged in the future.

XI.

ECONOMIC LEGISLATION, 1815-41.

Taxes to maintain the Continental War—The land tax—The tax on succession duties—The income tax—The inhabited house tax—Taxes on trades and professions—Taxes on consumables—Taxes on raw materials—The Merchants' Petition—The new departure—Canning—Sir Henry Parnell—Reduction of the taxes on raw material—Lord Monteagle—Rowland Hill and the Post Office—The beginning of the Anti-Corn Law agitation—Sir Robert Peel.

OTHER wars have been as long as that which this country waged with France between 1793 and 1815, but none have been so costly, none more desperate, none in which all maxims of financial justice and financial wisdom were more thoroughly cast aside. It had one characteristic, which has always been dwelt upon by those who have eulogised the men who promoted and waged it, a characteristic which is by no means without parallel, for it has been exhibited more than once before, the resolution of those who administered the affairs of the British nation. For the six years which intervened between Jena and Moscow, the British continued their struggle almost single-handed with France and her armies, which were recruited from the whole of Napoleon's conquests. During this period, as indeed before and after, English statesmen freely lavished the money and blood of the people, for it was a notable fact that the greater part of the taxes and loans raised were contributed by the workers, and that the landed interest steadily refused to make equivalent sacrifices from their own resources, which increased enormously during the time, for rents were trebled during the great French war, the recipients of those refusing to allow the taxation of their estates, though they freely gave those up to the tax-gatherer which had been accumulated by the industrial classes. In order to assist this financial plunder the State, through its ministers, inflicted on the people the additional injury of a forced and depreciated paper currency, attempted to deny and next to explain away the consequences of its action, but took care in the payment of its officials to give a practical refutation to its allegations in Parliament. Many of the mischiefs which were produced during that disastrous period still survive in their effects, the debt, the habits of official extravagance and excessive remuneration for public service, an administration of public affairs which is costly beyond parallel, and inefficient, one would have thought, beyond patience.

It is open to grave question whether the war of 1793, whatever may be the defence of its continuance, was not entirely unprovoked and gratuitous. Just a hundred years ago the rulers of France, aghast at the consequences of their own misgovernment, assembled, amid the approval of all wise and humane people, the *tiers état*, with a view of putting before this ancient and nearly forgotten Parliament the affairs of the kingdom. No one, I think, at the present time, doubts that the king and his advisers in taking this step hoped to arrive at a peaceful, though it might be a laborious, solution of the existing trouble. All classes it seems were willing to make sacrifices for the common end. The reasonings of Rousseau, the scepticism of the French savants, directed against many more social customs than were attacked elsewhere, and the spectacle of transatlantic freedom, predisposed all sections of society in favour of this new departure. Arthur Young, who was travelling in France during this eventful year, and has left what is on the whole the most graphic picture of the French capital and provinces during the summer and autumn of 1789, bears witness to the eagerness with which the gathering in Paris was welcomed. Even after the commons had quarrelled with the nobles and the clergy, and taking all affairs of State into their own hands, extinguished at a stroke the whole feudal system; even after the attack on the chateaux began, and the people rose against their old oppressors, sympathy with those who were rendered homeless and were impoverished by the winter risings was largely diluted by the satisfaction men felt at the total destruction of the ancient system. Many people in England, and those in quarters where one would least expect it, sympathized for a time, at least, with the insurgents. The friends of the people had allies and supporters in such men as the Duke of Richmond, Lord Stanhope, and Lord Orford, while not a few other members of the British aristocracy called themselves citizens, and affected republican principles and republican equality. Pitt, who had recently to his credit negotiated a very comprehensive treaty of commerce with France, might well have wished to see the result of this departure in commercial diplomacy.

All experience shows that a nation which has long been deprived of popular and representative institutions is exceedingly apt to misunderstand, misuse, and strain the powers which are suddenly put into their hands. The National Assembly of France was entirely unused to parliamentary action, and was sure to commit grave errors. The chaos which followed on the independence of the bureaucratically governed colonies of Spanish America is hardly reduced to order yet, after an interval of more than sixty years. The early parliamentary history of Greece is not satisfactory. No man in his senses would think of suddenly conferring representative institutions on India and China, great as is the material progress and educational intelligence which has been made in our Eastern dependency. The French assembly was sure to do many unwise and premature things, even if it had been left by the indifference of Europe to work out its own problems in profound peace. It was certain to depress and then to despoil the nobles and the clergy, though for a time, while it proclaimed war against the monastic orders, it was disposed to recognize allies in the parish priests. But very soon came an attempt at intervention, and what appears to be a characteristic of the French people, an overmastering suspicion of domestic treachery. If the founders of the French Revolution had done or attempted only a part of what they undertook, and had proceeded slowly and cautiously, they would in the end have done what had to be done far more effectually.

As the French Revolution was the natural outcome of the War of American Independence, so from the very beginning the progress of the French Revolution excited the most uneasy feelings among the hereditary monarchs of Europe. The French propaganda, on the one hand, was everywhere, and so were soon the *emigrés* or voluntary exiles, and the dispossessed priests. These two parties were counselling foreign intervention and domestic insurrection. The headquarters of the *emigrés* was at Coblentz. The clergy were fomenting disturbances in those parts of France which remained devoted to the old religion. Soon came the declaration of Pilnitz and the proclamation of war against Austria. The declaration does not indeed threaten war, but it made war inevitable.

It is very difficult to know what was the mind of Pitt at the time. I should certainly never take it from his eulogists. I can well understand that he desired peace, for after the singularly exhausting war with the American colonies he knew well enough that the country needed it. But it appears, from sources which have recently come to light, that he intrigued with the *emigrés* and the clergy, and fomented insurrections in Normandy and Brittany by money secretly supplied. So I do not doubt that Pitt desired parliamentary reform, but his action rather postponed than assisted that necessary change. Again, it seems that he sincerely wished to bring about Catholic Emancipation, but his subsequent attitude made the concession of it remote, difficult, and only the escape from a serious danger. But Pitt was a public man of all-devouring ambition. He was practically minister for twenty-two years consecutively, for Addington was a puppet whose strings he pulled. But there was one thing which might bring his power to a sudden end. If he lost the king's favour, or the king lost his own wits, his position would be perilous. His attitude on the Regency question had cost him the favour of the Prince of Wales, and he had no mind to fall like Walpole. We do not indeed as yet know the secret history of that time, for access is still denied to those national archives which contain that history. We had, beyond a general interest in monarchical institutions, none of those impulses which stirred hereditary and legitimate sovereigns. The King of England was a parliamentary sovereign, without a tittle of hereditary right. We had set aside a dozen families and chosen a German prince, who was most remotely descended from the royal state. The family alliances of our sovereigns had in the main been with the small German princelets of the Lutheran persuasion. Leopold had some reason in taking up the cause of his sister and brother-in-law. We had no such motive. Our policy was to let France alone, just as France let England alone, when she made war on, deposed, and executed her king. It seems to me impossible to doubt that if France had been let alone, and all interference in her domestic affairs discouraged or prohibited, the fire of revolution would have speedily burnt itself out. I conclude that we owe, as far as England is concerned, our intervention in French affairs and the twenty-two years' war to the obstinacy of George the Third, yielded to with culpable cowardice, just as we owed the war of American Independence to the same obstinacy, and to the same irrational and unconstitutional deference.

Whatever may have been the merits of the cause which he undertook, Pitt was a most unlucky war minister. The policy of the British Government had entirely destroyed the ancient amity between England and Holland, and the first movement against France was led by that Duke of Brunswick who was even more detested by the Dutch than the stadtholder was. The army which Frederic the Great had formed was demoralized in the hands of his foolish successors, and Europe at the outbreak of hostilities appears to have been almost worn out. Pitt had to bribe these people with subsidies, and he might as well have kept the money for all the good they did with it. Within four years the heaven-born minister had to sanction a forced paper currency. Before he died France had overrun Italy, Flanders, Holland, and both banks of the Rhine. It is said that the minister died of the battle of Austerlitz. Next year came an even greater disaster, the humiliation of Prussia at Jena. On sea, indeed, Great Britain was supreme, and without a rival after the victories of Nelson.

Pitt and his successors, up to and after the conclusion of the great war, cast aside every principle of finance for the purpose of procuring funds for this war. Every necessary and every convenience of life was taxed. Raw materials, staple manufactures, the earnings of the living and the savings of the dead were visited by the tax-gatherer. I have heard from those who lived through those times, how serious was the struggle for existence during the epoch of that finance. The sufferings of those who lived by wages, who were crippled in all their expenditure, starved by the Corn Laws, and reduced to that bare subsistence, of which the infallible index is the rise and fall of wages with the rise and fall in the price of food, were the greatest; for, as Mr. Porter has accurately stated, the principal burden of the war taxes fell on the working classes, who were exempted from the income tax, solely because the rate of wages never reached the minimum of annual income which Pitt, Addington, and the rest were constrained to spare. Most of the precedents of Pitt's taxation were borrowed from the Dutch excises, levied during the War of Independence; but with this marked difference between the two countries, that Holland kept to the principles of free trade, even in forms which seem to us grotesque, for it gathered its funds from consumers only, and from internal sources, leaving the ports free, while Pitt burdened trade with oppressive customs, and manufacture with disastrous excises. The Dutch took toll on shoes, on clothing, on every article, in short, which the individual purchased for his personal consumption, but they were not idiotic enough to burden the trader in foreign produce or the manufacturer of home products with vexatious and ruinous hindrances on imports.

Pitt had made the land tax, under an assessment framed at a period of great difficulty, of universal suspicion, and of widespread disloyalty to the principles of the Revolution, and therefore grossly unfair and inequitable, a perpetual charge, merely to effect a financial operation in connection with the public debt, for the land tax had been imposed at the highest rate for years before this operation was attempted. He was, therefore, precluded or thought he was precluded, except indirectly in levying any additional tax on land, and this at a time when high prices, aided by war and the Corn Laws, rapidly trebled agricultural rents. As consumers, and as payers of income tax, the landowners had to undertake some share of the burden, a burden which they could easily bear, as the source of their income was increasing by leaps and bounds. One of the reasons why so many of the larger yeomen, free and copyholders, disappeared after the war was over, was that their enormous gains habituated them to a scale of expense which they could neither endure nor abandon, after lower prices set in with peace. The great landowner paid a house tax it is true, but the rate at which their mansions were assured was nominal, on the absurd plea of their letting value. And when Pitt proposed, if he was serious, and only proposed what he did to save appearances, that their land should contribute like personal property to probate and succession duties, they threatened to desert him in a crisis, when, according to their talk, the country was struggling for its existence, unless he dropped this entirely equitable tax. But the tax on succession in England is so curiously illustrative of how notable a part historical events and practices play in the life of Englishmen, that it may be worth while to give you a brief account of the origin of the system.

The courts of law had divided property into what they called real and personal, and had assigned every form of it to one of these two heads. Some of the distinctions were grotesque enough. One of the most precarious estates which we can conceive is land held for the life of another. One of the most-enduring imaginable is a lease, say for 500 or 1,000 years, held under a small, even a nominal quit rent, as was by no means uncommon, even in the Middle Ages, and for certain intelligible reasons. But the courts of law insisted on calling the former real estate, the latter personal, or in their phrase, "chattels real." Now the courts of law took cognizance of real estate. Indeed, till the reign of Henry VIII., the freeholder could not devise an estate of inheritance, and there is one estate of inheritance which he cannot devise even now. But in the case of personal property, the Church was allowed to intervene. It took cognizance of wills, and in cases of intestacy of all those goods which came under its purview, alleging that in the former case the will was proved—*probatum est*, and dividing the personal estate of intestates, according to the rules of the civil code, from which body of law, indeed, all the learning, as it is called, about wills is derived. You will remember that in these early times, masses for the dead were an almost invariable obligation, and that to omit or disdain these offices on the part of a testator, or on the part of his representatives, if there were sufficient funds, was as distasteful to the sentiment of the age, as the neglect or omission of funeral solemnities would be now. There was a reason then, derived from the discipline of the Church, why ecclesiastics should supervise testamentary dispositions and intestate estates. Wills of personalty exist by thousands. I remember to have seen, years ago, a chest full of them in Hereford Cathedral, for they were consigned to the bishop's registry. Sometimes when an Englishman died abroad, say at the Papal court, where the barbarous rule of confiscating a stranger's goods did not prevail, a catalogue was made of his effects, a valuation given, and the account transmitted to the registry of the diocese whence he came, with an offer to send the price they fetched, or to take them at the valuation annexed, and transmit the proceeds. I have seen several such schedules from the court at Avignon in the fourteenth century. The probate was, therefore, a necessary solemnity, before the will was allowed to have validity ; and as was customary, the seal of the diocese was annexed to the instrument. But, as I have said, real estate passed through no such hands.

Now, by the Statute of Frauds, a will accompanied by certain formalities, was required for all testamentary dispositions, some few exceptions being allowed. In the Stamp Act of 1694, a duty was imposed on this certificate of proof, small in amount, and invariable. During the American war, the duty was increased by an *ad valorem* charge on the amount of the estate of which proof was tendered. But the tax was practically limited to England. Probates and letters of administration were unknown in Scotland, and only after Pitt's day was it imposed in Scotland. Nor has it been imposed on real estate. It is entirely an impost on what the law calls personal property. By a singular provision, one which, beyond its manifest injustice, is one which betrays a remarkable lack of humour, a considerable part of the probate duty is handed over to the new county councils. Thus the estate of deceased owners of personal property, which does not need a road to give it value, is expended in keeping roads in repair for the benefit of landowners, who do not contribute any probate duty whatever.

The probate duty mulcted the collected estate, but a further tax was imposed on it in its distributive aspect, *i.e.*, when it became a legacy. North, during the American War, attempted to impose such a tax in the form of a duty on receipts given for legacies; but as the law did not require such receipts, the tax produced next to nothing. Pitt, in 1796, determined to impose a duty on collateral legatees, not on direct descendants, and, as I have said, put forward an abortive project of extending the tax to real estate. He raised the duties in 1804, and included direct descendants in 1805. No attempt was made to include real estate till 1853, when Mr. Gladstone contrived to procure a very trivial contribution, and that on very easy terms from the succession of real estate. In 1885 an attempt to still further extend this liability was defeated on a division, and the Government had to resign.

In 1815, the population of the United Kingdom was between 19 and 20 millions. The taxation was $74\frac{1}{4}$ millions. The National Debt was 860 millions, and the annual charge was 32 millions. The people were no doubt exceedingly joyful at the final defeat of Napoleon and the humiliation of France, but they were staggering under the cost of the process. The war, too, and the circulation of inconvertible paper, had greatly raised all charges; and some of these charges, though justified at first for temporary reasons, became as the charges of government are apt to become, permanent. Of the revenue, about $25\frac{1}{4}$ millions was what is technically, but very often inaccurately, called direct, and of this more than $14\frac{1}{2}$ millions were derived from the 10 per cent. income tax. A little over 5 millions came from what Mr. Dowell calls eatables; $24\frac{1}{4}$ millions from alcoholic fluids, tea, coffee, and tobacco; a little more than 6 millions from raw materials; a little over 4 millions from manufactures and $2\frac{3}{4}$ millions from stamps. Everything conceivable was taxed, and several minor sources of revenue brought the sum up, with the Irish contribution, to the amount which I have named. Some people, to be sure, had done very well by the war, but the general condition of the people was fairly described by Sydney Smith in one of his contributions to the *Edinburgh Review* of 1820. I am indebted for these facts to Mr. Dowell's "History of Taxation in

England," *i.e.*, the United Kingdom, in which work with great accuracy as to the special details before him, there are introduced some of the most amazingly incorrect statements as to social history in England which I have ever encountered. But mistakes in this branch of study exist in plenty, and I suppose always will. "Our grandfathers," said the late Lord Derby, "had something about which to grumble." I think they had, but they have to thank Lord Derby's grandfather and the rest of his associates for the occasion of the grumbling which was given them.

Pledges had been given that the 10 per cent. income tax should cease with the war. The war was over, and people demanded the redemption of the pledge, *i.e.*, the people who paid it, and especially the rich traders, fundholders, and landowners. The Government wanted to keep half of it, for, as the Duke of Wellington said, without some part of it, "it seemed impossible to keep up the necessary peace establishment," this peace establishment being now nearly as costly as North's war establishment. The House of Commons determined that it should go, even at the risk of losing the invaluable services of Mr. Vansittart, Lord Castlereagh, and the rest. Now they had no mind to sacrifice themselves to their principles. Lord Castlereagh made a kind of stand. He charged his critics with "an ignorant impatience of taxation," and he irritated them the more. Nor did he do away with the impression when he changed from rebuke to entreaty, and "besought the British nation not to turn its back upon itself." The most expert gymnast would find it difficult to achieve this feat. But Lord Castlereagh was an Irish landlord, who had caught up an Irish habit, along with his Irish rents. The income tax had to go, root and branch.

There was another war tax, the repeal or reduction of which the landed interest insisted. After the war was over, the price of food fell. This used to be called agricultural distress, and some people call it so still. The tax on malt was 4s. 5d. the bushel, having been, up to 1802, 1s. 0¼d. Certain other war duties went with a moiety of the malt tax, and about 18 millions of revenue. But these remissions left the Treasury 56½ millions, of which 24 were to go to "the peace establishment." Our fathers thought this too much. Perhaps the economy enforced on the spending departments was worth the effort. I have known eminent politicians, who were not indifferent to the national defence, insist, up to thirty years ago, that we should make an effort after the old economy. But the sons of Zeruiah, who are described as mighty men of valour, were too strong for them, and are too strong for their descendants or successors. It is true that a Government ought to do its best to reduce the public debt, and therefore should always have an excess of revenue over expenditure, that excess being strictly devoted to this end. But it is also true that if one leaves a productive tax in the hands of a Government, it never will be at a loss for objects to spend it on. This fact is illustrated on the largest scale by the Government of the United States. It is similarly, though not so plainly, illustrated by the history of the modern income tax, as I hope to show in my next lecture.

In 1815, there were, besides these taxes on income and malt, others which were supposed to be on personal expenditure; those on houses and windows, on carriages, horses, and male servants, on the use of hair powder and armorial bearings. Taxes on houses have been generally defended by economists on the ground that a man's house is a fair index of his income. It is no such thing. It may be an index of another man's income, and commonly is. It is constantly a very heavy tax indeed on the process of earning an income. It would be much more fair, if it were a tax on the building cost of the house, the ground rent being separately assessed. Some few years ago, I was officially the tenant of a house in Charing Cross. The ground rent was £400 a year, the building rent £100. The parties whom I represented paid house tax and local rates on the whole rent. The ground landlord escaped everything but income tax. It is plain to every one that a ground rent is the outcome of increasing population, and increasing competition on those who are engaged in various kinds of town industry. The actual income of the occupier may very possibly be no more than his rent. To tax him, then, on what is essential to his earning an income at all, is either to make him pay a double income tax, or to compel him to transfer the tax he pays in the first instance to his customer. When house rents in towns were low, as they were in the days of

Adam Smith, there may have been some reason in the assertion that a house tax was a fair one. But it was very different when Mill wrote, and this latter author, omitting all inquiry into the incidence of the house tax, endorsed, I think rather rashly, the view of those older writers who approved it. Besides, the assessment of county mansions was, and is, notoriously fictitious, and upon this fictitious valuation the tax levied on the owner was calculated. Assessed taxes, as they are called, *i.e.*, taxes on voluntary, perhaps ostentatious expenditure are defensible. Some years ago, Mr. Gladstone jestingly declared that he would not remit the tax on the use of hair powder, as he deemed it the centre of constitutional finance—but he did remit it.

The tax on insurances, *i.e.*, taxes on forethought and prudence, yielded about a million sterling. There were taxes on auctions, taxes on advertisements, and taxes on newspapers. The first two of these pressed heavily on persons of moderate means, and in the case of auctions were in effect, nine cases out of ten, additional probate and legacy duties. The tax on newspapers, first imposed in Anne's reign, 1712, with the view of stifling criticism on the Ministry of Harley and Bolingbroke, had been greatly amplified by Pitt. If a Government is an entity, which is justified in using every expedient, as an individual might, to prolong its existence, a tax on those who might shorten that existence was a prudential measure. I am old enough to remember the time when a daily paper was a costly luxury. Taxes on locomotion were also levied, the tax being far heavier than that imposed on private carriages. Up to recent times, the tax on a hackney carriage was actually £18 5s. a year. Now, whatever may be said in favour of taxing the pleasures of people—and it is exceedingly hard to define and limit a luxury—to tax locomotion in the case of those who travel for business, is to impose an additional income tax on traders, which, of course, if they are to continue their calling on the ordinary condition of securing an average profit, they must recover from those who purchase their goods.

Licenses were exacted from several traders, and heavy duties were demanded from other members of what are called the two branches of the legal profession. A barrister paid £25 on admission to an Inn of Court, and £50 more at his call. Less fees were demanded from physicians, surgeons, and apothecaries. The attorney had to pay a tax of £120 on his articles of clerkship, £25 on admission, and £12 a year for license to practice. Such enormous fines paid for the bare permission to carry on a calling led to the doctrine that these practitioners had a vested interest, and justified the favour which has been shown to their function and to their charges. In the nature of things they recovered their outlay many times over from their clients. The taxes on traders were an indirect and most mischievous form of levying additional duties on consumption.

Pitt levied an enormous tax on salt, 15s. the bushel of 54 lbs. By this time nearly all the salt consumed in the United Kingdom was produced at home from brine springs. But the duty crippled the foreign trade in this article, and checked the manufacture of those soda products which the chemistry of the time had already discovered. Sugar paid 30s. a cwt., *i.e.*, a good deal more than its present price by retail, and pretty well a cent. per cent. tax at the time. The duty on alcoholic liquors was high, and was especially a tax on the poor, for the private brewer paid malt-and-hop taxes, while the brewer paid in addition a license on his calling, and an additional tax on the barrel. Wine and spirits were also heavily taxed. The total amount was nearly 18½ millions. Tea paid an *ad valorem* duty of 96 per cent., tobacco and snuff one of about 300 per cent. Coals and timber carried on coasters, or imported, 2¼ millions.

Raw materials, cotton, silk, hemp, soda, indigo, potash, iron, skins and furs yielded more than 1¾ millions. Manufactures were also taxed by the excise, leather, soap, bricks and tiles, glass, candles, and paper, to over 4 millions. But besides these near 1,200 other articles were in the tariff. The tax on some was simply destructive or prohibitory. But everything which people could use, everything on which ingenuity or improvement could be exhibited was starved by rigorous customs duties or a searching and vexatious excise. It was all but impossible for industry to make progress through these hindrances, and, as we shall see, the material progress of the country was very materially retarded by them. Finally, every transaction between man and man which could be carried on, or formed the necessary business of life, was visited with heavy stamp duties, imposed so unwisely, so unjustly, and so recklessly that the smaller the transaction was the heavier was the impost on it. So intricate and obscure were these Stamp Acts, that people who had no thought of defrauding the revenue incurred penalties, or at least were declared liable to them, and not infrequently the courts of law declared themselves unable to interpret the statutes which they were called on to enforce. Some of these liabilities the people flatly, but covertly, refused to incur, and the difficulty, arose as to how the whole people could be indicted, a difficulty which has arrested the course of the most vigilant advocates which law and order have ever had.

I have given you a brief, and yet I believe a sufficiently accurate, account of the financial position in the United Kingdom, when a report on British finance was presented on January 5, 1816. The situation, however, had its humorous side, its highly irregular corrective. The public revolted against the tariff, formed an alliance with the smuggler, assisted in baffling the exciseman and custom-house officer, and generally handed over these ministers of the law to the worst penalties which theologians have denounced. Statistical evidence on the subject could not, in the nature of things, be forthcoming, but it was credibly alleged that half the foreign goods, especially spirits, wine, tea, and tobacco, consumed in England were smuggled. In Scotland and Ireland there is reason to believe that the customs and excise laws were all but universally disregarded. I am not aware that my native village in Hampshire was more defiant than usual towards the finance of the heaven-born minister and his admirers, but smuggling in it was open, bold, and perpetual. Even those who wore medallions of Pitt, the political saint of the time, bought wine, spirits, tea, and tobacco which had paid no toll to the royal exchequer. Nor do I doubt that the London tradesmen, who apparently paid the customs, found out how to approach and deal with the irregular merchant. In this way, and in this alone, they could indirectly lessen the charges which successive chancellors of the exchequer, each more foolish than his predecessor, till the series sank down to Vansittart, put on them. In the arithmetic of the customs, said Swift, two and two do not always make four, and unless the trader was to be ruined by unlicensed and illicit competition, it was an overmastering influence with them to prevent two and two from making four. These financiers might, too, have known if they had studied the history of the English revenue, that the expedients which they had adopted had been tried before, and had been regularly baffled. Vigilant, too, and vexatious as the supervision of the exciseman was, the changes in the law, and the official instructions given to the revenue officers, show that they were constantly being outwitted by shrewd and desperate manufacturers. The exciseman was probably less frequently outmanœuvred than the custom-house officer, but illicit distillation was far from uncommon, and constantly undiscovered, and the fraudulent running of malt, to mention only one among several evasions, was common and successful. More harmless expedients were sometimes adopted. For instance, the excise on bricks was based on the dimensions of the product. When the Great Western Railway was being constructed between London and Bristol, and there was a great demand for bricks in order to construct arches, the contractor hit upon making his moulds of a larger size than ordinary, confident that the contraction in firing would bring them within the legal dimensions. So ingeniously and so accurately did he measure his moulds, that he actually, as he told me, saved the resultant duty in the excess of size. In those days men were exceedingly acute in evading fiscal imposts. In 1816 Vansittart even put an additional excise on soap; in 1819 fresh taxation was imposed to the amount of over 3 millions, and the revenue instead of being bettered was diminished.

The year 1820 is memorable for the presentation of the merchants' petition in both houses of Parliament. This historical document, drawn up by the late Mr. Thomas Tooke, and signed by many leading London merchants, was, as the custom went at that time, debated on its presentation. It contained the leading principles of the Free Trade theory. Its intrinsic truth and cogency was not disputed by Lord Liverpool, then at the head of the Government, but no hopes were held out that its prayer would be conceded. Lord Liverpool in a memorable passage declared that the hindrance to it was the vested interests which had grown up under the existing system, interests which would be imperilled if the petition became the test for practical politics.

Now there is no more serious peril which necessary economical and social changes incur, both in their inception and their course, than that of the vested interest, which is, nine cases out of ten, a demand that indefensible and mischievous privileges should be suffered to exist, or be compensated when extinguished. I have in a previous lecture shown how these claims were originated, what were the earliest occasions on which they were recognized, what defence is alleged for them, and how hollow and unreal it often is. But the cry has a natural attraction for those who think, like Demetrius of Ephesus, that their craft is in danger, and it excites only a very languid opposition from those who might be credited with the power of interpreting the facts, if they were not even prepared to yield to a clamour, either from sheer indifference, or because they are convinced that the benefit of reform could be more considerable than the loss involved in compensation. It is true that a stand has recently been made, and a project of recognition and compensation rejected, or at least postponed.

Animated with their success with the income tax, the country party attacked Mr. Vansittart's finance. The additional malt tax of 1819 was repealed, and on horses and in agriculture. Then went half the excise on leather, and soon provision was made for the reduction and the repeal of the salt duty. The remissions amounted to $3\frac{1}{2}$ millions. It was hoped that the deficiency would be covered by the Dead Weight Annuity, and by the conversion of certain 5 per cent. stocks into one of 4 per cent., an opportunity which arrives when capital is being steadily accumulated.

The Dead Weight Annuity was a scheme by which the Bank of England undertook to pay off the pensions contracted during the war, and those for the civil service. Now this charge was one which could have a limited and a calculable duration. The scheme was to make it the basis of an arrangement with the Bank of England, under which the duration of the charge was extended, and its termination fixed at a definite date, forty-five years after the operation, in 1867. The pensioners were very numerous, especially those of one Hanoverian regiment, which had run away at Waterloo, and seemed to be absolutely immortal after the action. But it was discovered at last that these interesting

Teutons had transmitted their claim on the British exchequer to their offspring, and that the parish clergy had assisted them in this praiseworthy, but fraudulent, attempt to procure a provision for their families. But in 1822 Lord Liverpool's ministry was recast, not before it was necessary, for it was becoming exceedingly unpopular. Peel took the place of Sidmouth, Canning that of Londonderry, better known as Lord Castlereagh, Robinson, whom Cobbett nicknamed Prosperity Robinson, that of Vansittart, who sank into obscurity on a sinecure and a peerage, while Huskisson went to the Board of Trade. These four persons began a new system of finance, which in a quarter of a century developed free trade, and bade, we may believe, a final adieu to protection. The leading advocate of these measures was Huskisson, who had long declared himself on the side of financial reform.

The first change was the abandonment of the sinking fund system, a project put out by Prior in the eighteenth century, accepted by Pitt, and continued with most disastrous effects, all through the Continental War. Briefly stated, it was a proposal that one's debts as a nation could be extinguished by borrowing more money, and therefore incurring more debt every year. It was, in fact, the perpetual renewal of accommodation bills, with the interest added to the principal when the liability became due. It is wonderful that any one so acute as Pitt could have been taken in by so transparent a project, and that at a time when he seriously applied himself to finance, and had not yet abandoned himself recklessly to mischievous taxation, as he did when he engaged in the Continental War. Now Huskisson had laid down the maxim that "the only source from which debt can be paid is the annual excess of revenue over expenditure." This new departure enabled Robinson in 1823 to repeal taxes to the annual amount of over 2¼ millions. In the next year the spirit duties in Scotland and Ireland were reduced, with the result that a greater revenue than before was derived from the lessened tax.

The years 1823, '24, and '25 were prosperous. Europe was beginning to recover from the effects of the great war, and to supply an outlet for British manufactures, though of course it was only a beginning. The spirits of the two advocates of fiscal reform rose, and Robinson actually began to contemplate the removal of all restrictions on British trade. The form which the first attempt (1824) in this direction took was the repeal of the duties on raw and thrown silk. The next was the reduction of the duty on wool. The third was on coals imported into London. The fourth was on rum, the increased yield of the lower duty soon making up the deficit, and the fifth was the abolition of a tax on legal proceedings. In 1825 Robinson continued his reductions, in this year on houses, and on articles of consumption, it being rendered pretty manifest that lessened duties not only increased the revenue, but rendered it possible that taxes on raw material could be abolished or lowered. This tariff was principally the work of Deacon and Huskisson.

Unluckily the progress which had been made was checked by a terrible financial crisis at the end of 1825 and the beginning of 1826, owing to the speculative trade attempted with the liberated Spanish Republics. I have commented on it in an earlier lecture. It was memorable as the occasion on which an attempt was made to affirm the principle and to suggest the adoption of bimetallism, when the subject was discussed with far more intelligence than will be found in a recent report. The convulsion, however, was entirely monetary. It produced no effect on the revenue. But the Budget of 1826 was marked by a curious incident. The draftsman of the Bill, says Mr. Dowell, allowed by an oversight one fourth of the tobacco duty to lapse in July. The effect of this accidental error was such a remarkable reduction in smuggling, that Robinson accepted the mistake, and acquiesced in the reduction.

Early in 1827 Lord Liverpool was stricken with apoplexy and soon died. Later in the year Canning, who had become Prime Minister, also died, and the administration passed into Wellington's hands. Then came the epoch of political agitation, of the repeal of the penal statutes against Roman Catholics, and of the first Reform Act. There was but little opportunity at such a crisis for the development of fiscal changes. But the tax on leather was repealed, and also that on beer. But in 1830 an important work on finance was published by Sir Henry Parnell, afterwards Lord Congleton, the son of the last Speaker of Grattan's Irish Parliament. Sir Henry Parnell is said to have been an impracticable colleague. But he had for years been chairman of the Finance Committee of the House of Commons, and had studied the subject on which he wrote with the care which is necessary before financial propositions can be announced or entertained. It is known that Parnell's conclusions made a deep impression on Sir Robert Peel's mind, and were the basis on which he established his changes after he came into office in 1841.

Parnell proposed the abolition of all taxes on raw material, using the word in the widest sense, so as not only to include products like cotton, wool, flax, and hemp, but those which, being the result of manufacture, are useful to the further end which is made of them, as leather, bricks, and tiles. He also advocated the same policy in the case of all excises on manufactures, on the ground that they were inevitably and invariably hindrances to industry. Such taxes were those on glass, paper, and printed fabrics. He further recommended a reduction of the taxes on foreign imports with a view of checking the practice of smuggling. In order to compensate the revenue for the loss it would sustain by these changes, he advised that a fair tax should be imposed on property and income. Some of his proposals were accepted, but the Tory party, after holding office practically for nearly half a century, was driven out in 1830. Then came Althorp's budget of 1831, only a part of which was carried; the repeal of the tax on coals and the excises on printed fabrics and candles.

When the reformed Parliament met, the Whigs were in the ascendency, and Althorp the finance minister. He reduced the house and window tax in the case of shopkeepers, lowered the insurance duty, took off the tax on fire insurances in the case of agricultural stocks, reduced the tax on soap, avowedly in order to check its illicit manufacture; abolished that on cotton and tiles, and lowered that on advertisements. To meet the proposal for a reduction of the malt tax, Althorp pointed out that to accede to this would be to render the imposition of a property tax necessary. In 1834 the house tax was repealed, the window tax retained, avowedly because the window tax touched the rich, while the house tax did not.

The malt tax was always a subject of vehement attack by the country party. The landowners were under the impression that the effect of the tax was to check the consumption and lower the price of barley, and so to arrest the growth of rent from light land. It is remarkable, however, that though they insisted on this change while in opposition, they never could procure it from the Conservative party when that party was in office. Under our fiscal system it was impossible to dispense with taxes on alcoholic drinks, and, in particular, to remit or reduce the tax on one kind, while it was maintained in full on another kind. Experience too has shown that if a revenue is the object of a Government, it is not possible to successfully attempt a high *ad valorem* tax on certain alcoholic fluids. At first sight it would seem fair to levy a high tax on foreign wines, especially those which bear a high price. But in practice it is found that such a tax defeats itself, that consumption is checked, and the revenue suffers. There is, and always will be, no fertile customs or excise which does not come from the habitual consumption of the poor. Now in alcoholic fluids that kind is always the most popular and most fruitful for revenue purposes of which the initial cost of production is the lowest. This is spirits, particularly English gin, which could be supplied from fermented barley, the operation being different from that of malting, at not more than two shillings a gallon. But the duty imposed on it is more than five times the cost of production. But if you take the average prices of strong wines at fifteen shillings a gallon, such wines containing 30 per cent. of the spirit which is charged at so high a rate when it is the product of distillation, the tax per gallon is one-fifth of the initial value; while in beer it is about one-half the same cost or charge. The proportion seems to be unfair in the highest degree; but experience has proved that the ratio given alone, or something very close to it, must be preserved, if the revenue is to be fruitful. If, therefore, taxation checks the consumption of barley and the profits of barley growing, the check is greatest where the taxation is highest, and the raw material is most exclusively barley. But this is the case with British-made spirits. I was greatly amused when the tax was repealed, and the demand of the landowners conceded, at the disappointment which was expressed at the substituted tax on beer, into which it was by no means certain that more malt would go, for even the dullest minds could see that unless the brewer were restrained from using anything but malt and hops, he would infallibly choose the cheapest material for his manufacture.

In 1834 the Whig government split in consequence of divisions on the Irish Church question, but was reconstructed under Lord Melbourne. But the new administration did not last long. It was succeeded by the first government of Sir Robert Peel, who, in order to test public feeling, dissolved the parliament. But this was not favourable to the new ministry, and in four months Peel resigned, and Melbourne returned to office. Spring Rice, afterwards Lord Monteagle, becoming Chancellor of the Exchequer. Lord Monteagle, whom I knew well in the later years of his life, was a very interesting person to a student of fiscal history, for he was exceedingly communicative as to his administrative career, and remained to the close of his life a representative of that financial school, which began with Huskisson and Robinson, and was continued by Althorp. The principle of those persons was to remit excises and taxes on raw materials, technically so called, and to reduce them in the case when they could not be wholly remitted, to such a point as would leave them available for purposes of revenue. He was scared, however, by excessive remissions of taxation, and was unable to discover that there were occasions on which the entire liberation of an industry from taxation would be followed by compensations in other quarters. He reduced, for example, the duty on paper; but he led the Opposition in the Lords when that House rejected the budget in which the paper duty was wholly repealed, an event which led to the latest collision between the two Houses, and the passage of the standing order under which the claim of the Lords to revise taxation was peremptorily negatived. But Lord Monteagle was convinced that he had taken a wise and judicious course, and he would dwell in treating this subject, on the enormous length at which he spoke in the Lords on the financial situation at this crisis. In fact, he had a good deal of that temper which was nicknamed the finality principle, which attempted to affirm that there were facts in finance and politics which must be taken as finally settled.

The five years 1837-42 were of great financial difficulty. The expenses of government, and especially of the services, increased, while the revenue was inelastic. It was believed that both parties had been too free in the remission of taxation. The harvests too, no unimportant factor in domestic prosperity, and tax-paying capacity as long as free trade in food was denied, were deficient, and there had been no little overtrading and speculation. There was every motive for economy and prudence, but the Whig government were, or believed themselves constrained to undertake the duty of putting down the Canadian insurrection, an event which was on a small scale, though the results were different, like that of American independence.

The French Canadians were French settlers, who had been compelled to transfer their allegiance from France to Great Britain during the Seven Years' War. They were treated with some consideration by the conquerors, and remained loyal to the British party during the War of Independence, probably from dislike to their American neighbours. Meanwhile a new colony, reinforced by loyalists from the States and immigrants from England, was formed in Upper Canada, and upon this and a detestable land company in which jobbery was rampant, the British Government heaped its favours. It would be a long story to show you how unwisdom created discontent, how discontent grew into indignation, and how the refusal on the part of the Colonial Office to listen to Lord Durham's judicious advice drew these people into rebellion. They were put down, for the home government had powerful allies in the English settlers. The leaders of the revolt were put on their trial for high treason, capitally convicted, pardoned, became leaders of public opinion, and one of them at least finally knighted. I do not dispute the wisdom with which the Government treated the revolt, and the leaders of it; and I have not time to explain in detail, even if it were relevant to the subject before me, the unwisdom which induced the outbreak, and the weakness which surrender after bluster invariably displays. Ever since that time there has been trouble in Canada, and the Colonial Office was the first cause of it.

With part of this trouble Spring Rice had to deal. It made its appearance in a series of deficits. In the first year the expenditure was in excess of revenue by one and a half millions, in the next half a million, in the third a million and three-quarters.

Early in 1839 the Government resigned, and Peel was again called on to form an administration. It broke down under what was called a palace intrigue, and Melbourne returned to office. His Chancellor of the Exchequer went to the refuge of failures, and Francis Baring succeeded him.

The Whig Government, however, in 1839, resolved on a most important financial reform. The Post Office was established during the Protectorate, partly as a convenience for the transmission of Government despatches, partly, as the Act avowed, for the purpose of detecting designs against the safety of Government. This part of the Commonwealth legislation was adopted by the restored Government; the conveyance of letters was made a monopoly, and the Crown of course began to quarter pensioners on the fund. As time went on the rates of postage were greatly increased, the charge being founded on a mileage which was arbitrary, because the routes over which letters were carried were settled on no principle whatever. In my youth, the postage from my native place to one town seven miles off was eightpence, that to another twelve miles off one penny.

Now for some time before the Act of 1839, Rowland Hill, then one of the Post Office secretaries, had urged that the real charge of the Post Office from the point of view of carriage was infinitesimal, the true cost of the service lying in the distribution of the letters. I am, I think, right in saying that my friend the late Sir Rowland Hill was the originator of this generality, though I believe that others have laid claim to it. It is quite certain that Hill was credited by those who were adverse to the change with the authorship, and one of the blemishes in Sir Robert Peel's administration was Mr. Hill's suspension from office, shortly after the new Government was formed in 1841, on some frivolous pretext. He was, however, speedily and wisely restored. The proposal had the warm support of a new school of politicians, which got the nickname of the Manchester Party, and consisted chiefly of the manufacturing classes in the north of England, and was treated with indifference or hostility by the country party, who were beginning on other grounds to feel the keenest animosity against their northern critics. The reason of the discrepancy was obvious. Easy and cheap communication by post was part, and a necessary part, of mercantile business; but was of less importance to country squires and farmers. The change of 1839 put an end to the privilege of franking, possessed up to that time by members of both houses, a privilege which, if we believe a story that a grand piano was once franked by a member to Ireland, was distinctly abused.

Baring, who had to succeed to the deficits of Spring Rice (and the new postal rates for a long time did not earn the income of the old system), had to meet a deficiency of a very serious character, no less than two and three-quarter millions. Of this deficit a million and a quarter was due to Post Office reform. To meet the emergency Baring had recourse to the worst expedients of Addington's and Vansittart's finance. He added 5 per cent. to customs and excise, an additional tax on spirits, and 10 per cent. on assessed taxes. The scheme was exceedingly unpopular. As it was contemporaneous with the Queen's marriage, the assessed taxes were, as I well remember, called Prince Albert's tax, and the Conservative party cut down the parliamentary grant, which the Government, guided by precedents, were disposed to give the Prince. Unfortunately too the projected failed, and the additional taxes failed to secure the expected revenue. In the year 1841 there was an anticipated deficiency of two and a half millions.

But before this fiscal crisis came a new force was rising, which was adding to the difficulties of the Government. An active and energetic party, amply provided with funds, and characterized by great perseverance, was engaged in agitating for the total repeal of the Corn Laws, and the entire abandonment of those principles which had governed English policy for more than a century and a half. The British nation had become the manufacturers of the world. But the Corn Laws stopped the exchange and paralyzed production. Corn-producing countries were eager to buy, and the northern manufacturers willing to produce; but the restraint on imports, virtually prohibitory, impeded the operation of trade. There was consequently great distress in the manufacturing districts, and much discontent. The interests of labour and the interests of trade were equally crippled by the protective system. The advocates of a change had a ready, a sympathetic, and finally a determined audience. Nor were the country party wise. Sometimes, it is true, they appealed to the fear of dependence on foreigners, but more frequently they stood on their private interests, or, as some boldly said, of the vested right which the landowners had to high prices and monopoly. As the advocates, of the new policy grew bolder they disclaimed all compromise, and declared themselves determined to destroy the Corn Laws, root and branch.

The Whigs were by no means disposed to yield. As for their rivals, the utterance of Lord Liverpool was remembered that the Corn Laws were a vested interest of the landowners. Lord Melbourne, an easy, genial, indolent politician, entirely imbued with the maxim of Walpole, "Quieta non movere," or, as he put it, "Why can't you leave it alone?" said that any one who proposed the repeal of the Corn Laws was mad. But the Government must either do something, or alienate a large section of those who had hitherto been their allies. They fancied that they had discovered a middle course. They proposed to reduce the duties on timber and sugar, in the hope that increased consumption could make up the immediate deficiency. They were defeated on the Sugar Bill after a prolonged debate, for the question of sugar was a good deal mixed up with that of slavery. The Government held on, and announced their determination to propose a fixed duty of eight shillings per quarter on wheat, with proportionate rates for other kinds of grain. They were met by a motion of want of confidence, proposed by Peel, and on a division were in a minority of one—312, 311. They resolved to dissolve Parliament and appeal to the country. The result of that appeal and its consequences will be dealt with in my last lecture for this term.

I am sensible that this sketch of British finance, from the conclusion of the great war to the election of 1841, is dull. But we cannot always expect liveliness in economic subjects, and least of all in finance. The experiments, however, of the period on which I have dwelt were of great importance in the greater and bolder experiments which were to be made hereafter by a man who had studied finance with anxious care, and had already made his mark, when he resisted successfully the attempt to tamper with the good faith of Government, for which too many of his associates were ready, at the resumption of cash payments, and had similarly been deaf to the blandishments of the bimetallists in 1825. He at any rate was determined to let no man describe him as he described Baring, as "seated on an empty chest, by the pool of bottomless deficiency, fishing for a budget."

XII.

ECONOMIC LEGISLATION SINCE 1841.

History of the Corn Laws—The Anti-Corn Law agitation—The rise of the Conservative party—Peel's finance—Reform in the customs tariff of 1842—The income tax reimposed—The Budget of 1845—The Irish famine—Peel and Cobden—The revolution of 1848—The Crimean War—Gladstone as finance minister—Direct and indirect taxation— The Budget of 1885—Mr. Lowe and the commercial prosperity— Mr. Goschen and local taxation—Division of local taxation between owners and occupiers.

THE Whigs of the Reform epoch, *i.e.*, of the period at which the first change was made in Parliamentary representation, were not fortunate, and their latest expedient, under Mr. Baring's action, was unwise and unlucky. But, in fact, their position was exceedingly difficult. The revenue was derived from customs and excises, from direct taxation on expenditure, and from stamps on commercial transactions. Now every one saw that customs levied on the materials of industry were in the last degree injurious to industry, that excises levied on manufactures were hindrances to improvement, and directly stimulated evasions, to counteract which an increasingly vexatious espionage was necessary. But only a few persons discerned that of all mischievous laws, that which interfered with the adequate supply of food was the greatest wrong and the greatest folly. Men are driven to industry by reason of the necessities of life, and primarily of subsistence. The economical theorists insisted on this with superfluous, and, as I think, with misdirected energy. But few persons seem to have insisted that to check the importation of food was to check the industry which would have been directed towards procuring it through the agency of commerce, and those who did see this truth, and urged its acceptance as a part, and an essential part, of practical politics, were credited with sinister designs against the agricultural interest, with the project of reducing the wages of labour, and with the unpatriotic, almost traitorous, anxiety of making the British nation dependent on the policy of foreign governments. The arguments derived from these considerations were the most courteous form of reply which was given to the advocates of free trade in food. There were plenty more, now fortunately refuted by events, or only revived in our days, because men have forgotten the miseries of a past generation, or because people are ready to assert that anything whatever is the cause of their trouble, except it be their own folly, incompetence, and shortsightedness. As it was, the whole landed interest, with rare exceptions, was averse to any modification in that part of our fiscal system which dealt with the prohibition of foreign food. The working classes, especially the most intelligent part of them, were entrapped by the gross fallacy that wages rise and fall as food is dearer or cheaper, and did not perceive that if this were true their actual wages could not be in excess of a bare existence; and all the foolish people, now it may be hoped fewer, who deemed that foreign trade would denude the country of its money, or compel it to unpatriotic deference to foreign governments, resisted the proposed reform.

No form of tax, it will be obvious, is more injurious to trade than that which puts an *ad valorem* import on a necessary of life, and is necessarily remitted when the price indicates dearth or even famine. Now this is precisely what the Corn Laws did. When food was at low or moderate prices the tax was prohibitive, when it was at scarcity prices the tax was almost remitted. Now foreign nations, like our own people, produce in the expectation of a market, and seek those places in which to sell their goods where the market is open. But no one could forecast the harvest in a foreign country, and therefore would not produce for it, or consign goods to a designedly uncertain market. It is true that under our warehousing system corn could be imported and stored under bond. But here an additional uncertainty was created. Neither consignor nor consignee could guess whether what they sent or stored would be allowed to come into the market or not. If the harvest was abundant and corn was cheap the foreign corn rotted in the warehouse, and the loss, viz., the cost of production, the freight, and the storage charges, was total. And in the same way the English manufacturer, who produced his own goods with the hope of exchanging them for these foreign products, was disabled by the uncertainty of the market : of course the foreign corn was exchanged against English goods, but when the chance of exchange depended on the caprice of the seasons, no reasonable manufacturer would incur the risks of so precarious a speculation. Hence there might be an urgent demand for food, and a foreign market eager to exchange food for English goods, the two prime elements or stimulants of industrial activity, and yet both might be prevented from completing the industrial circuit. In point of fact, as long as the Corn Laws and the sliding scale stopped the way, the remission of taxes on new materials, the abolition of excises on certain industrial processes, and the lessening of taxes on popular luxuries, were of little avail. For it is found out that no customs and excises are fruitful unless they are derived from general consumption, and it is plain that when the necessaries of life are stinted, and the industry which could indirectly procure those necessaries is transferred, the remissions of taxation are not likely to be followed by elasticity in the revenue. If governments want to get an income out of consumption it is their first interest to do all in their power to make the necessaries of life as cheap as possible, the market for them as open as possible.

The Corn Laws, in the form of a sliding scale, were first enacted in the interest of landowners by the Pensionary Parliament of Charles II., and when the farmers became a part of the electorate in 1832 were maintained presumably in their interest, or, at any rate, the farmers were advised to fight for them. But, like most of the gifts of government, they were of very doubtful benefit at any time to the landowners, and of still less good to the farmer. They were obviously of no value to one or the other, when the price of corn was so low at home that the prohibitory tax was in full force. When, on the other hand, bad harvests raised the price to that of dearth or famine, the ports were, by the operation of law, thrown open, and the price was suddenly reduced. In other words, the Corn Laws and sliding scale increased the risks of the farmers' calling, always considerable enough and vexatious enough. With low or moderate prices, which may however be fairly anticipated, the farmer could find out in what direction he could best turn his industry; with uncertain prices he was constrained to be a gambler. During the existence of the Corn Laws and sliding scale he was beset with the alternative terrors of plentiful and scanty harvests. If the former occurred there rose the cry of agricultural distress; prices would not pay rents, and either farmer or landlord had to suffer. If the latter, there was always the risk of a deluge of foreign corn, let loose by the operation of law from the bonded warehouses, a glut in the market, and a ruinous fall. The only chance for him was a price which would yield him a profit. But he was in the worst conceivable position for anticipating this. To forecast it demanded a large knowledge of foreign harvests and foreign markets, of the quantities already in bond, and the quantities which could be come at. To know this was the business of the corn merchant, and there is good reason to believe that he got these occasional profits. There was some reason too for his getting them, for the risks of his calling were very great, and he naturally made the most of his chances. Nor did the rent of land rise as it did after the repeal of those provisions which were intended to exalt and perpetuate it. From 1815 to 1846 rents were at best stationary, and were in some cases reduced. They had it is true risen, and partly, I allow, by reason of prices. But they owed much more to the growth of agricultural skill, *i.e.*, the diminished cost of production and the inevitable increase of profits. Now I need not say, that to increase risks is to discourage skill.

The landowners and farmers believed that the system secured fair rents and fair prices. But the former knew nothing about the causes of economic rent, and the latter never kept accounts, and therefore had but scanty means for arbitrating between the gains of one year and the losses of another. During the time when the agitation for the repeal of the Corn Laws was at its height, a Mr. Chonler, one of the Duke of Rutland's tenants, stated at an agricultural meeting that the farmers had all the horses, and could ride the free traders down. The retort that they had all the asses too was broad, but complete. Some twenty years after this utterance I made Mr. Chonler's acquaintance. He was then a jolly, prosperous farmer, who was turning his teams to better purpose, and often admitted to me that his fears had not been realized. I do not remember that he ever regretted not having exchanged the tools of peaceful agriculture for the flashing sabre of the yeomanry.

The repeal of this precious system, so fruitful of mischief, and so suggestive of deferred hope, was not to be thought of. Lord Melbourne said that any person who proposed the repeal of the Corn Laws would be mad, and the Whigs were as much interested in the contingency of high rents as the Tories were. But the Corn Laws and sliding scale produced no revenue. Nobody paid it when prices were low, and the law ceased to operate when prices were high. But it was very important in the face of annual deficits to get a revenue. If this could be got, and at the same time rents and corn prices could be kept up, a double stroke of business would be done. The landowners and farmers would obtain a benefit, the revenue would be increased. So Baring got his colleagues—in those days the budget was debated in the Cabinet—to let him propose a fixed duty of 8s. on wheat, and proportionate sums on other kinds of grain. He was beaten on his budget, and the government appealed to the country. The Free Traders would not go with the Whigs, for they alleged that a fixed duty was a fixed injustice. But the country party was thoroughly alarmed. The elections turned strongly in favour of the Conservative party, as the Tories, at Peel's instance it is said, began to call themselves. Peel came into power, and as was said subsequently, without pledges. That the landed interest believed he was there to maintain the restraints on the importation of food is however certain, and their belief is demonstrated by the exceeding bitterness with which they attacked him after he had announced and carried a contrary policy, one which went far beyond Baring's compromise. But as yet his position gave him a free hand for fiscal changes. He had the great advantage that his party had confidence in him, or rather perhaps in his ability as an agent in financial reforms. For Peel had succeeded in re-establishing a solid currency in 1819, and had resisted bimetallic crotchets in 1825, and had seen the necessity of yielding to Catholic claims in 1829, and had not, like the Crokers of the age, despaired of the republic in 1832, and had criticized with effect the Whig finance which succeeded it, and had kept his wrath secret when the new Postal system was carried in 1839, and had defeated Baring's budget in 1841, and had always gone with his party, and had never seceded, leaving others less astute to do that. On the whole, too, Peel was a very good judge of men, as well as of the opportunity of measures. All his previous policy had been successful, or, in other words, had disappointed sinister predictions. He made a mistake about one man, whose allegiance he rejected. But it was difficult to estimate that personage in 1841, and as difficult to estimate him forty years afterwards. Besides, Peel was a consummate parliamentary hand, to use modern slang, and an accurate judge of those forces which lie outside of Parliament. In 1841 he had *carte blanche*, and he knew how to use it, and to commend it to those whom he had trained, and to make his financial policy irreversible.

It is clear that he had accepted the principles of Parnell in his work on fiscal reform, in brief, the relief of trade and the sustentation of the revenue by an income or property tax. The principle of the change is one which it may be worth while for an economist to state. Parnell died in the spring of 1842, and did not therefore see the effect which was given to his reasonings. And, indeed, they who remembered the persistency with which all classes had resented the income tax of the war, and there were many living who had paid it a quarter of a century before, might well have deemed that the proposal to revive it was, in the House of Common's language, academical. It required a man with a very strong party, which trusted him, and would not or could not criticize his finance, and an opposition which was not implacably hostile, to revive the income tax as a financial expedient. But Peel was convinced that by this expedient only he could restore public credit, increase the revenue, and lessen the public debt, for you need not be told that public credit and the reduction of debt depend on an elastic revenue.

I hold, and always have held, that an income tax is unfair in principle and capricious in its incidence. It taxes uncertain or precarious income at the same rate that it does certain and permanent income. It levies the same rate on a professional income, which requires a great initial and a great continuous outlay, as it does on an income which needs no such expenditure. It gives to certain classes, retail traders notably, the opportunity of treating it as an occupation tax, and of transferring it to the price which they put on their goods. And when imposed on government securities it gives the impression of confiscation, for it is absurd to say that a government is fulfilling its contract of paying 3 per cent. on its loans, when it pays only £2 18s. 3d. on a 7d. income tax. And it taxes capital and interest in an annuity terminable at a given date, or with the life of the individual annuitant, interest only when the income is permanent. The great masters of finance have, it is true, uttered some plausible sophistries about this inequality, and perhaps the shallowest of them has been endorsed by Mr. Mill. But if the income tax of 1842 (it never was a property tax, and the phrase is not only misleading, but positively dishonest) be interpreted in the light of what a financier in Peel's position could do, and in that of the urgency of the case, it has the justification of necessity. Peel could not have imposed a property tax any more than Pitt could, or than Pitt or Childers could make real estate pay the same succession charges which personal property did and does. The territorial interest was too strong. How long it will be too strong is a topic which lies beyond my province to discuss. But the attempt has been made to equalize the succession duties, and though the attempt was a failure, some failures involve subsequent success. It is not agreeable to revive a rejected budget, but events march.

The details of Peel's income tax are peculiar, and suggests how anxious he was to avoid the sensitiveness of his party. It was impossible to levy a differential tax on rents and let the landowners, the value of whose property was constantly rising, pay less than the professional and trading classes. But it was expedient to show consideration to farmers who formed, under the

Chandos clause, the mass of the county voters. Their profits were estimated from this political point of view, at a lower rate than Pitt and Addington had set them. They were set then at half the rent in England, and one-third the rent in Scotland, and subsequently in Ireland. If this valuation had been sound, it would be a complete condemnation of the rents paid for land. But it was unsound and unequal; unsound, because it certainly let the farmer off at half his real income in England, and one-third in the rent of the United Kingdom; and unequal, because the rent of grass land is far higher than that of arable, and the cost of cultivating it to the acre is less. I do not find fault with Peel; he had to conciliate his party, and the most agreeable conciliation which a financier can find is that of showing them fiscal favour. The farmers did not, as some foolish people say, pay the landlord's income tax, for they deducted it by law from the rent, but taxation is an element in the cost of production, and in consequence of net profits; and thus, if the farmers were let off easily, they could pay more rent. Peel estimated that an income tax of sevenpence in the pound would yield about three and three-quarter millions, *i.e.*, less proportionately than Addington's tax had yielded. But the earlier scheme had taxed incomes from £50 to £150 on a graduated scale. Peel's did away with the liability up to £150 a year, and did not contemplate the taxation of incomes spent out of the United Kingdom. It was expedient to give an impression that the tax was a compensation on remissions of customs and excise which presumably pressed upon income, and this at a later date was made the defence of the tax. It was to continue for four years only, that is, till such time as the results of the new departure could be estimated by experience.

There were 1,200 articles in the customs tariff in 1842, and immediately Peel dealt with 750. He reduced taxes on raw materials, the word being used in a technical sense, general to nominal, or to what people called registration amounts. If the articles were partially manufactured, reductions were made. If they were manufactured the duties were not to exceed 20 per cent. of the value. As I have mentioned before, the expression "raw material" is ambiguous and not very easily definable. But conventionally it came to mean any product of value, *i.e.*, of demand, which was not in its present shape ordinarily available for human use. The estimated loss was £1,200,000. In the next year, further remissions were made to the amount of £400,000.

In 1845, a new factor in the industry of the country was being rapidly developed. I have often stated to you that the two forces which tend to lower prices are diminished cost of production and diminished cost of freight. If prices were lowered, the margin left for voluntary consumption was increased, for you never can tax necessary consumption. This new form of industry, marred indeed by rapine and folly, the fruits of which the present generation bears, was railway enterprise. The surplus revenue in 1844-5 was announced at five millions, and the experiment had been proved a success. In 1845-6, when the income tax was to cease, according to Peel's compact, the revenue would be sufficient. But the minister predicted a deficiency in 1846-7, and he therefore asked the House of Commons to extend the impost for three years more, so as to give an opportunity for entirely freeing commerce and manufactures from shackles, and " of adding to the comforts even of those who are called on to contribute it." For it must be allowed that Peel's early tariff reforms produced no appreciable effect on the expenditure of the consumer, but merely curtailed his resources.

In the budget of 1845, 450 items were taken out of the tariff, these being chiefly raw materials. All duties on exportation were repealed. The excise on glass was also abolished. It had on both occasions at which it was imposed, ruined the manufacture; in the days of William III., and during the war of the Austrian Succession. It was condemned even by the commissioners of excise; so was the duty on auctions—an entirely indefensible tax.

But in the autumn of 1845 a serious calamity had occurred. The harvest was wet beyond ordinary experience, and the crop was housed in bad condition. A new disease appeared in the potato which, for reasons too long to dwell on here, had become the staple food of the Irish. It was nearly as much the food of the Scottish crofters, though it was not the sole source of their livelihood, as the manufacture of kelp had not been yet superseded by the production of soda ash from salt. It was nearly the sole food of the Belgian peasantry, the most industrious and thrifty of races. Now when a community, however saving it may be, lives habitually on the cheapest kind of food, it is always within risk of dearth, and hardly less frequently of famine. Speaking roughly, the prices of wheat, barley, and rye, and oats, stand in the ratio of 100, 75, and 50. Now if a community habitually subsists on wheaten bread, as Englishmen did during the Middle Ages, a dearth may be met, as I have reason to know it was met, by having recourse to inferior grain, as rye, barley, or oats. But if a community lives from necessity or parsimony on the cheapest kind of food, it has nothing to betake itself to when this supply fails. The Belgian peasantry after the potato plague of 1845, suffered almost as much as the Irish peasantry did. They had to be driven back from the towns to which they flocked, by force. In Ireland, the people died by thousands, either directly by starvation or of famine fever. Great efforts were made to relieve them, but these efforts naturally fell short of the calamity. The University people were not friendly to Corn Law repeal. An undergraduate at the time, I never came across more than one person who, like myself, was an advocate of free trade in food. But the place was stirred by the determination to help the Irish peasantry, and the late Mr. Forster was the agent by whom the contributions collected here were distributed in the desolated west.

It was impossible for the Government to resist. Peel, by his own act, necessarily to be condoned by Parliament, threw open the ports to grain and other food, and foresaw that they never could be closed again. He entirely changed his front, acknowledged the cogency of the arguments against restrictions on the trade in food, and when some of his colleagues declined to endorse his views, resigned. But within a fortnight he was recalled to office; Mr. Stanley, afterwards the late Lord Derby, who had deserted the Whigs on the Irish Church Act, and now deserted the Conservatives on the importation of Food Act, declining to return to the Ministry. The Budget of 1846 repealed all duties on corn from February 1, 1849, except a shilling duty on entry. Nearly all other articles of food were exempted from duty. The repeal of the Corn Laws was carried by a large majority, and the Lords did no more than protest very numerously. I never saw Sir Robert Peel but once, and that was at his sister's house at

Brighton. He then said, what I make no doubt he had often said, that he had been in Parliament nearly forty years, and had never known a session without a Scotch Salmon Bill and an Irish Coercion Bill. His ministry was wrecked on one of these Bills. On the very day that the repeal of the Corn Duty Bill received the royal assent, his Government was defeated by a coalition of Protectionists, Whigs, and Irishmen. He left office rejoicing that his name would be associated with a necessary and important fiscal measure, the success of which he ascribed to the unwearied energies and the irresistible arguments of my late distinguished friend, Mr. Cobden. In course of time, the Protectionist party died of inanition, and modern attempts to revive it are futile and discredited. It was not to be expected that the reform which Peel effected would at once create supply and a market. Trade does not indeed require to be nursed, but trade may be so discouraged by unwise fiscal regulations, that it takes a long time to revive it. The harvest was bad in 1845, and not much better in 1846. The revenue would have suffered seriously, and Peel's changes would have been put to the severest strain had it not been for the impulse given to railway enterprise and the demand for labour paid generally at high rates. Great Britain was put into the hands of the navvies, and the contractors for the works found out that one well-fed workman was worth two ill-fed persons. Many of the projects to be sure were impracticable, many premature. Parliament in two years actually sanctioned the construction of near 8,000 miles of railway at a cost of near 200 millions. Then came a commercial crisis, the outcome of excessive gambling in new projects. But the fittest survived, and with them abundant employment and large expenditure. Eight millions were borrowed in order to meet the costs of the Irish famine. But no further change could be made.

In 1848, the revolutionary wars went over Europe, and half the thrones were shaken. In France the monarchy was overthrown. The only event which disturbed England was the Chartist agitation, which collapsed. But when the news of Louis Philippe's flight from France was told in the House of Commons, Sir Robert Peel walked across the floor of the House to Mr. Joseph Hume, who was sitting by Cobden, and said to him, no doubt for the edification of both, "This is what might have happened in England if I had listened to those Protectionists opposite." The story was told me by Cobden. The condition of Europe led to an increase in the estimates, and we were saddled, by the action of the so-called Cape Colonists, with a Kaffir war, which these Colonists had provoked, and for which we paid the bill. The expedient, of course, was the income tax, which was continued at sevenpence for three years more. It was only in 1850 that Wood was able to get rid of the tax on bricks, and to lessen the stamp duties. In 1851 the window tax was abolished, and an inhabited house duty revived.

In 1852 Lord Stanley, afterwards Lord Derby, came into power, and Mr. Disraeli became Chancellor of the Exchequer. In the winter of this year Disraeli brought forward his Budget, avowedly based on the principle of relieving the agricultural interest at the cost of the general body of taxpayers. It was at the meeting of a new Parliament that the final battle of Protection was fought. The Government was defeated, and Mr. Gladstone became finance minister. He extended the income tax, imposed it on Ireland, and permitted, up to one-sixth of the income, an abatement for life insurance. He contrived, too, to procure a very moderate duty on succession to real estate, the yield of which very much disappointed his expectations. The duty on soap and advertisements was repealed, the assessed taxes were revised, and the tax on tea was lowered. Some changes were made in the stamp duties, especially the substitution of a penny receipt stamp, which is paid, for an ascending scale of charges which never were paid. The penny receipt stamp was pressed successfully on Mr. Gladstone by the late Mr. Christie, the hatter, who found that the society of Quakers, to which he belonged, though just generally in rendering what was due to Cæsar, could not be induced to buy receipt stamps.

In 1853 the Crimean War broke out—our first quarrel with Russia. I do not enter into the causes which led to it, or to the reasons which made it popular in Great Britain. It had the effect of adding at once and, permanently, about ten millions annually to our expenditure, apart from the immediate charges of the war. In the commencement, Mr. Gladstone put the burden on taxation. He raised the income tax to 1s. 2d., put a war duty on malt, spirits, and sugar. But the Government was ill served at the public offices; the commissariat, which was still a highly effective organization for plundering the public, creating large fortunes for contractors, and entirely ruining, as far as human power could ruin the army, broke down. The Government had to resign, but the contractors, as they go now, went unpunished, and have, no doubt, begotten statesmen of more than average audacity, courage, and activity. Sir George Lewis undertook the finance of the country. The income tax was raised to 1s. 4d., and duties were put on articles of consumption, which were calculated to produce as much as the additional income tax did. The Crimean War cost seventy millions, of which about half was raised by loans. The Treaty of Paris was signed on March 30, 1856, but a cessation of war does not mean a cessation of war expenditure, and the income tax was reduced to one half the war rate, for the other taxes on consumption were continued till 1860. But in February, 1858, the Palmerston Government was overthrown, was succeeded by that of Lord Derby, which only lasted for fifteen months. Palmerston returned to office on June 18, 1859, and remained in power to his death, Mr. Gladstone again becoming Chancellor of the Exchequer. By this time the expenditure had risen to sixty-nine millions, and the deficit which the preceding Government had left was near upon five millions. Mr. Gladstone raised the income tax from 5d. to 9d.

In 1860, Mr. Gladstone had to accommodate his budget to the Commercial Treaty which Mr. Cobden had negotiated with France. He put another penny on the income tax and made a fresh revision of the tariff, altering, reducing, and extinguishing duties, bringing the customs and excise almost into the simplicity of their present form. In eighteen years the British tariff, which had been the most complicated and exhaustive conceivable, could be printed on half a page of Whitaker's Almanack, that repertory of useful information, to which the late Lord Beaconsfield declared that he owed so much. The same budget attempted to reduce the duty on paper; but the Lords, led by Monteagle, who often dilated on his achievement with modest pride, rejected the Bill for its repeal. But after an altercation with the Commons, they accepted it in the following year. For once, Mr. Gladstone had overestimated the revenue, and, as is said, by the amount of the paper duty. But the harvest was bad, and the deficiency of the harvest depressed the revenue. The next year's harvest was abundant, and the revenue exceeded the estimates by two millions. The result was a reduction of the income tax by a penny, and the repeal of the paper duties.

It was at this time that Mr. Gladstone, comparing direct and indirect taxation to two beautiful sisters, the Misses Gunning of finance, asserted that as a financier he could not allow himself to decide upon their respective charms; but, on the contrary, paid equal attention to both of them, that both were the daughters of Necessity and Invention, and that each had an equal claim on the public purse. I do not deny that it was an adroit piece of badinage, but I am convinced that the speaker was not serious. I can find a defence for an income tax, in spite of its unfairness and clumsiness in two conditions only. It may be necessary in order to meet a political emergency, or to be made the basis of a fiscal experiment. In this manner it was used by Peel, by Wood, and by Gladstone up to 1874. But as a permanent tax it is obviously unfair, does not visit equal capacity with equal sacrifices, and is only justified by the tyrant's plea. It may have an apology, but it has no defence.

The fact is, direct and indirect taxation are terms intended to imply that the taxgatherer visits the taxpayer immediately in the first case, and mediately, or through the instrumentality of another, in the other case. If imported commodities are taxed, they are rendered securer, and it depends upon the demand of a possible consumer as to whether he will submit to artificial sterility. If he declines to do so, the Government is *pro tanto* baffled, and its taxation becomes also sterile. To learn what articles will bear taxation and what will not, and if they will to what limit they will bear it and remain productive to the revenue, is the first and last problem to the financier. Some stupid financiers, like Dashwood and Vansittart, were untractable by the plainest evidence. The evidence comes in two ways. Will the consumer cease to procure the article at all? Will he have recourse to irregular means in order to satisfy his demand? Either alternative is injurious to the revenue. The case may be varied in terms. Will the tax destroy or cripple the trade? Will it evoke the intervention of the smuggler? If neither of these consequences ensues, the dealer, it is presumed, becomes the agent of the Government, and recovers from the consumer what has been paid to the Treasury. Of course the consumption will be checked, and so, *pro tanto*, the dealer will be injured, and I think it cannot be doubted that, though the dealer puts more than the tax on his customer, *i.e.*, makes him pay more than has been advanced to Government, he is not wholly free from loss or injury, for his trade transactions are curtailed. The proof of this is the advance of trade, and even of prices, when taxation is remitted. The former comes from the increase of consumers, the others from the demand of consumers. Now such a tax, in the loose language of economical politics, is called an indirect tax.

But people forget that men purchase services as well as manufactured products. The physician, the lawyer, the teacher, deal in services, as do a thousand other callings. The usage of financial language is to call a tax on such persons direct. The first may need a carriage and horses, may have to live in a high-rented house, and in a high-rented locality. The second may be charged a heavy license duty on his calling. So again a trader, who is competent and honest, conditions not invariably satisfied, sells a service. His customer relies on his skill in supplying genuine articles. Tax these people directly and they will strive to transfer the tax to those who use their services, and generally with success. Physicians declare that they cannot lived on the old scale of fees, solicitors stuff their documents with verbiage, and successfully claim a scale of charges for the privilege, too often exercised, of doing mischief, and traders transfer the tax on their callings, as well as on their goods, to their customers. As I have said, in the loose language of financiers, they have been visited by direct taxation, and they make every effort to secure that it should be indirect as far as they are concerned, and they are successful. Mr. Gladstone's beautiful sisters are twins in character as well as feature, or, to be precisely accurate, are the same person under different names. If they were not, the same person would be under a double burden. The fact is curiously illustrated by what happened during the suspension of cash payments. That prolonged suspension was a financial expedient. It was adopted by Pitt at a crisis of affairs, and prolonged by his incompetent successors when the actual crisis was over. Vansittart and Stanhope assured the country, and Parliament endorsed their nonsense, that gold was appreciated, and that the note had not fallen in value. But the judges knew better. They ascribed their shortened incomes to the policy of the Government, and they demanded and procured, as Cobbett tells us, an exaltation of their stipends from £3,000 to £5,000 a year. In other words, they transferred the tax.

The only tax which satisfies the conditions of a direct tax, *i.e.*, a tax which is in its beginning and its end paid wholly and solely by the person who is called on to contribute it, is a tax on property. British finance knows only one tax on property, and this is the probate and legacy duty, levied on personal estate, as defined by lawyers. This is not levied except in a ludicrously inefficient way on what the same people call real property. The tax on conveyances is one on a mercantile transaction, not levied on land only, but on stocks and shares. Now the person who pays a tax on property cannot shift it, for in the nature of the case it is not the material of economic exchange. If the property is sold it is made none the scarcer, as tea, tobacco, spirits, are by the tax; on the contrary, if anything happens, the imposition of the tax renders it more saleable by rendering its retention less desirable.

I need hardly say that all the force which power in Parliament, and of sophistry when power is threatened, can wield has been employed to save property from taxation. All local taxation has been put on occupancy. All charges which can be put on intermediaries in connection with ground-renting are put on them, for it is seen that as they have business, or exchange relations with occupiers, they will be able to shift them on the occupant. All new and permanent improvements are put on occupancy. By an absurd construction put by the magistrates in quarter sessions, from whose decision there is no appeal, the mansions of landowners are valued at nominal rents, for purposes of local taxation, of income tax, and of succession duty. The succession duty is based on the estimate made of the successor's expectation of life, is distributed over a number of years, and is remitted if the life drops during the period. The Government of 1885 was wrecked on the question in the budget as to whether a moderate approximation between the liabilities of real and personal property should be affirmed. And it should be remembered that while money devised for the purpose of purchasing land is treated as realty, land directed to be sold and divided between legatees, is treated in law as personalty. Of course this statement affects only one kind of property, but that kind is characteristic and dominant. When the sheer force by which these practices prevail and are permitted is weakened, appeals are made to sentiment, to self-interest among traders, and to the false and sophistical plea, that if land is more highly taxed, and the occupier be *pro tanto* relieved, the tax will be reimposed in an increased rent. But unless the tax causes a security in the article, and the demand is constant, it cannot be transferred. Now a tax on property would not make it scarcer, for it would make it less desirable, and thereupon more saleable.

It is neither just nor wise to exhaust the economic rent of land by taxation. If you do so, you must visit with the same tax the poor man's investment in land, as well as the rich man's ground-rents. It is even less just and wise to make the State the universal landlord, to increase the functions of Government, and to ensure corruption and jobbery. But it is wise to be equitable, and to do away with irrational and indefensible exemptions. It is proper to tax consumption, nor do I demur to the doctrine that there are enjoyments, never probably necessary, and certainly harmful, when taken in excess, which it is reasonable to tax up to the limit which will not extinguish consumption, and will not provoke frauds on the revenue. But above all things it is the duty of the economist, who is, as I have often alleged, only removed in a slight degree from the practical politician, to point out the incidence of taxation, and in these matters to insist that one should not confound names with things. Direct taxation is that which the person who pays it cannot transfer, indirect is that which he can and does ; and the test which distinguishes the two is that of whether the tax induces scarcity on an article in demand, and therefore can stint its use. Nor would I suggest that professional or industrial incomes should be exempted from taxation. No man has a right to accept the services of the State without contributing to its charges, unless, indeed, his receipts in the distribution of wealth leave him nothing but a bare subsistence, either by his misfortune or his fault, or possibly by the direct action of others. It is, in my opinion, entirely idle to discuss in what capacity a Government makes its demands upon those who owe it allegiance, but are competent to criticize, to modify it or recast it. It may represent part of the division of labour; it may be the mere engine of police; it may be a necessary service; it may be, as I incline to conceive it, a judge in equity, whose sentences are never final. It is sufficient to say that to the economist it is inevitable, and that if it abstain from being the instrument or agent of rapine, its benefits to all, even the most self-contained, are indisputable. But it cannot surely be beyond the reach of human intelligence to discover what is the fairest, and what is the most direct way in which the burdens which finance puts on men are to be imposed, and that it is in the last degree irregular to dismiss a recognized unfairness by a jest, a simile, or a metaphor. Generally, indeed, these explanations are an acknowledgment of incapacity, not perhaps of intelligence, but of power, and imply that certain private and unwarrantable interests are too strong to be grappled with, that the possible must be defended, not the true, and that an excuse of a more or less plausible kind must be found, by which a difficulty is not to be confessed, but shirked.

After 1863 the revenue increased, as Mr. Gladstone said, "by leaps and bounds." There was a solid reason for this. The free soil and the slavery party had at length come to blows, and a war was waged during the whole of Lincoln's first presidency, which was costly beyond parallel and beyond anticipation. It is true that the United States adopted in this war an utterly unwise fiscal system, and an equally unwise funding system, and so increased the cost of the war expenditure and the amount of the debt. They deliberately made everything dearer, and deliberately increased the eventual burden to the Republic by what was virtually a factitious funding system. But the resources of the country were too great, it seems, to be exhausted by any blunders, and the necessities of the situation enabled foreigners to overleap the barrier of what was believed to be a prohibitive tariff, which should enable the New England manufacturers and the Pennsylvanian iron masters to acquire the reputation of patriotism, and accumulate the profits of protection. And as the trade of this country grew by the exceptional demands of the combatants in the American War, industry was stimulated, was better paid, and had a larger margin to spend. The epoch of the American War was the beginning of that improvement in wages which went on with industrial activity. It checked foreign competition too in agricultural products, and gave occasion to that steady increase in agricultural rent which in the end has told so disastrously on tenant and landlord. The effect of the American Civil War was not over, when a brief but singularly destructive war broke out in Europe between France and Germany. The war was over within a year, but the losses incurred in it were enormous, and for its duration greater than that of the American struggle. Now when war breaks out, if the combatants have resources, the trade and manufactures of such non-combatants as can satisfy the inevitable void is greatly stimulated.

With the repeal of the duty on paper went that on hops, an agricultural product, the yearly amount of which is subject to prodigious variations. It was compensated by an additional tax on brewers, a class of traders who make, it seems, more profit than any one else, and can, therefore, be legitimately made the objects of taxation. They have been, probably because they know what their consolations are, tolerably patient, under the several imposts which have been put on them, and made no resistance to the arrangements which followed in more recent years, on the abolition of the malt duty, a boon which the farmers were always demanding, and in which they were abetted by their "friends," a boon which their friends never conferred on them, a boon with which they were instantly discontented when it was awarded them. But in 1885 they became restive, and since that time they have claimed to have a vested interest in the licensed public-houses which they virtually own. During the epoch of prosperous finance, and great surplusses on yearly budgets, taxes on fire insurance, on sugar, and on tea, were materially reduced, as well as on some other foreign imports.

When Mr. Disraeli came into office in 1866, the revenue again exceeded the estimates, and attention was now directed towards a systematic extinction of the public debt, by the creation of short annuities. In the interval, a new Reform Bill was carried, a fresh election became inevitable, and the result was, in 1868, the restoration of Gladstone's party to office. Again the revenue was declared to be in excess of the estimates, and the shilling duty on imported corn, which its advocates called a registration fee, was repealed. The old sliding scale had hardly ever aided the revenue, the shilling duty produced nearly a million when it was abolished. Of course it raised the price of all home-grown corn by the amount of the duty. But it also prevented the country from being a free port for corn. This was Mr. Lowe's plea, but he told me that he was surprised at the indifference with which the landowners viewed the extinction of the last protective duty on their produce. Mr. Lowe might easily have discovered the reason. Their rents were progressing more rapidly than they had under protection and fluctuating prices, for they were rising (you may find the fact in the schedule of the farmers' income tax) at the rate of $1\frac{1}{4}$ per cent. per annum. The protectionist cry has been revived under the shrinkage of rents and the fall of prices. The old assessed taxes were also modified, a license being substituted for an assessment. The sugar duties were also lowered.

Now, while it is true that a growing revenue enables a finance minister to recast his system of finance, it also stimulates the demands of those who wish to increase expenditure in any one of the three principal items of cost, the army, the navy, and the civil service, and sometimes the unwarrantable compensations for vested interests. The public defence cost ten millions more after the events of 1860, and the charge of the military and naval establishments kept steadily rising. The education of the people had been insisted on, and the charge, which should have been entirely a local obligation, was put mainly on the public revenue. It was determined to abolish purchase in the army, and to compensate those who resigned their commissions. But the services were strong enough to demand and secure that they who had broken the law by paying an extra or over-regulation price for their commission should be compensated because they had committed an entirely illegal act. Again, much of the civil service charge was for services of necessity and value, but it may be doubted whether, if the revenue had proved inelastic, that the Government of the day would have been very hasty in sanctioning these new charges. But nations, I presume, like individuals, are apt to increase their establishments with their fortunes, and it may be with no better reason than individuals occasionally act, from ostentation.

The budget of Mr. Lowe in 1871 was ambitious. It proposed to do away with the distinction between real and personal property in the legacy duties, and to increase the rates. This project was by itself sufficient to make the proposals generally unpalatable. But Mr. Lowe contrived to make his budget not only distasteful, but ridiculous. He proposed the well-known match tax, provoked the indignation and the remonstrances of a very poorly paid body of workpeople, and the laughter of every one else. He also proposed to alter the mode in which the income tax was voted, from so many pence in the pound, to a percentage. The change commends itself to the financier who has to handle the income tax, because it enables him to vary the fractional percentage, more easily than it is to vary the proportion in the pound, rated in pence and its divisions. But it involved elaborate calculations on the liability, though, of course, these could have supplied in print to the collectors. The budget was abandoned, and the income tax was raised from 4d. to 6d. The tax lasted for a year only, for the surplus was $3\frac{1}{4}$ millions. In the next year it was $4\frac{3}{4}$ millions, and a reduction in the sugar duties was effected. The income tax was reduced to 3d., and Mr. Gladstone proposed that it should be at last, since the experiment which had justified it had been abundantly successful, entirely extinguished. He had this reason for his action. He knew that there would be a great surplus. It was in the end six millions. But he had a further reason, which might have been advantageously promulgated. Had he avowed it, it would have taken away that appearance of a bribe, which the suggestion seemed to hold out.

As I have stated, the existence of a continuous surplus in the revenue suggests, on the one hand, remissions of taxation, on the other, spending on departments, and certain classes of persons.

The great elasticity of the revenue due, I am convinced, to the fact that Great Britain was working to fill up the void which war and waste had produced in America and Europe, was believed to be a continuous and recurrent phenomenon, and not an exceptional one, to be traced to its true causes. Now one of the forms which the demand for a portion of this progressive revenue took, was that of relieving the landowners, through the occupiers, of a part of those local charges which are necessarily incurred, in order that occupancy may be continuous and safe. Mr. Goschen, in 1869, had proposed that local taxation should be divided between owner and occupier. His proposal never went beyond a literary effort, or what is in effect the same thing, a parliamentary report. But it was sufficient to frighten the landowners. They began to urge that the incidence of local taxation, not levied on themselves the agricultural, and in towns the ground landlords, was onerous, that the duties discharged by local taxation were in great part rational, and that the weight should be lightened by transferring part of the charge to the owners of realized and untaxed wealth. They never pretended to discuss who really paid local taxation and who did not, who bore the loss, and who reaped the profit of the vicarious sacrifice. In consequence they made continual claims on the imperial revenue. One political party existed by, and for, the landowners, and a large minority of the other political party, whatever were their protestations in theory, were eager to mulct the taxpayers in practice. They put gradually burden on burden, justly due from land on the consolidated taxes. The instrument of the income tax was ready to their hand, and I am sure that if the income tax, when it came to 3d. in the pound in 1873, and it was clearly foreseen that there would be a surplus of six millions had been reduced, there would have been an end of the landowners' raids on the public purse. It is to be regretted that the case was not stated. When I stated it (as I state it to you now) twelve years after this crisis of 1874, no person who opposed what I said ventured to contradict my facts and my inferences, or disputed my criticism on the economical policy of the country party.

The Government which followed on the election of 1874 could

not help remitting a portion of the income tax. It was reduced to 2d. in the pound. The duty on sugar was repealed. A million was given, in the way which I have described, to the landowners. At this time came the turn of the tide. The cost of the three services was increased, and back went the penny. The relief to the landowners was increased, and twopence more went back on the income tax. Northcote put a very foolish additional tax on tobacco, the effects of which the dealers took care to evade, indeed, were taught by the budget how to evade it. Then came the terrible harvest of 1879, the rapid collapse of the farming class, and the return of Mr. Gladstone to the Exchequer. The deficit was two millions, and there was a wanton war at the Cape, with a charge for the Eastern Question.

The principal feature in the budget for 1880–81 was the repeal of the malt duty, and the substitution for it of a tax on the alcoholic powers of brewers' worts. It was an answer to an old-standing complaint, a concession to a farmers' grievance. But I well remember that it was not equally acceptable to the brewers. An additional penny was put on the income tax. In the year 1882–83, an additional 1½d. was put on for the expenses of the Egyptian trouble, the bombardment of Alexandria, and the war with Arabi. In 1884–85 another penny was put on to enable the British Government to deal with the Mahdi. But the Mahdi was more difficult to deal with than had been conceived, and the income tax was raised to 8d., the sinking fund being suspended, which seems to be the same thing as perpetuating a high income tax, of which the normal or peace rate was put at 5d., though five years before it might have been extinguished altogether. The budget of Mr. Childers contemplated an increase on the beer and spirit duties, and the equalization of the taxes on succession (not probate) of real and personal property. The budget was rejected, the country party preferring a deficit to meeting their share of taxation. A dissolution followed, and the Gladstone party was still in the ascendant. An attempt was made by myself to carry out Mr. Goschen's suggestions of 1869, *i.e.*, of dividing local taxation between owner and occupier. I carried my motion, and with it the doom of the Parliament, for it was plain to me speedily after my success, that the landed interest would never forgive a House which was resolved to do justly. No financial expedients of importance have occurred since, and we are close only to experiments, the significance of which had better not be handled.

Most of the facts which are collected in this lecture come from Mr. Dowell's work on taxation. The comments of course are my own. I am not conscious of any bias in what I have said, or say, when I allege that the extraordinary expenditure of Government seems likely to be provided, as it has been in recent years, from the most unfair, indefensible, and nearly the most mischievous tax that can be devised. But as the patriarch said, Issachar is a strong ass, and if, as some say, we are descended from the lost tribes, I make a shrewd guess at the particular tribe to which we must assign our origin.

INDEX.

ACCOUNTS kept by farmers, 229, 232, 341
Adulteration of goods due to competition, 388
———————— for African trade, 413
Agricultural inventions adopted slowly, 31, 253, 352
———— ——— rents, rise of, and bankers' loans, 84
———— ——— machinery in Ireland, 263, 315
———— ——— depression and emigration, 291
———— ——— labourer migrates to towns, 315
———— ——— labourer, wages of, 334, 356
———— ——— improvements of, in fourteenth century, 349, 352
Agriculture, importance of, to the Physiocrats, 188
———— ——— place of, in industry, 191
———— ——— the new, imported to England, 253
———— ——— in Scotland backward till recently, 256
———— ——— and division of employments, 26, 28-29
———— ——— an invariable employment in Middle Ages, 170, 348
Aislabie and the South Sea Co., 129
Aliens, English laws about, 301, 306
———— English laws about, gradually relaxed, 307
Allotments Act of 1589, 172, 257, 362
———— in modern times, 266-268, 343, 363
———— an assistance to wages, 364
Alton, robbers of, 296
American War of Independence destroys theory of sole market, 18

America, English settlements in, 276
Arable land, rent of, in Middle Ages, 209
Arguments against joint-stock enterprise, 145-7
———— in favour of joint-stock enterprise, 148-152
Army, English, in Middle Ages enlisted, 322
———— ———— cost of, 460
Arkwright's monopolies, 17
Artistic skill of Middle Ages, 27
Assiento Treaty, 128
Athenry, battle of, 274, 294
Atterbury's conspiracy, 80
Australasia as a home for emigrants, 282

BABBAGE on the division of employments, 31, 32
Badgers licensed by the king, 371
Bakewell's discovery in breeding, 227, 344
Balance of trade explained, 111
Baltimore, Roman Catholic State of, founded, 278
Bank Act of 1844, 87
Bank failures of 1825, 333
Bank of Amsterdam, 123
Bank of England, origin and career of, 123-132
———— ———— and English credit, 82, 133
Bankruptcy Law in France explained, 144-5
———— ———— and enforcement of contracts, 238
Baring described by Peel, 440
Benbow's captains guilty of cowardice, 102
Bentham's attack on Blackstone, 2
Bigod's Norfolk Estate, 9, 250, 274

31

INDEX

Bimetallism, theories on, 326
——— Tooke on, 327
——— in 1825, 331, 338
——— and old rents, 336
——— in France, 338
——— economic results of introduction of, 339
Blackburn, Archbishop, alleged to have been a pirate, 12
Bricks, tax on, levied by Vansittart, 429
Brick-making in England not known till end of fifteenth century, 11
Brigandage of Middle Ages, 295
Brodrick's Irish Code, 165
Budget, secrecy of the, explained, 85
Building land, rise in rent of, 209
Bullion, regulation of the trade of, 320
By-industries in peasant agriculture, importance of, 343

CAIRD, Sir James, on the depreciation of capital by dispossession, 233
Canning and the Holy Alliance, 332
Cannyng, birthplace of, 7
Capital unimportant as compared to labour, 25
——— divided into *annuelle* and *primitive* by the Physiocrats, 189
——— invested in agriculture depreciated by dispossession, 233
——— average, required per acre, 262, 314, 357
——— economic absurdity of the theory of the mobility of, 342
——— and capitalists, competition of, 376
Caravan routes blocked, ruin of Bruges, &c., 8, 93
Chadwick's sanitary crusade, 40
Chauvinism in politic science, 1
Chevalier on gold, 336
Chichele, birthplace and ancestry of, 7
Child's East India party in Parliament, 122
Chonler, Mr., and the repeal of the Corn Laws, 445
Cicero and the Collegia of Rome, 139
Clarendon, his history quoted, 13
Cloth as an English product, 396
Coal, variations in the price of, compared with variations in the price of wages, 180
Coercion for Ireland, Peel on, 451
Coinage of gold and silver in England, proportion of, 325

Colbert, effect of the policy of, on French trade, 186
Colleges of Oxford not founded in De Montfort's time, 6
——— of Oxford impoverished by bad management, 358
——— of Oxford buy tobacco for their Fellows, 398
Collegia of Roman Republic and Empire, 139
Colonial loans, extravagant nature of, 202, 288
——— trade of England in eighteenth century, 401
Commercial treaty with France, 453
Commercial bills, history of, 70–71
Competition, economic effects of, 365, 376
——— defended by Mill, 375
——— of capitals and capitalists, 375
——— causes trade to shift localities, 383
——— and adulteration, 389
——— abroad and Protection at home, 391
Conacre in Ireland, 252
Consolidation of farms, historical reasons for, given, 258
——— of farms, dangers of, 262, 264
Constitutional practices long precede historical notice, 5
Continental War, effect of, on English trade, 416
Contracts for use of land, 226–247
Convict colonies settled by the Government, 280
Co-operation, as used by Gibbon Wakefield, 31
——— described by Mr. Holyoake, 156
——— in Leicester, 160
——— in dairy farming, 246, 388
——— in agriculture, 268
Co-operative stores in London, 388
Corn exported from England in Middle Ages, 8
——— exported from England in eighteenth century, 14
——— Laws repealed, 450
Corn Laws in England, history of, 439–460
——— supply of England in fifteenth century, 47
Cornwall, mining system in, 153

Cornwall, land system in, 154
—— economic effect of Trade Unionism in, 182
Corruption of the Corporation of London, 122
Credit agencies, antiquity of, 66
Crimean war and taxation, 452
Cromwell's attempts to get sole market, 13
Cromwell and the navy, 116
—— and trade monopolies, 121
Currency, eight principles for regulating, 329

DEAD WEIGHT ANNUITY, the, 430
Defoe on the true-born Englishman, 293
Delusions sometimes as stimulating as realities, 16
Development of credit agencies, 65-88
—————————— transit, 89-112
Direct taxation, Gladstone on, 454
—— economies of, 457-8
Dissolution of the monasteries, extinguished rights of founders to reversion, 207
Dissolution of the Monasteries not reversed by Mary, 351
Distribution of wealth, inquiry into, should precede inquiry into production of wealth, 22
Division of employments, 2, 26, 31
—— of employments, effect on wages-earning power of labour, 32
Dowell's "History of Taxation," 423, 464
Duty, reduction of, causes rise in prices, 85
Dwight, Dr., on trusts in America, 372

EAST INDIA COMPANY, origin and career of, 118, 130-1
East India Company, monopoly of, 119
East India Company imports gold, 332
Ecclesiastical commissioners in Wales, 218
Ecclesiastics in England of fifteenth century computed, 48
Economic problems, solution of, becoming practical politics, 2
—— corruption, the destruction of the Roman Republic, 37-8

Economic corruption the destruction of the Stuart Dynasty, 39
—— History of chartered trade companies, 113-137
—— legislation, 1815-41, 415-440
—— legislation, 1842-89, 441, 464
—— doctrine of waste, 184-204
—— reforms since 1820, 355
Economists speculating on progress of human invention, 24, 216
Egyptian trade route destroyed by Selim I., 8, 93, 369, 400
Eight hours movement criticised, 158
Emery powder as a natural monopoly, 392
Emigration, modern reasons for, 287
—— and excess of population, 289
Empire, the, salvation of Roman civilization, 38
Enclosures of common land, 257
Engrossing defined, 371
Exceptional treatment of land, 206
Excise unpopular in Scotland, 319, 428
—— England, 386, 428
Exclusiveness of English life in Middle Ages, 7, 10
Executions in the seventeenth century, 166
Explorations of antiquity, 92
—— sixteenth century, 93-4, 400

FAIRS of the Middle Ages, 297
—— author's father purchased household goods at, 385
Famine of 1630, 13
—— endemic in Ireland before 1845, 59
—— 1845, 449
Farmers ruined by extravagant style of living, 231, 357
—— Club, paper on cost of production, read at, 334
Fertility of criminal classes, 59
Flemings, immigration of, 299-302
Flemish lease explained and recommended, 261
Foreigners unpopular in England, 396
Forestalling defined, 371
Forgery of trade marks by Germans, 391, 414
Fox, Henry, and the sole-market theory, 99.

Free coinage in England, impossibility of, 328
Free Trade restores sole market for England, 20, 407
——— policy of England criticised in America, 411
——— Education and efficiency of labour, 41
Freeholders, Gregory King's estimate of the number of, 253
Freights, effects of, on agriculture, 216
French Revolution and sole-market theory, 20
——— caused by temporizing of economists, 23
——— influence of the Physiocrats on, 190
——— English sympathizers with, 417
——— Bankruptcy Law, 144
Fruit, cultivation of, abroad, 234
Funds collected by Trade Unions, 163

GAME Laws, novel idea of, 171
Gastronomic waste, 204
George III.'s influence on English politics, 419
George and Malthus on increase of population, 61–64
——— on the profits of capital, 159
——— on the profits of landlords, 219
——— and "Progress and Poverty," 220
German migration to England, 312
——— weakness after Continental War, 406
Gibbon on *ex post facto* laws, 79
Giffen, second volume of essays, 2
Glasgow Bank, collapse of, 149
Godwin and Malthus on increase of population, 55–58
Gold currency, seignorage on, 327
——— England the first country to employ, 332
——— adopted on the Continent, 337
——— coinage of Middle Ages, 321
——— value of, as compared with silver, 324
Goldsmith's Company, bequest to the, 210
Government, proper functions of, 318
Greenways, the, of Leamington, career of, 149
Guilds of the Middle Ages, 138

Guilds of the Middle Ages restrain competition, 369

HANSEATIC League formed to suppress piracy, 4, 300
——— League full of vigour in the thirteenth century, 5
——— League in England, 300
Highlanders, emigration of, to Canada, 279
Holland, wealth of, not gained by agriculture, 192
Home trade and domestic competition, 365–389
——— international competition, 390–414
Hops, tax on, 459
House Tax, 426, 433
Hoveden, Walter, and the All Souls survey, 50
Huguenots, causes of enterprise of, 35
——— migrate to England, 304
——— descendants of, in England, 306
Hundreds of Kent, population of, in sixteenth century, 49
Huskisson's reforms of finance, 431

IMPEACHMENT as part of the English Constitution, 80
Immigration of Flemings in seventeenth century, 303
——— undesirable persons, 309
Imports and exports compared, 111
Income Tax, history of, 424, 430, 446, 449, 452–454, 461–464,
——— and Government credit, 447
Increase in rents due to improvement in agriculture, 214
Indirect taxation, Gladstone on, 454
Indian corn, price of, and the rupee, 339
Insurances, taxes on, 426, 459
Interest on land, rate of, compared with interest on stock, 230
Ireland, economic oppression of, 242
——— settlements in, 275
Irish, emigration of, to United States, 280, 292
Iron, prices of, in fourteenth century, 10
——— process of refining, discovered, 14
——— price of, compared with lead, 14, 369

JENKINS' ears and the war, 136
Jews migrate to England, 310

Joint-stock companies and regulated companies, 115
——— principle in capital, 138-161
——— enterprise, arguments against, 145-147
——— enterprise, arguments in favour of, 148-152
——— principle in labour, 162, 183
Judges demand increase of salary, 456
Jusserand on public peace of Middle Ages, 297

KENTISH HUNDREDS, population of, in sixteenth century, 49
Kenyon, Lord, on the offence of regrating, 372
——— granted powers of rating machinery, 383
King declares workmen a burden on the wealth of the country, 54
——— on the saving power of farmers, 352
King's Lynn, an important seaport, 383, 412
Knight service compared with villeinage, 347

LABOUR, importance of, to well-being of nation, 25
——— wage-earning power of, increased by division of employment, 32, 173
——— efficiency of, and sanitation, 40
——— and free education, 41
——— as a saleable commodity, 169
——— of farmer worth £100 per annum, 264
——— compared with hired labour, 364
——— laws and emigration, 290
Labourers' Act of 1563, 171
Land system in Cornwall, 154
——— ownership in, limited by common law, 207
——— system in Ireland, 241, 244
Land Tax made perpetual by Pitt, 420
Landless man regarded as a brigand, 251
Landlord cultivation continued till recent times, 252, 350
Landlords, good and bad, 236

Landlords and tenants, relation of, settled abroad, 239
——— and tenants, relation of, in England, 240
——— impose duty on foreign corn, 443
Landowners of the Middle Ages, their services to society, 208, 251
——— interest in production, 222
Large and Small Holdings, 248, 269
Latifundia perdidere Italiam, 248
Latimer on peasant agriculture, 348
Lead, price of, compared with iron, 14, 369
Lease of Lord Leicester, 247
——— Flanders, 261
Leicester, Lord, his lease, 247
Libel of English policy, 91, 411
Licenses, taxes on, 426, 455
Limitation of man's power over difficulties of nature, 24
Linschoten's voyages, 95
Local taxation, incidence of, 463
London more ready to admit strangers than other towns, 7
——— insanitary condition of, in seventeenth century, 40
Lovell, Lord, his accounts, 170

MACAULAY's inaccuracies, 47
MacCulloch, mischievous nonsense written by, 2, 243
Machinery introduced in trades, 382
Malt Tax, history of the, 424, 433, 434, 459
Malthus and Godwin, 55, 58
——— and Henry George, 61-64
Malthusian doctrine tested by history, 59, 60
——— and secondary wants, 368
Manor Court, antiquity of the, 5, 6, 346
——— the nature of the, 346
Marketing by private families extinct in England, 387
Match trade, strike in the, 181
Melbourne, Lord, on the Corn Laws, 445
Mercantile law, antiquity of, 68, 69
——— Marine of England, founded in South-eastern counties, 384
Merchandise Marks Act, 414
Merchant navy of England referred to by Barbarossa, 11

INDEX

Merchant navy of England sinks under the Tudors, 12
Merchants' petition presented in 1820, 429
Methuen Treaty, economic effects of the, 393, 397
Middleman, prices enhanced by the, 384
Milford Haven, advantages of, as a port, 411
Mill's political economy, 169
—— on unproductive labour, 194
—— on Ricardian doctrine of rent, 215
—— on House Tax, 426
Mining royalties, economic effect of, 153
—— system in Cornwall, 153
Mint, coinage at the, in seventeenth century, 325
—— coinage at the French, 336
Mohegans, the last of the, 278
Molyns, Adam du, the murder of, 91
Mompesson and trade monopolies, 118
Monopolies of chartered companies, 103
—— of chartered companies, *ex parte* defence of, 120
—— economic, conditions precedent of natural, 378
—— emery powder a natural, 392
Montague and the New East India Company, 124
Monteagle and Fiscal Reform, 435, 453
Morley, the late Samuel, on commercial integrity, 412
Mortality of London in seventeenth century, 198
Movements of labour, emigration, 270, 292
—— labour, immigration, 293, 316
—— currency, bi-metallism, 317-339
Muratori, on Italian commercial law, 69

NATIONAL character, economic importance of, 35
Naturalization of aliens, 307
Navigation Acts, 101, 105
Navy of England in Middle Ages, 91, 394
Newcastle, Duke of, on ownership of property, 208
Nonconformity in England, services to the State, 39

Nottingham Frame-breakers Act, 382
Nullum Tempus Act of 1768, 207

OFFICIALISM in Governments, dangers of, 36
Oldham Mills, success of, 157
Overend and Gurney, collapse of, 149
Overpopulation, dangers of, 25
—— economic checks on, 62
—— in certain classes of society, 64
Overstone, Lord, on banking, 65
—— on genius, 66
Ownership in land, right to, disputed, 209
—— in land limited according to common law, 207
—— of property, the Duke of Newcastle on, 208
—— in land always large in England, 249
—— large to be distinguished from large occupancy, 249, 260
Oxford Colleges subscribe for Huguenots, 305
—— buy tobacco, 398
—— University and the Guilds, 370

PACIFICATION of the Border, 52
Papal plunder of England, 323
Paper Duties repealed, 454
Panics of 1825, described by Mr. Tooke, 86-7
Parnell, Sir Charles, on Fiscal Reform, 433, 446
Partnership, early forms of, 140
Pasture land, rent of, in Middle Ages, 209
Paul, Sir John Dean, career of, 149
Peace, public, preserved within manors, 7, 208, 294-6
—— of Paris, progress of England dates from, 15, 403
Peasant proprietorship in Ireland due to political causes, 26, 362
—— proprietorship, literature on, 265
—— proprietorship elevates condition of labour, 314, 350
—— agriculture and manufacture, 340-364
Pecok, Bishop of Chichester, deprived by Bourchier, 164
Peek, Mr., on the "worthless" class, 64

Peel, Sir Robert, on money and credit, 72
——— Prime Minister in 1841, 446
——— repeals Corn Laws, 451
——— on Irish Coercion, 451
——— on the Revolution of 1848, 451
Penn's case quoted, 166
Physiocrats, rise of the, 187
——— reforms effected by the, 193
Piety in bankers, a prelude to insolvency, 84
Piracy suppressed by Hanseatic League, 4
——— in European waters, 114
Pitt and the Continental war, 418
Plantations settled by convicts, 280
Poets, great, have few descendants, 59
Political, not social, reasons for emigration of Puritans, 283
Politics becoming solution of economic problems, 2
Poll Tax of 1377, population estimated by, 47
Popularity of wasteful people, 185
Population in England in Middle Ages, 46–9
——— towns in Middle Ages, 48
——— Kentish Hundreds in sixteenth century, 49
——— seventeenth century, 51
——— the eighteenth century, 52
——— in 1815, 423
——— Ireland, 292
Porter on the incidence of taxation, 420
Portugal an English ally, 393
Post Office reform in England, 437
Poverty in England in fifteenth century, 10
Pretender and collapse of commercial credit, 126
Prices diminished by three causes, 334
——— not influenced by Bimetallism, 336
——— fixed by agreement in certain trades, 379
Prince Albert's Taxes, 438
Probate duty in England, 423
Protection to agriculture afforded by freights, 216, 390
——— to English goods against French, 319

Protection, economic effects of, 368
——— to agriculture by enactments, 404
Provisors and Præmunire, statutes of, 323
Puritan settlement in New England, 276

QUESNAI's parallel of Society, 191

RACKRENTING in England, 352
Railway mania of 1825, 83, 107, 449, 451
——— improvements and the Bessemer process, 109
——— enterprise and taxation, 449
Raw material, taxation of, 448
Realty and Personalty, laws on, 421
——— probate duties on, 423, 461
Receipt stamps, one penny, due to Mr. Christie, 452
Recreation as unproductive labour, 196
——— economic importance of, 366
"Registration tax," 448
Regrating defined, 371
Regulated companies and joint-stock companies, 115
Religious reasons for emigration of Puritans, 284
Rent of land in the Middle Ages, 208, 351, 352
——— justice of, attacked, 211
——— increase of, due to improvements in agriculture, 214
——— the outcome of profits, not prices, 215
——— exceptional position of, 223
——— economic defence of, 224
Rents, dangers of excessive, 227
——— rise in, up to 1874, 228, 234
——— in Ulster compared with those in England, 237
——— paid by small holders greater than those paid by large holders per acre, 245
——— modern, below economic value, 359, 361
——— affected by Corn Laws, 444
——— effect of taxing, up to full value, 457
Restraint of Trade, laws in, 381
Revolution of 1848, 451
Ricardian doctrine of rent attacked, 213
——— doctrine of rent, errors in explained, 214

INDEX

Ricardian doctrine of rent, and J. S. Mill, 215
Robinson's reforms in finance, 432
Roswag on the coinage of the French Mint, 336
Rupee, value of the, in India, 337

SALT industry revived in England, 379
—— deposits in Europe, 380
—— tax on, levied by Pitt, 427
Sanitary reform, economic importance of, 40
Scottish agriculture, 256
Seaport towns, relative importance of, in Middle Ages, 412
Secondary wants, expression of, 366
Security, uncalled capital as, 150
—— needed for farmer, 360
Senior on the precious metals, 324
Serfs position compared with the lords, 346
Shops, a development of modern times, 386
Silver, in Middle Ages, got from England, 321
—— in Middle Ages, exportation forbidden, 323
Sinclair, Sir John, and Scottish agriculture, 256, 359
Sinking Fund formed by Pitt, 431
Sitting tenant, economic condition of, 246, 360
Skill of agricultural labourer, 28, 29
—— of English farmer, 356
Small holdings, literature on, 265
—————— in thirteenth century, 345
Smith's "Wealth of Nations" comprehensive and cosmopolitan, 3
—— criticism of regulated and joint-stock companies, 117
—— doctrine of rent, 208
—— on endowments on education, 359
—— on regrating and forestalling, 374
—— on the sole-market theory, 402
—— on the House Tax, 426
Smoking in the Houses of Parliament, 397
—— in Oxford Colleges, 398
Smollet's account of the English navy in "Roderick Random," 102
Sole market for England, 14-21, 53, 99, 399
—— the object of Continental ambition, 402

South Sea Scheme, progress and collapse of, 75-77, 125-129
Spaniards in America, 277
Spanish Republics and English loans in 1825, 83, 332
Spring Rice, his deficits in 1839, 436
Stamp Act of 1694, 422
Standard of comfort for paupers, 366
State ownership of land, objections to, 217
—— regulation of currency, 327-329
Statute merchant and statute staple, 71
—— of Frauds and confiscation of land, 207
—————— and wills, 422
Strutt and Arkwright's machine, 17
Sugar trust in America declared illegal, 373
—— tax on, 427, 461
Swift on Irish misery, 59
—— on Irish tenants, 242
—— on the attitude of Whigs and Tories to the Church, 285

TAXATION, history of, by Stephen Dowell, 423, 464
Technical education and economic progress, 41
Tender, gold and silver alike legal, 332
Theory of economic rent, the, 205-225
Thring, Lord, on the Companies Act, 1862, 82
Throgmorton case quoted, 166
Tin, fluctuations in the price of, 153
—— fluctuations in the price of, compared with variations in wages, 156
Tithe, incidence and effect of, 218
Tobacco, price of, in England, 398
—— duty on, allowed to lapse by accident, 432
Torrens, Col., and the Bank Act of 1844, 65
Tooke, Mr., and the Bank Act of 1844, 65
—— and the Merchant's Petition, 429
—— on Bimetallism, 327
Towns, population of, in the fourteenth century, 48
Trade routes of antiquity, 91
—— ancient meaning of word, 162
—— Unions in Middle Ages, 164, 174
—————— in Middle Ages, first mention of, 175
—————— prescription of, 176

INDEX. 473

Trade Unions as industrial partnership, 177-179
——— and variations in wages, 180
——— and foreign immigration, 311
Tresham, Mr. Speaker, murdered in 1450, 7, 297
Trevor, Mr. Speaker, expelled the House, 122
Trusts declared illegal at common law, 372, 373
Turgot and the Physiocrats, 189
Turnips culture in England, delay in introduction of, 31

Ulster, economic condition of agriculture in, 172, 237
——— tenant right in, 243
Unearned increment and J. S. Mill, 215
United States as a home for emigrants, 281, 307
——— damaged commercially by Protection, 409
Universities Co-operative Association, collapse of, 151
Unlimited coinage, impossibility of, 328
"Unproductive" labour, 30, 194

Value of money in Middle Ages, 62
Vansittart's taxes, 429
Virginia and the tobacco trade, 399

Wadham, Dorothy, buys from the fore- of the works, 170
——— College designed by a mason, 27
Wages, variations of, compared with variations in price of tin, 155
——— variations of, compared with variations in price of coal, 180
——— variations of, compared with variations in price of food, 256

Wages of agricultural labourer, 335
——— assisted by allotments, 363
Wakefield, Gibbon, on distribution of employments, 2, 26, 30
War, economic effects of, on non-combatants, 459
Waste excusable sometimes, 200
Watson, Bishop of St. David's, deprived by Tenison, 164
Wheat crop of England in the fifteenth century, 47
Wills, origin of, due to the Church, 422
Wines, *ad valorem* tax on, 434
Window tax repealed, 452
Woods and Forest Department's lease in Cockspur Street, 210
Wool, English monopoly of, during Middle Ages, 9, 395
York, House of, strongest in Eastern Counties, 9, 298
——— popular in Ireland, 274
Young, and the French Revolution, 187, 239, 255, 416
——— on wages in north of England, 19
——— on misery in Ireland, 59
——— on the new agriculture, 254
——— on enclosures, 257
——— on the magic of property, 261
——— on rent of land, 268, 344, 354
——— on the amount of capital necessary per acre, 314
——— on small holdings, 343
——— on Bakewell's stock breeding, 344, 353
——— on the old agriculture, 353
——— his theories on political economy, 353
——— on gambling, 354
——— on profits of middle men, 385
——— on Corn Laws, 405
Younger son, redundant in fifteenth century, 63

The Gresham Press,
UNWIN BROTHERS,
CHILWORTH AND LONDON.

Catalogue of Select Books in Belles Lettres, History, Biography, Theology, Travel, Miscellaneous, and Books for Children.

Belles Lettres.

Gypsy Sorcery and Fortune Telling. Illustrated by numerous Incantations, Specimens of Medical Magic, Anecdotes and Tales, by CHARLES GODFREY LELAND ("Hans Breitman"), President of the Gypsy Lore Society, &c., &c. With numerous Illustrations and Initial Letters drawn by the Author. Small 4to., cloth, 16s. Limited Edition of 150 Copies, numbered and signed, demy 4to., price £1 11s. 6d. nett, to subscribers only.

This volume is one of the most important contributions of late years to the study of Folk Lore, and is drawn from the most interesting and curious sources, setting forth the magical practices of the Romany in different Countries, and their strange beliefs.

Dreams. By OLIVE SCHREINER, Author of "The Story of an African Farm." With Portrait. Fcap. 8vo. buckram, gilt, 6s.

CONTENTS :—1. The Lost Joy.—2. The Hunter.—3. The Gardens of Pleasure.—4. In a Far-off World.—5. Three Dreams in a Desert.—6. A Dream of Wild Bees.—7. In a Ruined Chapel.—8. Life's Gifts.—9. The Artist's Secret.—10. I Thought I Stood——.—11. The Moonlight Fell across my Bed.

Gottfried Keller : A Selection of his Tales. Translated, with a Memoir, by KATE FREILIGRATH KROEKER, Translator of "Brentano's Fairy Tales." With Portrait. Crown 8vo., cloth, 6s.

Keller is the greatest Swiss romancer of modern days.

The English Novel in the Time of

Shakespeare. By J. J. JUSSERAND, Author of "English Wayfaring Life." Translated by ELIZABETH LEE, Revised and Enlarged by the Author. Illustrated by Six Heliogravures by DUJARDIN, of Paris, and 21 full-page and many smaller Illustrations in facsimile. Demy 8vo., handsome cloth, gilt tops, 21s.

"Here we have learned, yet not at all wearisome, descriptions of the works which led up to the novel as we now understand it. . . . Dr. Jusserand's agreeable style in recounting the origin of the modern literary 'three decker' makes his book, though historically valuable, very pleasant reading."
Daily Telegraph.

English Wayfaring Life in the Middle

Ages (XIVth Century). By J. J. JUSSERAND. Translated from the French by LUCY A. TOULMIN SMITH. Illustrated. Third Edition. Demy 8vo., cloth, 12s.

"This is an extremely fascinating book, and it is surprising that several years should have elapsed before it was brought out in an English dress. However, we have lost nothing by waiting."—*Times.*

The Letters of Horace Walpole.

Selected and Edited, with Introduction and Notes, by CHARLES DUKE YONGE, M.A. Portraits and Illustrations. Limited Edition of 750 copies in Two Vols., medium 8vo., cloth, 32s.

"Have been carefully edited, and, moreover, contain admirable illustrations."
Guardian.

The Trials of a Country Parson: Some Fugitive

Papers by Rev. A. JESSOPP, D.D., Author of "Arcady," "The Coming of the Frairs," &c. Crown 8vo., cloth, 7s. 6d.

"Sparkles with fresh and unforced humour, and abounds in genial commonsense."—*Scotsman.*

The Coming of the Friars, And other Mediæval Sketches. By the Rev.

AUGUSTUS JESSOPP, D.D., Author of "Arcady: For Better, For Worse," &c. Third Edition. Crown 8vo., cloth, 7s. 6d.

"Always interesting and frequently fascinating."—*St. James's Gazette.*

Arcady: For Better, For Worse. By AUGUSTUS JESSOPP, D.D.,

Author of "One Generation of a Norfolk House." Portrait. Popular Edition. Crown 8vo., cloth, 3s. 6d.

"A volume which is, to our minds, one of the most delightful ever published in English."—*Spectator.*

The Twilight of the Gods. By RICHARD GARNETT, LL.D. Crown 8vo., cloth, 6s.

"If imagination and style constitute the true elixir of literary life, Dr. Garnett's 'Twilight of the Gods' should live."—*British Weekly.*

Light and Shadow: A Novel. By EDWARD GARNETT, Author of "The Paradox Club." Crown 8vo., cloth, 6s.

"An exceedingly clever book."—*Daily News.*

The Paradox Club. By EDWARD GARNETT. With Portrait of Nina Lindon. Second Edition. Crown 8vo., limp cloth, 3s. 6d.

"Mr. Garnett's dialogue is often quite as good as his description, and in description he is singularly happy. The mystery of London streets by night is powerfully suggested, and the realistic force of his night-pieces is enhanced by the vague and Schumann-like sentiment that pervades them."—*Saturday Review.*

Soul-Shapes. Crown 4to., with four coloured plates of Souls on hand-made paper, with Japanese vellum cover, 3s. 6d.

Robert Browning: Personal Notes. Frontispiece. Small crown 8vo., parchment, 4s. 6d.

"Every lover of Browning will wish to possess this exquisitely-printed and as exquisitely-bound little volume."—*Yorkshire Daily Post.*

Old Chelsea. A Summer-Day's Stroll. By Dr. BENJAMIN ELLIS MARTIN. Illustrated by JOSEPH PENNELL. Second Edition. Crown 8vo., cloth, 7s. 6d.

"Dr. Martin has produced an interesting account of old Chelsea, and he has been well seconded by his coadjutor."—*Athenæum.*

Euphorion: Studies of the Antique and the Mediæval in the Renaissance. By VERNON LEE. Cheap Edition, in one volume. Demy 8vo., cloth, 7s. 6d.

"It is the fruit, as every page testifies, of singularly wide reading and independent thought, and the style combines with much picturesqueness a certain largeness of volume, that reminds us more of our earlier writers than those of our own time."
Contemporary Review.

Studies of the Eighteenth Century in Italy. By VERNON LEE. Demy 8vo., cloth, 7s. 6d.

"These studies show a wide range of knowledge of the subject, precise investigation, abundant power of illustration, and hearty enthusiasm. . . . The style of writing is cultivated, neatly adjusted, and markedly clever."—*Saturday Review.*

Belcaro: Being Essays on Sundry Æsthetical Questions. By VERNON LEE. Crown 8vo., cloth, 5s.

Juvenilia: A Second Series of Essays on Sundry Æsthetical Questions. By VERNON LEE. Two vols. Small crown 8vo., cloth, 12s.

"To discuss it properly would require more space than a single number of 'The Academy' could afford."—*Academy.*

Baldwin: Dialogues on Views and Aspirations. By VERNON LEE. Demy 8vo., cloth, 12s.

"The dialogues are written with . . . an intellectual courage which shrinks from no logical conclusion."—*Scotsman.*

Ottilie: An Eighteenth Century Idyl. By VERNON LEE. Square 8vo., cloth extra, 3s. 6d.

"A graceful little sketch. . . . Drawn with full insight into the period described."—*Spectator.*

Introductory Studies in Greek Art. Delivered in the British Museum by JANE E. HARRISON. With Illustrations. Square imperial 16mo., 7s. 6d.

"The best work of its kind in English."—*Oxford Magazine.*

The Fleet: Its River, Prison, and Marriages. By JOHN ASHTON, Author of "Social Life in the Reign of Queen Anne," &c. With 70 Drawings by the Author from Original Pictures. Second and Cheaper Edition, cloth, 7s. 6d.

Romances of Chivalry: Told and Illustrated in Fac-simile by JOHN ASHTON. Forty-six Illustrations. New and Cheaper Edition. Crown 8vo., cloth, 7s. 6d.

"The result (of the reproduction of the wood blocks) is as creditable to his artistic, as the text is to his literary, ability."—*Guardian.*

The Dawn of the Nineteenth Century in England: A Social Sketch of the Times. By JOHN ASHTON. Cheaper Edition, in one vol. Illustrated. Large crown 8vo., 10s. 6d.

"The book is one continued source of pleasure and interest, and opens up a wide field for speculation and comment, and many of us will look upon it as an important contribution to contemporary history, not easily available to others than close students."—*Antiquary.*

Chopin, and Other Musical Essays. By HENRY T. FINCK, Author of "Romantic Love and Personal Beauty." Crown 8vo., cloth, 6s.

"The six essays are all written with great thoroughness, and the interest of each one is admirably sustained throughout."—*Freeman's Journal.*

The Temple: Sacred Poems and Private Ejaculations. By Mr. GEORGE HERBERT. New and fourth edition, with Introductory Essay by J. HENRY SHORTHOUSE. Small crown, sheep, 5s. *A fac-simile reprint of the Original Edition of 1633.*

"This charming reprint has a fresh value added to it by the Introductory Essay of the Author of 'John Inglesant.'"—*Academy.*

Songs, Ballads, and A Garden Play. By A. MARY F. ROBINSON, Author of "An Italian Garden." With Frontispiece of Dürer's "Melancholia." Small crown 8vo., half bound, vellum, 5s.

"The romantic ballads have grace, movement, passion and strength."—*Spectator.*
"Marked by sweetness of melody and truth of colour."—*Academy.*

Essays towards a Critical Method. Studies in English Literature. By JOHN M. ROBERTSON. Cr. 8vo., cloth, 7s. 6d.

"His essays are always shrewd and readable. His criticisms on the critics are enjoyable for the irony (conscious or unconscious) that is in them; and the book will not fail to please lovers of literature and literary history, and to prove suggestive to the critical."—*Scotsman.*

The Lazy Minstrel. By J. ASHBY-STERRY, Author of "Boudoir Ballads." Fourth and Popular Edition. Frontispiece by E. A. ABBEY. Fcap. 8vo., cloth, 2s. 6d.

"One of the lightest and brightest writers of vers de société."
St. James's Gazette.

Caroline Schlegel, and Her Friends. By Mrs. ALFRED SIDGWICK. With Steel Portrait. Crown 8vo., cloth, 7s. 6d.

"This is a singularly brilliant, delicate and fascinating sketch—one of the most skilful pieces of literary workmanship we have seen for a long time.... Mrs. Sidgwick is a writer of very unusual equipment, power and promise."
British Weekly.

Amos Kilbright: His Adscititious Adventures. With other Stories. By FRANK R. STOCKTON. 8vo., cloth, 3s. 6d.

"Mr. Stockton is the quaintest of living humorists."—*Academy.*

History.

The Vikings in Western Christendom, A.D. 789—888. By C. F. KEARY, Author of "Outlines of Primitive Belief," "The Dawn of History," &c. With Map and Tables. Demy 8vo., cloth, 16s.

National Life and Thought; Or, Lectures on Various Nations of the World. Delivered at South Place Institute by Professor THOROLD ROGERS, J. S. COTTON MINCHIN, W. R. MORFILL, F. H. GROOME, J. THEODORE BENT, Professor A. PÜLSKY, EIRIKE MAGNUSSON, and other Specialists. Demy 8vo., cloth, 10s. 6d.

These Lectures attracted much attention in the Session of 1889-90, and are now reprinted to meet the desire of a very large public. In each case the authors have striven to put their audience in thorough sympathy with the National Life and Thought of the Nations treated of.

Battles and Leaders of the American Civil War. An Authoritative History, written by Distinguished Participants on both sides. Edited by ROBERT U. JOHNSON and CLARENCE C. BUEL, of the Editorial Staff of "The Century Magazine." Four Volumes, Royal 8vo., elegantly bound, £5 5s.

LORD WOLSELEY, in writing a series of articles in the *North American Review* on this work, says: "The Century Company has, in my judgment, done a great service to the soldiers of all armies by the publication of these records of the great War."

Diary of the Parnell Commission. Revised with Additions, from *The Daily News*. By JOHN MACDONALD, M.A. Large crown 8vo., cloth, 6s.

"Mr. Macdonald has done his work well."—*Speaker*.

The End of the Middle Ages: Essays and Questions in History. By A. MARY F. ROBINSON (Madame Darmesteter). Demy 8vo., cloth, 10s. 6d.

"We travel from convent to palace, find ourselves among all the goodness, the wisdom, the wildness, the wickedness, the worst and the best of that wonderful time. We meet with devoted saints and desperate sinners... We seem to have made many new acquaintances whom before we only knew by name among the names of history... We can heartily recommend this book to every one who cares for the study of history, especially in its most curious and fascinating period, the later middle age."—*Spectator*.

Biography.

The Autobiography of Joseph Jefferson ("Rip Van Winkle"). With many full-page Portrait and other Illustrations. Royal 8vo., 16s.

This celebrated actor's autobiography is one of the most amusing ever penned. It abounds in droll stories and anecdotes of theatrical life, and is copious in recollections of the famous people of all ranks Jefferson mixed with.

Nelson: The Public and Private Life of Horatio, Viscount Nelson. By G. LATHOM BROWNE, Barrister-at-Law, Author of "Wellington," "Narratives of State Trials," &c. With Heliogravure frontispiece Portrait, 11 full-page Illustrations of portraits and relics of Nelson, hitherto unpublished, and 4 Maps. Demy 8vo., cloth, gilt tops, 18s.

Mr. Lathom Browne has had access to the documents and relics of Nelson in the possession of Earl Nelson and Viscount Bridport (Duke of Bronté); and by the thorough re-examination of all existing material has presented what has long been wanting—an impartial, exhaustive, and critical Life of Nelson, told largely from the point of view of his own letters and eye witnesses of his naval career.

Abraham Lincoln: A History. By JOHN G. NICOLAY and JOHN HAY. With many full-page Illustrations, Portraits, and Maps. Royal 8vo., complete in 10 vols., bound in cloth, price £6 the Set.

"We claim for our work that we have devoted to it twenty years of almost unremitting assiduity; that we have neglected no means in our power to ascertain the truth; that we have rejected no authentic facts essential to a candid story; that we have had no theory to establish, no personal grudge to gratify, no unavowed objects to subserve. We have aimed to write a sufficiently full and absolutely honest history of a great man and a great time."—*Extract from Author's Preface.*

Sir John Hawkwood (l'Acuto). Story of a Condottiere. Translated from the Italian of John Temple-Leader and Guiseppe Marcotti, by LEADER SCOTT. Illustrated. Royal 8vo., bound in buckram, gilt tops. Limited Edition.

"The career of such a man was well worth recording. . . . A valuable and interesting book."—*Glasgow Herald.*

The Life & Times of William Lloyd Garrison. From 1840—1879. By HIS CHILDREN. Vols. III. and IV., completing the work. Portraits and Illustrations. Demy 8vo., cloth, 30s.

"There is something to be learnt in every page, and the diversity of subjects taken up by this strong, resolute nature, make it altogether a book of the age."—*Daily Telegraph.*

Anne Gilchrist: Her Life and Writings. Edited by HERBERT HARLAKENDEN GILCHRIST. Prefatory Notice by WILLIAM MICHAEL ROSSETTI. Second edition. Twelve Illustrations. Demy 8vo., cloth, 16s.

Life and Times of Girolamo Savonarola. By PASQUALE VILLARI. Translated by LINDA VILLARI. Portraits and Illustrations. Two vols. Third Edition, with New Preface. Demy 8vo., cloth, 21s.

"We welcome the translation of this excellent work—which is all a translation ought to be."—*Spectator.*

Charles Dickens as I knew Him: The Story of the Reading Tours in Great Britain and America (1866-1870). By GEORGE DOLBY. New and cheaper edition. Crown 8vo., 3s. 6d.

"It will be welcome to all lovers of Dickens for Dickens' own sake."—*Athenæum.*

Ole Bull: A Memoir. By SARA C. BULL. With Ole Bull's "Violin Notes" and Dr. A. B. Crosby's "Anatomy of the Violinist." Portraits. Second edition. Crown 8vo., cloth, 7s. 6d.

Johannes Brahms: A Biographical Sketch. By Dr. HERMAN DEITERS. Translated, with additions, by ROSA NEWMARCH. Edited, with a Preface, by J. A. FULLER MAITLAND. Portrait. Small crown 8vo., cloth, 6s.

The Lives of Robert and Mary Moffat. By their Son, JOHN SMITH MOFFAT. Sixth edition. Portraits, Illustrations, and Maps. Crown 8vo., cloth, 7s. 6d.; Popular Edition, crown 8vo., 3s. 6d..

"The biographer has done his work with reverent care, and in a straightforward unaffected style."—*Contemporary Review.*

The German Emperor and Empress: The Late Frederick III. and Victoria. The Story of their Lives. By DOROTHEA ROBERTS. Portraits. Crown 8vo., cloth, 2s. 6d.

"A book sure to be popular in domestic circles."—*The Graphic.*

Arminius Vambéry: His Life and Adventures. Written by Himself. With Portrait and Fourteen Illustrations. Fifth and Popular Edition. Square Imperial 16mo., cloth extra, 6s.

"The work is written in a most captivating manner."—*Novoe Vremya, Moscow.*

The Federalist: A Commentary in the Form of Essays on the United States Constitution. By ALEXANDER HAMILTON, and others. Edited by HENRY CABOT LODGE. Demy 8vo., Roxburgh binding, 10s. 6d.

"The importance of the Essays can hardly be exaggerated."—*Glasgow Mail.*

The Story of the Nations.

Crown 8vo., Illustrated, and furnished with Maps and Indexes, each 5s.

"L'interessante serie l'Histoire des Nations formera . . . un cours d'histoire universelle d'une très grande valeur."—*Journal des Débats.*
"That useful series."—*The Times.*
"An admirable series."—*Spectator.*
"That excellent series."—*Guardian.*
"The series is likely to be found indispensable in every school library."
"This valuable series."—*Nonconformist.* *Pall Mall Gazette.*
"Admirable series of historical monographs."—*Echo.*
"Each volume is written by one of the most foremost English authorities on the subject with which it deals. . . . It is almost impossible to over-estimate the value of a series of carefully prepared volumes, such as are the majority of those comprising this library. . . . The illustrations make one of the most attractive features of the series."—*The Guardian.*

Rome. By ARTHUR GILMAN, M.A., Author of "A History of the American People," &c. Third edition.

The Jews. In Ancient, Mediæval, and Modern Times. By Prof. J. K. HOSMER. Second edition.

Germany. By Rev. S. BARING-GOULD, Author of "Curious Myths of the Middle Ages," &c. Second edition.

Carthage. By Prof. ALFRED J. CHURCH, Author of "Stories from the Classics," &c. Third edition.

Alexander's Empire. By Prof. J. P. MAHAFFY, Author of "Social Life in Greece." Fourth edition.

The Moors in Spain. By STANLEY LANE-POOLE, Author of "Studies in a Mosque." Third edition.

Ancient Egypt. By Canon RAWLINSON, Author of "The Five Great Monarchies of the World." Third edition.

Hungary. By Prof. ARMINIUS VAMBÉRY, Author of "Travels in Central Asia." Second edition.

The Saracens: From the Earliest Times to the Fall of Bagdad. By ARTHUR GILMAN, M.A., Author of "Rome," &c.

Ireland. By the Hon. EMILY LAWLESS, Author of "Hurrish." Third edition.

Chaldea. By Z. A. RAGOZIN, Author of "Assyria," &c. Second edition.

The Goths. By HENRY BRADLEY. Second edition.

Assyria. By ZÉNAÏDE A. RAGOZIN, Author of "Chaldea," &c.

Turkey. By STANLEY LANE-POOLE. Second edition.

Holland. By Professor THOROLD ROGERS. Second edition.

Mediæval France. By GUSTAVE MASSON. Second edition.

Persia. By S. G. W. BENJAMIN. Second edition.

Phœnicia. By CANON RAWLINSON.

Media. By Z. A. RAGOZIN.

The Hansa Towns. By HELEN ZIMMERN.

Early Britain. By Prof. A. J. CHURCH, Author of "Carthage," &c.

Russia. By W. R. MORFILL, M.A.

The Barbary Corsairs. By STANLEY LANE-POOLE.

The Jews under the Roman Empire. By W. DOUGLAS MORRISON, M.A.

Scotland. By JOHN MACINTOSH, LL.D.

Switzerland. By LINA HUG and R. STEAD.

Mexico. By SUSAN HALE.

(*For further information, see "Nation Series" Catalogue. Sent to any address on application to the Publisher.*)

www.ingramcontent.com/pod-product-compliance
Lightning Source LLC
Chambersburg PA
CBHW021423300426
44114CB00010B/613